ESSENTIALS OF ECONOMICS

ESSENTIALS OF ECONOMICS

SECOND EDITION

BRADLEY R. SCHILLER

THE AMERICAN UNIVERSITY

THE McGRAW-HILL COMPANIES, INC.

NEW YORK   ST. LOUIS   SAN FRANCISCO   AUCKLAND   BOGOTÁ   CARACAS   LISBON

LONDON   MADRID   MEXICO CITY   MILAN   MONTREAL   NEW DELHI

SAN JUAN   SINGAPORE   SYDNEY   TOKYO   TORONTO

ESSENTIALS OF ECONOMICS

This book is printed on acid-free paper.

3 4 5 6 7 8 9 0 VNH   VNH 9 0 9 8 7 6

ISBN 0-07-057220-8

This book was set in New Aster by York Graphic Services, Inc.
The editors were Lucille H. Sutton and Elaine Rosenberg;
the designer was Hermann Strohbach;
the production supervisor was Kathryn Porzio.
Cover photo and chapter openers—computer art by Marjory Dressler.
Von Hoffmann Press, Inc., was printer and binder.

Library of Congress Cataloging-in-Publication Data

Schiller, Bradley R., (date).
    Essentials of economics / Bradley R. Schiller.—2nd ed.
       p.   cm.
    Includes index.
    ISBN 0-07-057220-8
    1. Economics.   I. Title
HB171.5.S2923   1996
330—dc20   95-676

About the Author

Bradley R. Schiller has over two decades of experience teaching introductory economics in a variety of course formats, including guest lectures at nearly 100 colleges and universities. Dr. Schiller's unique contribution to teaching is his ability to relate basic principles to current socioeconomic problems, institutions, and public policy debates. This perspective is evident throughout *Essentials of Economics*.

Dr. Schiller derives this policy focus from his extensive experience as a Washington consultant. He has been a consultant to most major federal agencies, many congressional committees, and political candidates. In addition, he has evaluated scores of government programs and helped design others. His studies of discrimination, employment and training programs, tax reform, pensions, welfare, Social Security, entrepreneurship, and wage growth have appeared and been cited in both professional journals and popular media. Dr. Schiller is also a frequent commentator on economic policy for television, radio, and newspapers.

Dr. Schiller received his Ph.D. from Harvard in 1969. His B.A. degree, with great distinction, was completed at the University of California (Berkeley) in 1965. He is now a professor of economics in the School of Public Affairs at The American University.

Contents in Brief

Contents

Preface

Economics entails hard choices. No one knows this better than instructors assigned to teach a survey of economics in a single term. There are simply too many topics to cover in so short a time.

WELL-DEFINED FOCUS

Few textbooks confront this scarcity problem directly. Some one-semester books are nearly as long as full-blown principles texts. Those that are shorter tend to condense topics and omit the additional explanations, illustrations, and applications that are especially important in survey courses. Students and teachers alike get frustrated trying to pick out the essentials from abridged principles texts.

Essentials of Economics lives up to its name by making the difficult choices. The standard table of contents has been pruned to the core. The surviving topics are the very essence of economic concepts. In Section II on microeconomics, for example, the focus is on the polar models of perfect competition and monopoly. These models are represented as the endpoints of a spectrum of market structures (see figure on p. 120). Intermediate market structures—e.g., oligopoly, monopolistic competition—are noted but not analyzed. The goal here is simply to convey the sense that market structure is an important determinant of market outcomes. The contrast between the extremes of monopoly and perfect competition is sufficient to convey this essential message. The omission of other market structures from the outline also leaves more space for explaining and illustrating *how* market structure affects market behavior.

The same commitment to essentials is evident in the section on macroeconomics. Rather than attempt here to cover all the salient macro models, the focus is on a straightforward presentation of the aggregate supply-demand framework. The different interpretations of the classical, Keynesian, and Monetarist models are discussed. But there is no discussion of neo-Keynesianism, rational expectations, public choice, or Marxist models. The level of abstraction required for such models is simply not necessary or appropriate in an introductory survey course. Texts that include such models tend to raise more questions than survey instructors can ever hope to answer. In *Essentials* students are exposed only to the ideas needed for a basic understanding of how macroeconomies function.

REAL-WORLD EMPHASIS

The goal of this text is twofold: to focus on essential concepts and to make them *interesting* to students. In large part this is a question of style. But it's also a question of approach, particularly the choice between empirical examples and abstract ones. Students rarely get interested in stories about the mythical widget manufacturers that inhabit so many economics textbooks. But glimmers of interest—even some enthusiasm at times—appear when real-world illustrations are used.

The real world is in every nook and cranny of *Essentials*. Page 1 sets the tone by focusing on the central issue of how economies are directed—by market signals or government directives. The polar choices defined by Adam Smith and Karl Marx are illuminated by the wave of "privatizations" sweeping through the nations of the world and the terms of the Republican party's Contract with America. The recognition of both *market* failure and *government* failure complicates the choice of control mechanisms. Since neither the invisible hand of the marketplace nor the "visible foot" of the government works perfectly, there is plenty of room for debate on specific policy choices. *Essentials* highlights these policy debates. By the end of the first chapter students should feel that economics is very much a real-world conern.

The real-world approach of *Essentials* is reinforced by the boxed "Headlines" that appear in every chapter. The 60 Headlines offer up-to-date domestic and international applications of economic concepts. Some examples include 1994 public opinion on government's role in the economy (p. 4); ticket "scalping" for a U2 concert (p. 65); the entrepreneurial success of PowerBar (p. 154); the Fed's 1994–95 increase in interest rates (p. 298); and President Clinton's 1995 proposal for a $5.15 minimum wage (p. 175).

A PORTRAIT OF THE U.S. ECONOMY

In addition to scores of specific case applications, *Essentials* offers a unique portrait of the U.S. economy. Few students easily relate to the abstraction of "the economy." They hear about specific dimensions of the economy, but rarely see all the pieces put together. Chapter 2 tries to fill this void by providing a bird's-eye view of the U.S. economy. This descriptive chapter is organized around the three basic questions of WHAT, HOW, and FOR WHOM to produce. The current answer to the WHAT question is summarized with data on GDP and its components. Historical and global comparisons are provided to underscore the significance of America's $7 trillion economy. Similar perspectives are offered on the structure of production and the U.S. distribution of income. An early look at the role of government in shaping economic outcomes is also provided. This portrait is a critical tool in acquainting students with the broad dimensions of the U.S. economy and is unique to this text.

THEORY AND REALITY

In becoming acquainted with the U.S. economy, students will inevitably learn about the woes of the business cycle. As the course progresses, they will not fail to notice a huge gap between the pat solutions of economic theory and the dismal realities of recession. This experience will kindle one of the most persistent and perplexing questions students have, namely: "If the theory is so good, why is the economy such a mess?" Economists like to pretend that the theory is perfect but politicians aren't. That's part of the answer, to be sure. But it isn't entirely fair to either politicians or economists. In reality, the design and implementation of economic policy is impeded by incomplete information, changing circumstances, goal trade-offs, and— politics. Chapter 16 examines these real-world complications. In the process students get a much more complete explanation of the reasons why the real world doesn't always live up to the promises of economic theory.

SUPPORTIVE PEDAGOGY

The emphasis on real-world applications motivates students to read and learn basic economic concepts. This pedagogical goal is reinforced with several in-text student aids. These include:

- *Chapter-opening questions*   Each chapter begins with a short, empirically based introduction to key concepts. Three core questions are posed to motivate and direct student learning.
- *In-margin definitions*   Key concepts are highlighted in the text and defined in the margins. Key definitions are also repeated in subsequent chapters to reinforce proper usage.
- *Precise graphs*   All the analytical graphs are plotted and labeled with precision. This shouldn't be noteworthy, but other texts are surprisingly deficient in this regard.
- *Synchronized tables and graphs*   The graphs are made more understandable with explicit links to accompanying tables. Notice in Figure 3.2 (p. 55), for example, how the lettered rows of the table match the lettered points on the graph.
- *Complete annotations*   *All* the graphs and tables have self-contained annotations. These captions facilitate both initial learning and later review.
- *Chapter summaries*   Key points are summarized in bulleted capsules at the end of each chapter.
- *Key-term review*   A list of key terms (the ones defined in the margin) is provided at the end of each chapter. This feature facilitates review and self-testing.
- *Questions for discussion*   These are intended to stimulate thought and discussion about the nature of core concepts and their application to real-world settings.
- *Numerical problems*   Numerical problems are set out at the end of each chapter. These problems often require students to use material from earlier tables, graphs, or Headlines. Answers to all problems are provided in the *Instructor's Resource Manual* along with clarifying annotations.
- *End-of-text glossary*   The chapter-specific definitions and key-term reviews are supplemented with a comprehensive glossary at the end of the text.

CONTENTS: MICROECONOMICS

The micro sequence of the text includes only six chapters. In this brief space students get an introduction to the essentials of consumer demand, producer supply decisions, market structure (competition vs. monopoly), and labor market behavior. In each case, the objective is to spotlight the essential elements of market behavior, e.g., the utility-maximizing behavior of consumers, the profit-maximizing quest of producers, and the interactions of supply and demand in setting both wages and prices. The monopoly chapter (Chapter 7) offers a step-by-step comparison of competitive and monopoly behavior, in both the short and long run. Contrasts with centrally planned economies are also strewn throughout the discussion to highlight the unique character of *market* outcomes.

The final chapter in the micro core examines the purposes of government intervention. The principal sources of market failure (public goods, externalities, market power, inequity) are explained and illustrated. So, too, is the nature of government intervention and the potential for *government* failure. Students should end the micro core with a basic understanding of how markets work and when and why government intervention is sometimes necessary.

CONTENTS: MACROECONOMICS

The macro sequence begins with an historical and descriptive introduction to the business cycle, including the 1990–1991 recession. The rest of the opening macro chapter explains and illustrates the nature and consequences of unemployment and inflation. This discussion is predicated on the conviction that students have to understand *why* business cycles are feared before they'll show any interest in the policy tools designed to tame the cycle. The standard measures of unemployment and inflation are explained, along with specific numerical goals set by Congress and the President.

The basic analytical framework of aggregate supply and aggregate demand (AS/AD) is introduced in Chapter 11. The focus is on how different shapes and shifts of AS and AD curves affect macro outcomes. The AS/AD framework is also used to illustrate the basic policy options that decision makers confront. The stylized model of the economy illustrated in Figure 11.1 (p. 232) is used repeatedly to show how different macro determinants affect macro outcomes (e.g., see the highlighting of fiscal policy in Figure 12.1 on p. 252).

The fiscal-policy chapter surveys the components of aggregate demand and shows how changes in government spending or taxes can alter macro equilibrium. The multiplier is illustrated in the AS/AD framework and the potential consequences for price inflation are discussed. The chapter ends with a discussion of budget deficits.

The monetary dimensions of the macroeconomy get two chapters. The first introduces students to modern concepts of money and the process of deposit creation. Chapter 14 focuses on how the Federal Reserve regulates bank reserves and lending to influence macro outcomes.

Supply-side concerns are addressed in Chapter 15. The potential of tax cuts, deregulation, and other supply-side policy options to improve both short- and long-term macro performance is explored. The chapter also offers a discussion of why economic growth is desirable, despite mounting evidence of environmental degradation and excessive consumption.

The final chapter in the macro section is every student's favorite. It starts out with a brief review of the nature and potential uses of fiscal, monetary, and supply-side policy options. Then the economic record is examined to highlight the contrast between theory and reality. The rest of the chapter identifies the obstacles that prevent us from eliminating the business cycle in the real world. These obstacles include everything from faulty forecasts to pork-barrel politics.

CONTENTS: INTERNATIONAL PERSPECTIVE

No introduction to economics can omit discussion of the global economy. But how can international topics be included in such a brief survey? *Essentials* resolves this dilemma with a two-pronged approach. The major thrust is to integrate global perspectives throughout the text. Half of the Headline boxes feature international illustrations of core concepts. In addition, the basic contrast between market and command economies that sets the framework for Chapter 1 is referred to repeatedly in both the micro and macro sections. The U.S. economy is described in a global context (Chapter 3) and analyzed throughout as an open economy with substantial foreign trade and investment sectors. Students will not think of the U.S. economy in insular terms as they work through this text.

The second global dimension to this text is a separate chapter on international trade. Chapter 17 describes U.S. trade patterns, then explains trade on the basis of comparative advantage. Consistent with the real-world focus of the text, a discussion of protectionist pressures and obstacles is also included. The objective is to convey a sense not only of why trade is beneficial, but also why trade issues are so politically sensitive.

TEXT SUPPLEMENTS

Issue Modules

The paring of the table of contents to 17 core chapters gives instructors more flexibility to pursue specific policy issues of interest. To facilitate such discussions, separately bound issue modules are available. These chapter-length modules are self-contained and formatted just like text chapters (with definitions in the margin, summary, questions for discussion, etc.). Available modules include:

- Welfare: Too Much or Too Little?
- Owls vs. Loggers: The Economics of Species Preservation
- Social Security: The Economics of an Aging Population
- Budget Deficits: Outcomes, Process, Theory
- Financial Markets: The Links to Economic Outcomes
- The California Economy Today
- The Texas Economy Today
- State and Local Finances
- Poverty in America
- The Economics of Discrimination

These modules can be ordered shrink wrapped with the text or can be incorporated into a bound custom-designed book. Your local McGraw-Hill sales representative can provide details.

Study Guide

From the student's perspective, the most important text supplement is the *Study Guide*, prepared by Professors Lawrence Ziegler and Linda Wilson at the University of Texas at Arlington. The *Study Guide* develops quantitative skills and the use of economic terminology, and enhances critical thinking capabilities. Each chapter of the *Study Guide* contains these features:

Quick Review. Key points in the text chapter are restated at the beginning of each *Study Guide* chapter. The reviews are parallel to and reinforce the chapter summaries provided in the text.

Learning Objectives. The salient lessons of the text chapters are noted at the outset of each *Study Guide* chapter. These objectives focus the student's efforts and help to ensure that key points will not be overlooked.

Key-Term Review. Early in each chapter the students are asked to match definitions with key terms. This relatively simple exercise is designed to refresh the student's memory and provide a basis for subsequent exercises.

True-False Questions. Fifteen true–false questions are provided in each chapter. These questions have been class tested to ensure their effectiveness in highlighting basic principles.

Multiple-Choice Questions. Twenty multiple-choice questions per chapter are provided. These questions allow only one correct answer and also focus on basic principles.

Problems and Applications. Exercises in each chapter of the *Study Guide* stress current issues and events, and problem-solving techniques.

Media Exercises. Each of the Headline boxes in the text are the focus of questions and problems. These exercises help integrate the Headline applications into the core material of the text.

Common Errors. In each chapter of the *Study Guide*, errors that students frequently make are identified. The bases for those errors are then explained, along with the correct principles. This unique feature is very effective in helping students discover their own mistakes.

Answers. Answers to *all* problems, exercises, and questions are provided at the end of each chapter. Difficult problems have annotated answers. These answers make the *Study Guide* self-contained, thus allowing students to use it for self-study.

Instructor's Resource Manual

The *Instructor's Resource Manual* has been prepared by Dillon Sanders of Oregon State University. The *Instructor's Resource Manual* is designed to assist instructors as they cope with the demands of teaching a survey of economics in a single term. There are suggestions for lecture launchers for each chapter. There is an annotated outline of each chapter which can be used as core material for lectures. There is also a brief description of some of the most common problems that arise when covering the material in each chapter. All of these sections should be helpful in deciding which topics to emphasize and which to omit as instructors cope with the reality of not being able to cover all they want.

In addition to these core lecture aids, the *Instructor's Resource Manual* contains suggestions for generating discussion on the Headlines in each chapter. It provides answers to the end-of-chapter problems in the text, along with explanations of how the answers were derived. A brief inventory of potential quiz questions is also provided for each chapter. Finally, it provides a list of supplementary materials (articles, videos, and films) for both instructor use and classroom showing.

Test Bank. The *Test Bank to accompany Essentials of Economics* follows the lead of the textbook in its application of economic concepts to worldwide economic issues, current real-world examples, and the role of government in the economy. The *Test Bank* has been prepared by *Study Guide* authors Lawrence Ziegler and Linda Wilson. This team helps assure a high level of quality and consistency of the test questions and the greatest possible correlation with the content of the text and the *Study Guide*. The *Test Bank* contains roughly 1,700 objective, predominantly multiple-choice questions. Each multiple-choice question is coded as to level of difficulty and is given a text-page reference where the student will find a discussion of the concept on which the question is based. Questions based on the boxed Headline material are segregated to facilitate their use.

News Flashes

As up-to-date as *Essentials of Economics* is, it can't foretell the future. As the future becomes the present, however, I will write News Flashes describing major economic events and relating them to specific topics in the text. Adopters of *Essentials* have the option of receiving News Flashes by mail or nearly instantaneously via fax. Four to six News Flashes are sent to adopters each year.

Spanish Edition

Essentials has been translated into Spanish. The Spanish edition also offers a chapter-length description of Spain's economy, paralleling the description of the U.S. economy in Chapter 2.

ACKNOWLEDGMENTS

Users of the first edition were generous in sharing their experiences and offering suggestions for revision. In addition, the edition benefited from very detailed reviews provided by:

John Altazan, University of New Orleans
Shirley Cassing, University of Pittsburgh
James E. Clark, Wichita State University
Bruce Domazlicky, Southeast Missouri State
Elizabeth Elmore, Stockton State College
Charlotte Hixson, Midlands Technical College
William Rawson, University of South Carolina
Arthur Raymond, Muhlenberg College
Roger Riefler, University of Nebraska
Ted Scheinman, Mt. Hood Community College

At McGraw-Hill, I was fortunate to have Elaine Rosenberg again assume the Editing Supervisor's responsibility of keeping all the pieces together as the book and supplements worked their way through the production process. The text also continues to benefit from the lively and engaging design created by Hermann Strohbach.

FINAL THOUGHTS

Hopefully, the brevity, content, style, and novel supplements of *Essentials* will induce you to try it out in your introductory survey course. The ultimate measure of the book's success will be reflected in student motivation and learning. As the author, I would appreciate hearing how well *Essentials* lives up to that standard.

Bradley R. Schiller

SECTION I

BASICS

Chapter 1

An Overview

Every nation grapples with a fundamental economic issue: Should the government determine economic outcomes, or should society rely instead on "the market" to fashion economic results? Historically, the pendulum of control has swung in both directions. The eighteenth-century economist Adam Smith argued that nations would prosper with less government interference and more reliance on the "invisible hand" of the marketplace. As he saw it, markets were efficient mechanisms for deciding what goods to produce, how to produce them, and what wages to pay. Smith's writings (*The Wealth of Nations*, 1776) encouraged governments to take a more passive role in "the business of business."

Karl Marx saw things differently. In his view, a freewheeling marketplace would cater to the whims of the rich and neglect the needs of the poor. Workers would be exploited by industrial barons and great landowners. To "leave it to the market," as Smith had proposed, would encourage exploitation. In the mid-nineteenth century, Karl Marx proposed a radical alternative: overturn the power of the elite and create a communist state in which everyone's needs would be fulfilled. Marx's writings (*Das Kapital*, 1848) encouraged communist revolutions and the development of central planning systems. The (people's) government, not the market, assumed responsibility for deciding what goods were produced, at what prices they were sold, and even who got them.

The choices have not always been so dramatic. In the history of the United States there haven't been any "all-or-nothing" transformations like those in Russia, China, Cuba, Burma, or Eastern Europe. The alternatives of government control or market reliance have been a question of degree, not revolution. The New Deal was about as big a change as America has experienced. In the depths of the Great Depression of the 1930s, President Franklin Roosevelt greatly expanded the government's role in providing income security, regulating working conditions, and limiting the power of large corporations. The English economist John Maynard Keynes (*The Gen-*

eral Theory of Employment, Interest and Money, 1936) also encouraged governments both here and abroad to play a more active role in reducing unemployment.

The pendulum of control hasn't always swung in the direction of more government. In the 1990s, the central planning systems of Central and Eastern Europe were largely dismantled. As communism collapsed, people in Russia and Eastern Europe turned to the marketplace for direction. State enterprises were sold to private investors. The central planners lost their control over prices. Jobs and wages were no longer guaranteed by the state.

The pendulum swung in the same direction in Western Europe, Latin America, and Asia. In the mid-1980s, Italy, France, and Great Britain privatized formerly government-run enterprises in railroads, steel, telephones, and electricity. Mexico moved in a similar direction, as did India, Vietnam, and a host of other countries. In every case, the motivation for change was the belief that market-directed economies would outperform government-directed ones.

The Republican sweep of the 1994 U.S. congressional elections also represented a movement away from government regulation. Public-opinion polls such as the one in the accompanying Headline showed that Americans were dissatisfied with the pace of economic advancement and increasingly skeptical of the government's ability to fix things. When the Republican party offered to reduce the role of government and rely more on

HEADLINE

MARKET VS. GOVERNMENT RELIANCE

Government Gets Blame for Bad Economy

An October 1994 Gallup poll reveals that Americans are dissatisfied with economic conditions and don't foresee much improvement. Who do they blame? They say the government is trying to do too much and that we need to rely more on the private sector.

Current Economy

Question:	How would you rate economic conditions in this country today?	
Response:	Excellent	1%
	Good	25
	Fair	52
	Poor	21
	No opinion	1

The Outlook

Question:	Do you think that economic conditions in

the country as a whole are getting better, getting worse, or staying about the same?

Response:	Getting better	22%
	Getting worse	28
	About the same	49
	No opinion	1

Government Role

Question:	Some people think the government is trying to do too many things that should be left to individuals and businesses. Others think that government should do more to solve our country's problems. Which comes closer to your own view?

Response:	Doing too much	57%
	Not doing enough	37
	Other/No opinion	6

The Gallup Poll Monthly, October 1994.

the marketplace to create jobs, raise incomes, and promote prosperity, voters responded positively.

THREE BASIC ECONOMIC QUESTIONS

The continuing controversy over government control versus market reliance is not just a debate about the price of bread or the number of available jobs. Politically, the choice between different systems of control also represents a decision on who will have more power in society and who will have less. Philosophically, the issue of government versus market control raises questions of basic liberty: Which decisions can be left to individual members of society and which should be made collectively (for the "public good")?

This text focuses on those issues that have a decidedly economic content. In this context three central questions stand out:

- *WHAT to produce*
- *HOW to produce*
- *FOR WHOM to produce*

WHAT to Produce

opportunity cost: The most desired goods and services that are foregone in order to obtain something else.

factors of production: Resource inputs used to produce goods and services; e.g., land, labor, capital, entrepreneurship.

scarcity: Lack of available resources to satisfy all desired uses of those resources.

The WHAT question is quite simple. People want more clothes, fancier cars, bigger houses, and loads of electronic gadgetry. We also want better schools, more roads, and cleaner streets. Unfortunately, we can't have it all. Our ability to produce goods and services is limited. It's the same kind of problem you have with your time. You might like to go to the movies, go shopping, hang out with friends, even attend class. With only 24 hours in a day, you've got to make choices. If you decide to go to the movies, you have less time to study. In effect, the sacrificed study time is a cost of going to the movies. In general, whatever you decide to do will entail an **opportunity cost,** i.e., the sacrifice of a next-best alternative. Faced with such tradeoffs, you must decide how *best* to use your scarce time.

For the larger economy, time is also limited. So, too, are the resources needed to produce desired goods and services. To get more houses, more cars, or more movies, we need not only time but also resources to produce these things. These resources—land, labor, capital, and entrepreneurship—are the basic ingredients of production. They are called **factors of production.** The more factors of production we have, the more we can produce in a given period of time.

Even in a country as rich as the United States, there is only so much land, labor, and machinery available. There is also a limited number of people with the creativity and skill (entrepreneurial talent) to use these resources in production. These *resource* limits constrain our *output* possibilities. Similar but smaller limits to production exist in Japan, Russia, Brazil, and South Africa—in fact, in all countries.

Because our capacity to produce is limited, we must make hard choices about what goods and services to produce. The problem here is **scarcity,** a situation where our desires exceed our resources. Do we want to build more homes this year or more schools? Do we want more cars or more transit systems? Should we devote our farmland to corn production or to soybeans? ***Because wants exceed resources, we must make difficult choices about WHAT to produce.***

**FIGURE 1.1
A Production-Possibilities Curve**

A production-possibilities curve describes the various combinations of final goods or services that could be produced in a given time period with available resources and technology. It represents a "menu" of output choices an economy confronts. Point *C* indicates that we could produce a *combination* of *OD* units of consumer goods and the quantity *OE* of military output. To get more military output (e.g., at point *X*), we have to reduce consumer output. Our objective is to select the best possible mix of output.

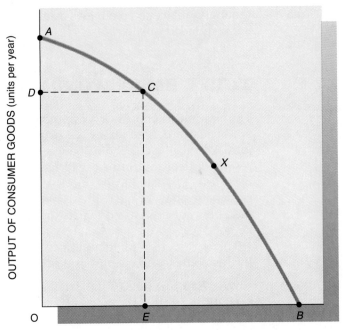

OUTPUT OF MILITARY GOODS (units per year)

Production Possibilities. Figure 1.1 illustrates this basic dilemma. Suppose there are only two kinds of goods, "consumer goods" and "military goods." In this case, the question of WHAT to produce boils down to finding the most desirable combination of these two goods.

To make that selection, we first need to know how much of each good we *could* produce. That will depend on how many resources we have available and our ability to use them. The first thing we need to do, then, is to count up our factors of production—the land, labor, capital (buildings and machinery), and entrepreneurial talent that are needed to produce goods and services. Then we must assess our technology—our technical and managerial abilities—to use these factors of production to produce specific goods. By doing this, we will discover what the *limits* to production are.

Suppose that the limit to our production of consumer goods is represented by point *A* in Figure 1.1. That is to say, the vertical distance from the origin (point O) to point *A* represents the maximum quantity of consumer goods that could be produced this year. To produce the quantity *A* of consumer goods, we would have to use *all* available factors of production. At point *A* no resources would be available for producing military goods. The choice of *maximum* consumer output implies *zero* military output.

We could make other choices about WHAT to produce. Point *B*, for example, illustrates another extreme. The horizontal distance from the origin (point O) to point *B* represents our maximum capacity to produce military goods. To get that much military output, we would have to devote all available resources and know-how to that single task. It could be done, however; point *B* represents a production *possibility*. If we chose it, we wouldn't be producing *any* consumer goods. We would be well protected, but ill-nourished and poorly clothed (wearing last year's clothes).

Our choices about WHAT to produce are not limited to the extremes of points *A* and *B*. We could instead produce a *combination* of consumer and military goods. Point *C* represents one such combination. To get to point *C*, we have to forsake maximum consumer goods output (point *A*) and use some of our scarce resources to produce military goods. At point *C* we are producing only *OD* of consumer goods and *OE* of military goods.

Point *C* is just one of many combinations we *could* produce. We could produce *any* combination of output represented by points along the curve in Figure 1.1. For this reason we call it the **production-possibilities** curve; it represents the alternative combinations of goods and services that could be produced in a given time period with all available resources and technology. It is, in effect, an economic "menu" from which some combinations of goods and services must be selected.

production possibilities: The alternative combinations of goods and services that could be produced in a given time period with all available resources and technology.

The production-possibilities curve puts the basic issue of WHAT to produce in graphic terms. We can only produce *one* specific combination of goods in any time period. Accordingly, the question of WHAT to produce boils down to choosing a single point on the production-possibilities curve.

Who Should Decide? Which point should we select? Every mix of output will help fulfill our collective desires. They are not equally desirable, however, for some combinations are better than others. In fact, one combination is likely to be better than all others. That *optimal* mix of output is what every economy strives to produce.

Locating the best possible (optimal) mix of output isn't an easy task. There are bound to be sharp disagreements. Pacifists might prefer to produce at point *A*, eliminating any military output. Military hawks, on the other hand, might see some urgency in producing more weapons, even if doing so forced consumers to tighten their belts. In such circumstances, it won't be easy to reach a consensus on which mix of output is best.

During the Cold War that persisted from 1948 to 1989, there was a general consensus that the United States needed to maintain a huge arsenal of weapons. Not everyone agreed with that conclusion, but both the Republican and Democratic political parties supported the proposition. As a result, national defense spending absorbed as much as 6.5 percent of total output in the mid-1980s. Producing that arsenal required the use of scarce resources that would have otherwise been employed to produce consumer goods.

When the Soviet Union collapsed, the need for American military preparedness diminished. This scenario presented the opportunity to change the mix of output—to produce fewer weapons and more consumer goods. The nature of the resulting "peace dividend" is illustrated in Figure 1.2. The accompanying Headline illustrates some specific forms the peace dividend might have taken.

POLITICAL CHOICES. The initial decision to support a military buildup and the later decision to reduce military output were political decisions. Ultimately, it was the U.S. Congress that made those decisions. Congress also makes decisions about how many interstate highways to build, how many Head Start classes to offer, and how much space exploration to pursue. All of these decisions entail the use of scarce resources and thus affect the mix of output we produce.

Should Congress also decide how much ice cream will be produced, and how many CD players? What about essentials, like food and shelter? Should decisions about the production of those goods be made in Washington, D.C., or should the mix of output be selected some other way?

FIGURE 1.2
A Peace Dividend

A reduction in military output releases factors of production that can be used to produce consumer goods. The military builddown associated with the move from point S to point R enables consumption output to increase from C_1 to C_2.

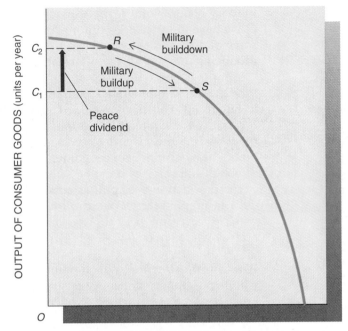

THE MARKET MECHANISM. The market mechanism offers an alternative decision-making process. In a market-driven economy the process of selecting a mix of output is as familiar as grocery shopping. If you desire ice cream and have sufficient income, you simply buy ice cream. Your purchases act as a signal to producers that ice cream is desired. By expressing the *ability and willingness to pay* for ice cream, you are effectively telling ice cream producers that their efforts are going to be rewarded. If enough consumers feel the same way you do—and are able and willing to pay the price of ice cream—ice cream producers will produce more ice cream.

The same kind of interactions helps determine which crops we grow. There is only so much good farmland available. Should we grow corn or beans? If consumers prefer corn, they will buy more corn and shun the beans. Farmers will quickly get the market's message and devote more of their land to corn, cutting back on bean production. In the process, the mix of output will change—moving us closer to the choice consumers have made.

The central actor in this reshuffling of resources and outputs is the **market mechanism.** *Market sales and prices send a signal to producers about what mix of output consumers want.* If you want something and have sufficient income, you buy it. If enough people do the same thing, the total sales of that product will rise, and perhaps its price will as well. Producers, seeing sales and prices rise, will be inclined to increase production. To do so, they will attempt to acquire a larger share of our available resources and use it to produce the goods we desire. No direct communication between us and the producer is required; market sales and prices convey the message and direct the market, much like an "invisible hand." It was this ability of "the market" to select a mix of output desired by consumers that so impressed Adam Smith. He urged governments to pursue a policy of **laissez faire**—leaving the market alone to make basic economic decisions.

market mechanism: The use of market prices and sales to signal desired outputs (or resource allocations).

laissez faire: The doctrine of "leave it alone," of nonintervention by government in the market mechanism.

HEADLINE

OPPORTUNITY COSTS

The Peace Dividend

During the military buildup of the 1980s, as much as 6.5 percent of total output consisted of military goods and services. The end of the Cold War in 1989 created an historic opportunity to change that mix of output. Former Defense Secretary Richard Cheney said the United States could safely cut $120 billion from defense spending over five years. What kind of civilian goods might be produced with that "peace dividend"? Some possible uses of those resources were estimated by Data Resources, Inc., an economic consulting firm based in Lexington, Massachusetts. By 1995, the defense share of total output had fallen to 4 percent.

Produce this . . .

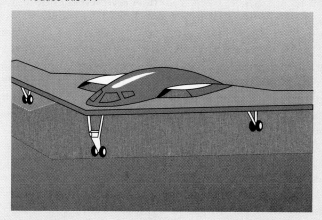

or this?

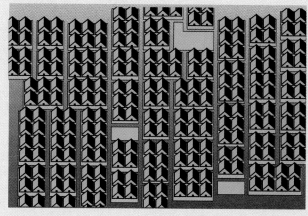

8% of estimated military spending	$120 billion	Cost of cleaning up and modernizing nuclear weapons plants
Advanced technology fighter	$40 billion	Cost of repairing the nation's 240,000 deficient bridges
Navy's V-22 Osprey program	$25 billion	Cost of modernizing the air-traffic control system
SDI expenditures (1991)	$5 billion	50% increase in all university research budgets
One B-2 bomber	$532 million	Cost of buying housing for 8,000 families
One M-1 tank	$2.6 million	Full four-year college costs for 50 students
One Phoenix air-to-air missile	$1 million	Cost of nursing home care for 35 elderly citizens

Source: Data Resources, Inc.

CENTRAL PLANNING. We could leave it to the government to decide what goods to produce. In the extreme, this would entail a system of central planning. In the former Soviet Union, the central planners decided how many cars to produce and how much bread. They then assigned workers and other resources to those industries to implement their decisions. They also decided who would get the bread and the cars that were produced.

MIXED ECONOMIES. Few countries now depend on either central planning or the market mechanism to make all the output decisions. Instead, **mixed economies** use a combination of market signals and government directives to select a mix of output. In the United States, for example, we let the market decide how much ice cream will be produced and how many cars. We

> **mixed economy:** An economy that uses both market and non-market signals to allocate goods and resources.

use the political process, however, to decide how many highways to construct, how many schools to build, and how much military output to produce.

Market Failure. Our use of both market signals and government directives to select the mix of output suggests a certain ambivalence. Why don't we let the market make *all* our output decisions? If the market does such a good job in producing the right amount of ice cream, couldn't it also decide how many highways to build or how much weaponry to produce?

The market does not work equally well in all situations. In fact, in some circumstances, the market mechanism might actually fail to produce the goods and services society desires. National defense is an example. Most people want to feel that their nation's borders are secure and that law and order will prevail in their communities. But few people can afford to buy an army or maintain a legal system. Even if someone were rich enough to pay for such security, he might decline to do so. After all, a military force and a legal system would benefit everyone in the community, not just those individuals who paid for it. Recognizing this, few people would willingly pay for national security or a system of criminal justice. They would rather spend their income on ice cream and CD players, hoping someone else would pay for law and order. If everyone waited for a "free ride," no money would be spent on national defense or a legal system. Society would end up with neither output, even though both services were widely desired.

In other situations, the market might produce *too much* of a good or service. If there were no government regulation, then anyone who had enough money could purchase and drive a car. Little kids from wealthy families could hit the highways, and so could adults with a history of drunken driving. Moreover, no one would have to spend money on emissions-control systems, lead-free gasoline, or mufflers. We could drive as fast as we wanted.

Some people would welcome unregulated roadways as a new utopia. Others, however, would be concerned about safety and pollution. They would realize that the *market's* decisions about who could drive and what kinds of cars were produced might not be so perfect. They would want the government to intervene. To assure safer and cleaner driving, people might agree to let the government regulate speed, auto emissions, and even drivers.

These and other situations suggest that the market alone might not always pick the best possible mix of output. The problem is illustrated in Figure 1.3. Suppose point *X* represents the best possible mix of output, based on some sort of societal consensus. The market, however, produces a different mix of output, at point *M*. In that case, we would conclude that the market had *failed*. **Market failure** means that the market does not produce the best possible mix of output. In Figure 1.3, the market produces too much civilian output and too little military output. When the market fails to produce the right mix of output, government intervention may be required to get to point *X*.

market failure: An imperfection in the market mechanism that prevents optimal outcomes.

Government Failure. Faced with the possibility of market failure, the desirability of some government regulation becomes clear. But how much government intervention do we want? And how can we be sure that government intervention will *improve* market outcomes? Maybe government bureaucrats will be more interested in enhancing their own careers than in serving the public. They might be more attuned to serving powerful pri-

FIGURE 1.3
Market Failure

The market mechanism will allocate resources to produce a specific mix of output. In this case, however, the market-generated mix (point *M*) is not consistent with society's most desired mix (point *X*). When this happens, the market has failed.

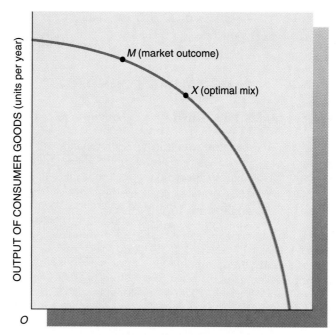

OUTPUT OF MILITARY GOODS (units per year)

vate interests than to serving the general public interest. Maybe they will just make mistakes.

The possibility for **government failure**—intervention that fails to improve (possibly even worsens) market outcomes—is illustrated in Figure 1.4. Again, we assume the optimal mix of output is located at point *X* and that the market itself produces the suboptimal mix at point *M*. In this case, the goal of government intervention is to move the economy closer to point *X*. It is possible, however, that misguided intervention might move the econ-

government failure: Government intervention that fails to improve economic outcomes.

FIGURE 1.4
Government Failure

The goal of government intervention is to correct market failure. It is possible, however, that government policy might move the economy farther away from the optimal mix (to point G_1) or even inside the production-possibilities curve (point G_2).

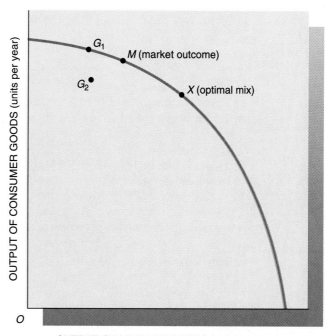

OUTPUT OF MILITARY GOODS (units per year)

HEADLINE

COMMAND ECONOMIES

Where Communist Economies Fell Short

It's not over till it's over, Yogi admonished. But with Muscovites salivating over the arrival of McDonald's and Hungary celebrating the embrace of General Electric, it is hard to deny that the long ideological war between capitalism and socialism has ended in a decisive win for the home team.

Economists across the political spectrum agree that central planning has proved a bust in recent decades. Most would also agree that decentralized economic decision-making offers Communist countries the best hope for catching up with the affluent West.

Under the purest versions of centralized planning, administrators decide what goods will be produced and what economic resources will be used to make them. Unemployment is, in effect, abolished by decree. And inflation is suppressed, with excess demand showing up as shortages rather than as rising prices.

But in practice, the performance of planned economies is mixed. Their inherent strength, the ability to mobilize resources for a few national goals, is familiar to anyone who remembers the way the American economy rallied to support the Allied armies in World War II. By organizing what amounts to a permanent war economy, Stalin was able to transform a backward land into a great military power with an impressively large industrial base. And by forcing Soviet citizens to invest a high percentage of income, planners could maintain very high growth rates through the 1960's.

The New York Times, December 17, 1989, p. E3. Copyright © 1989 by the New York Times Company. Reprinted by permission.

Drowning in Detail

Soviet economists once thought they could use computer models to simulate the decentralized workings of markets, but that idea has proved far beyond the capacities of the speediest supercomputer. As the Soviet economy grew more complex, the lack of accurate signals of cost and value began to cut more deeply. Production goals set in tons, for example, have led Soviet pipe manufacturers to use far more steel than necessary. Consumer prices held far below cost have led to colossal waste: it often pays farmers to sell their grain to the state, and then buy back the subsidized bread made from the grain, to use as animal feed.

Correcting such obvious misincentives is not easy. Planners, with thousands of interdependent production sectors to coordinate, drown in detail. Even the Soviet Congress, convened last week to debate momentous issues of policy, was reduced to quarreling over the poor quality of washing machines and the scarcity of school desks.

Scale and complexity seem to magnify another weakness of planned economies—the lack of financial incentives for personal initiative. In Stalin's day it might have been sufficient to set quotas for numbers of tractors assembled or tons of coal dug, rewarding overachievers with New Year's vodka and punishing shirkers with holidays in the gulag.

But in a modern economy whose long-term prospects depend on the creation and rapid diffusion of technology, such crude incentives cannot work.

—Peter Passell

omy to point G_1, farther away from the optimal mix. That worsening of the mix of output would represent government failure. Government intervention would also fail if it moved the economy to point G_2, *inside* the production-possibilities curve. At point G_2, the inefficiencies associated with government intervention prevent the economy from fully utilizing its productive capacity. This kind of government failure helped to precipitate the collapse of communism, as discussed in the accompanying Headline.

HOW to Produce

The second basic economic issue, HOW to produce, can also be resolved by the market alone, by government directives, or by some mix of the two methods. Here, again, the possibility of both market failure and government failure exists.

Consider the message that unregulated markets communicate to producers. In an unregulated market, no price would be charged for using air or waterways, since neither are owned by any individual. Producers, therefore, would regard the use of air and waterways as a "free" good. Under such circumstances it would be a lot cheaper for a factory to dump its waste into nearby waterways than to dispose of it more carefully. It would also be cheaper for power plants to let waste gases and soot go up in smoke than to install environmental safeguards. Were profit-and-loss considerations the only determinant of HOW goods were produced, we might end up destroying the environment. If the market encouraged such an outcome, we could conclude that it had failed to select the best possible way for producing desired goods and services.

If the market fails to answer the HOW question correctly, we may turn to government for help. But will the government have the right answers? The centrally planned economies of Eastern Europe have experienced some of the world's worst environmental problems. The huge steel mills outside Krakow, Poland, spewed more sulfur into the air than all of Western Europe's steel mills combined. The air in Budapest was so polluted that Hungarians paid for brief inhalations of compressed clean air. The factory and sewage waste from Hungary, Czechoslovakia, and Bulgaria made the Danube Europe's most polluted waterway. Worse yet, Soviet planners allowed Chernobyl to become a nuclear nightmare. Clearly, ***there is no guarantee that the visible hand of government will be any cleaner than the invisible hand of the marketplace.***

The challenge here is to determine the most desirable methods of production, then ensure that they are put into place. In the United States, and other mixed economies, this challenge is pursued with a combination of market incentives and government regulation.

FOR WHOM to Produce

Similar considerations influence our decisions on FOR WHOM to produce. A market system rewards people according to their value in the marketplace. Sports stars, entertainers, and corporate executives end up with huge paychecks while others toil for meager wages. Big paychecks provide access to more output; people with little paychecks get much less of what is produced.

Is this market-based system of distributing output fair? Should rich people live in mansions while poor people sleep in abandoned cars? Many observers object that the market should not be the sole arbiter of who gets shelter.

Centrally planned economies try to resolve this problem by letting the government determine how much each worker will be paid and who will get to purchase the goods produced. This central control is again predicated on the assumption that government knows best and can attain the (centrally) desired distribution of income in an efficient way. But central planning may dull people's incentives and so reduce total output. The slices may become more equal, but the pie shrinks. Central control of the distribution of income and goods also creates irresistible opportunities for political favoritism and personal gain.

Mixed economies use a combination of market forces and government policies to determine FOR WHOM output is produced. The government redistributes income by taxing the rich and giving transfer payments to the poor (welfare, food stamps), the jobless (unemployment benefits), and the aged (Social Security benefits). The government also redistributes goods and services directly by providing shelters for the homeless and medical and legal assistance for the poor, not to mention public schools. All of these interventions reflect the conviction that the invisible hand of the market shouldn't be the sole determinant of FOR WHOM our output is produced.

Although the intention of government tax and transfer policies is laudatory, such intervention may have undesired side effects. The poor could end up paying more taxes, and the rich could end up with the income transfers. Since the political process is more responsive to rich people than to poor people, such a perverse outcome is not unthinkable. Even if the redistribution were from rich to poor, the process of redistribution might reduce total output. Both transfer recipients and tax-burdened rich people might decide to work or produce less. Here, again, the possibility of government failure must be recognized.

WHAT ECONOMICS IS ALL ABOUT

economics: The study of how best to allocate scarce resources among competing uses.

There is a lot at stake in our collective decisions about WHAT, HOW, and FOR WHOM to produce. To make the right decisions, we have to know how economies function. That is the motivation for studying economics. The science of **economics** focuses on the central problem of scarcity. The goal of economic theory is to figure out how society can best allocate its scarce resources. How can society attain the best possible mix of output, the most efficient methods of production, and the optimal distribution of income?

End vs. Means

Economists do not formulate the answers to the three basic questions themselves. Instead, they focus on the means available for achieving given goals. If society decides it wants a certain mix of output, economists can show how to attain that combination most efficiently. If the community demands less pollution, economists can show the least costly ways of achieving that goal. Economists can also describe the consequences for investment, work effort, and output of taxing the rich to provide welfare benefits for the poor.

The distinction between ends and means doesn't imply that economists have no personal opinions. It does emphasize, however, that economists—like all scientists—have a professional responsibility to distinguish subjective opinion from objective observation. To do this, economists recognize two different kinds of economic analysis, normative economics and positive economics.

Normative economics is subjective and expresses what *ought* to be. The decision of the U.S. Congress to make full employment a policy goal is a reflection of normative economics. The members of Congress decided that everyone who is able and willing to work ought to have the opportunity to do so. Designating a point on the production-possibilities curve as the most desirable mix of output is likewise a normative judgment.

Positive economics tries to stick to the facts. The function of positive economics is to describe the mechanisms for achieving full employment or the preferred mix of output. Positive economic analysis may enumerate the costs of pursuing a specific goal but won't render a judgment on whether those costs are too high.

It would be wonderful if we could always keep a clear line between normative and positive economics. In reality, however, an economist's "positive" analysis may be influenced by his or her "normative" judgments. Hence economists may offer conflicting policy advice even where "objective" theory suggests unanimity.

Macro vs. Micro

> **macroeconomics:** The study of aggregate economic behavior, of the economy as a whole.

> **microeconomics:** The study of individual behavior in the economy, of the components of the larger economy.

The study of economics is typically divided into two parts: macroeconomics and microeconomics. Macroeconomics focuses on the behavior of an entire economy—the "big picture." In macroeconomics we worry about such national goals as full employment, control of inflation, and economic growth, without worrying about the well-being or behavior of specific individuals or groups. The essential concern of **macroeconomics** is to understand and improve the performance of the economy as a whole.

Microeconomics is concerned with the details of this "big picture." In microeconomics we focus on the individuals, firms, and government agencies that actually make up the larger economy. Our interest here is in the behavior of individual economic actors. What are their goals? How can they best achieve these goals with their limited resources? How will they respond to various incentives and opportunities?

A primary concern of macroeconomics, for example, is to determine the impact of aggregate consumer spending on total output, employment, and prices. Very little attention is devoted to the actual content of consumer spending or its determinants. Microeconomics, on the other hand, focuses on the specific expenditure decisions of individual consumers and the forces (tastes, prices, incomes) that influence those decisions.

The distinction between macro- and microeconomics is also reflected in discussions of business investment. In macroeconomics we want to know what determines the aggregate rate of business investment and how those expenditures influence the nation's total output, employment, and prices. In microeconomics we focus on the decisions of individual businesses regarding the rate of production, the choice of factors of production, and the pricing of specific goods.

The distinction between macro- and microeconomics is a matter of convenience. In reality, macroeconomic outcomes depend on micro behavior, and micro behavior is affected by macro outcomes. Hence one cannot fully understand how an economy works until one understands how all the participants behave and why they behave as they do. But just as you can drive a car without knowing how its engine is constructed, you can observe how an economy runs without completely disassembling it. In macroeconomics we observe that the car goes faster when the accelerator is depressed and that it slows when the brake is applied. That is all we need to know in most situations. There are times, however, when the car breaks down. When it does, we have to know something more about how the pedals work. This leads us into micro studies. How does each part work? Which ones can or should be fixed?

Theory vs. Reality

The distinction between macroeconomics and microeconomics is one of many simplifications we make in studying economic behavior. The economy is much too vast and complex to describe and explain in one course (or one lifetime). Accordingly, we focus on basic relationships, ignoring annoying detail. In so doing, we isolate basic principles of economic behavior, then use those principles to predict economic events and formulate economic policies. What this means is that we formulate theories, or *models*, of economic behavior, then use those theories to evaluate and design economic policy.

Because all economic models entail simplifying assumptions, they never *exactly* describe the real world. Nevertheless, the models may be useful. If our models are *reasonably* consistent with economic reality, they may yield good predictions of economic behavior. Likewise, if our simplifications do not become distortions, they may provide good guidelines for economic policy.

Our theory of consumer behavior assumes, for example, a distinct relationship between the price of a good and the quantity people buy. As prices increase, people buy less. In reality, however, people *may* buy *more* of a good at increased prices, especially if those high prices create a certain "snob appeal" or if prices are expected to increase still further. In predicting consumer responses to price increases, we typically ignore such possibilities by *assuming* that the price of the good in question is the *only* thing that changes. This assumption of "other things remaining equal (unchanged)" (in Latin, **ceteris paribus**) allows us to make straightforward predictions. If instead we described consumer responses to increased prices in any and all circumstances (allowing everything to change at once), every prediction would be accompanied by a book full of exceptions and qualifications. We would look more like lawyers than economists.

Although the assumption of *ceteris paribus* makes it easier to formulate economic theory and policy, it also increases the risk of error. Obviously, if other things do change in significant ways, our predictions (and policies) may fail. But, like weather forecasters, we continue to make predictions, knowing that occasional failure is inevitable. In so doing, we are motivated by the conviction that it is better to be approximately right than to be dead wrong.

ceteris paribus: The assumption of nothing else changing.

Politics vs. Economics

Politicians cannot afford to be quite so complacent about predictions, however. Policy decisions must be made every day. And a politician's continued survival may depend on being more than approximately right. Economists can contribute to those policy decisions by offering measures of economic impact and predictions of economic behavior. But in the real world, those measures and predictions will always contain a substantial margin of error. That is to say, economic policy decisions are always based on some amount of uncertainty. Even the best economic minds cannot foretell the future.

Even if the future were known, economic policy could not rely completely on economic theory. There are always political choices to be made. The choice of more consumer goods ("butter") or more military hardware ("guns"), for example, is not an economic decision. Rather it is a sociopolitical decision based in part on economic tradeoffs (opportunity costs). The "need" for more butter or more guns must be expressed politically—ends versus means again. Political forces are a necessary ingredient in economic policy decisions. That is not to say that all "political" decisions are right. It does suggest, however, that economic policies may not always conform to economic theory.

Both politics and economics are involved in the continuing debate about laissez faire and government intervention. The pendulum has swung from laissez faire (Adam Smith) to central government control (Karl Marx) and to an ill-defined middle ground where the government assumes major responsibilities for economic stability (John Maynard Keynes) and for answers to the WHAT, HOW, and FOR WHOM questions. In the 1980s the Reagan administration pushed the pendulum a bit closer to laissez faire by cutting taxes, reducing government regulation, and encouraging market incentives. The Bush administration pushed the pendulum back a bit by expanding the government's role in education, regulation, and research. When the economy slumped in 1990–91, however, President Bush rejected advice to intervene, preferring to let the market right itself.

President Clinton thought the government should play a more active role in resolving basic economic issues. Just after he was elected, he published a "Vision for America" that spelled out a greater role for government in assuring health care, providing skills training, protecting the environment, and regulating working conditions. In his vision, well-intentioned government officials could correct market failures. The Democratic-controlled Congress of 1993–94 offered little support for Clinton's visions, however, and the Republican-controlled Congress of 1995–96 rejected it.

In part, this enduring controversy about markets versus government reflects diverse political, rather than strictly economic, views. Some people think a big public sector is undesirable, even if it improves economic performance. They see government intervention as a threat not only to economic performance but to individual liberties as well. They prefer the "invisible hand" of the market to the visible hand of government intervention almost every time. On the other hand, some advocates of government intervention feel that the market mechanism is inherently corrupting of human values and call on the government to limit greed, to guarantee economic security, and to protect the environment.

The debate over markets versus government also persists because of gaps in our economic understanding. For over 200 years economists have been arguing about what makes the economy tick. None of the competing theories has performed spectacularly well. Indeed, few economists have successfully predicted major economic events with any consistency. Even annual forecasts of inflation, unemployment, and output are regularly in error. Worse still, there are never-ending arguments about what caused a major economic event long after it has already occurred. In fact, economists are still arguing over the causes of the Great Depression of the 1930s!

Modest Expectations

In view of all these debates and uncertainties, you should not expect to learn everything there is to know about the economy in this text or course. Our goals are more modest. We want to develop a reasonable perspective on economic behavior, an understanding of basic principles. With this foundation, you should acquire a better view of how the economy works. Daily news reports on economic events should make more sense. Congressional debates on tax and budget policies should take on more meaning. You may even develop some insights that you can apply toward running a business or planning a career.

SUMMARY

- Every nation confronts the three basic economic questions of WHAT to produce, HOW, and FOR WHOM.
- The three questions can be answered by the interplay of decentralized markets, by a system of central planning, or by a mixed system of market signals and government intervention.
- Price signals are the key feature of the market mechanism. Consumers signal their desires for specific goods by paying a price for these goods. Producers respond to the price signal by assembling factors of production to produce the desired output.
- The need to select a single mix of output is necessitated by our limited capacity to produce. Scarcity results when our wants exceed our resources.
- The production-possibilities curve illustrates the limits to output dictated by available factors of production and technology. The production-possibilities curve is the menu of different output mixes from which we may choose.
- All production entails an opportunity cost: We can produce more of output A only if we produce less of output B. The implied reduction in output B is the opportunity cost of output A.
- Market failure occurs when the market mechanism generates the wrong mix of output, inefficient methods of production, or an inequitable distribution of income. Government intervention may fail, too, however, by not improving (or even worsening) economic outcomes.
- The study of economics focuses on the broad question of resource allocation. Macroeconomics is concerned with allocating the resources of an entire economy to achieve broad economic goals (e.g., full employment). Microeconomics focuses on the behavior and goals of individual market participants.
- Normative economics entails subjective judgments of what *ought* to be. Positive economics entails objective analysis of how to attain desired goals.

Terms to Remember

Define the following terms:

opportunity cost	laissez faire	economics
factors of production	mixed economy	macroeconomics
scarcity	market failure	microeconomics
production possibilities	government failure	*ceteris paribus*
market mechanism		

Questions for Discussion

1. What opportunity costs did you incur in reading this chapter?
2. Why must an economy choose a specific mix of output? How can the best mix be identified?
3. In Figure 1.4, government failure causes output to fall below its full potential. How might this happen?
4. We currently allocate about 4 percent of our resources to military output. Is this too much or too little? How can we decide?
5. Should the government build more shelters for the homeless? Where will it get the resources to do so?

6. If auto-emissions controls weren't required, would people willingly buy and install them? Explain.
7. Which government income transfers do rich people receive? Who pays for them?
8. If taxes on the rich were raised to provide more housing for the poor, how would the willingness to work be affected? What would happen to total output?

Problems

1. Redraw Figure 1.1 and show the opportunity cost of moving from
   (a) point A to point C
   (b) point C to point X
   (c) point X to point B
2. Assume that it takes 4 hours of labor time to paint a room and 3 hours to sand a floor. Illustrate the production possibilities for a single worker in a 24-hour period. What is the opportunity cost of painting six rooms?
3. Suppose in problem 2 that a second worker became available. Illustrate the resulting change in production possibilities. Now what would be the opportunity cost of painting 6 rooms?
4. Assume that the schedule below describes the production possibilities confronting an economy. Using the information from the table:
   (a) Draw the production-possibilities curve. Be sure to label each alternative output combination (A through E).
   (b) Calculate and illustrate on your graph the opportunity cost of producing one CD player per week.
   (c) What is the cost of producing a second CD player? What might account for the difference?
   (d) Which point on the curve is the most desired one? How will we find out?

Potential Weekly Output Combinations	Pianos	CD players
A	10	0
B	9	1
C	7	2
D	4	3
E	0	4

APPENDIX

USING GRAPHS

Economists like to draw graphs. In fact, we didn't even make it through the first chapter without a few graphs. The purpose of this appendix is to look more closely at the way graphs are drawn and used.

The basic purpose of a graph is to illustrate a relationship between two *variables*. Consider, for example, the relationship between grades and studying. In general, we expect that additional hours of study time will lead to higher grades. Hence we should be able to see a distinct relationship between hours of study time and grade-point average.

Suppose that we actually surveyed all the students taking this course with regard to their study time and grade-point averages. The resulting information can be compiled in a table such as Table A.1.

TABLE A.1
Hypothetical Relationship of Grades to Study Time

Study Time (hours per week)	Grade-Point Average
16	4.0 (A)
14	3.5 (B +)
12	3.0 (B)
10	2.5 (C +)
8	2.0 (C)
6	1.5 (D +)
4	1.0 (D)
2	0.5 (F +)
0	0 (F)

According to the table, students who don't study at all can expect an F in this course. To get a C, the average student apparently spends 8 hours a week studying. All those who study 16 hours a week end up with an A in the course.

These relationships between grades and studying can also be illustrated on a graph. Indeed, the whole purpose of a graph is to summarize numerical relationships.

We begin to construct a graph by drawing horizontal and vertical boundaries, as in Figure A.1. These boundaries are called the *axes* of the graph. On the vertical axis we measure one of the variables; the other variable is measured on the horizontal axis.[1]

In this case, we shall measure the grade-point average on the vertical axis. We start at the *origin* (the intersection of the two axes) and count upward, letting the distance between horizontal lines represent half (0.5) a grade point. Each horizontal line is numbered, up to the maximum grade-point average of 4.0.

The number of hours each week spent doing homework is measured on the horizontal axis. We begin at the origin again, and count to the right. The *scale* (numbering) proceeds in increments of 1 hour, up to 20 hours per week.

When both axes have been labeled and measured, we can begin to illustrate the relationship between study time and grades. Consider the typical student who does 8 hours of homework per week and has a 2.0 (C) grade-point average. We illustrate this relationship by first locating 8 hours on the horizontal axis. We then move up from that point a distance of 2.0 grade points, to point *M*. Point *M* tells us that 8 hours of study time per week is typically associated with a 2.0 grade-point average.

The rest of the information in Table A.1 is drawn (or *plotted*) on the graph in the same way. To illustrate the average grade for people who study 12 hours per week, we move upward from the number 12 on the horizontal axis until we reach the height of 3.0 on the vertical axis. At that intersection, we draw another point (point *N*).

Once we have plotted the various points describing the relationship of study time to grades, we may connect them with a line or curve. This line (curve) is our summary. In this case, the line slopes upward to the right—that is, it has a *positive* slope. This slope indicates that more hours of study time are associated with *higher* grades. Were higher grades associated with *less* study time, the curve in Figure A.1 would have a *negative* slope (downward from left to right).

---

[1] The vertical axis is often called the *Y* axis; the horizontal axis, the *X* axis.

FIGURE A.1
The Relationship of Grades to Study Time

The upward (positive) slope of the curve indicates that additional studying is associated with higher grades. The average student (2.0, or C grade) studies 8 hours per week. This is indicated by point M on the graph.

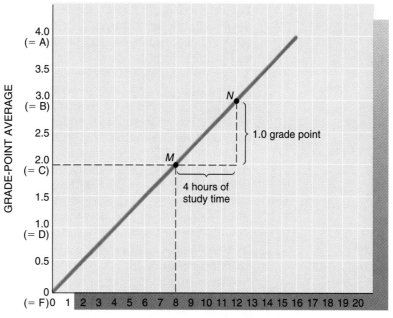

Slopes

The upward slope of Figure A.1 tells us that higher grades are associated with increased amounts of study time. That same curve also tells us *by how much* grades tend to rise with study time. According to point M in Figure A.1, the average student studies 8 hours per week and earns a C (2.0 grade-point average). In order to earn a B (3.0 average), students apparently need to study an average of 12 hours per week (point N). Hence an increase of 4 hours of study time per week is associated with a 1-point increase in grade-point average. This relationship between *changes* in study time and *changes* in grade-point average is expressed by the steepness, or *slope,* of the graph.

The slope of any graph is calculated as

$$\bullet \ \text{Slope} = \frac{\text{vertical distance between two points}}{\text{horizontal distance between two points}}$$

Some people simplify this by saying

$$\text{Slope} = \frac{\text{the rise}}{\text{the run}}$$

In our example, the vertical distance (the "rise") between points M and N represents a change in grade-point average. The horizontal distance (the "run") between these two points represents the change in study time. Hence the slope of the graph between points M and N is equal to

$$\text{Slope} = \frac{3.0 \ \text{grade} - 2.0 \ \text{grade}}{12 \ \text{hours} - 8 \ \text{hours}} = \frac{1 \ \text{grade point}}{4 \ \text{hours}}$$

In other words, a 4-hour increase in study time (from 8 to 12 hours) is associated with a 1-point increase in grade-point average (see Figure A.1).

Shifts

The relationship between grades and studying illustrated in Figure A.1 is not inevitable. It is simply a graphical illustration of student experiences, as revealed in our hypothetical survey. The relationship between study time and grades could be quite different.

Suppose that the university decided to raise grading standards, making it more difficult to achieve every grade other than an F. To achieve a C, a student now would need to study 12 hours per week, not just 8 (as in Figure A.1). Whereas students could previously expect to get a B by studying 12 hours per week, now they have to study 16 hours to get that grade.

Figure A.2 illustrates the new grading standards. Notice that the new curve lies to the right of the earlier curve. We say that the curve has *shifted* to reflect a change in the relationship between study time and grades. Point *R* indicates that 12 hours of study time now "produces" a C, not a B (point *N* on the old curve). Students who now study only 4 hours per week (point *S*) will fail. Under the old grading policy, they could have at least gotten a D. ***When a curve shifts, the underlying relationship between the two variables has changed.***

A shift may also change the slope of the curve. In Figure A.2, the new grading curve is parallel to the old one; it therefore has the same slope. Under either the new grading policy or the old one, a 4-hour increase in study time leads to a 1-point increase in grades. Therefore, the slope of both curves in Figure A.2 is

$$\text{Slope} = \frac{\text{vertical change}}{\text{horizontal change}} = \frac{1}{4}$$

This, too, may change, however. Figure A.3 illustrates such a possibility. In this case, zero study time still results in an F. But now the payoff for additional studying is reduced. Now it takes 6 hours of study time to get a D (1.0 grade point), not 4 hours as before. Likewise, another 4 hours of study

FIGURE A.2
A Shift

When a relationship between two variables changes, the entire curve *shifts*. In this case a tougher grading policy alters the relationship between study time and grades. To get a C one must now study 12 hours per week (point *R*), not just 8 hours (point *M*).

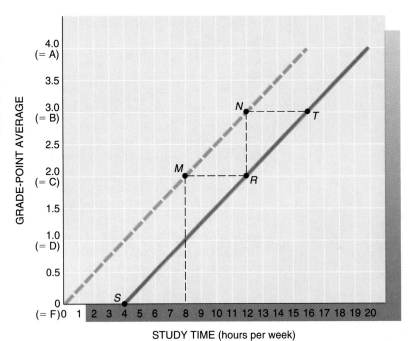

STUDY TIME (hours per week)

FIGURE A.3
A Change in Slope

When a curve shifts, it may change its slope as well. In this case, a new grading policy makes each higher grade more difficult to reach. To raise a C to a B, for example, one must study 6 additional hours (compare points *J* and *K*). Earlier it took only 4 hours to move up the grade scale a full point. The slope of the line has declined from 0.25 (= 1 ÷ 4) to 0.17 (= 1 ÷ 6).

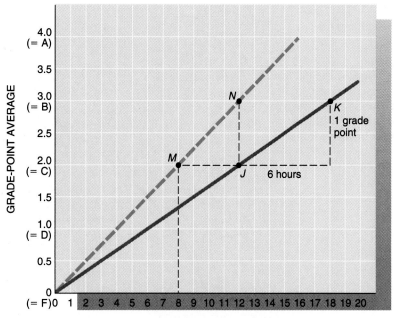

time (to a total of 10) raises the grade by only two-thirds of a point. It takes 6 hours to raise the grade a full point. The slope of the new line is therefore

$$\text{Slope} = \frac{\text{vertical change}}{\text{horizontal change}} = \frac{1}{6}$$

The new curve in Figure A.3 has a smaller slope than the original curve and so lies below it. What all this means is that it now takes a greater effort to *improve* your grade.

Linear vs. Nonlinear Curves

In Figures A.1–A.3, the relationship between grades and studying is represented by a straight line—that is, a *linear* curve. A distinguishing feature of linear curves is that they have the same (constant) slope throughout. In Figure A.1, it appears that *every* 4-hour increase in study time is associated with a 1-point increase in average grades. In Figure A.3, it appears that every 6-hour increase in study time leads to a 1-point increase in grades. But the relationship between studying and grades may not be linear. Higher grades may be more difficult to attain. You may be able to raise a C to a B by studying 4 hours more per week. But it may be harder to raise a B to an A. According to Figure A.4, it takes an additional 8 hours of studying to raise a B to an A. Thus the relationship between study time and grades is *nonlinear* in Figure A.4; the slope of the curve changes as study time increases. In this case, the slope decreases as study time increases. Grades continue to improve, but not so fast, as more and more time is devoted to homework. You may know the feeling.

Causation

Figure A.4 does not itself guarantee that your grade-point average will rise if you study 4 more hours per week. In fact, the graph drawn in Figure A.4

FIGURE A.4
A Nonlinear Relationship

Straight lines have a constant slope, implying a constant relationship between the two variables. But the relationship (and slope) may vary. In this case, it takes 6 extra hours of study to raise a C (point *W*) to a B (point *X*) but 8 extra hours to raise a B to an A (point *Y*). The slope is decreasing as we move up the curve.

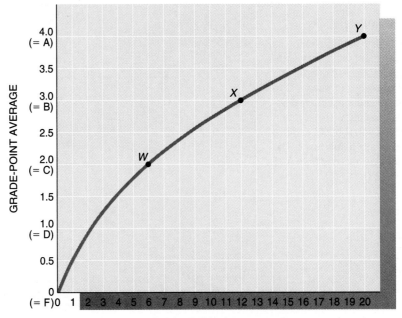

does not prove that additional study ever results in higher grades. The graph is only a summary of empirical observations. It says nothing about cause and effect. It could be that students who study a lot are smarter to begin with. If so, then less able students might not get higher grades if they studied harder. In other words, the *cause* of higher grades is debatable. At best, the empirical relationship summarized in the graph may be used to support a particular theory (e.g., that it pays to study more). Graphs, like tables, charts, and other statistical media, rarely tell their own story; rather, they must be *interpreted* in terms of some underlying theory or expectation.

Chapter 2

The U.S. Economy

We are surrounded by the economy but never really see it. We see only fragments, never the entirety. We see boutiques at the mall, never total retail sales. We pump gas at the service station but have no notion of how many millions of barrels of oil are consumed each day. We know the details of our paychecks, but we never encounter the nation's aggregate income. For most people, the "economy" is at best a vague reference to the sum of all our individual parts.

The intent of this chapter is to provide a graphic picture of the U.S. economy. This profile of the economy is organized around the three core questions of WHAT, HOW, and FOR WHOM. Our interest here is to see how these questions are answered at present in the United States—that is,

- What goods and services does the U.S. produce?
- How is that output produced?
- For whom is the output produced?

As we look at the answers to these questions, we will also see how the dimensions of the U.S. economy compare to those of the rest of the world.

WHAT AMERICA PRODUCES

The output of the American economy is so enormous that no one could describe it in detail. We can, however, get a sense of how much output is produced and what its basic contents are.

How Much Output

The output of the economy consists of physical *goods*, like cars, jeans, and compact discs, as well as *services*, like entertainment, education, and accounting. To get some sense of how much output these goods and services add up to, we need a mechanism for adding them up. We could add up our output in *physical* terms, but such a list would be endless. We need a summary measure of all our output activity.

The top panel of Table 2.1 illustrates the problem of obtaining a summary measure of output. Even if we only produced three goods—oranges, disposable razors, and insurance policies—there is no obvious way of summarizing total output in *physical* terms. Should we count *units* of output? In that case, oranges would appear to be the most important good produced. Should we count the *weight* of different products? In that case, insurance policies wouldn't count at all. Should we tally their *size?* As you ponder these various physical measures of output, the hopelessness of a summary statement becomes clear.

If we use monetary *value* instead of physical units to compute total output, we would have more success. In a market economy, every good and service commands a specific price. Hence, the value of each product can be observed easily. By multiplying the physical output of each good by its price, we can determine the total value of each good produced. Notice in the top panel of Table 2.1 how easily these separate values can be added up. The resultant sum ($4.2 billion, in this case) is a measure of the value of *total* output.

gross domestic product (GDP): The total value of goods and services produced within a nation's borders in a given time period.

Gross Domestic Product. The summary measure of output most frequently used is called **gross domestic product (GDP).** GDP takes advantage of the fact that every good or service produced commands a price in the marketplace. Those prices are the mechanism used for adding up the total *value* of all goods and services produced. *GDP refers to the total value of all final goods and services produced in a country during a given time period; it is a summary measure of a nation's output.* GDP enables us to add apples and razors and even insurance policies into a meaningful summary of economic activity (see Table 2.1).

TABLE 2.1
The Measurement of Output

It is impossible to add up all output when it is counted in *physical* terms. Accordingly, total output is measured in *monetary* terms, with each good or service valued at its market price. GDP refers to the total market value of all goods and services produced in a given time period. According to the numbers in this table, the total *value* of the oranges, razors, and insurance policies produced was $4.2 billion. If prices rise, the value of measured total output rises as well. *Real* GDP is an inflation-adjusted measure of total output.

Output	Amount
MEASURING OUTPUT . . .	
. . . **in physical terms**	
Oranges	6 billion
Disposable razors	3 billion
Insurance policies	7 million
Total	?
. . . **in monetary terms**	
6 billion oranges @ 20¢ each	$1.2 billion
3 billion razors @ 30¢ each	0.9 billion
7 million policies @ $300 each	2.1 billion
Total	$4.2 billion
INFLATION DISTORTIONS	
6 billion oranges @ 40¢ each	$2.4 billion
3 billion razors @ 60¢ each	1.8 billion
7 million policies @ $600 each	4.2 billion
Total	$8.4 billion

Real GDP. Although GDP is a convenient summary of total output produced in a year, it has some shortcomings when used to compare the output of different years. GDP is based on both physical output and prices. Accordingly, from one year to the next either rising prices or an increase in physical output could cause GDP to increase.

Notice in the lower panel of Table 2.1 what happens when all prices double. The measured value of total output also doubles—to $8.4 billion. That sounds like an impressive jump in output. In reality, however, no more goods are being produced; *physical quantities* are unchanged. So the apparent jump in GDP is an illusion caused by rising prices (inflation).

To provide a clearer picture of how much output we are producing, GDP numbers are routinely adjusted for inflation. These inflation adjustments delete the effects of rising prices by valuing output in constant prices of a selected base year. The end result of this effort is referred to as **real GDP,** an inflation-adjusted measure of total output.

> **real GDP:** The inflation-adjusted value of GDP; the value of output measured in constant prices.

In 1995, the U.S. economy produced over $7 *trillion* of output. That was a lot of oranges, razors, and insurance policies—not to mention the tens of thousands of other goods and services produced. Indeed, even when reduced to a single value, the dimensions of our collective production are incomprehensible. We can get a better sense of how much output this really is by making a few comparisons.

International Comparisons. The $7 trillion of output that the United States produced in 1995 looks particularly impressive in a global context. Together all the nations of the world produced less than $30 trillion of output. Hence, the United States—with just 5 percent of the world's population—produced nearly one-fourth of the entire world's output.

Figure 2.1 provides some specific country comparisons. The U.S. economy is two and a half times larger than Japan's, the world's second largest. It is 25 times larger than Mexico's. In fact, the U.S. economy is so large that its output exceeds by a wide margin the *combined* production of *all* countries in Africa and South America.

Per Capita GDP. Another way of putting these trillion-dollar figures into perspective is to relate them to individuals. This can be done by dividing total GDP by the population, a calculation that yields **per capita GDP.** Per capita GDP tells us how much output is potentially available to the average person. It doesn't tell us how much any specific person gets. ***Per capita GDP is simply an indicator of how much output the average person would get if all output were divided evenly among the population.***

> **per capita GDP:** Total GDP divided by total population; average GDP.

In 1995, per capita GDP in the United States was approximately $27,000—more than five times as much as the average in the rest of the world. By international standards, the average American enjoys an unmatched standard of living. Table 2.2 provides a global perspective on American living standards.

Historical Comparisons. Still another way of digesting the dimensions of the American economy is to compare today's living standards with those of earlier times. People who the U.S. government currently classifies as "poor" live as well today as the *average* American family did in the 1950s. The average American today has a standard of living that is *five* times higher than that of the 1930s. Although many of us complain that we don't have "enough," we enjoy an array of goods and services that earlier generations only dreamed of.

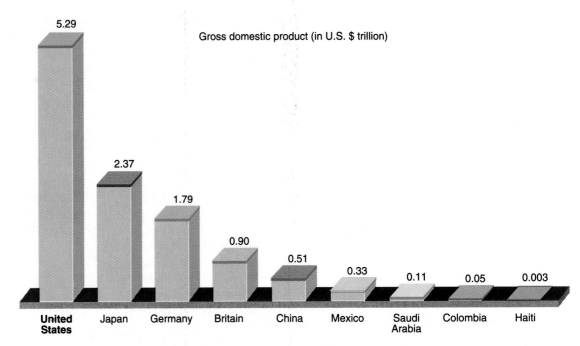

Gross domestic product (in U.S. $ trillion)

United States	Japan	Germany	Britain	China	Mexico	Saudi Arabia	Colombia	Haiti
5.29	2.37	1.79	0.90	0.51	0.33	0.11	0.05	0.003

FIGURE 2.1
Comparative Economic Output of Specific Countries (1992)

The United States is by far the world's largest economy. America's annual output of goods and services is more than twice that of Japan's and equal to all of Western Europe. The output of Third World countries is only a tiny fraction of U.S. output.

Source: World Bank, *World Development Report, 1994.*

> **economic growth:** An increase in output (real GDP); an expansion of production possibilities.

The source of our increased affluence lies in the process of **economic growth**—recurrent increases in real GDP. As Figure 2.2 illustrates, output has grown by 3 percent a year while our population has increased by only 1 percent a year. If this growth difference of two percentage points persists, per capita incomes will double again in approximately thirty-five years. If that happens, your children will have twice as much output per year as you now enjoy.

TABLE 2.2
GDP per Capita Around the World (1992)

The American standard of living is over five times higher than the world average. People in the poorest nations of the world (e.g., Haiti, Ethiopia) barely survive on per capita incomes that are a tiny fraction of U.S. standards.

United States	$23,400
Japan	19,860
France	18,850
Spain	13,970
Greece	7,290
Puerto Rico	6,590
World average	**4,280**
Mexico	3,470
Jordan	1,120
Philippines	770
Haiti	340
India	310
Ethiopia	110

Source: World Bank, *World Development Report, 1994,* and U.S. Central Intelligence Agency.

FIGURE 2.2
U.S. Output and Population Growth, 1900–95

Over time, the growth of output in the United States has greatly exceeded population growth. As a consequence, GDP per capita has grown tremendously. GDP per capita was five times higher in 1995 than in 1900.

Source: U.S. Department of Commerce.

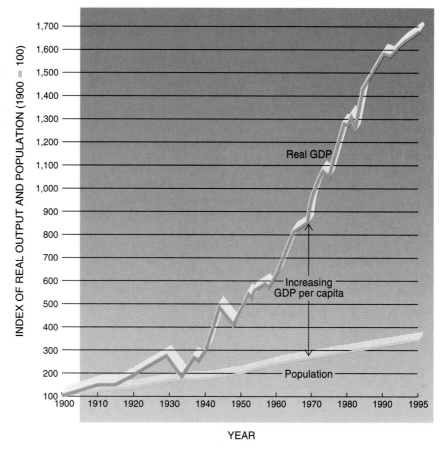

The Mix of Output

It would be interesting to know what kinds of goods and services will be included in the mix of output thirty-five years from today. Many goods we now consume weren't even created a generation ago. Indeed, some of today's most popular consumer goods (compact discs, pocket telephones, miniature TVs, virtual reality games, notebook computers) didn't exist ten years ago. We can only guess what people will produce and consume in future decades.

One way to summarize the mix of output we are currently producing is to examine the uses to which it is put. The major uses of total output include consumption, business investment, government services, and exports.

Consumer Goods. Consumer goods account for two-thirds of America's total output. Consumer goods include everything from breakfast cereals to videos—anything and everything consumers buy.

Three types of consumer goods are often distinguished: *durable goods, nondurable goods,* and *services.* Consumer durables are expected to last at least three years. They tend to be "big-ticket" items like cars, appliances, and furniture. They are generally expensive and, when purchased, absorb a big chunk of consumer incomes. Because of this, consumers tend to postpone buying durables when they are worried about their incomes. Conversely, consumers tend to go on durables-spending sprees when times are good. This spending pattern makes durable goods output highly *cyclical,* that is, very sensitive to economic trends.

Nondurables and services are not as cyclical. Nondurables include clothes, food, gasoline, and other "staples" that consumers buy frequently. Services are the largest and fastest growing component in consumption. At present, over half of all consumer output consists of medical care, entertainment, utilities, and other services.

Investment Goods. Investment goods are a completely different type of output. **Investment** goods include the plant, machinery, and equipment that are produced for use in the business sector. These investment goods are used

1. To replace worn-out equipment and factories, thus *maintaining* our production possibilities.
2. To increase and improve our stock of capital, thereby *expanding* our production possibilities.

We also count as investment goods those that businesses hold as inventory for later sale to consumers.

The economic growth that has lifted our living standards so high was fueled by past investments. To attain even higher living standards, we must continue to devote some of our scarce resources to the production of new plant and equipment. This requires us to limit our immediate consumption (that is, save) so scarce resources can be used for investment. Only 15 percent of America's GDP today consists of investment goods (see Figure 2.3). This investment rate is below the ratio of many other developed countries, putting America at a disadvantage in the continuing quest for economic growth.

Note that the term "investment" here refers to real output—plant and equipment produced for the business sector. This is not the way most people use the term. People often speak, for example, of "investing" in the stock market. Purchases of corporate stock, however, do not create goods and services. Such *financial* investments merely transfer ownership of a corporation from one individual to another. Such financial investments may at times enable a corporation to purchase real plant and equipment. Tangible

> **investment:** Expenditures on (production of) new plant and equipment (capital) in a given time period, plus changes in business inventories.

FIGURE 2.3
The Uses of GDP

Total GDP amounted to $7 trillion in 1995. Over two-thirds of this output consisted of private consumer goods and services. The next largest share (17 percent) of output consisted of public-sector goods. Investment goods made up 15 percent of GDP. Finally, because imports exceeded exports, we ended up consuming 1 percent more than we produced.

Source: *Economic Report of the President, 1995.*

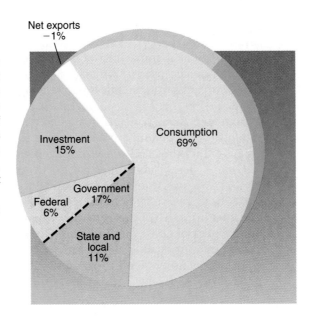

FIGURE 2.4
Federal Outlays, by Type

The federal government spent nearly $1.6 trillion in fiscal year 1995. Just over half of all this spending was for goods and services (including national defense, health programs, and all other services). Over $500 billion was spent on income transfers (Social Security benefits, welfare, unemployment benefits, etc.). Interest payments on the national debt accounted for the rest of the budget.

Source: U.S. Office of Management and Budget, fiscal year 1995 estimates.

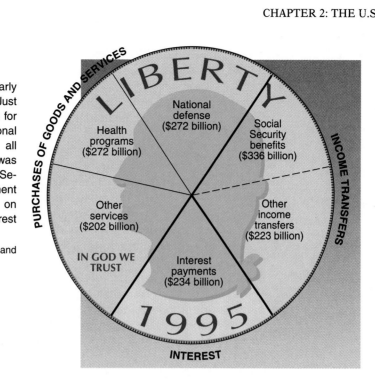

income transfers: Payments to individuals for which no current goods or services are exchanged; e.g., Social Security, welfare, unemployment benefits.

(economic) investment does not occur, however, until that plant and machinery are actually produced. Only tangible investment is counted in the mix of output.

Government Services. The third type of output included in GDP is government services. Federal, state, and local governments purchase resources to police the streets, teach classes, write laws, and build highways. The resources used by the government sector for these purchases are unavailable for either consumption or investment. The production of government services currently absorbs nearly one-fifth of total output (Figure 2.3).

Notice the emphasis again on the production of real goods and services. The federal government *spends* roughly $1.6 trillion a year. Much of that spending, however, is in the form of income transfers, not resource purchases. **Income transfers** are payments to individuals for which no direct service is provided. Social Security benefits, welfare checks, food stamps, and unemployment benefits are examples of income transfers. Such transfer payments account for nearly half of all federal spending (see Figure 2.4). This spending is *not* part of our output of goods and services. ***Only that part of federal spending used to acquire resources and produce services is counted in GDP.*** In 1995, federal purchases (production) of goods and services accounted for only 8 percent of total output.

State and local governments use far more of our scarce resources than does the federal government. Consider just one factor of production, labor. State and local governments employ more than five times as many people (16 million) as the federal government does (3 million). As a consequence, state and local governments also produce more goods and services than the federal government does (see Figure 2.3). The dominant position of state and local governments in deciding WHAT is produced is often obscured by the relatively small size of individual jurisdictions. Sheer numbers, however, give state and local governments great power over the mix of output.

In addition to the 50 state governments, there are 3,000 counties, 18,000 cities, 17,000 townships, 21,000 school districts, and over 20,000 special districts. These are the government entities that build roads; provide schools, police, and firefighters; administer hospitals; and provide social services. The output of all these state and local governments accounts for roughly 11 percent of total GDP.

Net Exports. Finally, we should note that some of the goods and services we produce each year are used abroad rather than at home. That is to say, we **export** some of our output to other countries, for whatever use they care to make of it. Thus GDP—the value of output produced within the United States—can be larger than the sum of our own consumption, investment, and government purchases if we export some of our output.

exports: Goods and services sold to foreign buyers.

International trade is not a one-way street. While we export some of our own output, we also **import** goods and services from other countries. These imports may be used for consumption (Scotch whiskey, Japanese CD players), investment (German ball bearings), or government (French radar screens). Whatever their use, imports represent goods and services that were used by Americans but not produced in the United States.

imports: Goods and services purchased from foreign sources.

The GDP accounts subtract imports from exports. The difference represents *net* exports. In 1995, the value of exports was less than the value of imports. This implies that we used more goods and services than we produced in 1995. Hence, we have to subtract net imports from consumption, investment, and government services to figure out how much we actually produced. That is why net exports appear as a negative item in Figure 2.3.

Changing Industry Structure

As we noted earlier, the mix of output we consume today includes goods and services that did not exist ten or even two years ago. We have also observed (Figure 2.2) how much the volume of output has grown over time. Throughout this process of economic growth, the patterns of production have changed dramatically, as Figure 2.5 illustrates.

Decline in Farming. At the beginning of this century, the farm sector played a huge role in the American economy. In 1900, four out of ten workers were employed in agriculture. Constant improvements in agricultural productivity made it possible to feed the nation with fewer and fewer farmers. Between 1900 and 1990, over 25 *million* people left the farms and sought jobs in the cities and suburbs. Today there are fewer than 2 million farms, and even their number continues to decline. First the "Green Revolution" (chemical fertilizers), then computerization, and now biotechnology have made the farm sector one of the most productive high-tech industries in America. As productivity has outpaced consumption, the number of farmers needed in production has dropped sharply.

Decline of Manufacturing. Most of the farmers displaced by technological advances in the early 1900s found jobs in the expanding manufacturing sector. The Industrial Revolution that flourished in the late 1800s led to a massive increase in manufacturing activity (e.g., steel, transportation systems, automobiles, airplanes). Between 1860 and 1920, the manufactured share of GDP doubled, reaching a peak at 27 percent. World War II also created a huge demand for ships, airplanes, trucks, and armaments,

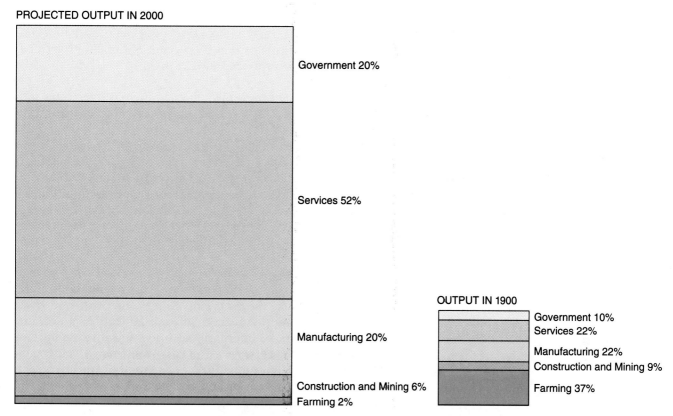

PROJECTED OUTPUT IN 2000

Government 20%

Services 52%

Manufacturing 20%

Construction and Mining 6%

Farming 2%

OUTPUT IN 1900

Government 10%

Services 22%

Manufacturing 22%

Construction and Mining 9%

Farming 37%

FIGURE 2.5
A Century of GDP Changes

In this century the total output of the U.S. economy has increased thirteenfold. As the economy has grown, the farm sector has shrunk and the manufactured *share* of total output has declined. Since 1930 the American economy has been predominantly a "service economy," with output and job growth increasingly concentrated in retail trade, education, health care, entertainment, personal and business services, and government. The share of publicly provided services (government) in total output has doubled in this century. The share of services provided by the private sector has increased even faster.

Source: U.S. Departments of Commerce and Labor.

requiring an enlarged manufacturing sector. After World War II, the manufactured share of output declined, and now accounts for less than 20 percent of total output.

The *relative* decline in manufacturing does not mean that the manufacturing sector has actually shrunk. Some industries like iron and steel do produce less today than a generation ago. Other manufacturing industries—for example, machinery, chemicals, and publishing—have grown tremendously, however. The net result has been a fourfold increase in manufacturing output since just 1950.

Growth of Services. The relative decline in manufacturing is due primarily to the rapid expansion of the service sector. America has largely become a "service economy." A hundred years ago less than 25 percent of the labor force was employed in the service sector; today service industries (including government) generate over 70 percent of total output. Among the fastest growing service industries are health care, computer science and software, financial services, retail trade, business services, and law. According to the U.S. Department of Labor, this trend will continue into the twenty-first century. The Labor Department projects that 98 percent of net job growth between 1995 and 2005 will be in service industries.

Growth of Trade. International trade also plays an increasingly important role in how goods are produced. In 1995, roughly one-eighth of the output America consumed was imported. In addition, a small but growing share of GDP was produced by foreign-owned companies operating in the United States (e.g., Toyota plants in Ohio, Nissan in Tennessee, BP and Shell service stations everywhere). This foreign direct investment represents capital, technology, and labor resources that help produce American gross domestic product.

What is remarkable about these international transactions is how they have grown. The import ratio—imports divided by GDP—has increased from 5 percent in the 1920s to over 13 percent today. Just in the last ten years, direct foreign investment has quadrupled. This increasing "globalization" of the U.S. economy is likely to continue. The slow but continuing removal of trade barriers (e.g., the emerging North American free trade zone) facilitates this globalization. Advances in communications and transportation technologies also make international trade and investment easier. Finally, the growing share of services (e.g., travel, finance, entertainment, insurance, advertising, computer software) in the mix of output makes cross-border transactions easier and cheaper.

HOW AMERICA PRODUCES

The growth and transformation of the U.S. economy reflect the consumption and production decisions of millions of market participants. The economy today also reflects collective decisions about the role of government in providing services and regulating private business.

Business Organization

Private-sector output in the United States is produced by roughly 20 million business firms that differ greatly in structure, number, and size.

Business Types. Business firms come in all shapes and sizes. A basic distinction is made, however, among three different legal organizations:

- Corporations
- Partnerships
- Proprietorships

The primary distinction among these three business forms lies in their ownership characteristics. A single proprietorship is a firm owned by one individual. A partnership is owned by a small number of individuals. A corporation is typically owned by many—even hundreds of thousands of—individuals, each of whom owns shares (stock) of the corporation. An important characteristic of corporations is that their owners (stockholders) are not personally responsible (liable) for the debts or actions of the company. This limited liability makes it easier for corporations to pool the resources of thousands of individuals.

Numbers vs. Size. As a rule, corporations tend to be much larger than the other two forms, because they bring together the financial resources of so many more individuals. Single proprietorships are typically quite small, because few individuals have vast sources of wealth or credit. The typical proprietorship has less than $10,000 in assets, whereas the average corporation has assets in excess of $4 million. As a result of their size, corporations dominate market transactions, accounting for 90 percent of all business sales.

We can describe who's who in the business community, then, in two very different ways. In terms of numbers, the single proprietorship is the most common type of business firm in America. Proprietorships are particularly dominant in agriculture (the family farm), retail trade (the corner grocery store), and services (your dentist). In terms of size, however, the corporation is the dominant force in the economy (see Figure 2.6). The four largest nonfinancial corporations in the country (GM, ATT, Exxon, Ford) alone have more assets than *all* the 15 million proprietorships doing business in the United States. Just one of the four, General Motors, commands nearly $200 billion in assets, over $150 billion in sales, and employs more than 500,000 workers (and pays its president ten times as much as we pay the president of the country). Even in agriculture, where corporate entities are still comparatively rare, the few "agribusiness" corporations are so large as to dominate many thousands of small farms.

One way to grasp the dimensions of the largest corporations is to compare them to countries. As the accompanying Headline reveals, GM's annual sales exceed the entire output of Denmark, South Africa, and most other countries. Indeed, General Motors ranks as the thirtieth "country" in this comparison. The largest U.S. corporations dominate not only American industries but many foreign markets as well.

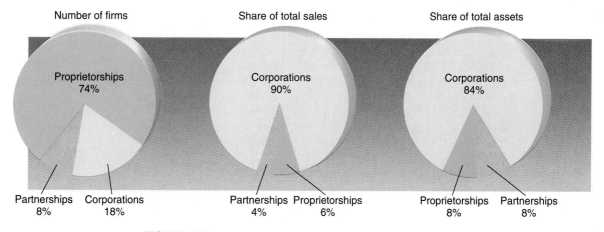

FIGURE 2.6
U.S. Business Firms: Numbers vs. Size

Proprietorships (individually owned companies) are the most common form of American business firm. Corporations are so large, however, that they account for most business sales and assets. Although only 18 percent of all firms are incorporated, corporations control 90 percent of all sales and 95 percent of all assets.

Source: U.S. Department of Commerce, *Statistical Abstract of the United States, 1994.*

HEADLINE

FIRM SIZE

Market Power

The largest firms in the United States are also the dominant forces in global markets. They export products to foreign markets and produce goods abroad for sale there or to import back into the United States. In terms of size alone, these business giants rival most of the world's nations. GM's gross sales, for example, would make it the thirtieth largest "country."

American corporations are not the only giants in the global markets. Toyota (Japan) and Shell Oil (Netherlands) are among the foreign giants that contest global markets.

Corporate Sales and World Output, by Rank
(1992 data, in billions of dollars)

Rank	Country or Corporation	Sales or Output	Rank	Country or Corporation	Sales or Output
1	United States	$5,951	27	**Prudential Insurance**	**155**
2	Japan	2,469	28	Switzerland	152
3	Germany	1,398	29	Sweden	146
4	France	1,080	30	**General Motors**	**133**
5	Italy	1,012	31	Indonesia	126
6	United Kingdom	920	32	Denmark	124
7	Canada	537	33	Egypt	120
8	Spain	515	34	**Metropolitan Life**	**118**
9	China	506	35	Norway	113
10	Russia	388	36	Hong Kong	111
11	South Korea	361	37	Iran	110
12	Brazil	360	38	Thailand	110
13	Mexico	329	39	**Exxon**	**104**
14	Australia	294	40	South Africa	103
15	The Netherlands	260	41	**Ford Motor**	**101**
16	India	233	42	Turkey	100
17	Austria	185	43	**Royal Dutch/Shell**	**95**
18	Taiwan	182	44	Algeria	88
19	Saudi Arabia	181	45	Finland	94
20	Belgium	178	46	Chile	87
21	Argentina	173	47	**Toyota**	**85**
22	Nigeria	173	48	Portugal	80
23	Poland	162	49	Israel	70
24	Venezuela	161	50	**Hitachi**	**69**
25	Columbia	156	51	Greece	67
26	Philippines	156	52	**IBM**	**65**

Sources: U.S. Central Intelligence Agency, World Bank, and *Fortune* Magazine.

Government Regulation Although some American firms are immense, none of them operates with total independence. On the contrary, the government has always played a significant role in deciding HOW goods and services are produced. Before America became an independent nation, royal charters bestowed the right to produce and trade specific goods. Even the European discovery of America was dependent on government financing and the establishment of exclusive rights to whatever resources and treasures were found. Today, over

50 federal agencies and thousands of state and local government entities regulate the production of goods. In the process, they profoundly affect HOW goods are produced.

Protecting Consumers. Much government regulation is intended to protect the interests of consumers. One way to do this is to prevent individual business firms from becoming too powerful. In the extreme case, a single firm might have a **monopoly** on the production of a specific good. As the sole producer of that good, a monopolist could dictate the price, the quality, and the quantity of the product. In such a situation, consumers would likely end up with the short end of the stick—paying too much for too little.

> **monopoly:** A firm that produces the entire market supply of a particular good or service.

To protect consumers from monopoly exploitation, the government tries to prevent individual firms from dominating specific markets. Antitrust laws prohibit mergers or acquisitions that would threaten competition. The U.S. Department of Justice and the Federal Trade Commission also regulate pricing practices, advertising claims, and other behavior that might put consumers at an unfair disadvantage in product markets.

Government also regulates the safety of many products. Consumers don't have enough expertise to assess the safety of various medicines, for example. If they rely on trial and error to determine drug safety, they might not get a second chance. To avoid this calamity, the government requires rigorous testing of new drugs, food additives, and other products.

Protecting Labor. The government also regulates how our labor resources—ourselves and fellow humans—are used in the production process. As recently as 1920, well over a million children between the ages of 10 and 15 were employed in mines, factories or farms, and in private homes. They picked cotton and cleaned shrimp in the South, cut sugar beets and pulled onions in the Northwest, processed coal in Appalachia and pressed tobacco leaves in the Mid-Atlantic states. They often worked six days a week, in abusive conditions, for a pittance in wages. Private employers got cheap labor, but society lost valuable resources when so much human capital remained uneducated and physically abused. It was also patently unfair to the children, who had no means of refusing work their families told them to do. First the state legislatures, then the U.S. Congress intervened to protect children from such abuse by limiting or forbidding the use of child labor and making school attendance mandatory.

Government regulations also set standards for workplace safety and even minimum pay, fringe benefits, and overtime provisions. After decades of bloody confrontations, the government also established the right of workers to organize and set rules for union–management relations. Unemployment insurance, Social Security benefits, disability insurance, and guarantees for private pension benefits also had the effect of protecting labor from the vagaries of the marketplace. They have had a profound effect on how much people work, when they retire, and even on how long they live.

Protecting the Environment. In earlier times, producers didn't have to concern themselves with the impact of their production activities on the environment. The steel mills around Pittsburgh blocked out the sun with clouds of sulfurous gases that spewed out of their furnaces. Timber companies laid waste to broad swaths of forestland, without regard to animal habitats or ecological balance. Paper mills used adjacent rivers as disposal sites, and ships at sea routinely dumped their waste overboard. Neither cars nor airplanes were equipped with controls for noise or air pollution.

In the absence of government intervention, such side effects would be common. Decisions on how to produce would be based on costs alone, not on how the environment is affected. However, such **externalities**—"spillover" costs imposed on the broader community—affect our collective well-being. To reduce the external costs of production, the government limits air, water, and noise pollution and regulates environmental use.

> **externalities:** Costs (or benefits) of a market activity borne by a third party.

Striking a Balance

All of these government interventions are designed to change the way in which resources are used. Such interventions reflect the conviction that the market alone would not select the best possible way of producing goods and services. The market's answer to the HOW question would be based on narrow, profit-and-loss calculations, not on broader measures of societal well-being. To redress this market failure, the government regulates production behavior. There is no guarantee that government regulation of HOW goods are produced always makes us better off. Excessive regulation may inhibit production, raise product prices, and limit consumer choices. In other words, *government* failure might replace *market* failure, leaving us no better off and possibly even worse off.

Public-opinion polls reveal that most Americans feel that we may have reached the point of government failure. As the accompanying Headline confirms, people now feel that government intervention is more likely to *worsen* outcomes rather than improve them. Although public attitudes aren't the only test of government efficacy, they do underscore the importance of striking the right balance between market reliance and government regulation.

HEADLINE

PUBLIC OPINION

Uncle Sam is No Mr. Fix-It

Few people put their faith in government. That's the clear message of public-opinion polls designed to gauge popular sentiment about government performance. A May 1994 ABC poll revealed the extent of the public's concern:

The Confidence Gap

Question: When the government in Washington decides to solve a problem, how much confidence do you have that the problem actually will be solved?

Response:	A lot of confidence	4%
	Some confidence	31
	Just a little	42
	None at all	22

Reinventing Government

Question: Do you think this country needs to make major changes in the way the Federal government works, minor changes, or what?

Response:	Major changes	74%
	Minor changes	22
	Other/no opinion	4

National Journal, June 11, 1994, p. 1370.

FOR WHOM AMERICA PRODUCES

Whatever failings we may have in our responses to the WHAT and HOW questions, they cannot obscure how rich America is. As we have observed, the American economy produces a $7 trillion economic "pie." The final question we have to address is how that pie will be sliced. Will everyone get an equal slice, or will some Americans be served gluttonous slices while others get only crumbs?

Were the slices of the pie carved by the market mechanism, the slices surely would not be equal. Markets reward individuals on the basis of their contribution to output. **In a market economy,** *an individual's income depends on*

- *The quantity and quality of resources owned, and*
- *The price that those resources command in the market.*

That's what concerned Karl Marx so much. As Marx saw it, the capitalists (owners of capital) had a decided advantage in this market-driven distribution. By owning the means of production, capitalists would continue to accumulate wealth, power, and income. Members of the proletariat would get only enough output to assure their survival. Differences in income within the capitalist class or within the working class were of no consequence in the face of these class divisions. All capitalists were rich, all workers poor.

Marx's predictions of how output would be distributed turned out to be wrong in two ways. First, labor's share of total output has risen greatly over time. Second, differences within the labor and capitalist "classes" have become more important than differences between the classes. Many "workers" are rich and a good many "capitalists" are poor. Moreover, the distinction between "workers" and "capitalists" has been blurred by profit-sharing plans, employee ownership, and widespread ownership of corporate stock.

The Functional Distribution

> **functional distribution of income:** The division of income among factors of production, especially between capital and labor.

The division of total income between labor and capital is now called the **functional distribution of income.** No one is quite sure what the functional distribution looked like in the mid-nineteenth century (when Marx was writing). Recent estimates suggest, however, that wage and salary workers were getting less than 40 percent of total output. This low labor share was explained largely by the prevalence of small farmers, whose income was derived primarily from their own labor and was not paid in wages and salaries. No matter how poor, the small family farmer has always been considered part of the capitalist class.

By 1929 labor's share of total income was 60 percent (see Table 2.3). Since then, labor's share of total income has increased further and now accounts for nearly three-fourths of total income. In part this trend is explained by the substantial shift in our GDP away from heavy manufacturing (which is capital-intensive) to labor-intensive services (including government services and education). As the mix of output continues to shift toward services, labor's share of total income will keep rising.

The Personal Distribution

The functional distribution tells us that "labor" gets roughly three-fourths of America's output. That doesn't tell us anything, however, about how output is distributed among individuals. For a closer look at the FOR WHOM

TABLE 2.3
Changes in the Functional Distribution of Income, 1929–93

Labor's share of total income has risen substantially in the last fifty years. Much of this increase is due to the shift away from manufacturing to more labor-intensive service industries. Increased capital investment, education, skill training, and labor organization have also contributed to a rising labor share of income.

Year	Total Labor Share (percent)	Total Capital Share	Capital Share (percent)*				
			Farmers	Nonfarm Proprietors	Rental Income	Corporate Profits	Interest Income
1929	60.3	39.7	7.2	9.8	5.8	11.3	5.5
1933	75.1	24.9	6.3	7.4	5.1	−3.8†	10.4
1943	64.6	35.4	7.0	9.9	2.7	14.1	1.6
1953	68.6	31.4	4.2	9.9	3.5	12.3	1.4
1963	69.1	30.9	2.4	9.1	3.4	12.7	3.3
1973	72.4	27.6	3.0	7.6	1.6	10.1	5.3
1983	74.3	25.7	0.5	6.5	0.5	7.9	10.3
1993	73.7	26.3	0.7	7.9	0.5	9.5	7.8

*Includes income of farmers, landowners, and landlords, as well as those who own plant and equipment.
†In 1933, corporate profits were negative, as was net investment.
Source: *Economic Report of the President, 1995.*

personal distribution of income: The way total personal income is divided up among households or income classes.

issue, we need to examine the **personal distribution of income**—that is, the way total income is divided up among households.

Table 2.4 summarizes the personal distribution of income. The 97 million households in the United States are grouped into five income classes (quintiles), each of equal size. The median household income in 1993 was just about $31,000. To be in the highest class, a household needed an income of at least $60,000. The average income for these "rich" households was far above that threshold, exceeding $100,000. The top 1 percent of all households—the "super-rich"—had average incomes of over $600,000.

The standard of living is very different at the bottom of the income distribution. Households in the lowest income class received no more than $12,967 in 1993. Many of these low-income households, in fact, got by on a lot less; their average income was only $7,400.

The rich in America obviously fare far better than the poor. As Table 2.4 shows, the rich receive nearly half of all the income, while low-income households receive less than 4 percent of all income. These *income disparities translate into access to output*. With more income, the rich are able to buy a far greater share of output than the poor.

As large as income inequalities are in the United States, incomes are dis-

TABLE 2.4
Distribution of Personal Income, 1993

The size distribution of income indicates how total income is distributed among income classes. That fifth of our population with the lowest incomes received only 3.6 percent of total income. The highest income class (fifth) received over 48 percent of total income.

Income Group	1993 Income (dollars)	Average Income	Share of Total Income (percent)
Lowest fifth	0–12,967	$ 7,400	3.6
Second fifth	12,968–24,679	18,700	9.0
Third fifth	24,680–38,793	31,000	15.1
Fourth fifth	38,794–60,300	48,600	23.5
Highest fifth	above 60,300	101,300	48.9

Source: U.S. Department of Commerce, Bureau of the Census.

HEADLINE

INEQUALITY

Income Share of the Rich

Incomes are distributed much less equally in poor countries than in rich ones. In most developing countries the

top tenth of all households receives 30–50 percent of all income. In the United States and other developed countries inequality is much less severe.

Country	Per Capita Income	Percentage of Total Income Received by Highest Decile
Honduras	$580	47.9
Kenya	310	47.9
Tanzania	110	46.5
Mexico	3,470	39.5
Thailand	1,840	35.3
Philippines	770	32.1
Great Britain	17,790	27.8
Australia	17,260	25.8
United States	**23,240**	**25.0**
Spain	13,970	21.8
Sweden	27,000	20.8

Source: World Bank, *World Development Report, 1994.*

tributed even less equally in many other countries. The accompanying Headline displays the share of total income received by the top decile (tenth) of households in various countries. In general, inequalities tend to be larger in poorer countries. As countries develop, inequalities tend to diminish.

In-Kind Income

in-kind income: Goods and services received directly, without payment in a market transaction.

Although income buys access to goods and services, output is not distributed exclusively on the basis of money income. Many goods and services are distributed directly as **in-kind income,** rather than through market purchases. Many poor people, for example, live in public housing and pay little or no rent. As a consequence, they receive a larger share of total output than their money incomes imply. People with low incomes also receive food stamps, which allow them to purchase more food than their money incomes would allow. In this sense, food-stamp recipients are better off than the distribution of personal income (which omits food stamps) implies.

Similarly, students who attend public schools and colleges consume more goods and services than they directly pay for; public education is subsidized by all taxpayers. As a consequence, the distribution of money income understates the share of output received by students in public schools. All older Americans, regardless of income, also get subsidized health care from the Medicare program.

So long as some goods and services need not be purchased in the marketplace, *the distribution of money income is not synonymous with the distribution of goods and services.* Accordingly, the distribution of money receipts is not a complete answer to the question of FOR WHOM we produce. This measurement problem is particularly important when comparisons are made over time. For example, the federal government officially classifies people as "poor" if their money income is below a certain threshold. By this standard, we have made little progress in reducing the number of poor people in America during the last fifteen years. In that time, however, we have provided a vastly increased amount of in-kind benefits to low-income people. Hence their living standards (*real* income) have risen much more than the *money* statistics indicate. In this case, money statistics give a misleading picture of the changing income distribution.

The distinction between money incomes and real incomes also affects international comparisons. Many people in less developed countries rely more on home production than on market participation for essential goods and services. As a consequence, the measured distribution of money income may look more unequal than it really is. This overstatement affects comparisons between the United States and such countries as Sweden and Great Britain. In those countries, the governments provide more direct goods and services (e.g., housing, medical care) than the U.S. government does. Hence *real* income is more evenly distributed in those countries than money incomes imply.

Taxes and Transfers

In-kind benefits like food stamps, Medicaid, and public housing are examples of government intervention in the FOR WHOM question. Their goal is to increase the share of output received by people who receive little income from the market. Such in-kind benefits are part of the larger tax–transfer system.

> **progressive tax:** A tax system in which tax rates rise as incomes rise.

Taxes. A major goal of the tax system is to redistribute income. This is done by taxing people on the basis of their ability to pay. A **progressive tax** does this by imposing higher tax rates on people with larger incomes. Under such a system a rich person pays not only more taxes but also a larger *portion* of his or her income. Thus ***a progressive tax makes after-tax incomes more equal than before-tax incomes.***

The federal income tax is designed to be progressive. Individuals with less than $6,000 of income paid no income tax in 1993 and might even have received a spendable tax credit from Uncle Sam. Middle-income households confronted an average tax rate of 25 percent, and rich households faced a tax rate of 30 percent or more. Hence the federal income tax changes the FOR WHOM decision in favor of lower income families.

> **regressive tax:** A tax system in which tax rates fall as incomes rise.

The rest of the American tax system is less progressive. Social Security payroll taxes and state and local sales taxes have the opposite effect on the FOR WHOM question. These are **regressive taxes** that impose higher tax rates on lower income households. This may seem strange, but this reverse redistribution results from the way such taxes are levied. The amount of sales tax you pay, for example, depends on how much you spend. As a rule, poor people spend nearly all of their income whereas rich people save a lot. As a consequence, poor people end up spending a greater percentage of their incomes on sales taxes. Thus sales and other regressive taxes tend to make the after-tax distribution of income less equal.

When all taxes are added up the tax system appears to have little impact on the FOR WHOM question. The progressive nature of the federal income tax is just about offset by the regressive nature of other sales, payroll, and property taxes. As a result, ***the tax system does not equalize incomes very much.***

Transfers. Taxes are only half of the redistribution story. Equally important is who gets the income the government collects. The government completes the redistribution process by transferring income to consumers and providing services. The largest income-transfer program is Social Security, which pays over $300 billion a year to 40 million older or disabled persons. Although rich and poor alike get Social Security benefits, low-wage workers get more retirement benefits for every dollar of earnings. Hence the benefits of the Social Security program are distributed in a progressive fashion. Income transfers reserved exclusively for poor people—welfare benefits, food stamps, Medicaid, and the like—are even more progressive. Overall, ***the income-transfer system gives lower income households more output than the market itself would provide.***

Taken together, then, the tax–transfer system does alter the market's answer to the FOR WHOM question. In the absence of transfer payments and taxes the lowest income quintile would get only 1 percent of total income. The tax–transfer system raises their share to 5 percent. This may still not be "enough," but it confirms that the system changes the market's answer to the FOR WHOM question.

SUMMARY

- The answers to the WHAT, HOW, and FOR WHOM questions are reflected in economic statistics. These answers are the product of market forces and government intervention.
- Gross domestic product (GDP) is the basic measure of how much an economy produces. Real GDP measures the inflation-adjusted value of output.
- The United States produces roughly $7 trillion of output, approximately one-fourth of the world's total. American GDP per capita is five times the world average.
- The high level of U.S. per capita GDP reflects the high productivity of American workers. Abundant capital, education, technology, training, and management all contribute to high productivity.
- Over 70 percent of U.S. output consists of services. The service industries continue to grow faster than goods-producing industries.
- Most of America's output consists of consumer goods and services. Investment goods account for only 15 percent of total output.
- Proprietorships and partnerships outnumber corporations nearly five to one. Nevertheless, "corporate America" produces 90 percent of total output.
- Government intervenes in the economy to correct the market's answers to the WHAT, HOW, and FOR WHOM questions. The risk of government failure spurs the search for the right mix of market reliance and government regulation.
- Wages and salaries absorb nearly three-fourths of total income. Incomes are distributed very unequally among households, however, with households in the highest income class (quintile) receiving ten times more income than the average low-income (quintile) household.
- The tax system alone does little to equalize incomes. Tax-financed transfer payments like Social Security and welfare do redistribute a significant amount of income, however.

Terms to Remember

Define the following terms:

gross domestic product	exports	personal distribution
real GDP	imports	of income
per capita GDP	monopoly	in-kind income
economic growth	externality	progressive tax
investment	functional distribution	regressive tax
income transfers	of income	

Questions for Discussion

1. Americans already enjoy living standards that far exceed world averages. Do we have enough? Should we even try to produce more?
2. Why do we measure output in value terms rather than in physical terms? For that matter, why do we bother to measure output at all?
3. Why do people suggest that the United States needs to devote more output to investment goods? Why not produce just consumption goods?
4. The U.S. farm population has shrunk by over 25 million people since 1900. Where did they all go? Why did they move?
5. "Rich" people have over ten times as much income as "poor" people. Is that fair? How should output be distributed?

Problems

1. Suppose the following data describe output in two different years:

Item	Year 1	Year 2
Apples	20,000 @ 25¢ each	30,000 @ 30¢ each
Computers	700 @ $800 each	650 @ $900 each
Video rentals	6,000 @ $1.50 each	7,000 @ $2.00 each

(a) Compute GDP in each year.
(b) By what percentage did GDP increase between Year 1 and Year 2?
(c) Now compute *real* GDP in Year 2 by using the prices of Year 1.
(d) How has real GDP changed from Year 1 to Year 2?

2. GDP per capita in the United States was approximately $27,000 in 1995. What will it be in the year 2000 if GDP per capita grows each year by
(a) 0 percent
(b) 2 percent
(c) 4 percent

3. In 1994, the federal income tax schedule for individuals was as follows:

Bracket	Taxable Income	Tax Rate
1	0–$22,750	15% of amount over $0
2	$22,750–$55,100	$3,412 + 28% of amount over $22,950
3	$55,100–$115,000	$12,470 + 31% of amount over $55,100

Use this schedule to determine
(a) How much tax is owed for an individual with an income of
   i. $25,000
   ii. $50,000
   iii. $100,000
(b) What *percentage* of income is paid by each of the individuals.

4. Suppose that the following table describes the spending behavior of individuals at various income levels:

Income	Total Spending	Sales Tax	Sales Tax Paid as Percentage of Income
$ 1,000	$ 1,000	_____	_____
2,000	1,800	_____	_____
3,000	2,400	_____	_____
5,000	3,500	_____	_____
10,000	6,000	_____	_____
100,000	40,000	_____	_____

Assuming that a sales tax of 10 percent is levied on all purchases, calculate
   (a) The amount of taxes paid at each income level
   (b) The fraction of income paid in taxes at each income level
Is the sales tax progressive or regressive in relation to income?
5. Using Table 2.4, determine how much income each income class would have to gain or lose to make all average incomes equal.

Chapter 3

Supply and Demand

The dismantling of the Berlin Wall in November 1989 was a symbol of the Cold War's end and the reintegration of Europe. It also provided a quick lesson in the economics of supply and demand. Millions of East Germans flocked to West Berlin to buy goods that were not available in the east. Electronic toys, radios, cosmetics, tropical fruit, and chocolate were at the top of the shopping list. The East Germans had to pay high prices, but at least they had the chance to buy the goods they desired.

West Berliners went on a shopping spree as well. Fewer goods were available in East Berlin, but the prices of those necessities were kept low by the East German government. So West Berliners rushed into East Berlin to buy boots, sausages, women's lingerie, children's clothes, and Christmas geese. So much merchandise was being carted off to West Berlin that the East German government had to halt sales to foreigners and impose border controls to slow the outflow of available goods.

The cross-border shopping frenzy reflected a basic difference in the way production and prices were established in the two Germanys. West Germany had relied on *decentralized markets* to determine the production and prices of consumer goods; it was a *market economy*. East Germany relied instead on *central planners* to determine which goods to produce and at what prices to sell them; it was a *command economy*. When the Berlin Wall fell, consumers on both sides got a clear view of the differences between market and command economies. We can't provide such a vivid picture of the difference between market-driven and plan-driven economies in a textbook. We can try, however, to get a clearer view of how markets work. How does the market mechanism decide WHAT to produce, HOW to produce, and FOR WHOM to produce? Specifically

- What determines the price of a good or service?
- How does the price of a product affect its production or consumption?
- Why do prices and production levels often change?

MARKET PARTICIPANTS

Over 260 million individual consumers, about 20 million business firms, and tens of thousands of government agencies participate directly in the U.S. economy. Millions of foreigners also participate by buying and selling goods in American markets. Fortunately, we can summarize much of this activity by classifying market participants into four distinct groups—consumers, business firms, government agencies, and foreigners—and then analyzing their behavior.

Goals

Individual consumers, business firms, and government agencies participate in the market in order to achieve specific goals. Consumers strive to maximize their own happiness by purchasing the most satisfying bundle of goods and services with their available incomes. Businesses try to maximize profits by using the most efficient combination of resources to produce the most profitable products. Government agencies are supposed to maximize the general welfare by using available resources to produce desired public goods and services and to redistribute incomes. Foreigners pursue these same goals, as consumers, producers, or governmental agencies.

Market participants sometimes lose sight of their respective goals. Consumers, for example, sometimes buy something impulsively and later wish they had used their income more wisely. Likewise, a producer may take a two-hour lunch, even at the sacrifice of maximum profits. A foreign tourist may belatedly decide that Las Vegas is not worth a visit. And vested economic or political interests can easily cause a government agency to neglect the public's general welfare. In all sectors of the economy, however, the basic goals of utility maximization (maximum satisfaction), profit maximization, or welfare maximization explain most economic activity.

Constraints

The desire of all market participants to maximize something—profits, private satisfaction, or social welfare—is not their only common trait. Another element common to all participants is their *limited resources*. You and I cannot buy everything we desire; we simply don't have enough income. As a consequence, we must make *choices* among available products, always hoping to get the most satisfaction for the few dollars we have to spend. Likewise, business firms and government agencies must decide how best to use their limited resources to maximize profits or public welfare. This is the scarcity problem that is central to all economic decisions.

Specialization and Exchange

Our desire to maximize the returns on our limited resources leads us to participate in the market, buying and selling various goods and services. Our decision to participate in these exchanges is prompted by two considerations. First, most of us are incapable of producing everything we desire to consume. Second, even if we *could* produce all our own goods and services, it would still make sense to specialize, producing only one product and trading it for other desired goods and services.

Suppose you were capable of growing your own food, stitching your own clothes, building your own shelter, and even writing your own economics text. Even in this little utopia, it would still make sense to decide how *best* to expend your limited time and energy, and to rely on others to fill in the gaps. If you were *most* proficient at growing food, you would be best off spending your time farming. You could then exchange some of your food output for the clothes, shelter, and books you desired. In the end, you'd be able to consume more goods than if you had tried to make everything yourself.

Our economic interactions with others are thus necessitated by two constraints:

● Our inability as individuals to produce all the things we desire
● The limited amount of time, energy, and resources we possess for producing those things we could make for ourselves

Together, these constraints lead us to specialize and interact. Most of the interactions that result take place in the market.

MARKET INTERACTIONS

Figure 3.1 summarizes the kinds of interactions that occur among market participants. Note, first of all, that we have identified *four separate groups of market participants:*

● *Consumers*
● *Business firms*
● *Governments*
● *Foreigners*

FIGURE 3.1
Market Interactions

Business firms participate in markets by supplying goods and services to product markets and purchasing factors of production in factor markets. Individual consumers participate in the marketplace by supplying factors of production (e.g., their own labor) and purchasing final goods and services. Federal, state, and local governments also participate in both factor and product markets. Foreigners also participate by supplying imports, purchasing exports, and buying and selling resources.

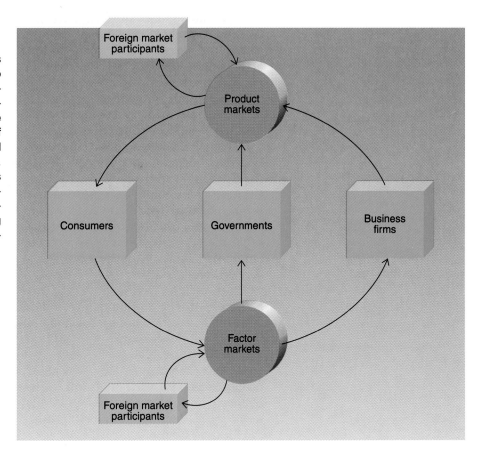

Domestically, the "Consumers" rectangle includes all 260 million consumers in the United States. In the "Business firms" box we have grouped all of the domestic business enterprises that buy and sell goods and services. The third participant, "Governments," includes the many separate agencies of the federal government, as well as state and local governments. Figure 3.1 also illustrates the role of foreigners.

The Two Markets

> **factor market:** Any place where factors of production (e.g., land, labor, capital, entrepreneurship) are bought and sold.

> **product market:** Any place where finished goods and services (products) are bought and sold.

The easiest way to keep track of all this market activity is to distinguish two basic markets. Figure 3.1 does this by portraying separate circles for product markets and factor markets. In **factor markets,** factors of production are exchanged. Market participants buy or sell land, labor, or capital that can be used in the production process. When you go looking for work, for example, you are making a factor of production—your labor—available to producers. You are offering to *sell* your time and talent. The producers will hire you—*buy* your services in the factor market—if you are offering the skills they need at a price they are willing to pay.

Interactions within factor markets are only half the story. At the end of a hard day's work, consumers go to the grocery store (or the movies) to purchase desired goods and services—that is, to buy *products*. In this context, consumers again interact with business firms. This time, however, their roles are reversed: consumers are doing the *buying* and businesses are doing the *selling*. This exchange of goods and services occurs in **product markets.** Foreigners also participate in the product market by supplying goods and services (imports) to the United States and buying some of our output (exports).

Governments also supply goods and services to product markets. The consumer rarely buys national defense, schools, or highways directly; instead, such purchases are made indirectly through taxes and government expenditure. In Figure 3.1, the arrows running from governments through product markets to consumers serve to remind us, however, that all government output is intended "for the people." In this sense, the government acts as an intermediary, buying factors of production and providing certain goods and services consumers desire.

In Figure 3.1, the arrow connecting product markets to consumers emphasizes the fact that consumers, by definition, do not supply products. To the extent that individuals produce goods and services, they do so within the government or business sector. An individual who is a doctor, a dentist, or an economic consultant functions in two sectors. When selling services in the market, this person is regarded as a "business"; when away from the office, he or she is regarded as a "consumer." This distinction is helpful in emphasizing the role of the consumer as the final recipient of all goods and services produced.

Locating Markets. Although we will refer repeatedly to two kinds of markets, it would be a little foolish to go off in search of the product and factor markets. Neither a factor market nor a product market is a single, identifiable structure. The term "market" simply refers to any place where an economic exchange occurs—where a buyer and seller interact. The exchange may take place on the street, in a taxicab, over the phone, by mail, or through the classified ads of the newspaper. In some cases, the market used may in fact be quite distinguishable, as in the case of a retail store, the Chicago Commodity Exchange, or a state employment office. But whatever it looks like, *a market exists wherever and whenever an exchange takes place.* The market is simply a place or medium where buyer and seller get together; which market they are in depends on what they are buying or selling.

Dollars and Exchange

Figure 3.1 is a useful summary of market activities, but it neglects one critical element of market interactions: dollars. Each of the arrows in the figure actually has two dimensions. Consider again the arrow linking consumers and product markets. It is drawn in only one direction because consumers, by definition, do not provide goods and services directly to product markets. But they do provide something: dollars. If you want to obtain something from a product market, you must offer to pay for it (typically, with cash, check, or credit card). Consumers exchange dollars for goods and services in product markets.

The same kinds of exchange occur in factor markets. When you go to work, you are exchanging a factor of production (your labor) for income, typically a paycheck. Here, again, the path connecting consumers to factor markets really goes in two directions, one of real resources, the other of dollars. Consumers receive wages, rent, and interest for the labor, land, and capital they bring to the factor markets. Indeed, nearly *every market transaction involves an exchange of dollars for goods (in product markets) or resources (in factor markets).* Money thus plays a critical role in facilitating market exchanges and the specialization they permit.

Supply and Demand

supply: The ability and willingness to sell (produce) specific quantities of a good at alternative prices in a given time period, *ceteris paribus.*

demand: The ability and willingness to buy specific quantities of a good at alternative prices in a given time period, *ceteris paribus.*

The two sides of each market transaction are called **supply** and **demand.** As noted earlier, we are *supplying* resources to the market when we look for a job—that is, when we offer our labor in exchange for income. But we are *demanding* goods when we shop in a supermarket—that is, when we are prepared to offer dollars in exchange for something to eat. Business firms may *supply* goods and services in product markets at the same time that they are *demanding* factors of production in factor markets.

Whether one is on the supply side or the demand side of any particular market transaction depends on the nature of the exchange, not on the people or institutions involved.

DEMAND

Although the concepts of supply and demand are useful for explaining what's happening in the marketplace, we are not yet ready to summarize the countless transactions that occur daily in both factor and product markets. Recall that *every market transaction involves an exchange and thus some element of both supply and demand.* Then just consider how many exchanges you alone undertake in a single week, not to mention the transactions of the other 260 million or so consumers among us. To keep track of so much action, we need to summarize the activities of many individuals.

Individual Demand

We can begin to understand how market forces work by looking more closely at the behavior of a single market participant. Let us start with Tom, a sophomore at Clearview College. Tom is currently experiencing the torment of writing a paper for his English composition class. To make matters worse, Tom's professor has insisted on typed papers, and Tom cannot type with his fingers much better than he can write with his toes. Under the circumstances, Tom is desperate for a typist.

Although it is apparent that Tom has a strong desire for a typist, his demand for typing services is not yet evident. ***A demand exists only if someone is willing and able to pay for the good***—that is, exchange dollars for a good or service in the marketplace. Is Tom willing and able to pay for typing?

Let us assume that Tom has some income and is willing to spend some of it to get his English paper typed. Under these assumptions, we can claim that Tom is a participant in the *market* for typing services.

But how much is Tom willing to pay? Surely, Tom is not prepared to exchange all his income for the typing of a single English paper. After all, Tom could use his income to buy more desirable goods and services. If he spent all his income on typing, his one English paper would have an extremely high **opportunity cost.** He would be giving up all the other goods and services he could have purchased with his income. Doesn't sound like a good idea. Even though Tom says he would be willing to pay *anything* to get that paper typed, he probably has lower prices in mind. Indeed, it would be more reasonable to assume that there are *limits* to the amount Tom is willing to pay for any given quantity of typing. These limits will be determined by how much income Tom has to spend and how many other goods and services he must forsake in order to pay for typing services.

We assume, then, that when Tom starts looking for a typist, he has in mind some sort of **demand schedule,** like that described in Figure 3.2. According to row *A* of this schedule, our tormented English compositionist is willing and able to buy only 1 page of typing per semester if he must pay $5 per page. At such an outrageous price, he will have only the first page of his paper typed professionally and will peck out or print the remaining pages himself. That way, the paper will make a good first impression, and Tom won't have to sacrifice so many other goods and services for his paper.

At lower prices, Tom would behave differently. According to Figure 3.2, Tom would get more pages typed if the price of typing were less. At lower prices, he would not have to give up so many other goods and services for each page of professional typing. The reduced opportunity costs implied by lower typing prices increase the attractiveness of professional typing. Indeed, we see from row *I* of the demand schedule that Tom is willing to have 20 pages per semester—an entire paper—typed professionally if the price per page is as low as $1.

Notice that the demand schedule doesn't tell us anything about *why* this consumer is willing to pay specific prices for various amounts of typing. Tom's expressed willingness to pay for typing may reflect a desperate need to finish his paper, a lot of income to spend, or a relatively small desire for other goods and services. All the demand schedule tells us is what the consumer is *willing and able* to buy, for whatever reasons.

Also observe that the demand schedule doesn't tell us how many pages of typing the consumer will *actually* buy. Figure 3.2 simply states that Tom is *willing and able* to pay for one page of typing per semester at $5.00 per page, for two pages at $4.50 each, and so on. How much typing he purchases will depend on the actual price of typing in the market. Until we

opportunity cost: The most desired goods or services that are forgone in order to obtain something else.

demand schedule: A table showing the quantities of a good a consumer is willing and able to buy at alternative prices in a given time period, *ceteris paribus*.

FIGURE 3.2
A Demand Schedule and Curve

A demand schedule indicates the quantities of a good a consumer is able and willing to buy at alternative prices (*ceteris paribus*). The demand schedule indicates that Tom would buy 5 pages of typing per semester if the price of typing were $3.50 per page (row *D*). If typing were less expensive (rows *E–I*), Tom would purchase a larger quantity.

A demand curve is a graphical illustration of a demand schedule. Each point on the curve refers to a specific quantity that will be demanded at a given price. If, for example, the price of typing were $3.50 per page, this curve tells us the consumer would purchase 5 pages per semester (point *D*). If typing cost $3 per page, 7 pages per semester would be demanded (point *E*). Each point on the curve corresponds to a row in the schedule.

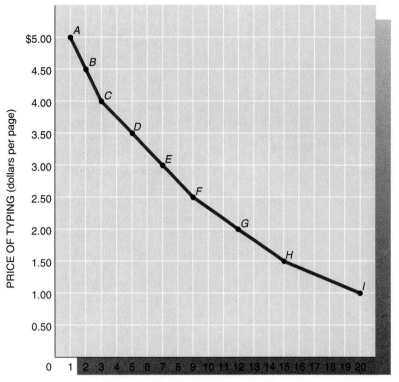

QUANTITY OF TYPING DEMANDED (pages per semester)

	Demand Schedule	
	Price of Typing (per page)	**Quantity of Typing Demanded (pages per semester)**
A	$5.00	1
B	4.50	2
C	4.00	3
D	3.50	5
E	3.00	7
F	2.50	9
G	2.00	12
H	1.50	15
I	1.00	20

know that price, we cannot tell how much typing will be purchased. Hence *"demand" is an expression of consumer buying intentions, of a willingness to buy, not a statement of actual purchases.*

A convenient summary of buying intentions is the **demand curve,** a graphical illustration of the demand schedule. The demand curve in Figure 3.2 tells us again that this consumer is willing to pay for only one page of professional typing per semester if the price is $5.00 per page (point *A*), for two if the price is $4.50 (point *B*), for three at $4.00 a page (point *C*), and so on. Once we know what the market price of typing actually is, a glance at the demand curve tells us how much typing this consumer will buy.

demand curve: A curve describing the quantities of a good a consumer is willing and able to buy at alternative prices in a given time period, *ceteris paribus*.

What the notion of "demand" emphasizes is that the amount we buy of a good depends on its price. We seldom if ever decide to buy only a certain quantity of a good at whatever price is charged. Instead, we enter markets with a set of desires and a limited amount of money to spend. How much we actually buy of any good will depend on its price.

A common feature of demand curves is their downward slope. As the price of a good falls, people tend to purchase more of it. In Figure 3.2 the quantity of typing demanded increases (moves rightward along the horizontal axis) as the price per page decreases (moves down the vertical axis). This inverse relationship between price and quantity is so common we refer to it as the **law of demand.**

> **law of demand:** The quantity of a good demanded in a given time period increases as its price falls, *ceteris paribus*.

Determinants of Demand

The demand curve in Figure 3.2 has only two dimensions—quantity demanded (on the horizontal axis) and price (on the vertical axis). This seems to imply that the amount of typing demanded depends only on the price of typing. This is surely not the case. A consumer's willingness and ability to buy a product at various prices depend on a variety of forces. *The determinants of demand include*

- *Tastes* (desire for this and other goods)
- *Income* (of the consumer)
- *Other goods* (their availability and price)
- *Expectations* (for income, prices, tastes)

If Tom didn't have to turn in a typed English composition, he would have no taste (desire) for typing services and thus no demand. If he had no income, he would not have the ability to pay and thus would still be out of the typing market. Other goods shape the opportunity cost of typing, while expectations for income, grades, and graduation prospects would all influence his willingness to buy typing services.

Ceteris Paribus

> *ceteris paribus:* The assumption of nothing else changing.

If demand is in fact such a multidimensional decision, how can we reduce it to only two dimensions? This is the *ceteris paribus* trick we encountered earlier. To simplify their models of the world, economists focus on only one or two forces at a time and *assume* nothing else changes. We know a consumer's tastes, income, other goods, and expectations all affect the decision to buy typing services. But *we focus on the relationship between quantity demanded and price.* That is to say, we want to know what *independent* influence price has on consumption decisions. To find out, we must isolate that one influence, price, and assume that the determinants of demand remain unchanged.

The *ceteris paribus* assumption is not as far-fetched as it may seem at first. People's tastes (desires) don't change very quickly. Income tends to be fairly stable from week to week. Even expectations for the future are slow to change. Accordingly, the price of a good may be the only thing that changes in the short run. In that case, a change in price may be the only thing that prompts a change in consumer behavior.

Shifts in Demand

The determinants of demand do change, of course, particularly as the time frame is expanded. Accordingly, *the demand schedule and curve remain unchanged only so long as the underlying determinants of demand re-*

shift in demand: A change in the quantity demanded at any (every) given price.

main constant. If the *ceteris paribus* assumption is violated—if tastes, income, other goods, or expectations change—the ability or willingness to buy will change. When this happens, the demand curve will **shift** to a new position.

Suppose, for example, that Tom won the state lottery. This increase in his income would greatly increase his ability to pay for typing services. Figure 3.3 shows the effect of this windfall on Tom's demand for typing. The old demand curve, D_1, is no longer relevant. Tom's lottery winnings enable him to buy more pages at any price. This is illustrated by the new demand curve, D_2. According to this new curve, lucky Tom is now willing and able to buy 11 pages per semester at the price of \$3.50 per page (point d_2). This is a large increase in demand, as previously (before winning the lottery) he demanded only 5 pages at that price (point d_1).

With his higher income, Tom can buy more typing at every price. Thus *the entire demand curve shifts to the right when income goes up.* Both the old (prelottery) and the new (postlottery) demand curves are illustrated in Figure 3.3.

Income is only one of four basic determinants of demand. Changes in any of the other determinants of demand would also cause the demand curve to shift. Tom's taste for typing might increase dramatically, for example, if his parents promised to buy him a new car for passing English composition. In that case, he might be willing to forgo other goods and spend more of his income on typing. *An increase in taste (desire) also shifts the demand curve to the right.*

Movements vs. Shifts

It is important to distinguish shifts of the demand curve from movements along the demand curve. *Movements along a demand curve are a response to price changes for that good.* Such movements assume that determinants of demand are unchanged. By contrast, *shifts of the demand curve occur when the determinants of demand change.* When tastes, income, other goods, or expectations are altered, the basic relationship between price and quantity demanded is changed (shifts).

FIGURE 3.3
A Shift in Demand

A demand curve shows how the quantity demanded changes in response to a change in price, *if* all else remains constant. But the determinants of demand may themselves change, causing the demand curve to shift. In this case, an increase in income increases demand from D_1 to D_2. After this shift, Tom demands 11 pages (d_2), rather than 5 (d_1), at the price of \$3.50. The quantity demanded at all other prices increases as well.

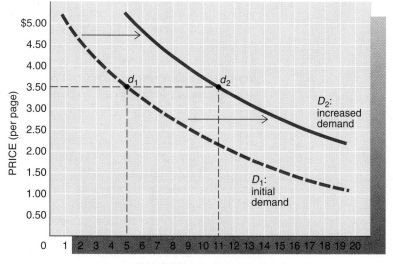

For convenience, the distinction between movements along a demand curve and shifts of the demand curve have their own labels. Specifically, take care to distinguish

- *Changes in quantity demanded:* movements along a given demand curve, in response to price changes of that good
- *Changes in demand:* shifts of the demand curve due to changes in tastes, income, other goods, or expectations

Tom's behavior in the typing market will change if either the price of typing changes or the underlying determinants of his demand for typing are altered. Demand curves help us predict those behavioral changes.

Market Demand

What we can say about demand for typing on the part of one harassed English major we can say about the demand of all other market participants. That is, we can identify the demand for typing services associated with every student at Clearview College (or, for that matter, with all 260 million consumers in the United States). Some students, of course, have no need or desire for professional typing and are not willing to pay anything for such services; they do not participate in the typing market. Other students have a desire for such services but not enough income to pay for them; they, too, are excluded from the typing market. A large number of students, however, not only have a need (or desire) for typing services but also are willing and able to purchase such services.

market demand: The total quantities of a good or service people are willing and able to buy at alternative prices in a given time period; the sum of individual demands.

What we start with in product markets, then, is many individual demand curves. Fortunately, it is possible to combine all the individual demand curves into a single **market demand** for typing services. The aggregation process is no more difficult than simple arithmetic. In fact, simple arithmetic is all that's needed, once you know the buying intentions of all consumers. Suppose you would be willing to buy 1 page of typing per semester at a price of $8 per page. George, who is desperate to make his English essays at least *look* good, would buy 2 at that price; and I would buy none, since I only grade papers and needn't type the grades. What would our combined (market) demand for typing services be at that price? Clearly, our individual inclinations indicate that we would be willing to buy a total of 3 pages of typing per semester if the price were $8 per page. Our combined willingness to buy—our collective market demand—is nothing more than the sum of our individual demand schedules. The same kind of aggregation can be performed for all consumers, leading to a summary of the total market demand for typing services at Clearview College. This ***market demand is determined by the number of potential buyers and their respective tastes, incomes, other goods, and expectations.***

The Market Demand Curve

Table 3.1 provides the basic market demand schedule for a situation in which only four people participate on the demand side of the market. Figure 3.4 illustrates the same market situation with demand curves. The four individuals who participate in the market demand for typing at Clearview College obviously differ greatly, as suggested by their respective demand schedules. Tom has to turn in several papers each semester, has a good income, and is willing to purchase typing services. His demand schedule is portrayed in the first column of Table 3.1 (and is identical to the one we examined in Figure 3.2). George, as we already noted, is desperate to im-

TABLE 3.1
The Market Demand Schedule

Market demand represents the combined demands of all market participants. To determine the total quantity of typing demanded at any given price, we add up the separate demands of the individual consumers. Row *G* of this schedule indicates that a *total* quantity of 39 pages per semester will be demanded at a price of $2 per page.

	Price per Page	Quantity Demanded (pages per semester)				Total Demand
		Tom +	George +	Lisa +	Me =	
A	$5.00	1	4	0	0	5
B	4.50	2	6	0	0	8
C	4.00	3	8	0	0	11
D	3.50	5	11	0	0	16
E	3.00	7	14	1	0	22
F	2.50	9	18	3	0	30
G	2.00	12	22	5	0	39
H	1.50	15	26	6	0	47
I	1.00	20	30	7	0	57

prove the appearance of his papers and is willing to pay relatively high prices for typing services. His demand schedule is summarized in the second column under "Quantity Demanded" in Table 3.1. The third consumer in this market is Lisa. She has a very limited budget and can do her own typing if she must; she is not willing to buy any typing at higher prices. As prices drop below $3.50 per page, however, her demand schedule indicates that she will get some of her work professionally typed. Finally, there is my demand schedule (the fourth column under "Quantity Demanded" in Table 3.1), which confirms that I really don't participate in the local typing market.

The differing personalities and consumption habits of Tom, George, Lisa, and me are expressed in our individual demand schedules and associated curves, as depicted in Table 3.1 and Figure 3.4. To determine the *market* demand for typing from this information, we simply add up these four sep-

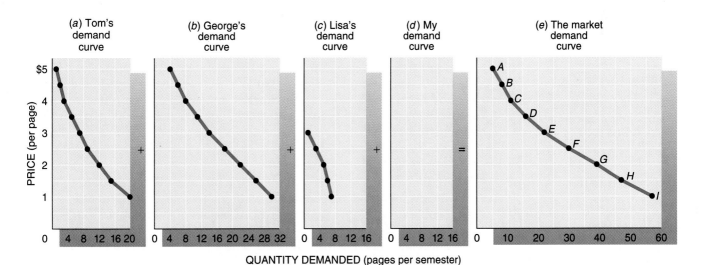

QUANTITY DEMANDED (pages per semester)

FIGURE 3.4
Construction of the Market Demand Curve

The market demand curve expresses the *combined* demands of all market participants. At a price of $3 per page, the total quantity of typing demanded would be 22 pages per semester (point *E*): 7 pages demanded by Tom, 14 by George, and 1 by Lisa.

arate demands. The end result of this aggregation is, first, a *market* demand schedule (the last column in Table 3.1) and, second, the resultant *market* demand curve (the curve in Figure 3.4*e*). These market summaries describe the various quantities of typing that Clearview College students are *willing and able* to purchase each semester at various prices.

The Use of Demand Curves

So why does anybody care what the demand curve for typing looks like? What's the point of doing all this arithmetic and drawing so many graphs?

If you owned a typing service at Clearview College, you'd certainly like to have the information depicted in Figure 3.4. What the market demand curve tells us is how much typing could be sold at various prices to Clearview students. Suppose you hoped to sell 30 pages at a price of $3 per page. According to Figure 3.4 (point *E*), students will buy only 22 pages at that price. Hence, you won't attain your sales goal. You could find that out by posting ads on campus and waiting for a response. It would be a lot easier, however, if you knew in advance what the demand curve looked like.

People who promote music concerts need the same kind of information. They want to fill the stadium with screaming fans. But fans have limited income and desires for other goods. Accordingly, the number of fans who will buy concert tickets depends on the price. If the promoter sets the price too high, there will be lots of empty seats at the concert. If the price is set too low, the promoter may lose potential sales revenue. What the promoter wants to know is what price will induce a quantity demanded that conforms to the number of available seats. If he could consult a demand curve, the correct price would be evident.

SUPPLY

Even if we knew what the demand for every good looked like, we couldn't predict what quantities would be bought. The demand curve only tells us how much consumers are willing and able to buy at specific prices. We don't know the price yet, however. To find out what price will be charged, we've got to know something about the motivations and behavior of people who *sell* goods and services. That is to say, we need to examine the *supply* side of the marketplace. The **market supply** of a good reflects the collective behavior of all firms that are willing and able to sell that good at various prices.

market supply: The total quantities of a good that sellers are willing and able to sell at alternative prices in a given time period, *ceteris paribus*.

Determinants of Supply

Let's return to the Clearview campus for a moment. What we need to know now is how much typing people are willing and able to do. Generally speaking, people don't like to type. Word processors and computers have made the job easier, but they haven't made it fun. So few people offer to supply typing services just for the fun of it. People who supply typing services do it for money. Specifically, they do it to earn income that they, in turn, can spend on goods and services they desire.

How much income one can make from typing depends on a number of things. As a consequence, the ***determinants of market supply include***

- *Technology*
- *Factor costs*
- *Other goods*
- *Taxes*
- *Expectations*
- *Number of sellers*

Word processors, for example, are a technological improvement over standard typewriters. By making it easier to "produce" typing, they induce people to supply more typing services at every price.

How many pages of typing are offered at any given price also depends on the cost of factors of production. If ribbons, software, or paper costs are high, typists will have to charge more per page in order to earn some income.

Other goods can also affect the willingness to supply typing services. If you can make more income waiting tables than you can typing, why type? As the prices paid for other goods and services change, they will influence people's decision about whether to offer typing services.

In the real world, the decision to supply goods and services is also influenced by the long arm of Uncle Sam. Federal, state, and local governments impose taxes on income earned in the marketplace. When tax rates are high, people get to keep less of the income they earn. Some people may conclude that typing is no longer worth the hassle and withdraw from the market.

Expectations are also important on the supply side of the market. If typists expect higher prices, lower costs, or reduced taxes, they may be more willing to perfect their typing skills. On the other hand, if they have bad expectations about the future, they may just sell their word processors and find something else to do.

Finally, we note that the number of available typists will affect the quantity of typing offered for sale at various prices. If there are lots of willing typists on campus, a large quantity of typing will be available.

The Market Supply Curve

> **law of supply:** The quantity of a good supplied in a given time period increases as its price increases, *ceteris paribus*.

Figure 3.5 illustrates the market supply curve of typing at Clearview College. Like market demand, the market supply curve is the sum of all the individual supplier decisions about how much to produce at any given price. The market supply curve slopes upward to the right, indicating that *larger quantities will be offered at higher prices.* This basic **law of supply** reflects the fact that increased output typically entails higher costs and so will be forthcoming only at higher prices. Higher prices may also increase profits and so entice producers to supply greater quantities.

Note that Figure 3.5 illustrates the *market* supply. We have not bothered to construct separate supply curves for each person who is able and willing to supply typing services on the Clearview campus. We have skipped over that first step and gone right to the market supply curve. Like the mar-

FIGURE 3.5
The Market Supply Curve

The market supply curve indicates the *combined* sales intentions of all market participants. If the price of typing were $2.50 per page (point *e*), the *total* quantity of typing supplied would be 62 pages per semester. This quantity is determined by adding together the supply decisions of all individual producers.

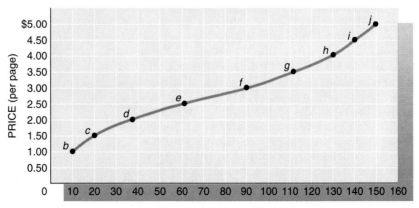

ket demand curve, however, the market supply curve is based on the supply decisions of individual producers. The curve itself is computed via simple arithmetic, by adding up the quantities each producer is willing and able to supply at every given price. Point *f* in Figure 3.5 tells us that those individuals are collectively willing and able to produce 90 pages of typing per semester at a price of $3 per page. The rest of the points on the supply curve tell us how many pages of typing will be offered at other prices.

None of the points on the market supply curve (Figure 3.5) tells us how much typing is actually being sold on the Clearview campus. ***Market supply is an expression of sellers' intentions, of the ability and willingness to sell, not a statement of actual sales.*** My next-door neighbor may be *willing* to sell his 1986 Honda Civic for $8,000, but it is most unlikely that he will ever find a buyer at that price. Nevertheless, his *willingness* to sell his car at that price is part of the *market supply* of used cars.

Shifts in Supply

As with demand, there is nothing sacred about any given set of supply intentions. Supply curves *shift* when the underlying determinants of supply change. Thus we again distinguish

* ***Changes in quantity supplied:*** movements along a given supply curve
* ***Changes in supply:*** shifts of the supply curve

Our Latin friend *ceteris paribus* is once again the decisive factor. If the price of typing is the only thing changing, then we can **track changes in quantity supplied along the supply curve** in Figure 3.5. But if *ceteris paribus*

HEADLINE

SUPPLY SHIFT

California Floods and Lettuce Prices

Winter storms battered California so badly in early 1995 that 39 of the state's 56 counties were declared disaster areas. Over a dozen people were killed and thousands of residents were evacuated from flooded areas.

The 1995 floods had a major impact on crop prices. California farmers grow nearly all of the nation's lettuce, artichokes, and almonds. About 10,000 acres of almond trees were wrecked in the area around Fresno, and 30,000 acres of prime farmland in the Salinas Valley—known as America's "salad bowl" because so much of the nation's lettuce, cabbage, cauliflower, and similar crops are grown there—were submerged. Many ripening vegetables were destroyed and a lot of land was lost for the season. This lost production capacity caused a sudden leftward shift of market supply. The reduced supply, in turn, caused lettuce prices to jump sharply from point *A* to point *B* in the accompanying graph.

The Wall Street Journal, March 14, 1995, p. A2.

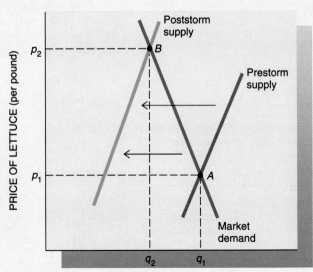

is violated—if technology, factor costs, other goods, taxes, or expectations change—then ***changes in supply are illustrated by shifts of the supply curve.*** The accompanying Headline illustrates a shift in the supply of lettuce that occurred when storms damaged California's farms in 1995.

EQUILIBRIUM

We can now determine the price and quantity of typing being sold at Clearview College. The market supply curve expresses the *ability and willingness* of producers to sell typing at various prices. The market demand curve illustrates the *ability and willingness* of Tom, George, Lisa, and me to buy typing at those same prices. When we put the two curves together, we see that ***only one price and quantity are compatible with the existing intentions of both buyers and sellers.*** This **equilibrium** occurs at the intersection of the two curves in Figure 3.6. Once it is established, typing will cost $2 per page. At that price, campus typists will sell a total of 39 pages of typing per semester—the same amount that students wish to buy at that price.

> **equilibrium price:** The price at which the quantity of a good demanded in a given time period equals the quantity supplied.

FIGURE 3.6
Market Surplus or Shortage

Only at equilibrium is the quantity demanded equal to the quantity supplied. In this case, the equilibrium price is $2 per page, and 39 pages is the equilibrium quantity. At higher prices, a market surplus exists—the quantity supplied exceeds the quantity demanded. At prices below equilibrium, a market shortage exists.

The intersection of the demand and supply curves in the graph represents equilibrium price and output in this market.

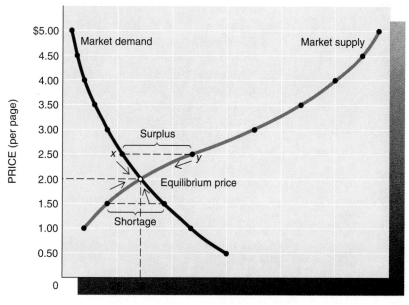

Price per Page	Quantity Supplied (pages per semester)		Quantity Demanded (pages per semester)
$5.00	148		5
4.50	140		8
4.00	130	market	11
3.50	114	surplus	16
3.00	90		22
2.50	62		30
2.00	39	equilibrium	39
1.50	20	market	47
1.00	10	shortage	57

An important characteristic of the equilibrium price is that it is not determined by any single individual. Rather it is determined by the collective behavior of many buyers and sellers, each acting out his or her own demand or supply schedule. It is this kind of impersonal price determination that gave rise to Adam Smith's characterization of the market mechanism as "the invisible hand." In attempting to explain how the market mechanism works, the famed eighteenth-century economist noted a certain feature of market prices. The market behaves as if some unseen force (the invisible hand) were examining each individual's supply or demand schedule, then selecting a price that assured an equilibrium. In practice, the process of price determination is not so mysterious; rather, it is a simple one of trial and error.

Surplus and Shortage

> **market surplus:** The amount by which the quantity supplied exceeds the quantity demanded at a given price; excess supply.

Suppose for the moment that campus typists believed typing could be sold for $2.50 per page rather than the equilibrium price of $2.00 and offered it only at this higher price. From the demand and supply schedules depicted in Figure 3.6, we can foresee the consequences. At $2.50 per page, campus typists would be offering more typing services (point y) than Tom, George, and Lisa were willing to buy (point x) at that price. A **market surplus** of typing services would exist, in that more typing was being offered for sale (supplied) than students cared to purchase at the available price.

As Figure 3.6 indicates, at a price of $2.50 per page, a market surplus of 32 pages per semester exists. Under these circumstances, campus typists would be spending many idle hours at their typewriters, waiting for customers to appear. Their waiting will be in vain, because the quantity of typing demanded will not increase until the price of typing falls. That is the clear message of the demand curve. The tendency of quantity demanded to increase as price falls is illustrated in Figure 3.6 by a movement along the demand curve from point x to lower prices and greater quantity demanded. As we move down the market demand curve, the desire for typing does not change, but the quantity people are able and willing to buy increases.

Typists at Clearview would have to reduce price from $2.50 (point y) to $2.00 per page in order to attract enough buyers. Cruise ships confronted the same dilemma in 1995. The accompanying Headline shows how a sur-

HEADLINE

MARKET SURPLUS

Ocean Cruise Prices Relax

America's love affair with cruising may be losing some steam—and that has some cruise lines lowering prices to keep vacationers coming.

We're seeing softness in the Caribbean market and unexpected softness in Europe. It's causing better deals than we expected," says Rick Kaplan of CruiseMasters, a cruise-only travel agency in Los Angeles.

Best bargains, he and other experts say, are for summer cruises to Europe. Holland America, for example, offers a 12-day cruise around Scandinavia and Russia

starting at $2,762 per person, including round-trip airfare from the East Coast—about $450 less than a year ago....

Reason for discounts: Not enough vacationers to fill all the new ships, Kaplan says.

New ships coming on line this year will boost capacity 7.3%, says Hence Orme of NatWest Securities. But the number of people taking cruises has leveled off after tripling from 1982 to 1993.

—By Gene Sloan

HEADLINE

MARKET SHORTAGE

For Fans, What's 4 Nights for U2?

After an 80-hour ordeal—four nights stuffed in a car, three days breathing bus exhaust, scarfing Cokes and franks, running blocks for pit stops—the three University of Maryland seniors who camped out at RFK Stadium prevailed. They beat the scalpers to U2 concert tickets.

At 8 a.m. today they would be, if all went as planned, first on line at the RFK box office. By 9 a.m. the 52,000-seat stadium will sell out, predicted a Ticketmaster official.

"It's what you got to do to get good seats," said Crawford Conniff, 22, stretched out near the stadium among traffic island dandelions.

"We have unlimited time," said Mike Collins, 22. "If we had a job making 50 grand, we could pay $150 to scalpers."

Actually, $150 sounds cheap for the $28.50 face-value tickets. Today's ticket sale for the Aug. 15 concert, one of the summer's hottest, is likely to ignite an orgy of profiteering.

When the band played Los Angeles, scalpers scored up to $1,200 a ticket for prime seats. In Washington, as early as Tuesday, ticket brokers had stationed students, unemployed and even homeless people at ticket outlets to snap up hundreds of choice seats.

—Laura Blumenfeld

The Washington Post, April 25, 1992, p. A1. ©1992 The Washington Post. Reprinted with permission.

---

plus of cruise ships in world markets forced sellers to reduce cruise prices substantially.

A very different sequence of events would occur if a market shortage existed. Suppose someone were to spread the word that typing services were available at only $1.50 per page. Tom, George, and Lisa would be standing in line to get their papers typed, but campus typists would not be willing to supply the quantity desired at that price. As Figure 3.6 confirms, at $1.50 per page, the quantity demanded (47 pages per semester) would greatly exceed the quantity supplied (20 pages per semester). In this situation, we may speak of a **market shortage,** that is, an excess of quantity demanded over quantity supplied. At a price of $1.50 a page, the shortage amounts to 27 pages of typing.

market shortage: The amount by which the quantity demanded exceeds the quantity supplied at a given price; excess demand.

When a market shortage exists, not all consumer demands can be satisfied. In other words, some people who are *willing* to buy typing at the going price ($1.50) will not be able to do so. To assure themselves of sufficient typing, Tom, George, Lisa, or some other consumer may offer to pay a *higher* price, thus initiating a move up the demand curve of Figure 3.6. The higher prices offered will in turn induce other enterprising students to type more, thus ensuring an upward movement along the market supply curve. Thus a higher price tends to call forth a greater quantity supplied, as reflected in the upward-sloping supply curve. Notice, again, that the *desire* to type has not changed; only the quantity supplied has responded to a change in price.

The accompanying Headline illustrates what happens at music concerts when tickets are priced below equilibrium. When the quantity demanded exceeds the quantity supplied, people have to stand in line to get tickets. Those who are lucky (and patient) enough to get tickets can turn around and sell them at the market-clearing price. Such "scalping" represents income that the U2 concert promoter could have gotten if the tickets had initially been priced closer to equilibrium.

What we observe, then, is that **whenever the market price is set above or below the equilibrium price, either a market surplus or a market shortage will emerge.** To overcome a surplus or shortage, buyers and sellers will change their behavior—that is, the prices charged or paid and the quantities demanded or sold. Only at the *equilibrium* price will no further adjustments be required. The equilibrium price is the only price at which the amount consumers are willing to buy equals the amount producers are willing to sell. We can count on market participants to find this equilibrium.

Business firms can discover equilibrium market prices in the same way. If they find that consumer purchases are not keeping up with production, they may conclude that their price is above the equilibrium price. They will have to get rid of their accumulated inventory. To do so they will have to lower their price (by a Grand End-of-Year Sale, perhaps) or convince consumers (via advertising) that they have underrated a most indispensable product. In the happy situation where consumer purchases are outpacing production, a firm might conclude that its price was a trifle too low and give it a nudge upward. Or it might expand production facilities. In any case, the equilibrium price can be established after a few trials in the marketplace.

Changes in Equilibrium

The collective actions of buyers and sellers will quickly establish an equilibrium price for any product. We should not regard any particular equilibrium price as permanent, however. The equilibrium price established in the Clearview College typing market, for example, was the unique outcome of specific demand and supply schedules. Those schedules themselves were based on our assumption of *ceteris paribus*. Specifically, we assumed that the "taste" (desire) for typing was given, as were consumers' incomes, the price and availability of other goods, and expectations. But any of these determinants of demand could change. When one does, the demand curve has to be redrawn. Such a shift of the demand curve will lead to a new equilibrium price and quantity. Indeed, **the equilibrium price will change whenever the supply or demand curve shifts.**

We can illustrate how equilibrium prices change by taking one last look at the Clearview College typing market. Our original supply and demand curves, together with the resulting equilibrium (point E_1), are depicted in Figure 3.7. Now suppose that the professors at Clearview begin assigning additional papers and homework, all of which must be typed. The increased need (desire) for typing services will affect market demand. Tom, George, and Lisa are suddenly willing to buy more typing at every price than they were before. That is to say, the *demand* for typing has increased. We can represent this increased demand by a rightward *shift* of the market demand curve, as illustrated in Figure 3.7.

Note that the new demand curve intersects the (unchanged) market supply curve at a new price (point E_2); the equilibrium price is now $3 per page. This new equilibrium price will persist until either the demand curve or the supply curve shifts again.

The kinds of price changes we are describing here are quite common. Indeed, equilibrium prices change as often as significant changes occur in the behavior of buyers or sellers. A few moments in a stockbroker's office or a glance through the stock pages of the daily newspaper should be testimony enough to the fluid character of market prices. If thousands of stock-

FIGURE 3.7
A New Equilibrium

A rightward shift of the demand curve indicates that consumers are willing and able to buy a larger quantity at every price. As a consequence, a new equilibrium is established (point E_2), at a higher price and greater quantity. A shift of the demand curve occurs only when the assumption of *ceteris paribus* is violated—when one of the determinants of demand changes.

The equilibrium would also be altered if the determinants of supply changed, causing a shift of the market supply curve.

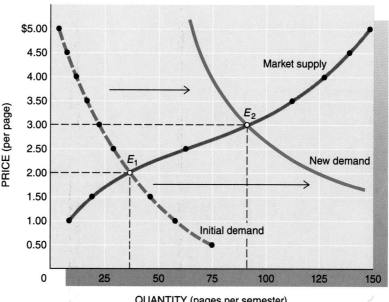

QUANTITY (pages per semester)

holders decide to sell IBM shares tomorrow, you can be sure that the market price of that stock will drop.

DISEQUILIBRIUM PRICING

The ability of the market to achieve equilibrium price and quantity is evident. Nevertheless, people are often upset with those outcomes. At Clearview College, the consumers of typing services are likely to feel that the price of typing is too high. On the other hand, campus typists may feel that they are getting paid too little for their services.

Price Ceilings

price ceiling: Upper limit imposed on the price of a good.

Sometimes consumers are able to convince the government to intervene on their behalf by setting a limit on prices. In many cities, for example, poor people and their advocates have convinced local governments that rents are too high. High rents, they argue, make housing prohibitively expensive for the poor, leaving them homeless or living in crowded, unsafe quarters. They ask government to impose a *limit* on rents in order to make housing affordable for everyone. Two hundred local governments—including New York City, Boston, Washington, D.C., and San Francisco—have responded with rent controls. In all cases, rent controls are a **price ceiling**—an upper limit imposed on the price of a good or service.

Rent controls have the immediate effect of making housing more affordable. But such controls are *disequilibrium* prices and will change housing decisions in unintended ways. Figure 3.8 illustrates the problem. In the absence of government intervention, the quantity of housing consumed (q_e) and the prevailing rent (p_e) would be established by the intersection of market supply and demand curves. Not everyone would be housed to their satisfaction in this equilibrium. As the demand curve indicates, more housing would be consumed if rents were lower. Some of those people on the low end of the demand curve simply do not have enough income to pay the

FIGURE 3.8
Price Ceilings Create Shortages

Many cities impose rent controls to keep housing affordable. Consumers respond to the below-equilibrium price ceiling (p_c) by demanding more housing (q_d vs. q_e). But the quantity of housing supplied diminishes as landlords convert buildings to other uses (e.g., condos) or simply let rental units deteriorate. New construction also slows. The result is a housing shortage ($q_d - q_s$) and an actual reduction in available housing.

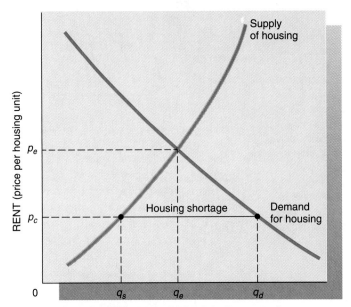

equilibrium rent p_e. They may be living with relatives or roommates they would rather not know. Or they may be homeless.

To remedy this situation, the city government imposes a rent ceiling of p_c. This lower price seemingly makes housing more affordable for everyone, including the poor. At the controlled rent p_c, people are willing and able to consume a lot more housing: the quantity demanded increases from q_e to q_d.

But what about the quantity of housing supplied? Rent controls do not increase the number of housing units available. On the contrary, price controls tend to have the opposite effect. Notice in Figure 3.8 how the quantity *supplied* falls from q_e to q_s when the rent ceiling is enacted. There is now less housing available than there was before. Thus ***price ceilings tend to***

- ***Increase the quantity demanded***
- ***Decrease the quantity supplied***
- ***Create a market shortage***

You may well wonder where the "lost" housing went. The houses did not disappear. However, some landlords decided that renting their units was no longer worth the effort. They chose, instead, to sell the units, convert them to condominiums, or even live in them themselves. Other landlords stopped maintaining their buildings, letting the units deteriorate. The rate of new construction slowed, too, as builders decided that rent control made new construction less profitable. Slowly but surely the quantity of housing declines from q_e to q_s. Hence ***there will be less housing for everyone when rent controls are imposed to make housing more affordable for some.***

Figure 3.8 illustrates another problem. As we have seen, the rent ceiling p_c has created a housing shortage—a gap between the quantity demanded (q_d) and the quantity supplied (q_s). Who will get the increasingly scarce housing? The market would have settled this FOR WHOM question by permitting rents to rise and allocating available units to those consumers willing and able to pay the rent p_e. Now, however, rents cannot rise and we have lots of people clamoring for housing that is not available. A different method of distributing goods must be found. Vacant units will go to those who learn of them first, patiently wait on waiting lists, or offer a gratuity to the landlord or renting agent. In New York City, where rent control was the law for forty years, people "sold" their rent-controlled apartments when they moved elsewhere.

Price Floors

price floor: Lower limit imposed on the price of a good.

Artificially high (above-equilibrium) prices create similar problems in the marketplace. A **price floor** is a minimum price imposed by the government for a good or service. The objective is to raise the price of the good and create more income for the seller. Federal minimum wage laws, for example, forbid most employers from paying less than $4.25 an hour for labor.

Price floors are also common in the farm sector. To stabilize farmers' incomes while ensuring a steady flow of food, the government offers price guarantees for certain crops. In 1995, for example, the government set a price guarantee ("target price") of $2.75 per bushel for corn. If the market price of corn were to fall below $2.75, the government promised to pay farmers the difference. Hence farmers knew they could sell their corn for $2.75 per bushel, regardless of market demand.

Figure 3.9 illustrates the consequences of the price floor. The price guarantee p_f lies above the equilibrium price p_e (otherwise it would have no effect). At that higher price, farmers supply more corn (q_s vs. q_e). However, consumers are not willing to buy that much corn: at the price p_f they demand only the quantity q_d. Hence, a *price floor*

- *Increases the quantity supplied*
- *Reduces the quantity demanded*
- *Creates a market surplus*

The problem now is to dispose of all that excess corn. For years, the U.S. government simply purchased the surplus corn and stored it. This got too expensive, and tons of corn were wasted through spoilage and rat pillage. We even tried giving it to poor countries, but the surplus disrupted their

FIGURE 3.9
Price Floors Create Surplus

The U.S. Department of Agriculture sets a "target price" for corn (p_f). If the market price drops below p_f, the government pays farmers the difference. Hence the target price is a guaranteed price floor for farmers.

Farmers respond by producing the quantity q_s. Consumers will purchase the quantity q_s, however, only if the market price drops to p_m (point *a* on the demand curve). The government thus must either purchase and store the surplus $q_s - q_d$ or pay farmers the difference between p_f and p_m for each bushel of corn.

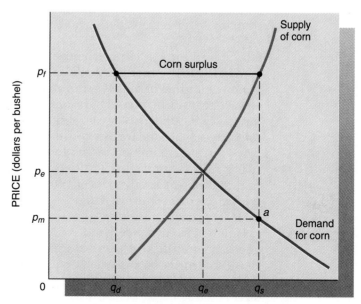

QUANTITY OF CORN (bushels per harvest)

own agricultural markets. Finally, we decided to sell it. But notice what happened to the market price. Consumers would purchase the quantity q_s only if the price of corn fell to p_m (point a in Figure 3.9). Hence, corn prices in the marketplace have to fall *below* the true equilibrium (p_e) in order to dispose of the excess corn grown for sale at the guaranteed price p_f. That sounds like a great deal for both consumers (now paying a below-equilibrium price) and farmers (now receiving an above-equilibrium price). But the outcome is not as good as it looks. The government must collect enough taxes to pay farmers the difference between the price floor (p_f) and the resulting market price (p_m). Furthermore, the mix of output now includes more corn than people would want if they had to pay the true costs of corn (p_f) directly. This is a classic case of **government failure**: society ends up with the wrong mix of output, an increased tax burden, and an altered distribution of income.

> **government failure:** Government intervention that fails to improve economic outcomes.

POLICY PERSPECTIVES

Laissez Faire

> **laissez faire:** The doctrine of "leave it alone," of nonintervention by government in the market mechanism.

The apparent inefficiencies of price ceilings and floors imply that market outcomes are best left alone. This is a conclusion reached long ago by Adam Smith, the founder of modern economic theory. In 1776 he advocated a policy of **laissez faire**—literally, "leave it alone." As he saw it, the market mechanism was an efficient procedure for allocating resources and distributing incomes. Interference with the market—through price ceilings, floors, or other regulation—was likely to cause more problems than it could hope to solve.

The policy of laissez faire is motivated not only by the potential pitfalls of government intervention but also by the recognition of how well the market mechanism can work. Recall our visit to Clearview College, where the price and quantity of typing services had to be established. There was no central agency that set the price of typing or determined how much typing would be done at Clearview College. Instead, both the price of typing and its quantity were determined by the **market mechanism**—the interactions of many independent (decentralized) buyers and sellers.

> **market mechanism:** The use of market prices and sales to signal desired outputs (or resource allocations).

WHAT, HOW, FOR WHOM

Notice how the market mechanism resolved the basic economic questions of WHAT, HOW, and FOR WHOM. The WHAT question refers to how much typing to include in society's mix of output. The answer at Clearview College was 39 pages per semester. This decision was not reached in a referendum, but instead in the market equilibrium (see Figure 3.6). In the same way but on a larger scale, millions of consumers and a handful of auto producers decide to include 6 million to 7 million cars in each year's mix of output.

The market mechanism will also determine HOW these goods are produced. Profit-seeking producers will strive to produce typing and automobiles in the most efficient way. They will use market prices to decide not only WHAT to produce but also what resources to use in the production process.

Finally, the "invisible hand" of the market will determine who gets the goods produced. At Clearview College, who got their papers typed? Only those students who were willing and able to pay $2 per page for that service. FOR WHOM are all those automobiles produced each year? The answer is the same: those consumers who are willing and able to pay the market price for a new car.

Optimal, Not Perfect

Not everyone is happy with these answers, of course. Tom would like to pay only $1 a page for his typing. And some of the Clearview students do not have enough income to buy any typing. They think it is unfair that they have to type their own papers while richer students can have someone else do their typing for them. Students who cannot afford cars are even less happy with the market's answer to the FOR WHOM question.

Although the outcomes of the marketplace are not perfect, they are likely to be optimal. Optimal outcomes are the best possible, given the level and distribution of incomes and scarce resources. In other words, we expect the choices made in the marketplace to be the best possible choices for each participant. Why do we draw such a conclusion? Because Tom and George and everybody in our little Clearview College drama had (and continue to have) absolute freedom to make their own purchase and consumption decisions. And also because we assume that sooner or later they will make the choices they find most satisfying. The results are thus *optimal*, in the sense that everyone has done as well as they can, given their income and talents.

The optimality of market outcomes provides a powerful argument for *laissez faire*. In essence, the laissez-faire doctrine recognizes that decentralized markets not only work, but also give individuals the opportunity to maximize their satisfaction. In this context, government interference is seen as a threat to the attainment of the "right" mix of output and other economic goals. The evident efficiency of the market mechanism allocating scarce resources seems to dictate against government intervention. Since its development by Adam Smith in 1776, the laissez-faire doctrine has had a profound impact on the way the economy functions and what government does (or doesn't do).

SUMMARY

- Individual consumers, business firms, government agencies, and foreigners participate in the marketplace by offering to buy or sell goods and services, or factors of production. Participation is motivated by the desire to maximize utility (consumers), profits (business firms), or the general welfare (government agencies).
- All interactions in the marketplace involve the exchange of either factors of production or finished products. Although the actual exchanges can take place anywhere, we may say that they take place in product markets or factor markets, depending on what is being exchanged.
- People who are willing and able to buy a particular good at some price are part of the market demand for that product. All those who are willing and able to sell that good at some price are part of the market supply. Total market demand or supply is the sum of individual demands or supplies.
- Supply and demand curves illustrate how the quantity demanded or supplied changes in response to a change in the price of that good, if nothing else changes (*ceteris paribus*). Demand curves slope downward; supply curves slope upward.
- The determinants of market demand include the number of potential buyers and their respective tastes (desires), incomes, other goods, and expectations. If any of these determinants changes, the demand curve shifts. Movements along a demand curve are induced only by a change in the price of that good.

- The determinants of market supply include technology, factor costs, other goods, taxes, expectations, and the number of sellers. Supply shifts when these underlying determinants change.
- The quantity of goods or resources actually exchanged in each market will depend on the behavior of all buyers and sellers, as summarized in market supply and demand curves. At the point where the two curves intersect, an equilibrium price—the price at which the quantity demanded equals the quantity supplied—will be established.
- A distinctive feature of the equilibrium price and quantity is that it is the only price–quantity combination that is acceptable to buyers and sellers alike. At higher prices, sellers supply more than buyers are willing to purchase (a market surplus); at lower prices, the amount demanded exceeds the quantity supplied (a market shortage). Only the equilibrium price clears the market.
- Price ceilings and floors are disequilibrium prices imposed on the marketplace. Such price controls create an imbalance between quantities demanded and supplied.
- The market mechanism is a device for establishing prices and product and resource flows. As such, it may be used to answer the basic economic questions of WHAT to produce, HOW to produce it, and FOR WHOM. Its apparent efficiency prompts the call for laissez faire—a policy of government nonintervention in the marketplace.

Terms to Remember

Define the following terms:

factor market	law of demand	market surplus
product market	*ceteris paribus*	market shortage
supply	shift in demand	price ceiling
demand	market demand	price floor
opportunity cost	market supply	government failure
demand schedule	law of supply	laissez faire
demand curve	equilibrium price	market mechanism

Questions for Discussion

1. In our story of Tom, the nontypist confronted with a typing assignment, we emphasized the great urgency of his desire for typing services. Many people would say that Tom had an "absolute need" for typing and was therefore ready to "pay anything" to get his paper typed. If this were true, what shape would his demand curve have? Why isn't this realistic?
2. Illustrate the market situation for the U2 concert (p. 65). Why didn't the concert promoters set an equilibrium price?
3. Word-processing machines make typing easier and improve the appearance of the final product as well. How have word processors altered the supply and demand for typing services?
4. Explain the practice of "scalping" tickets for major sporting events in terms of market shortages. How else might tickets be distributed?
5. If rent controls are so counterproductive, why do cities impose them? How else might the housing problems of poor people be solved?

Problems

1. Using Figure 3.7 as a guide, determine the approximate size of the market surplus or shortage that would exist at a price of (*a*) $4, (*b*) $2.

2. Given the following data, (a) construct market supply and demand curves and identify the equilibrium price; and (b) identify the amount of shortage or surplus that would exist at a price of $4.

Participant	Quantity Demanded (per week)				
A. Price	$5	$4	$3	$2	$1
B. Demand side					
Al	1	2	3	4	5
Betsy	0	1	1	1	2
Casey	2	2	3	3	4
Daisy	1	3	4	4	6
Eddie	1	2	2	3	5
Market total	__	__	__	__	__

Participant	Quantity Supplied (per week)				
A. Price	$5	$4	$3	$2	$1
C. Supply side					
Alice	3	3	3	3	3
Butch	7	5	4	4	2
Connie	6	4	3	3	1
Dutch	6	5	4	3	0
Ellen	4	2	2	2	1
Market total	__	__	__	__	__

3. Suppose that the good described in problem 2 became so popular that every consumer demanded one additional unit at every price. Illustrate this increase in market demand and identify the new equilibrium. Which curve has shifted? Along which curve has there been a movement of price and quantity?

4. The following events shift either the supply or the demand curve for American-made automobiles. Illustrate each situation on the graphs below.

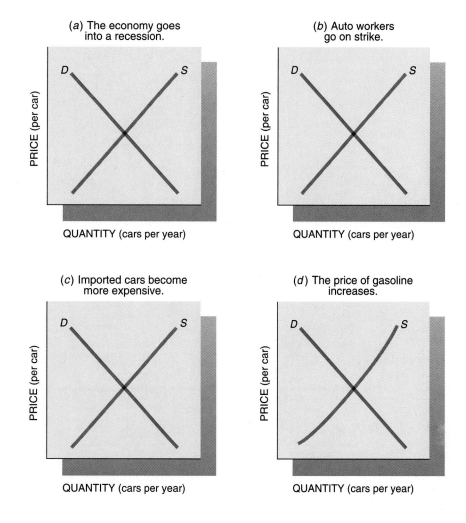

(a) The economy goes into a recession.

QUANTITY (cars per year)

(b) Auto workers go on strike.

QUANTITY (cars per year)

(c) Imported cars become more expensive.

QUANTITY (cars per year)

(d) The price of gasoline increases.

QUANTITY (cars per year)

SECTION II

MICROECONOMICS

The prices and products we see every day emerge from decisions made by millions of individual consumers and firms. A primary objective of microeconomic theory is to explain how those decisions are made. How do consumers decide which products to buy and in what quantities? How do business firms decide how much to produce? How are market outcomes affected by the structure of markets—that is, the number and size of producers? When should the government intervene to change market outcomes? These are the issues addressed in microeconomics.

Chapter 4

Consumer Demand

"**S**hop until you drop" is apparently a way of life for many Americans. The *average* American (man, woman, or child) spends roughly $19,000 per year on consumer goods and services. This adds up at the cash register to a consumption bill of nearly $5 *trillion* a year.

A major concern of microeconomics is to explain all of this activity. What drives us to department stores, grocery stores, and every Big Sale in town? More specifically,

- How do we decide how much of any good to buy?
- How does a change in price affect the quantity we purchase or the amount of money we spend on a good?
- What factors other than price affect our consumption decisions?

The law of demand, first encountered in Chapter 3, gives us some clues for answering these questions. But we need to look beyond that law to fashion more complete answers. Knowing that demand curves are downward-sloping is important, but that knowledge won't get us very far in the real world. In the real world, producers need to know the exact quantities demanded at various prices. Producers also need to know what forces will alter consumer demand.

The specifics of consumer demand are also important to public policy decisions. Suppose the city wants to relieve highway congestion and encourage more people to use public transit. Will public appeals be effective in changing commuter behavior? Or should the city try to change commuter habits by altering relative prices? Experience shows that raising the price of private auto use (e.g., higher parking fees, bridge tolls) and lowering transit fares are effective in relieving highway congestion. Economists try to predict just how much prices should be altered to elicit the desired response.

Your school worries about the details of consumer demand as well. If tuition goes up again, some students will go elsewhere. Other students may take fewer courses. As enrollment begins to drop, school administrators may ask economics professors for some advice on tuition pricing. Their advice will be based on studies of consumer demand.

PATTERNS OF CONSUMPTION

A good way to start a study of consumer demand is to observe how consumers spend their income. Figure 4.1 provides a quick summary of how the average consumer dollar is spent. Note that half of all consumer spending is for food and shelter. Out of the typical consumer dollar, 34 cents is devoted to housing—everything from rent and repairs to utility bills and grass seed. Another 16 cents is spent on food, including groceries and trips to McDonald's. We also spend a lot on cars: transportation expenditures (car payments, maintenance, gasoline, insurance) eat up 19 cents out of the typical consumer dollar.

Taken together, housing, transportation, and food expenditures account for nearly 70 percent of the typical household budget. Most people regard these items as the "basic essentials." However, there is no rule that says 16 cents of every consumer dollar must be spent on food, or that 34.1 percent of one's budget is "needed" for shelter. What Figure 4.1 depicts is how the average consumer has *chosen* to spend his or her income. We could choose to spend our incomes in other ways and even change our view of what is "essential" and what is not.

A closer examination of consumer patterns reveals that we do in fact change our habits on occasion. In the last ten years, our annual consumption of red meat has declined from 125 pounds per person to 115 pounds. In the same time, our consumption of chicken has increased from 47 pounds to 70 pounds. We now consume less coffee, whiskey, beer, and eggs, but more wine, asparagus, and ice cream compared to ten years ago. Car phones and CD players are often regarded as "essentials" today, even though no one had these products ten years ago. What prompted these changes in consumption patterns?

Some changes in consumption are more sudden. In the recession of

FIGURE 4.1
How the Consumer Dollar is Spent

Consumers spend their incomes on a vast array of goods and services. This figure summarizes those consumption decisions by showing how the average consumer dollar is spent. The goal of economic theory is to explain and predict these consumption choices.

Source: U.S. Department of Labor, 1993 Consumer Expenditure Survey.

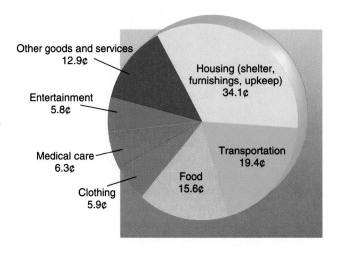

Other goods and services
12.9¢

Entertainment
5.8¢

Medical care
6.3¢

Clothing
5.9¢

Housing (shelter, furnishings, upkeep)
34.1¢

Transportation
19.4¢

Food
15.6¢

1990–91, Americans abruptly stopped buying new cars. Does that mean that cars were no longer "essential"? Did people suddenly decide to walk to work, rather than drive? Or did other factors change consumption patterns in those years?

DETERMINANTS OF DEMAND

What determines the mix of goods and services we buy in a certain time period? What leads us to buy some goods while rejecting others?

The Sociopsychiatric Explanation

As one might expect, psychiatrists and psychologists have had a virtual field day formulating explanations of our behavior in the supermarket. Sigmund Freud was among the first to describe us poor mortals as bundles of subconscious (and unconscious) fears, complexes, and anxieties. From a Freudian perspective, we strive for ever higher levels of consumption to satisfy basic drives for security, sex, and ego gratification. Like the most primitive of people, we seek to clothe and adorn ourselves in ways that assert our identity and worth. We eat and smoke too much because we need the oral gratifications and security associated with mother's breast. Self-indulgence, in general, creates in our minds the safety and satisfactions of childhood. Oversized homes and cars provide us with a source of warmth and security remembered from the womb. On the other hand, we often buy and consume some things we expressly don't desire, just to assert our rebellious feelings against our parents (or parent substitutes). In Freud's view, it is the constant interplay of id, ego, and superego drives that motivates us to buy, buy, buy.

Sociologists offer additional explanations for our consumption behavior. They emphasize our yearning to stand above the crowd, to receive recognition from the masses. For those of truly exceptional talents, such recognition may come easily. But for the ordinary person, recognition may depend on conspicuous consumption. A larger car, a newer fashion, a more exotic vacation become expressions of identity that provoke recognition, even social acceptance. Thus we strive for ever higher levels of consumption—so as to *surpass* the Joneses, not just to keep up with them.

Not *all* consumption is motivated by ego or status concerns, of course. Some food is consumed for the sake of self-preservation, some clothing for warmth, and some housing for shelter. The typical American consumer has more than enough income to satisfy these basic needs, however. In today's economy, consumers have a lot of *discretionary* income that can be used to satisfy psychological or sociological longings. As a result, single women are able to spend more money on clothing and pets, while men spend more on entertainment, food, and drink (see the accompanying Headline). As for teenagers, they express their affluence in purchases of electronic goods, cars, and clothes (see Figure 4.2).

The Economic Explanation

Although psychiatrists and sociologists offer many reasons for these various consumption patterns, their explanations all fall a bit short. At best, sociopsychiatric theories tell us why teenagers, men, and women *desire* certain goods and services. They don't explain which goods will actually be

HEADLINE

CONSUMPTION PATTERNS

Men vs. Women: How They Spend

Are men really different from women? If spending habits are any clue, males do differ from females. That's the conclusion one would draw from the latest Bureau of Labor Statistics (BLS) survey of consumer expenditure. Here's what BLS found out about the spending habits of young (under age 25) men and women who are living on their own:

Common Traits

* Young men have slightly more income to spend ($9,945) than do young women ($8,867). Both sexes go deep into debt, however, by spending $3,000–$4,000 more than their income.

* Neither sex spends much on charity, reading, or health care.

Distinctive Traits

* Young men spend 50 percent more at fast-food outlets, restaurants, and carryouts.
* Men spend three times as much on alcoholic beverages and twice as much on smoking.
* Men spend twice as much as women do on television and stereo equipment.
* Young women spend a lot more money on clothing and also devote more of their income to their pets.

U.S. Bureau of Labor Statistics, 1993 Consumer Expenditure Survey.

---

purchased. Desire is only the first step in the consumption process. To acquire goods and services, one must be willing and able to *pay* for one's wants. Producers won't give you their goods just because you want to satisfy your Freudian desires. They want money in exchange for their goods. Hence prices and income are just as relevant to the consumption decision as are more basic desires and preferences.

In explaining consumer behavior, then, economists focus on the demand for goods and services. To say that someone **demands** a particular good means that he or she is able and willing to buy it at some price(s). In the marketplace, money talks: *the willingness and ability to pay* are critical. Many people with a strong desire for a Rolls-Royce have neither the ability nor the willingness actually to buy it; they do not *demand* Rolls-Royces. Similarly, there are many rich people who are willing and able to buy goods they only remotely desire; they *demand* all kinds of goods and services.

What determines a person's willingness and ability to buy specific goods? Desire alone is clearly not enough. Nor does income alone determine which goods will be demanded or in what quantities. Economists have identified four different influences on consumer demand. In particular, ***an individual's demand for a specific product is determined by***

* *Tastes* (desire for this and other goods)
* *Income* (of the consumer)
* *Expectations* (for income, prices, tastes)
* *Other goods* (their availability and prices)

Note again that desire (tastes) is only one determinant of demand. Other determinants of demand (income, expectations, and other goods) also influence whether a person will be willing and able to buy a certain good at a specific price.

> **demand:** The ability and willingness to buy specific quantities of a good at alternative prices in a given time period, *ceteris paribus*.

FIGURE 4.2
Affluent Teenagers

Teenagers spend over $70 billion a year. Much of this spending is for cars, stereos, and other durables. The percentage of U.S. teenagers owning certain items is shown here.

Source: Teenage Research Unlimited (1994 data).

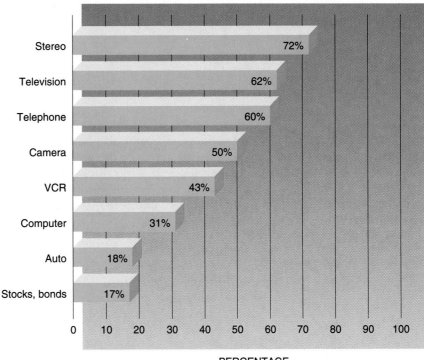

PERCENTAGE

---

market demand: The total quantities of a good or service people are willing and able to buy at alternative prices in a given time period; the sum of individual demands.

The **market demand** for a good is simply the sum of all individual consumer demands. As we observed in Chapter 3, the market demand curve is simply the aggregation of individual demand curves. Hence *the market demand for a specific product is determined by*

- *Tastes*
- *Income*
- *Expectations*
- *Other goods*
- *The number of consumers in the market*

In the remainder of this chapter we shall see how these determinants of demand give the demand curve its downward slope. Our objective is not only to explain consumer behavior but also to see (and predict) how consumption patterns change in response to *changes* in the price of a good, or to *changes* in the underlying determinants of demand.

THE DEMAND CURVE

Utility Theory

The starting point for an economic analysis of demand is quite simple. Economists accept consumer tastes as the outcome of sociopsychiatric and cultural influences. They don't look beneath the surface of expressed desires to see how those tastes originated. Economists simply note the existence of certain tastes (desires), then look to see how those tastes affect consumption decisions. We assume that the more additional pleasure a product gives us, the higher the price we would be willing to pay for it. If the oral sensation of buttered popcorn at the movies really turns you on, you're likely to be willing to pay dearly for it. If you have no great taste or desire for popcorn, the theater might have to give it away before you'd eat it.

Total vs. Marginal Utility. Economists use the term **utility** to refer to the expected pleasure, or satisfaction, obtained from goods and services. Instead of asking someone how much he or she "likes" popcorn, an economist might ask how much "utility" a person gets from consuming popcorn. An economist would also be more specific about the source of the utility. **Total utility** refers to the amount of satisfaction obtained from your *entire* consumption of a product. By contrast, **marginal utility** refers to the amount of satisfaction you get from consuming the *last* (i.e., "marginal") unit of a product. More generally, note that

$$\bullet \quad \frac{\text{Marginal}}{\text{utility}} = \frac{\text{change in total utility}}{\text{change in quantity}}$$

Diminishing Marginal Utility. The concepts of total and marginal utility explain not only why we buy popcorn at the movies but also why we stop eating it at some point. Even people who love popcorn (i.e., derive great utility from it), and can afford it, don't eat endless quantities of popcorn. Why not? Presumably because the thrill diminishes with each mouthful. The first box of popcorn may bring sensual gratification, but the second or third box is likely to bring a stomachache. We express this change in perceptions by noting that the marginal utility of the first box of popcorn is higher than the additional or marginal utility derived from the second box.

The behavior of popcorn connoisseurs is not that unusual. Generally speaking, the amount of additional utility we obtain from a product declines as we continue to consume larger quantities of it. The third pizza is not so desirable as the first, the sixth soda not so satisfying as the fifth, and so forth. Indeed, this phenomenon of diminishing marginal utility is so nearly universal that economists have fashioned a law around it. This **law of diminishing marginal utility** states that each successive unit of a good consumed yields less *additional* utility.

The law of diminishing marginal utility does *not* say that we won't like the third box of popcorn, the second pizza, or the sixth soda; it just says we won't like them as much as the ones we've already consumed. Note also that time is important here: if the first pizza was eaten last year, the second pizza, eaten now, may taste just as good. The law of diminishing marginal utility is most relevant to short time periods.

The expectation of diminishing marginal utility is illustrated in Figure 4.3. The graph on the left depicts the *total* utility obtained from eating popcorn. Notice that total utility continues to rise as we consume the first five boxes (ugh!) of popcorn. But total utility increases by smaller and smaller increments. Each successive step of the total utility curve in Figure 4.3 is a little shorter.

The height of each step of the total utility curve in Figure 4.3 represents *marginal* utility—the increments to total utility. The graph on the right in Figure 4.3 illustrates these increments—the height of each step of the total utility curve (left graph). This graph shows more clearly how *marginal* utility diminishes.

(a) Total utility

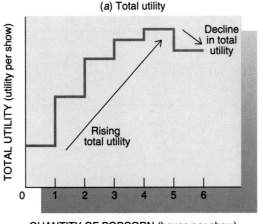

(b) Marginal utility

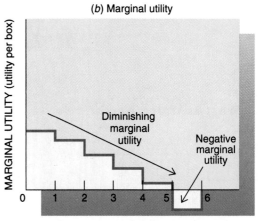

FIGURE 4.3
Total vs. Marginal Utility

The *total* utility derived from consuming a product comes from the *marginal* utilities of each successive unit. The total utility curve shows how each of the first five boxes of popcorn contributes to total utility. Note that each successive step is smaller. This reflects the law of diminishing marginal utility.

The sixth box of popcorn causes the steps to descend; the sixth box actually *reduces* total utility. This means that the sixth box has *negative* marginal utility.

The marginal utility curve (*b*) shows the change in total utility with each additional unit. It is derived from the total utility curve. Marginal utility here is positive but diminishing for the first five boxes.

Do not confuse *diminishing* marginal utility with dislike. Figure 4.3 doesn't imply that the second box of popcorn isn't desirable. It only says that the second box isn't as satisfying as the first. It still tastes good, however. How do we know? Because its *marginal* utility is positive (right graph), and therefore *total* utility (left graph) rises when the second box is consumed. ***So long as marginal utility is positive, total utility must be increasing.***

The situation changes abruptly with the sixth box of popcorn. According to Figure 4.3, the good sensations associated with popcorn consumption are completely forgotten by the time the sixth box arrives. Nausea and stomach cramps dominate. Indeed, the sixth box is absolutely *distasteful*, as reflected in the downturn of total utility and the *negative* value for marginal utility. We were happier—in possession of more total utility—with only five boxes of popcorn. The sixth box—yielding negative marginal utility—has reduced total satisfaction.

Marginal utility not only explains why we stop eating popcorn before we explode but also why we pay so little for drinking water. As the accompanying Headline suggests, water has a high *total* utility: we would die without it. But its *marginal* utility is low, so we're not willing to pay much for another glass of it.

Not all goods approach zero (much less negative) marginal utility. Yet the more general principle of diminishing marginal utility is experienced daily. That is to say, ***additional quantities of a good tend to yield increasingly smaller increments of satisfaction.*** Total utility continues to rise, but at

HEADLINE

MARGINAL UTILITY

What Is Water Worth?

Water is vital to human life. But we waste water all the time and often get angry when anyone tries to charge us a price for it.

The concept of marginal utility helps explain this paradox. If only a small amount of water were available, we would store it carefully and use it only to sustain life. As more water becomes available, however, we use it for less valued purposes, like washing hands, brushing teeth, and bathing. These uses of water are valuable, too, but

of less *marginal* utility than water's first use (sustaining life). With still more water, we can wash the car, water the garden, and even have water fights on a hot day. Eventually, the marginal utility of water gets so low that we fill water glasses and set them on the table but don't even drink the water that has been served. We have consumed so much water that the additional water offers little if any marginal utility. Water remains tremendously valuable—its *total* utility is enormous—but we're not prepared to pay much for an additional glass of it; its *marginal* utility is negligible.

an ever slower rate as more of a good is consumed. Marginal utility may even approach zero for very valuable goods (see Headline). For our purposes, it does not matter whether marginal utility can be measured (it cannot), just so long as it declines with continued consumption of a good. There are exceptions to the law of diminishing marginal utility, but not many. (Can you think of any?)

Price and Quantity

ceteris paribus: The assumption of nothing else changing.

law of demand: The quantity of a good demanded in a given time period increases as its price falls, *ceteris paribus*.

demand curve: A curve describing the quantities of a good a consumer is willing and able to buy at alternative prices in a given time period, *ceteris paribus*.

How much of a certain good we are willing to buy at any particular price depends not only on its marginal utility (a measure of our "taste") but also on our income, our expectations, and the prices of alternative goods and services. Rather than try to explain all these forces at once, however, let us focus on the relationship between the *price* of the good and the amount of it we are willing to buy. This doesn't mean that other forces are unimportant, just that we want to proceed one step at a time. In effect, we are assuming that everything else is constant, or unchanging. This is the **ceteris paribus** assumption first encountered in Chapter 1.

The concepts of marginal utility and *ceteris paribus* enable us to explain the downward slope of demand curves. The more marginal utility a good delivers, the more you're willing to pay for it. But marginal utility *diminishes* as increasing quantities of a product are consumed. Hence you won't be willing to pay so much for additional quantities of the same good. The moviegoer who is willing to pay 50 cents for that first mouth-watering ounce of buttered popcorn may not be willing to pay so much for a second or third ounce. The same is true for the second pizza, the sixth soda, and so forth. **With given income, taste, expectations, and prices of other goods and services, people are willing to buy additional quantities of a good only if its price falls.** In other words, as the marginal utility of a good diminishes, so does our willingness to pay. This inverse relationship between the quantity demanded of a good and its price is referred to as the **law of demand.** Figure 4.4 illustrates this relationship again, for the case of popcorn. Notice that the **demand curve** slopes downward.

FIGURE 4.4.
A Demand Schedule and Curve

Because marginal utility diminishes, consumers are willing to buy larger quantities of a good only at lower prices. This demand schedule and curve illustrate the specific quantities demanded at alternative prices. Notice that points *A* through *J* on the curve correspond to the rows of the demand schedule. If popcorn sold for 25 cents per ounce, this consumer would buy 12 ounces per show (point *F*). More popcorn would be demanded only if the price were reduced (points *G–J*).

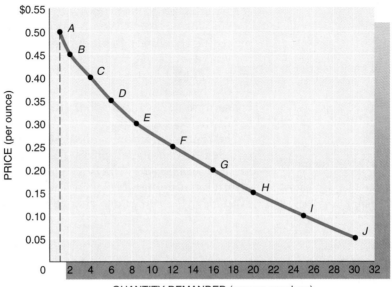

	Price (per ounce)	Quantity Demanded (ounces per show)
A	$0.50	1
B	0.45	2
C	0.40	4
D	0.35	6
E	0.30	9
F	0.25	12
G	0.20	16
H	0.15	20
I	0.10	25
J	0.05	30

The law of demand and the law of diminishing marginal utility tell us nothing about why we crave popcorn or why our cravings subside. They simply describe our market behavior.

PRICE ELASTICITY

The theory of demand gives us some general insights into consumer behavior. Often, however, much more specific information is desired. Imagine you owned a theater and were actually worried about popcorn prices and sales. Knowing that the demand curve is downward-sloping wouldn't tell you a whole lot about what price to charge. What you'd really want to know is *how much* popcorn sales would change if you raised or lowered the price.

Airlines want the same kind of hard data. Airlines know that around Christmas they can charge full fares and still fill all their planes. After the holidays, however, people have less of a desire to travel. To fill planes in February, the airlines must offer discount fares. But how far should they lower ticket prices? That depends on *how much* passenger traffic *changes* in response to reduced fares.

A similar problem arises with water conservation. People pay little or nothing for tap water. As a result, they tend to waste a lot of water (see the preceding Headline). In times of drought, however, water must be conserved for vital uses like agriculture and safe drinking. If a price were charged for each gallon of water, people would use less of it. But how high a price should be charged? What price will induce a substantial change in water consumption? To answer that question, we need more specific information about the demand curve.

The central question in all these decisions is the response of quantity demanded to a change in price. ***The response of consumers to a change in price is measured by the price elasticity of demand.*** Specifically, the **price elasticity of demand** refers to the *percentage* change in quantity demanded divided by the *percentage* change in price—that is

price elasticity of demand: The percentage change in quantity demanded divided by the percentage change in price.

$$\bullet \; \text{Price elasticity } (E) = \frac{\text{percentage change in quantity demanded}}{\text{percentage change in price}}$$

Suppose we increased the price of popcorn by 20 percent. We know from the law of demand that the quantity of popcorn demanded will fall. But we need to observe market behavior to see how far sales drop. Suppose that unit sales (quantity demanded) fall by 10 percent. We could then compute the price elasticity of demand as

$$E = \frac{\text{percentage change in quantity demanded}}{\text{percentage change in price}} = \frac{10}{20} = 0.5$$

Since price and quantity demanded always move in opposite directions, E is a negative value (-0.5 in this case). For convenience, however, the absolute value of E (without the minus sign) is used. What we learn here is that popcorn sales decline at half (0.5) the rate of price increases. Moviegoers cut back grudgingly on popcorn consumption when popcorn prices rise.

Elastic vs. Inelastic Demand

We characterize the demand for various goods as being elastic or inelastic or unitary elastic. If E is larger than 1, we say demand is elastic. Consumer response is large relative to the change in price.

If E is less than 1, we say demand is inelastic. This is the case with popcorn, where E is only 0.5. ***If demand is inelastic, consumers aren't very responsive to price changes.***

If E is equal to 1, demand is unitary elastic. In this case, the percentage change in quantity demanded is exactly equal to the percentage change in price.

Consider the case of smoking. Many smokers claim they'd "pay anything" for a cigarette after they've run out. But would they? Would they continue to smoke just as many cigarettes if prices doubled or tripled? Research suggests not: higher cigarette prices *do* curb smoking (see Headline). There is at least *some* elasticity in the demand for cigarettes. But the elasticity of demand is low, so price hikes don't curb cigarette purchases very much.

Table 4.1 on page 88 indicates that the elasticity of cigarette demand is only 0.4. On the other hand, demand is highly elastic in the case of airline

HEADLINE

CHANGING CONSUMPTION

Curbing Smoking

Nations around the world have tried to curb cigarette smoking. Consumption theory has provided some useful ideas about how this might be done.

Changing Tastes

The cigarette industry has spent billions of dollars on advertising to convince consumers that smoking is smart, elegant, and pleasurable. To counter this effort, governments have restricted cigarette advertising, forced manufacturers to issue health warnings, and undertaken antismoking campaigns in the media. All such efforts attempt to *shift the demand curve to the left.* Some examples:

USA. Television advertising was prohibited in 1971. Health warnings are required on cigarette packs, printed advertising, and billboards.
Sweden. Print advertisements may portray only a cigarette pack against a plain background; no billboard or poster advertising is permitted.
Sudan. All cigarette advertising is prohibited.
Cuba. Fidel Castro gave up smoking in 1985 and urged his countrymen to follow his example.

Raising Prices

Higher prices also can deter people from smoking by *changing the quantity demanded.* Some examples:

USA. Between 1981 and 1987, the price of cigarettes in the United States increased from 67 cents to $1.10 a pack. This large price increase reduced the quantity demanded, especially among young teenagers. According to Professor Jeffery Harris of MIT, the price increase induced 2 million Americans to quit smoking and 600,000 teenagers not to start.
Canada. Between 1984 and 1991, taxes on cigarettes quadrupled; prices rose above $5 a pack.
Great Britain. The British government imposes an extra tax on high-tar and high-nicotine cigarettes.
Poland. In Poland cigarettes cost only 22 zlotys in 1990, or about 65 cents a pack. With the world's lowest prices, Poland also has one of the highest levels of consumption. Per capita cigarette consumption exceeds 3,500 in Poland, versus roughly 2,200 in the United States.

Bans on Smoking

Outright bans on smoking represent an effort to *circumvent the market,* preventing smokers from consuming as many cigarettes as they are willing and able to buy. Some examples:

USA. Smoking is prohibited on domestic air flights and restricted in federal offices and military facilities. In 37 states and 400 cities smoking is limited in public places.
Spain. Smoking is prohibited on public transportation; segregated smoking areas are designated in public buildings and large commercial establishments.
Germany. Smoking is not permitted on public transportation or at railway stations; smoking is restricted in restaurants.

travel. Accordingly, fare discounts are a very effective mechanism for filling available airplanes. If fares are discounted by 25 percent, the number of passengers may increase by as much as 60 percent. As Table 4.1 shows, the elasticity of airline demand is 2.4, meaning that the percentage change in quantity demanded (60 percent) will be 2.4 times larger than the price cut (25 percent).

Price Elasticity and Total Revenue

The concept of price elasticity is useful for destroying the popular misconception that producers often charge the "highest price possible." Except in the very rare case of completely inelastic demand ($E = 0$), this notion makes no sense. Indeed, higher prices may actually *lower* total sales revenue.

TABLE 4.1
Elasticity Estimates

Price elasticities vary greatly. When the price of gasoline increases, consumers reduce their consumption only slightly. When the price of fish increases, however, consumers cut back their consumption substantially. These differences reflect the availability of immediate substitutes, the prices of the goods, and the amount of time available for changing behavior.

Type of Elasticity	Estimate
Relatively elastic ($E > 1$)	
Airline travel, long run	2.4
Fresh fish	2.2
New cars, short run	1.2–1.5
Unitary elastic ($E = 1$)	
Private education	1.1
Radios and televisions	1.2
Shoes	0.9
Relatively inelastic ($E < 1$)	
Cigarettes	0.4
Coffee	0.3
Gasoline, short run	0.2

Sources: Compiled from Hendrick S. Houthakker and Lester D. Taylor, *Consumer Demand in the United States, 1929–1970* (Cambridge, MA: Harvard University Press, 1966); and F. W. Bell, "The Pope and Price of Fish," *American Economic Review*, December 1968.

total revenue: The price of a product multiplied by the quantity sold in a given time period: $p \times q$.

The **total revenue** of a seller is the amount of money received from product sales. It is determined by the quantity of the product sold and the price at which it is sold. Specifically

$$\bullet \quad \frac{\text{Total}}{\text{revenue}} = \text{price} \times \frac{\text{quantity}}{\text{sold}}$$

If the price of popcorn is 20 cents per ounce and 16 ounces are sold (point *G* in Figure 4.5), total revenue equals $3.20 per show. This total revenue is illustrated by the shaded rectangle in Figure 4.5. (Recall that the area of a rectangle is equal to its height *p*, times its width, *q*.)

Now consider what happens to total revenue when the price of popcorn is reduced. From the law of demand, we know that a cut in price will lead to an increase in quantity demanded. Without Figure 4.5 it is not apparent whether total revenue will rise or fall, however. The change in total revenue depends on *how much* quantity demanded goes up when price goes down. This brings us back to the concept of elasticity.

Suppose we reduce popcorn prices from 20 cents to only 15 cents per ounce. What happens to total revenue? We know from Figure 4.5 that total revenue at point *G* was $3.20. At the lower price of 15 cents, unit sales increase (point *H*). But total revenue actually declines, to $3.00 (20 ounces × 15 cents per ounce). This shrinkage in total revenue is illustrated by the dashed rectangle in Figure 4.5 and rows *G* and *H* of the accompanying table.

Price cuts don't always reduce total revenue. Total revenue fell in this case because the consumer response to a price reduction was small in comparison to the relative size of the price cut. In other words, demand was price *inelastic*. If demand had been elastic ($E > 1$), consumers would have increased their popcorn purchases by a larger percentage and total revenue would have increased. Thus we can conclude that

- *A price cut reduces total revenue if demand is inelastic ($E < 1$).*
- *A price cut increases total revenue only if demand is elastic ($E > 1$).*
- *A price cut does not change total revenue if demand is unitary elastic ($E = 1$).*

FIGURE 4.5
Elasticity and Total Revenue

Total revenue is equal to the price of the product times the quantity sold. It is illustrated by the area of the rectangle formed by $p \times q$. The shaded rectangle illustrates total revenue ($3.20) at a price of 20 cents and a quantity demanded of 16 ounces. When price is reduced to 15 cents, the rectangle and total revenue shrink (see dashed lines) because demand is inelastic in that price range. Price cuts increase total revenue only if demand is elastic.

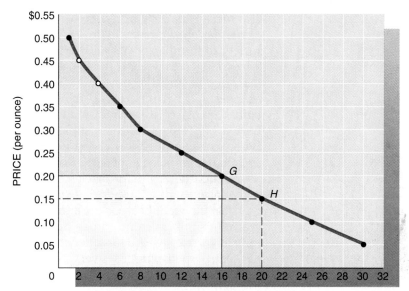

QUANTITY DEMANDED (ounces per show)

	Price	×	Quantity Demanded	+	Total Revenue
A	$0.50		1		$0.50
B	0.45		2		0.90
C	0.40		4		1.60
D	0.35		6		2.10
E	0.30		8		2.40
F	0.25		12		3.00
G	0.20		16		3.20
H	0.15		20		3.00
I	0.10		25		2.50
J	0.05		30		1.50

Table 4.2 summarizes these responses as well as responses to price increases.

Once we know the price elasticity of demand, we can predict quite accurately how consumers will respond to changing prices. By the same token, we can also predict what will happen to the total revenue of the seller. However, elasticity, like the demand curve itself, is subject to the vagaries of changing tastes, changing incomes, and changes in the prices or availability of alternative goods. All of these potential changes are ignored when we calculate elasticity along a given demand curve.

TABLE 4.2
Price Elasticity of Demand and Total Revenue

The impact of higher prices on total revenue depends on the price elasticity of demand. Higher prices result in higher total revenue only if demand is inelastic. If demand is elastic, *lower* prices result in *higher* revenues.

If demand is:	and price increases, total revenue will:	and price decreases, total revenue will:
Elastic ($E > 1$)	decrease	increase
Inelastic ($E < 1$)	increase	decrease
Unitary elastic ($E = 1$)	not change	not change

Determinants of Elasticity

The price elasticity of demand is influenced by all of the determinants of the demand curve. Table 4.1 indicated the actual price elasticity for a variety of familiar goods and services. These large differences in elasticity are explained by several factors. One of them is *price* relative to income. If the price of an item is very high in relation to one's income, then price changes will be important. Airline travel and new cars, for example, are quite expensive, so even a small percentage change in their prices could have a big impact on a consumer's budget (and consumption decisions). By contrast, coffee is so cheap for most people that even a large percentage change in price is of little real significance.

A second determinant of elasticity is the *availability of substitutes*. The high elasticity of demand for fish reflects the fact that consumers can always eat chicken, beef, or pork if fish prices rise. On the other hand, most cigarette smokers cannot imagine any other product that could substitute for a cigarette. As a consequence, when cigarette prices rise, smokers do not reduce their purchases very much at all. The price elasticity of demand for cigarettes is very low.

Finally, *time* affects the price elasticity of demand. Car owners cannot switch to coal-fired autos every time the price of gasoline goes up. In the short run, consumers are stuck with their gasoline-powered automobiles and can only vary the amount of driving they do. Even that can't be varied much, however, unless one relocates one's home or job. Hence the quantity of gasoline demanded doesn't drop much immediately when gasoline prices increase. In the short run, the elasticity of demand for gasoline is quite low. With more time to adjust, however, consumers can buy more fuel-efficient cars, relocate homes or jobs, and even switch fuels. As a consequence, ***the long-run price elasticity of demand is higher than the short-run elasticity.***

POLICY PERSPECTIVES

Caveat Emptor

No discussion of consumer demand would be complete without considering the role that advertising plays in shaping our consumer behavior. As noted earlier, psychiatrists see us as complex bundles of basic drives, anxieties, and layers of consciousness. They presume that we enter the market with confused senses of guilt, insecurity, and ambition. Economists, on the other hand, regard the consumer as the rational *Homo economicus*, aware of his or her wants and knowledgeable about how to satisfy them. In reality, however, we do not always know what we want or which products will satisfy us. This uncertainty creates a vacuum into which the advertising industry has eagerly stepped.

The efforts of producers to persuade us to buy, buy, buy are as close as the nearest television, radio, magazine, or billboard. American producers now spend over $100 *billion* per year to change our tastes. This spending works out to over $450 per consumer, one of the highest per capita advertising rates in the world (see Headline). Much of this advertising (including product labeling) is intended to provide information about existing products or to bring new products to our attention. A great deal of advertising, however, is also designed to exploit our senses and lack of knowledge. Recognizing that we are guilt-ridden, insecure, and sex-hungry, advertisers offer us pictures and promises of exoneration, recognition, and love; all we have to do is buy the right product.

HEADLINE

ADVERTISING

Where the Pitch Is Loudest

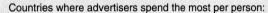

Countries where advertisers spend the most per person:

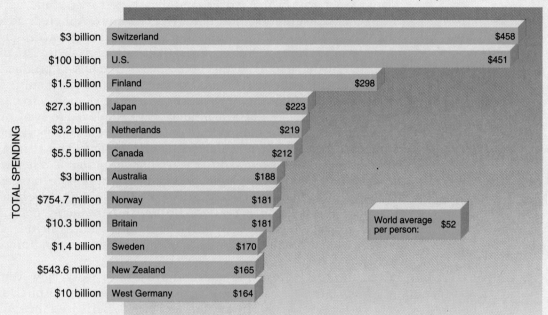

TOTAL SPENDING		
$3 billion	Switzerland	$458
$100 billion	U.S.	$451
$1.5 billion	Finland	$298
$27.3 billion	Japan	$223
$3.2 billion	Netherlands	$219
$5.5 billion	Canada	$212
$3 billion	Australia	$188
$754.7 million	Norway	$181
$10.3 billion	Britain	$181
$1.4 billion	Sweden	$170
$543.6 million	New Zealand	$165
$10 billion	West Germany	$164

World average per person: $52

Figures reflect advertising expenditures for 68 countries in 1987.

Source: Adapted from *U.S. News & World Report*, March 20, 1989, p. 90. Copyright © March 20, 1989 *U.S. News & World Report*. Basic data: Starch INRA Hooper, Inc.

One of the favorite targets of advertisers is our sense of insecurity. Thousands of products are marketed in ways that appeal to our need for identity, most often by creating a specific identity image for each product. Thousands of brand images are designed to help the consumer answer the nagging question "Who am I?" The answers, of course, vary. *Playboy* magazine says I'm a virile man of the world; Marlboro cigarettes say I'm a rugged individualist who enjoys "man-sized flavor." Users of Tide detergent are worthy homemakers, whereas Virginia Slims cigarette smokers are liberated women. The right bourbon or scotch is reserved for the successes among us, of either sex.

Other needs and drives are equally susceptible to the blandishments of promoters. Those who fear rejection can find solace and confidence in the right mouth freshener or deodorant; exhibitionist urges can be sublimated with the Wonder Bra. A measure of immortality may be achieved through insurance plans that will exercise our wishes and control in our absence. On the other hand, eternal youth can be preserved with a proper mix of vitamin supplements, face lotions, and laxatives.

Are Wants Created?

Advertising cannot be blamed for all of our "foolish" consumption. The dynamics of personality structure and social interaction give rise to drives and needs that operate in any economic context. Even members of the most primitive tribes, uncontaminated by the seductions of advertising, adorned themselves with rings, bracelets, and pendants. Furthermore, advertising has grown to massive proportions only in the last three decades, but regular increases in consumption spending have taken place throughout recorded history. Accordingly, it is a mistake to attribute the growth of consumption to the persuasions of advertisers.

This is not to say that advertising has necessarily made us happier or directed consumption into preferred channels. Although advertising cannot be charged with creating our needs, it does provide specific (if not necessarily correct) outlets for satisfying those needs. The objective of all advertising is to alter the choices we make. Just as product images are used to attract us to particular commodities, so are pictures of hungry, ill-clothed children used to persuade us to give money to charity. In the same way, public-relations gimmicks are employed to sway our votes for public servants. In the case of consumer products, advertising seeks to increase tastes for particular goods and services and therewith our willingness to pay. *A successful advertising campaign is one that shifts the demand curve to the right,* inducing consumers to increase their purchases of a product at every price (see Figure 4.6). Advertising may also make the demand curve less elastic, thus reducing consumer responses to price increases. By influencing our choices in this way, advertising alters the distribution of our consumption expenditures, if not their level.

Even the best advertising efforts don't always work, however. As the Coca-Cola Company learned, consumers may resist the pitch for new products (see Headline). Turkey farmers have experienced the same problem. By packaging turkey in new ways (e.g., turkey hot dogs) and trumpeting its low fat content, producers hoped to persuade consumers to eat more turkey. So far, however, consumer behavior hasn't responded: the demand curve for turkey hasn't budged. People eat turkey at Thanksgiving and Christmas but continue to eat chicken and ribs the rest of the year.

FIGURE 4.6
The Impact of Advertising on a Demand Curve

Advertising seeks to increase our taste for a particular product. If our taste (the product's perceived marginal utility) increases, so will our willingness to buy. The resulting change in demand is reflected in a rightward shift of the demand curve, often accompanied by diminished elasticity.

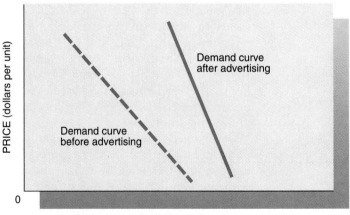

HEADLINE

UNCHANGED TASTES

The New Coke: An Advertising Flop

In April 1985 the Coca-Cola Company announced that it was changing the 99-year-old formula of its world-famous product. Coca-Cola spent millions of advertising dollars trying to convince consumers that the new, sweeter Coke was better. But consumer tastes didn't budge. The Coca-Cola Company was besieged with letters and phone calls from consumers demanding a return to the old formula. The cries of protest did not di-minish with time: in June the company said it was still receiving 1,500 calls a day. In July the company succumbed to consumer pressure, announcing that it would revive the original formula and market it under the name Coca-Cola Classic. By 1990, Coca-Cola Classic was the best-selling soft drink, outselling "New Coke" by a margin of eight to one. In early 1990 the company renamed ("Coke II") and repackaged the "new" Coke in an effort to bolster lagging sales.

SUMMARY

- Our desires for goods and services originate in the structure of personality and social dynamics and are not explained by economic theory. Economic theory focuses on *demand*—that is, our ability and willingness to buy specific quantities of a good at various prices.
- "Utility" refers to the satisfaction we get from consumer goods and services. Total utility refers to the amount of satisfaction associated with all consumption of a product. *Marginal* utility refers to the satisfaction obtained from the last unit of a product.
- The law of diminishing marginal utility says that the more of a product we consume, the smaller the increments of pleasure we tend to derive from additional units of it. This provides a basis for the law of demand.
- The price elasticity of demand is a numerical measure of consumer response to a change in price (*ceteris paribus*). It equals the percentage change in quantity demanded divided by the percentage change in price.
- If demand is elastic ($E > 1$), a small change in price induces a large change in quantity demanded. "Elastic" demand indicates that consumer behavior is very responsive to price changes.
- If demand is *elastic*, a price increase will reduce total revenue. Price and total revenue move in the same direction only if demand is *inelastic*.
- The shape and position of any particular demand curve depend on a consumer's income, tastes, expectations, and the price and availability of other goods. Should any of these things change, the assumption of *ceteris paribus* will no longer hold, and the demand curve will *shift*.
- Advertising seeks to change consumer tastes and thus the willingness to buy. If tastes do change, the demand curve will shift.

Terms to Remember Define the following terms:

demand	marginal utility	law of demand
market demand	law of diminishing	demand curve
utility	marginal utility	price elasticity of demand
total utility	*ceteris paribus*	total revenue

Questions for Discussion

1. If you could afford to buy every new CD released, would you do so? What considerations might limit your consumption?
2. Is it possible to have a great taste for French cooking and still eat at McDonald's? What is the relationship of tastes, income, prices, and consumer behavior in this case?
3. What does the demand for education at your college look like? What is on each axis? Is the demand elastic or inelastic? How could you find out?
4. If you were promoting a new music group, how would you decide what price to charge for concert tickets?
5. Identify three goods each for which your demand is (*a*) elastic or (*b*) inelastic. What accounts for the differences in elasticity?
6. Utility companies routinely ask state commissions for permission to raise utility rates. What does this suggest about the price elasticity of demand? Why is demand so (in)elastic?

Problems

1. The following is a demand schedule for shoes:

Price (per pair)	$100	$80	$60	$40	$20
Quantity demanded (in pairs per year)	10	14	18	22	26

Illustrate the demand curve on the graph below.

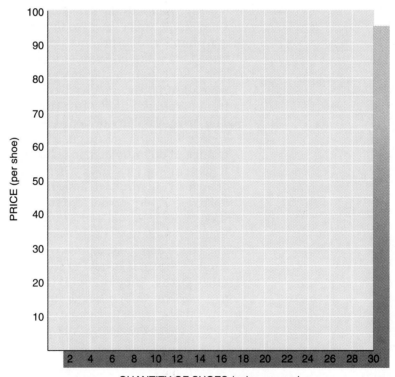

PRICE (per shoe) — QUANTITY OF SHOES (pairs per year)

2. According to the information in problem 1, how much will consumers spend on shoes at the price of (*a*) $80 and (*b*) $60? As the price drops from $80 to $60 a pair, is demand elastic or inelastic?

3. If advertisers convinced people that to be stylish they needed more shoes, how would the demand curve in problem 1 be altered? Illustrate this change.

4. How large a tax would it take to reduce cigarette consumption by 20 percent. (See Table 4.1 for a clue.)

5. Suppose the following table reflects the total satisfaction (utility) derived from eating pizza:

Quantity consumed	1	2	3	4	5	6	7
Total utility	47	92	122	135	137	120	70

    (*a*) What is the marginal utility of each pizza?
    (*b*) What causes the marginal utility to diminish?

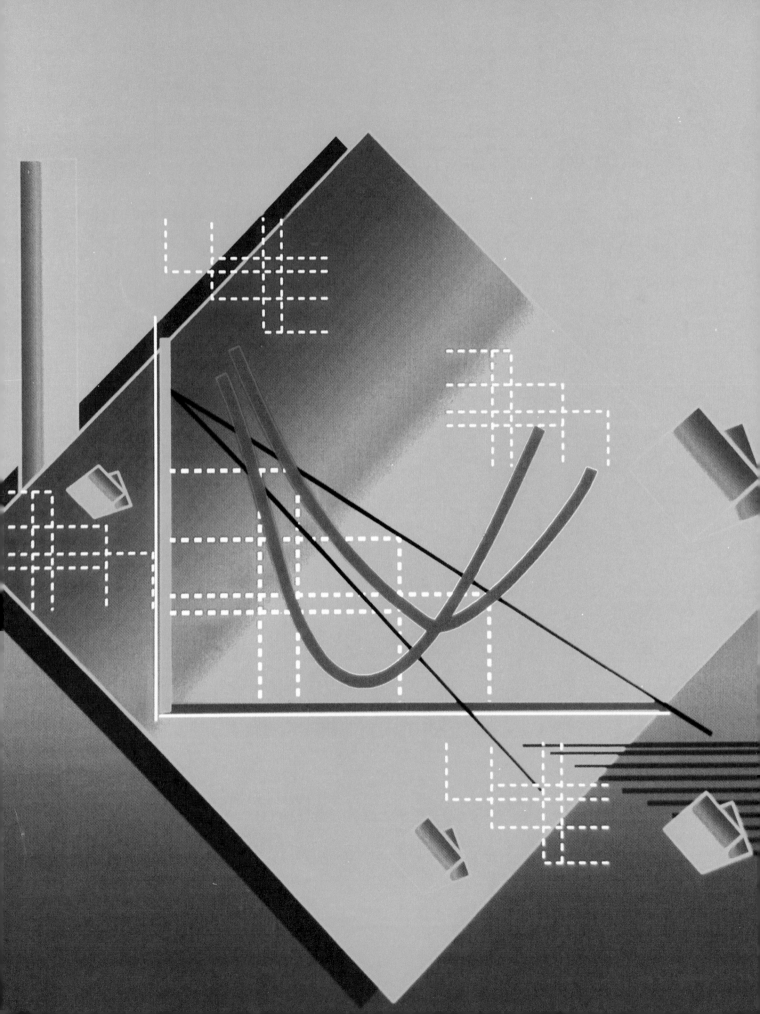

Chapter 5

Supply Decisions

Most consumers think producers reap huge profits from every market sale. Most producers wish that were true. The average producer earns a profit of only four to six cents on every sales dollar. And those profits don't come easily. Producers earn a profit only if they make the correct supply decisions. They have to keep a close eye on prices and costs and produce the right quantity at the right time. If they do all the right things, they *might* make a profit. Even when a producer does everything right, however, profits are not assured. Over 50,000 businesses failed in 1995, despite their owners' best efforts to make a profit.

In this chapter we look at markets from the supply side, examining two distinct concerns. First, how much output *can* a firm produce? Second, how much output will it *want* to produce? As we'll see, the answers to these two questions are rarely the same. The capacity to produce is determined by resources and technology. By contrast, the choice of how much capacity to use is dictated by profit-and-loss considerations. If costs escalate as capacity is approached, it might make profit sense to produce less than capacity output. In some situations, the costs of production might even be so high that it doesn't make profit sense to produce *any* output from available facilities.

The question of how much *can* be produced is largely an engineering and managerial problem. The question of how much *should* be produced is an *economic* issue. The producer is confronted with a *choice* about resource utilization. That behavioral choice will be influenced by profit-and-loss calculations. The end result will be a **supply** decision, that is, an expressed *ability* and *willingness* to produce a good at various prices.

This chapter focuses on those supply decisions. We first look at the capacity to produce, then at how choices are made about how much to supply. The analysis revolves around three questions:

supply: The ability and willingness to sell (produce) specific quantities of a good at alternative prices in a given time period, *ceteris paribus.*

97

- What limits a firm's ability to produce?
- What costs are incurred in producing a good?
- How do costs affect production decisions?

Once we have answered these questions, we will be able to make sense of supply decisions. We will then look at how supply and demand decisions come together in various markets to determine WHAT goods are produced, HOW they are produced, and FOR WHOM.

CAPACITY CONSTRAINTS: THE PRODUCTION FUNCTION

To supply goods and services to the market, you need more than ambition. No matter how large a business is or who owns it, all businesses confront one central fact: it costs something to produce goods. To produce corn, a farmer needs land, water, seed, equipment, and labor. To produce fillings, a dentist needs a chair, a drill, some space, and labor. Even the "production" of educational services (e.g., this economics class) requires the use of labor (your teacher), land (on which the school is built), and some capital (the building and blackboard). In short, unless you are producing unrefined, unpackaged air, you need **factors of production**—that is, resources that can be used to produce a good or service.

> **factors of production:** Resource inputs used to produce goods and services, e.g., land, labor, capital, entrepreneurship.

The factors of production used to produce a good or service provide the basic measure of economic cost. The costs of your economics class, for example, are measured by the amounts of land, labor, and capital it requires. These are *resource* costs of production.

An essential question for production is how many resources are actually needed to produce a given product. The answer depends on our technological know-how and how we organize the production process. At any moment, however, there is sure to be some minimum amount of resources needed to produce a good. Likewise, there will always be some *maximum* amount of output attainable from a given quantity of resources. These limits to the production of any good are reflected in the **production function.** The production function tells us the maximum amount of good X producible from various combinations of factor inputs. With one chair and one drill, a dentist can fill a maximum of 32 cavities per day. With two chairs, a drill, and an assistant, a dentist can fill up to 55 cavities per day.

> **production function:** A technological relationship expressing the maximum quantity of a good attainable from different combinations of factor inputs.

A production function is a technological summary of our ability to produce a particular good. Table 5.1 provides a partial glimpse of one such function. In this case, the desired output is designer jeans, as produced by Tight Jeans Corporation. The essential inputs in the production of jeans are land, labor (garment workers), and capital (a factory and sewing machines). With these inputs, Tight Jeans can produce and sell fancy jeans to status-conscious consumers.

As in all production endeavors, we want to know how many pairs of jeans we can produce with available resources. To make things easy, we shall assume that the factory is already built, with fixed space dimensions. The only inputs we can vary are labor (the number of garment workers per day) and additional capital (the number of sewing machines we lease per day).

As you would expect, the quantity of jeans we can produce depends on the amount of labor and capital we employ. *The purpose of a production function is to tell us just how much output we can produce with varying amounts of factor inputs.* Table 5.1 provides such information for jeans production.

TABLE 5.1
A Production Function
(pairs of jeans per day)

A production function tells us the maximum amount of output attainable from alternative combinations of factor inputs. This particular function tells us how many pairs of jeans we can produce in a day with a given factory and varying quantities of capital and labor. With one sewing machine, and one operator, we can produce a maximum of 15 pairs of jeans per day, as indicated in the second column of the second row. To produce more jeans, we need more labor or more capital.

Capital Input (sewing machines per day)	Labor Input (workers per day)								
	0	1	2	3	4	5	6	7	8
	Output (pairs per day)								
0	0	0	0	0	0	0	0	0	0
1	0	15	34	44	48	50	51	51	47
2	0	20	46	64	72	78	81	82	80

Consider the simplest option, that of employing no labor or capital (the upper left corner of Table 5.1). An empty factory cannot produce any jeans; maximum output is zero per day. The lesson here is quite simple: no inputs, no outputs. Even though land, capital (an empty factory), and even denim are available, some essential labor and capital inputs are missing, and jeans production is impossible.

Suppose now we employ some labor (a machine operator) but do not lease any sewing machines. Will output increase? Not according to the production function. The first row of Table 5.1 illustrates the consequences of employing labor without any capital equipment. Without sewing machines (or needles or other equipment), the operators cannot make jeans out of denim. Maximum output remains at zero, no matter how much labor is employed in this case.

The dilemma of machine operators without sewing machines illustrates a more general principle of production. ***The output of any factor of production depends on the amount of other resources available to it.*** Industrious, hardworking machine operators cannot make designer jeans without sewing machines.

We can increase the productivity of garment workers by providing them with machines. The production function again tells us by *how much* jeans output could increase if we leased some sewing machines. Suppose we leased just one machine per day. Now the second row of Table 5.1 is the relevant one. It says jeans output will remain at zero if we lease one machine but employ no labor. If we employ one machine *and* one worker, however, the jeans will start rolling out the front door. Maximum output under these circumstances (row 2, column 2) is 15 pairs of jeans per day. Now we're in business!

The remaining columns of row 2 tell us how many additional jeans we can produce if we hire more workers, still leasing only one sewing machine. With one machine and two workers, maximum output rises to 34 pairs per day. If a third worker is hired, output could increase to 44 pairs.

This information on our production capabilities is illustrated in Figure 5.1. The production function drawn here mirrors the second row of Table 5.1, where only one sewing machine is available. Point *A* illustrates the cold, hard fact that we can't produce any jeans without some labor. Points *B* through *I* show how production increases as additional labor is employed.

Efficiency

Every point on the production function in Figure 5.1 represents the *most* output we could produce with a given number of workers. Point *D*, for example, tells us we could produce as many as 44 pairs of jeans with three workers. We must recognize, however, that we might also produce less. If the workers goof off or the sewing machines aren't maintained well, total output might be less than 44 pairs per day. In that case, we wouldn't be making the best possible use of scarce resources: we would be producing *inefficiently*. In Figure 5.1 this would imply a rate of output *below* point *D*. Only if we produce with maximum *efficiency* will we end up at point *D* or some other point on the production function.

Capacity

Every point on the production function tells us how much output we could produce with a given amount of input—using our inputs efficiently. We could not keep increasing output forever, however, by hiring more workers. We have other production constraints. In this case, we have only a small factory and one sewing machine. If we keep hiring workers, we will quickly run out of space and available equipment. ***Land and capital constraints place a ceiling on potential output.***

Notice in Figure 5.1 how total output peaks at point *G*. We can produce a total of 51 pairs of jeans at that point by employing six workers. What happens if we hire still more workers? According to Figure 5.1, if we employed a seventh worker, total output would not increase further. At point *H*, total output is 51 pairs, just as it was at point *G*, when we hired only six workers.

FIGURE 5.1
Short-Run Production Function

In the short run some inputs (e.g., land, capital) are fixed in quantity. Output then depends on how much of a variable input (e.g., labor) is used. The short-run production function shows how output changes when more labor is used. This figure is based on the second (one-machine) row of Table 5.1.

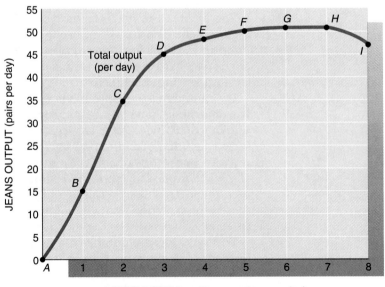

LABOR INPUT (machine operators per day)

Were we to hire an *eighth* worker, total jeans output would actually *decline*, as illustrated by point *I*. An eighth worker would actually *reduce* total output by increasing congestion on the factory floor, delaying access to the sewing machine, and just plain getting in the way. Given the size of the factory and the availability of only one sewing machine, no more than six workers can be productively employed. Hence, the *capacity* production of this factory is 51 pairs of jeans per day. We could hire more workers, but output would not go up.

Marginal Physical Product

The land and capital constraints that limit output have some interesting effects on the productivity of individual workers. Consider that seventh worker at the jeans factory. If he were hired, total output would not increase. Accordingly, that seventh worker contributes nothing to total input.

The contribution of each worker to production is measured by the change in *total* output that results when the worker is employed. The name for this concept is **marginal physical product (MPP)** and is measured as

> **marginal physical product (MPP):** The change in total output associated with one additional unit of input.

- Marginal physical product (MPP) = $\dfrac{\text{change in total output}}{\text{change in input quantity}}$

In this case, total output doesn't change when the seventh worker is hired, so his MPP equals zero.

Contrast that experience with that of the *first* worker hired. Notice again what happens when the first worker is employed at the jeans factory: total output jumps from zero (point *A*) to 15 pairs of jeans per day (point *B*). This increase in output reflects the marginal physical product (MPP) of that first worker—that is, the *change* in total output that results from employment of one more unit of (labor) input.

If we employ a second operator, jeans output more than doubles, to 34 pairs per day (point *C*). Whereas the marginal physical product of the first worker was only 15 pairs, a second worker increases total output by 19 pairs.

The higher MPP of the second worker raises a question about the first. Why was the first's MPP lower? Laziness? Is the second worker faster, less distracted, or harder working?

The higher MPP of the second worker is not explained by superior talents or effort. We assume in this exercise that all "units of labor" are equal—that is, one worker is just as good as another. Their different marginal products are explained by the structure of the production process, not by their respective abilities. The first garment worker had not only to sew jeans but also to unfold bolts of denim, measure the jeans, sketch out the patterns, and cut them to approximate size. A lot of time was spent going from one task to another. Despite the worker's best efforts (and assuming perfect efficiency), this person simply could not do everything at once.

A second worker alleviates this situation. With two workers, less time is spent running from one task to another. Now there is an opportunity for each worker to specialize a bit. While one is measuring and cutting, the other can continue sewing. This improved ratio of labor to other factors of production results in the large jump in total output. The superior MPP of the second worker is not unique to this person: it would have occurred even if we had hired the workers in the reverse order. What matters is the amount of other factors of production each unit of labor must work with.

Law of Diminishing Returns

Unfortunately, these large increases in output cannot be maintained as still more workers are hired. Look what happens when a third worker is hired. Total jeans production continues to increase. But the increase from point *C* to point *D* in Figure 5.1 is only 10 pairs per day. Hence the MPP of the third worker (10 pairs) is *less* than that of the second (19 pairs). Marginal physical product is *diminishing*.

What accounts for this decline in MPP? The answer again lies in the ratio of labor to other factors of production. A third worker begins to crowd our facilities. We still have only one sewing machine. Two people cannot sew at the same time. As a result, some time is wasted as the operators wait for their turns at the machine. Even if they split up the various jobs, there will still be some downtime, since measuring and cutting are not as time-consuming as sewing. In this sense, we cannot make full use of a third worker. The relative scarcity of other inputs (capital and land) constrains the marginal physical product of labor.

Resource constraints are even more evident when a fourth worker is hired. Total output increases again, but the increase this time is very small. With three workers, we got 44 pairs of jeans per day (point *D*); with four workers, we get a maximum of 48 pairs (point *E*). Thus the marginal physical product of the fourth worker is only 4 pairs of jeans. A fourth worker really begins to strain our productive capacity to the limit. There simply aren't enough machines to make productive use of so much labor.

If a seventh worker is hired, the operators get in each other's way, argue, and waste denim. As we observed earlier, total output does not increase at all when a seventh worker is hired. The MPP of the seventh worker is zero. The seventh worker is being wasted, in the sense that she contributes nothing to total output. This waste of scarce resources (labor) was commonplace in communist countries, where everyone was guaranteed a job (see Headline). At Tight Jeans, however, they do not want to hire someone who doesn't contribute to output. And they certainly wouldn't want to hire an *eighth* worker, since total output actually *declines* from 51 pairs of jeans (point *H* in Figure 5.1) to 47 pairs (point *I*) when an eighth worker is hired. In other words, the eighth worker has a *negative* MPP.

HEADLINE

MARGINAL PHYSICAL PRODUCT

"We Pretend to Work, They Pretend to Pay Us"

One of the attractions of communist nations was their promise of employment. Passing through the factory gate was not proof of productive employment, however. Ordered to hire all comers, state-run enterprises became bloated with surplus workers. Although payrolls climbed, output stagnated.

As it turned out, the paychecks handed out to the workers weren't very good anyway. Runaway inflation and a scarcity of consumer goods rendered the paychecks almost worthless. The futility of the situation was summed up by one worker who explained that "we pretend to work and they pretend to pay us."

When communism collapsed, the factory gates were no longer open to all. New profit-oriented owners were unwilling to pay workers whose marginal physical product was zero. In East Germany alone, over 400,000 workers lost their jobs when 126 state-owned enterprises were sold to private investors—without any decline in output.

The problem of crowded facilities applies to most production processes. In the short run, a production process is characterized by a fixed amount of available land and capital. Typically, the only factor that can be varied in the short run is labor. Yet, *as more labor is hired, each unit of labor has less capital and land to work with.* This is simple division: the available facilities are being shared by more and more workers. At some point, this constraint begins to pinch. When it does, marginal physical product starts to decline. This situation is so common that it is the basis for an economic principle: the **law of diminishing returns.** This law says that the marginal physical product of any factor of production (e.g., labor) will begin to diminish at some point, as more of it is used in a given production setting.

> **law of diminishing returns:** The marginal physical product of a variable input declines as more of it is employed with a given quantity of other (fixed) inputs.

Short Run vs. Long Run

> **short run:** The period in which the quantity (and quality) of some inputs cannot be changed.

> **long run:** A period of time long enough for all inputs to be varied (no fixed costs).

The limited availability of space or equipment is the cause of diminishing returns. Once we have purchased or leased a specific factory, it sets a limit to current jeans production. When such commitments to fixed inputs (e.g., the factory) exist, we are dealing with a **short-run** production problem. If no land or capital were in place—if we could build or lease any size factory—we would be dealing with a *long-run* decision. In the **long run** we might also learn new and better ways of making jeans and so increase our production capabilities. For the time being, however, we must accept the fact that the production function in Figure 5.1 defines the short-run limits to jeans production. Our short-run objective is to make the best possible use of the factory we have acquired.

COSTS OF PRODUCTION

A production function tells us how much output a firm *could* produce with its existing plant and equipment. It doesn't tell us how much the firm will *want* to produce, however. The level of desired output depends on prices and costs. A firm *might* want to produce at capacity if the profit picture were bright enough. On the other hand, a firm might not produce *any* output if costs always exceeded sales revenue. The most desirable rate of output is the one that maximizes total **profit**—the difference between total revenue and total costs.

> **profit:** The difference between total revenue and total cost.

The production function, then, is just a starting point for supply decisions. To decide how much output to produce with that function, a firm must next examine the dollar costs of production.

Total Cost

> **total cost:** The market value of all resources used to produce a good or service.

The **total cost** of producing a product includes the market value of all the resources used in its production. To determine this cost we simply identify all the resources used in production, compute their value, then add everything up.

In the production of jeans, these resources include land, labor, and capital. Table 5.2 identifies these resources, their unit values, and the total costs associated with their use. This table is based on an assumed output of 15 pairs of jeans per day, with the use of one machine operator and one sewing machine (point *B* in Figure 5.1). The rent on the factory is $100 per day, a sewing machine costs $20 per day, the wages of a garment worker are $80 per day. We shall assume Tight Jeans Corporation can purchase bolts of

TABLE 5.2
The Total Costs of Production
(total cost of producing 15 pairs of jeans per day)

The total cost of producing a good equals the market value of all the resources used in its production. In this case, we have assumed that the production of 15 pairs of jeans per day requires resources worth $245.

Resource	Price	Total Cost
1 factory	$100 per day	$100
1 sewing machine	20 per day	20
1 operator	80 per day	80
1.5 bolts of denim	30 per bolt	45
Total cost		$245

denim for $30 apiece, each of which provides enough denim for 10 pairs of jeans. In other words, one-tenth of a bolt ($3 worth of material) is required for one pair of jeans. We shall ignore any other potential expenses. With these assumptions, the total cost of producing 15 pairs of jeans per day amounts to $245, as shown in Table 5.2.

Total costs will change, of course, as we alter the rate of production. But not all costs increase. In the short run, some costs don't increase at all when output is increased. These are **fixed costs,** in the sense that they do not vary with the rate of output. The factory lease is an example. Once you lease a factory, you are obligated to pay for it, whether you use it or not. The person who owns the factory wants $100 per day, whether you produce any jeans or not. Even if you produce no jeans, you still have to pay the rent. That is the essence of fixed costs.

The leased sewing machine is another fixed cost. When you rent a sewing machine, you must pay the rental charge. It doesn't matter whether you use it for a few minutes or all day long—the rental charge is fixed at $20 per day.

Labor costs are another story altogether. The amount of labor employed in jeans production can be varied easily. If we decide not to open the factory tomorrow, we can just tell our only worker to take the day off. We will still have to pay rent, but we can cut back on wages. On the other hand, if we want to increase daily output, we can also get additional workers easily and quickly. Labor is regarded as a **variable cost** in this line of work—that is, a cost that *varies* with the rate of output.

The denim itself is another variable cost. Denim not used today can be saved for tomorrow. Hence how much we "spend" on denim today is directly related to how many jeans we produce. In this sense, the cost of denim input varies with the rate of jeans output.

Figure 5.2 illustrates how these various costs are affected by the rate of production. On the vertical axis are the costs of production, in dollars per day. Notice that the total cost of producing 15 pairs per day is still $245, as indicated by point *B*. This figure consists of $120 of fixed costs (factory and sewing machine rents) and $125 of variable costs ($80 in wages and $45 for denim). If we increase the rate of output, total costs will rise. *How fast total costs rise depends on variable costs only,* however, since fixed costs remain at $120 per day. (Notice the horizontal fixed cost curve in Figure 5.2.)

With one sewing machine and one factory, there is an absolute limit to daily jeans production. The capacity of a factory with one machine is roughly 51 pairs of jeans per day. If we try to produce more jeans than this by hiring additional workers, our total costs will rise, but our output will

fixed costs: Costs of production that do not change when the rate of output is altered, e.g., the cost of basic plant and equipment.

variable costs: Costs of production that change when the rate of output is altered, e.g., labor and material costs.

FIGURE 5.2
The Costs of Jeans Production

Total cost includes both fixed and variable costs. Fixed costs must be paid even if no output is produced (point *A*). Variable costs start at zero and increase with the rate of output. The total cost of producing 15 pairs of jeans (point *B*) includes $120 in fixed costs (rent on the factory and sewing machines) and $125 in variable costs (denim and wages). Total cost rises as output increases, because additional variable costs must be incurred.

In this example, the short-run capacity is equal to 51 pairs (point *G*). If still more inputs are employed, costs will rise but not total output.

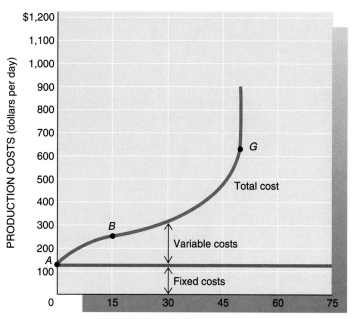

RATE OF OUTPUT (pairs of jeans per day)

not. In fact, we could fill the factory with garment workers and drive total costs sky-high. But the limits of space and one sewing machine do not permit output in excess of 51 pairs per day. This limit to productive capacity is represented by point *G* on the total cost curve. Further expenditure on inputs will increase production costs but not output.

Although there is no upper limit to costs, there is a lower limit. If output is reduced to zero, total costs fall only to $120 per day, the level of fixed costs. This is illustrated by point *A* in Figure 5.2. As before, ***there is no way to avoid fixed costs in the short run.***

Which Costs Matter?

The different nature of fixed and variable costs raises some intriguing questions about how to measure the cost of producing a pair of jeans. In figuring how much it costs to produce one pair, should we look only at the denim and labor time used to produce that pair? Or should we also take into account the factory rent and lease payments on the sewing machines?

A similar problem arises when you try to figure out whether a restaurant overcharges you for a steak dinner. What did it cost the restaurant to supply the dinner? Should only the meat and the chef's time be counted? Or should the cost include some portion of the rent, the electricity, and the insurance?

The restaurant owner, too, needs to figure out which measure of cost to use. She has to decide what price to charge for the steak. She wants to earn a profit. Can she do so by charging a price just above the cost of meat and wages? Or must she charge a price high enough to cover some portion of all her fixed costs as well?

Before deciding which costs are most important for production and pricing decisions, we need to clarify a couple of key cost measures. We will focus on two: average cost and marginal cost.

Average Cost

> **average total cost (ATC):** Total cost divided by the quantity produced in a given time period.

Average total cost (ATC) is simply total cost divided by the rate of output; that is

$$\text{Average total cost (ATC)} = \frac{\text{total cost}}{\text{total output}}$$

If the total cost of supplying 10 steaks is $62, then the *average* cost of the steaks is $6.20.

As we observed in Figure 5.2, total costs change as the rate of output increases. Hence, both the numerator and the denominator in the ATC formula change with the rate of output. This complicates the arithmetic a bit, as Figure 5.3 illustrates.

FIGURE 5.3
Average Costs

Average total cost (ATC) in column 5 equals total cost (column 4) divided by the rate of output (column 1). ATC tends to fall initially, then later rise. This gives the ATC curve a U shape, as illustrated in the graph.

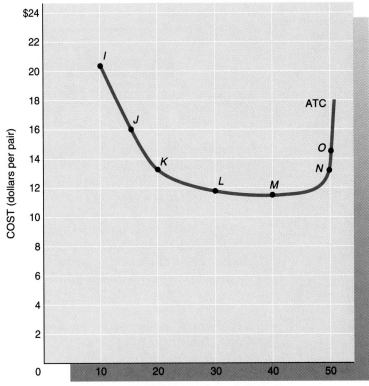

RATE OF OUTPUT (pairs per day)

	(1) Rate of Output	(2) Fixed Costs	+	(3) Variable Costs	=	(4) Total Cost	(5) Average Cost
H	0	$120		$ 0		$120	—
I	10	120		85		205	$20.50
J	15	120		125		245	16.33
K	20	120		150		270	13.50
L	30	120		240		360	12.00
M	40	120		350		470	11.75
N	50	120		550		670	13.40
O	51	120		633		753	14.76

Figure 5.3 shows how average costs change as the rate of output varies. Row *J* of the cost schedule, for example, again indicates the fixed, variable, and total costs of producing 15 pairs of jeans per day. Fixed costs are still $120 (for factory and machine rentals); variable costs (denim and labor) are $125. Thus the total cost of producing 15 pairs per day is $245. The *average* cost for this rate of output is simply total cost ($245) divided by quantity (15), or $16.33 per day. This ATC is indicated in column 5 of the table and by point *J* on the graph.

An important feature of the ATC curve is its shape. ***Average costs start high, fall, then rise once again, giving the ATC curve a distinctive U shape.***

The initial decline in ATC is largely due to fixed costs. At low rates of output, fixed costs are a high proportion of total costs. Quite simply, it's very expensive to lease (or buy) an entire factory to produce only a few pairs of jeans. The entire cost of the factory must be averaged out over a small quantity of output. This results in a high average cost of production. To reduce *average* costs, we must make fuller use of our leased plant and equipment.

The same problem of cost spreading would affect a restaurant that only served two dinners a day. The *total* cost of operating a restaurant might easily exceed $500 a day. If only two dinners were served, the *average* total cost of each meal would exceed $250. That's why restaurants need a high volume of business to keep meal prices low.

As output increases, the fixed costs of production are distributed over an increasing quantity of output. Fixed costs no longer dominate total costs as production increases (compare columns 2 and 3 in Figure 5.3). As a result, average total costs tend to decline.

Average total costs don't fall forever, however. They bottom out at point *M* in Figure 5.3, then start rising. What accounts for this turnaround?

Marginal Cost

> **marginal cost (MC):** The increase in total cost associated with a one-unit increase in production.

The upturn of the ATC curve is caused by rising *marginal* costs. **Marginal cost (MC) *refers to the change in total costs when one more unit of output is produced.*** In practice, marginal cost is easy to measure; just observe how much total costs increase when one more unit of output is produced. For larger increases in output, marginal cost can also be approximated by the formula

$$\bullet \text{ Marginal cost} = \frac{\text{change in total cost}}{\text{change in total output}}$$

Using this formula and Figure 5.3 we could confirm how marginal costs rise in jeans production. As jeans production increases from 20 pairs (row *K*) to 30 pairs (row *L*) per day, total costs rise from $270 to $360. Hence, the change in total cost ($90) divided by the change in total output (10) equals $9. This is the marginal cost of jeans in that range of output (20 to 30 pairs).

As output continues to increase further from 30 to 40 pairs per day, marginal costs rise. Total cost rises from $360 (row *L*) to $470 (row *M*), a *change* of $110. Dividing this by the change in output (10) reveals that marginal cost is now $11. Marginal costs are rising as output increases.

Rising marginal cost implies that each additional unit of output becomes more expensive to produce. Why is this? Why would a third pair of jeans cost more to produce than a second pair did? Why would it cost a restaurant more to serve the twelfth dinner than the eleventh dinner?

The explanation for this puzzle of rising marginal cost lies in the production function. As we observed earlier, output increases at an ever slower pace as capacity is approached. The law of diminishing marginal product tells us that we need an increasing amount of labor to eke out each additional pair of jeans. The same law applies to restaurants. As more dinners are served, the waiters and cooks get pressed for space and equipment. It takes a little longer (and, hence, more wages) to prepare and serve each meal. Hence, the *marginal* costs of each meal increase as the number of patrons rises.

The MC Curve. Figure 5.4 illustrates a simplified marginal cost curve. In this case, output increases one unit at a time. This makes it easier to see how costs change with a single unit of added output. Notice in the table what happens to total cost when output increases from 3 units (row *s*) to 4 units (row *t*). Total cost increases from $19 to $25, yielding a *marginal* cost of $6 for the fourth unit. This marginal cost is illustrated by point *t* on the graph. The remaining points show how marginal costs increase at higher rates of output.

FIGURE 5.4
The Marginal Cost Curve

Marginal cost (MC) is the increase in *total* cost resulting from a one-unit increase in the rate of production. MC is the additional cost of producing one more unit. These hypothetical numbers indicate that total cost increases from $25 to $34 when a fifth unit is produced (compare rows *u* and *t*). Hence the MC of the fifth unit is $9, as illustrated by point *u* on the marginal cost curve. The MC curve generally rises (as a consequence of the law of diminishing returns).

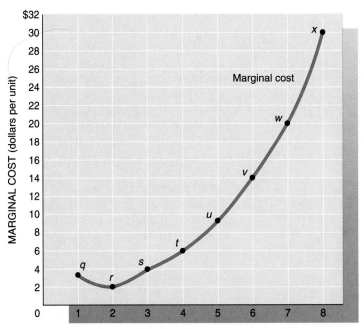

	Rate of Output	Total Cost	Marginal Cost
p	0	$10	
q	1	13	3
r	2	15	2
s	3	19	4
t	4	25	6
u	5	34	9
v	6	48	14
w	7	68	20
x	8	98	30

The Relationship of MC to ATC

Figure 5.5 brings together the average and marginal cost curves. The centerpiece of Figure 5.5 is the U-shaped ATC curve. What is of special significance is its relationship to marginal costs. Notice that ***the MC curve intersects the ATC curve at its lowest point*** (point *m*). This will always be the case. So long as the marginal cost of producing one more unit is less than the previous average cost, average costs must fall. Thus average costs decline as long as the marginal cost curve lies below the average cost curve, as to the left of point *m* in Figure 5.5.

We have already observed, however, that marginal costs themselves tend to rise as output expands, largely because additional workers reduce the amount of land and capital available to each worker (in the short run, the size of plant and equipment is fixed). Consequently, at some point (*m* in Figure 5.5) marginal costs will rise to the level of average costs.

As marginal costs continue to rise beyond point *m*, they begin to pull average costs up, giving the average cost curve its U shape. Average costs increase whenever marginal costs exceed average costs. This is the case to the right of point *m*, since the marginal cost curve always lies above the average cost curve in that part of Figure 5.5.

FIGURE 5.5
Basic Cost Curves

With total cost and the rate of output, all other cost concepts can be computed. The MC curve typically rises, sometimes after a brief decline. The ATC curve has a U shape. And the MC curve will always intersect the ATC curve at its lowest point (*m*).

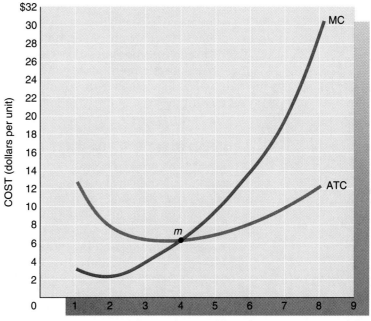

RATE OF OUTPUT (units per time period)

Rate of Output	TC	MC	ATC
0	$10.00	—	—
1	13.00	$ 3.00	$13.00
2	15.00	2.00	7.50
3	19.00	4.00	6.33
4	25.00	6.00	6.25
5	34.00	9.00	6.80
6	48.00	14.00	8.00
7	68.00	20.00	9.71
8	98.00	30.00	12.25

TABLE 5.3
A Guide to Costs

Total costs of production include **fixed costs** and **variable costs:**

$$\bullet \; TC = FC + VC$$

Dividing total costs by the quantity of output yields the **average total cost:**

$$\bullet \; ATC = \frac{TC}{q}$$

The most important measure of changes in cost is **marginal cost,** which equals the increase in total costs when one additional unit of output is produced:

$$\bullet \; MC = \frac{\text{change in total cost}}{\text{change in output}}$$

To visualize the relationship between marginal cost and average cost, imagine computing the average height of people entering a room. If the first person who comes through the door is 6 feet tall, then the average height of people entering the room is 6 feet at that point. But what happens to average height if the second person entering the room is only 3 feet tall? *Average* height declines because the last (marginal) person entering the room is shorter than the previous average. Whenever the last entrant is shorter than the average, the average must fall.

The relationship between marginal costs and average costs is also similar to that between your grade in this course and your grade-point average. If your grade in economics is better (higher) than your other grades, then your overall grade-point average will rise. In other words, a high *marginal* grade will pull your *average* grade up. If you don't understand this, your grade-point average is likely to fall.

ECONOMIC VS. ACCOUNTING COSTS

An essential characteristic of the cost curves we have observed is that they are based on *real* production relationships. The dollar costs we compute are a direct reflection of underlying resource costs—the land, labor, and capital used in the production process. Not everyone counts this way. On the contrary, accountants and businesspeople typically count dollar costs only and ignore any resource use that doesn't result in an explicit dollar cost.

Return to Tight Jeans for a moment to see the difference. When we computed the dollar cost of producing 15 pairs of jeans per day, we noted the following resource inputs:

INPUTS	COST
1 factory rent	@ $100
1 machine rent	@ 20
1 machine operator	@ 80
1.5 bolts of denim	@ 45
Total cost	$245

The total value of the resources used in the production of 15 pairs of jeans was thus $245 per day. But this figure need not conform to *actual* dollar costs. Suppose the owners of Tight Jeans decided to sew jeans. Then they would not have to hire a worker or pay $80 per day in wages. *Dollar* costs would drop to $165 per day. The producers and their accountant would consider this to be a remarkable achievement. They would assert that the costs of producing jeans had fallen.

Economic Cost

An economist would draw no such conclusions. ***The essential economic question is how many resources are used in production.*** This has not changed. One unit of labor is still being employed at the factory; now it's simply the owners, not a hired worker. In either case, one unit of labor is not available for the production of other goods and services. Hence society is still paying $245 for jeans, whether the owners of Tight Jeans write checks in that amount or not. We really don't care who sews jeans—the essential point is that someone (i.e., a unit of labor) does.

The same would be true if Tight Jeans owned its own factory rather than rented it. If the factory was owned rather than rented, the owners probably would not write any rent checks. Hence accounting costs would drop by $100 per day. But society would not be saving any resources. The factory would still be in use for jeans production and therefore unavailable for the production of other goods and services. The economic (resource) cost of producing 15 pairs of jeans would still be $245.

The distinction between an economic cost and an accounting cost is essentially one between resource and dollar costs. *Dollar cost* refers to the actual dollar outlays made by a producer; it is the lifeblood of accountants. **Economic cost,** in contrast, refers to the dollar *value* of all resources used in the production process; it is the lifeblood of economists. The accountant's dollar costs are usually *explicit*, in the sense that someone writes a check. The economist takes into consideration *implicit* costs as well, that is, even those costs for which no direct payment is made. In other words, economists count costs as

> • Economic cost = explicit costs + implicit costs

As this formula suggests, ***economic and accounting costs will diverge whenever any factor of production is not paid an explicit wage (or rent, etc.).***

The Cost of Homework. These distinctions between economic and accounting costs apply also to the "production" of homework. You can pay people to write term papers for you, and at large schools you can often buy lecture notes. But most students end up doing their own homework, so that they will learn something and not just turn in required assignments.

Doing homework is expensive, however, even if you don't pay someone to do it. The time you spend reading this chapter is valuable. You could be doing something else if you weren't reading right now. What would you be doing? The forgone activity—the best alternative use of your time—represents the economic cost of doing homework. Even if you don't pay yourself for reading this chapter, you'll still incur that *economic* cost.

economic cost: The value of all resources used to produce a good or service; opportunity cost.

SUPPLY HORIZONS

All these cost calculations can give you a real headache. They can also give you second thoughts about jumping into Tight Jeans, restaurant management, or any other business. There are tough choices to be made. A given firm can produce many different rates of output, each of which entails a distinct level of costs. Someone has to choose which level of output to produce and thus how many goods to supply to the market. That decision has to be based not only on the *capacity* to produce (the production function) but also on the *costs* of production (the cost functions). Only those who make the right decisions will succeed in business.

The Production Decision

production decision: The selection of the short-run rate of output (with existing plant and equipment).

The supply decision has two dimensions, a short-run horizon and a long-run horizon. The *short run* is characterized by the existence of fixed costs. A commitment has been made: a factory has been built, an office leased, or machinery purchased. The only decision to make is how much output to produce with these existing facilities. This is the **production decision,** the choice of how intensively to use available plant and equipment. This choice is typically made daily (e.g., jeans production), weekly (e.g., auto production), or seasonally (e.g., farming).

The most important factor in the production decision is marginal costs. Producers will be willing to supply output only if they can at least cover marginal costs. If the marginal cost of a pair of jeans is $11, then there is no profit in producing an additional pair unless the price of jeans is at least $11. Accordingly, the marginal cost curve is a basic determinant of short-run production decisions.

Marginal costs may also dictate short-run pricing decisions. Suppose the average cost of serving a steak dinner is $12, but the marginal cost is only $7. How low a price can the restaurant charge for the dinner? Ideally, it would like to charge at least $12 and cover all of its costs. It could at least cover *marginal* costs, however, if it charged only $7. At that price the restaurant would be no worse or better off for having served an extra dinner. The additional cost of serving that one meal would be covered. As we'll see in Chapter 6, such marginal cost considerations play a critical role in supply behavior.

The Investment Decision

investment decision: The decision to build, buy, or lease plant and equipment; to enter or exit an industry.

The long run opens up a whole new range of options. In the *long run,* we have no lease or purchase commitments. We are free to start all over again, with whatever scale of plant and equipment we desire. *There are no fixed costs in the long run.* Accordingly, long-run supply decisions are more complicated. If no commitments to production facilities have been made, a producer must decide how large a facility to build, buy, or lease. Hence the size (scale) of plant and equipment becomes an additional option for long-term supply decisions. In a long-run (no fixed costs) situation, a firm can make the **investment decision.**

Note that the distinction between short- and long-run supply decisions is not based on time. The distinction instead depends on whether commitments have been made. If no leases have been signed, no construction contracts awarded, no acquisitions made, a producer still has a free hand. With no fixed costs, the producer can walk away from the potential business at a moment's notice.

Once fixed costs are incurred, the options narrow. Then the issue becomes one of making the best possible use of the assets (e.g., factory, office space, equipment) that have been acquired. Once fixed costs have been incurred, it's hard to walk away from the business at a moment's notice. The goal then becomes to make as much profit as possible from the investments already made. The following Headline illustrates the distinction between these production and investment decisions. The weekly decisions of automakers about how many cars to produce is a short-run production decision. They are deciding how fully to utilize their production capacity. By contrast, Matsushita is trying to decide whether to *increase* its production capacity; an investment decision.

HEADLINE

PRODUCTION AND INVESTMENT DECISIONS

The first news clip indicates how many cars GM and other automakers planned to produce in a single week. This weekly *production decision* refers to the use of *existing* plant and equipment.

In the second news clip, the decision of Matsushita to build a factory for producing microwave ovens is an *investment decision*. New plant and equipment is being acquired. Matsushita will later decide how many ovens to produce each week from its new factory.

GM's Main Cadillac Plant to Cut Output

DETROIT—General Motors Corp. said it will slow production in mid-January at its main Cadillac plant, in Hamtramck, Mich., in response to an expected slowdown in luxury-car sales.

GM says it will slow the production line at the Cadillac plant in Hamtramck by about 6% to 7%. Currently, the plant makes an average of 900 vehicles a day, operating on a two-shift basis . . .

Separately, the ten domestic auto makers said they planned to build 158,154 cars and trucks last week, down 35.7% from 246,040 vehicles built in the same week a year ago.

—Gabriella Stern

The Wall Street Journal, November 28, 1994, p. A12. Reprinted by permission of *The Wall Street Journal*, © 1994 Dow Jones & Company, Inc. All Rights Reserved Worldwide.

Matsushita Electric Industrial to Build Factory Near Chicago

Matsushita Electric Industrial announced plans to build what it is calling the world's largest microwave oven factory near Chicago. The $25 million plant will add 800 new jobs to the current 1,200 at Matsushita in Franklin Park, Ill.

Washington Post, March 5, 1992, p. B11. Reprinted by permission of The Associated Press.

POLICY PERSPECTIVES

Productivity Improvements

In the 1990s, the U.S. labor force will continue to grow by more than a million workers per year. If capital investments don't keep pace, these added workers will strain production facilities. The law of diminishing marginal productivity would push wages lower and reduce living standards.

To beat the Law of Diminishing Marginal Productivity, we have to *increase* the productivity of all workers. This means that we have to shift production functions upward, as shown graphically in Figure 5.6a.

How can we achieve such across-the-board productivity gains? There are several possibilities. Increased education generates smarter workers. Vocational training imparts specific job skills. More capital investment relieves capacity bottlenecks and raises output per worker.

During the 1980s, the productivity of the average U.S. worker increased by about 1 percent a year. This enabled living standards to rise, despite a growing population. In the 1990s, the productivity advances started out slowly but then accelerated. This will not only foster higher wages and living standards but also keep America competitive in world markets. As Figure 5.6b reminds us, falling costs are the flip side of rising productivity. This is why Robert Reich, President Clinton's secretary of labor, highlighted

(a) When the production
function shifts up

(b) Cost curves shift down

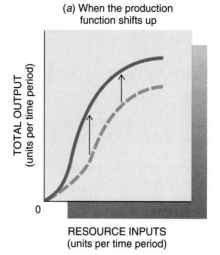

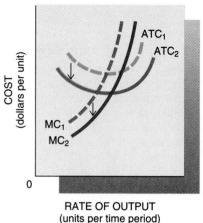

FIGURE 5.6
Improvements in Productivity
Reduce Costs

Advances in technological or managerial knowledge increase our productive capability. This is reflected in upward shifts of the production function (part *a*) and downward shifts of production cost curves (part *b*).

education and training as the decisive factors in determining America's future position in the world economy.

SUMMARY

- Supply decisions are constrained by the *capacity* to produce and the *costs* of using that capacity.
- In the short run, some inputs (e.g., land and capital) are fixed in quantity. Increases in (short-run) output result from more use of variable inputs (e.g., labor).
- A production function indicates how much output can be produced from available facilities, using different amounts of variable inputs. Every point on the production function represents efficient production. Capacity output refers to the maximum quantity that can be produced from a given facility.
- Output tends to increase at a diminishing rate when more labor is employed in a given facility. Additional workers "crowd" existing facilities, leaving each worker with less space and machinery to work with.
- The costs of production include both fixed and variable costs. Fixed costs (e.g., space and equipment leases) are incurred even if no output is produced. Variable costs (e.g., labor and material) are incurred when plant and equipment are put to use.
- Average cost is simply total cost divided by the quantity produced. The ATC curve is typically U shaped.
- Marginal cost is the increase in total cost that results when one more unit of output is produced. Marginal costs increase because of diminishing returns in production.
- The economic costs of production include the value of *all* resources used. Accounting costs typically include only those dollar costs actually paid (explicit costs).
- The production decision is the short-run choice of how much output to produce with existing facilities. At a minimum, a producer will be willing to supply output only if price at least covers marginal cost.
- The long run is characterized by an absence of fixed costs. The invest-

ment decision entails the choice of whether to acquire fixed costs, that is, whether to build, buy, or lease plant and equipment.

● Historically, advances in technology and the quality of our inputs have been the major source of productivity growth. These advances have shifted production functions up and pushed cost curves down.

Terms to Remember

Define the following terms:

supply	short run	average total cost
factors of production	long run	(ATC)
production function	profit	marginal cost (MC)
marginal physical product	total cost	economic cost
(MPP)	fixed costs	production decision
law of diminishing returns	variable costs	investment decision

Questions for Discussion

1. Is your school currently producing at capacity (i.e., teaching as many students as possible)? What considerations might inhibit full capacity utilization?
2. What are the production costs of your economics class? What are the fixed costs? The variable costs? What is the marginal cost of enrolling more students?
3. Suppose you set up a lawn-mowing service and recruit friends to help you. Would the law of diminishing returns apply? Explain.
4. If you get a grade of B in this class, how will it affect your grade-point average? If all future grades are higher than your existing average, what will happen to your average grade?
5. Owner-operators of small gas stations rarely pay themselves an hourly wage. Does this practice reduce the economic cost of dispensing gasoline?
6. In the Headline on p. 102, why did MPP fall to zero? What was the opportunity cost of those surplus workers?

Problems

1. Complete the following table, then plot the marginal cost and average total cost curves on the same graph. Identify the lowest per-unit cost on the graph.

Rate of Output	Total Cost	Marginal Cost	Average Total Cost
0	$100	_____	_____
1	110	_____	_____
2	130	_____	_____
3	165	_____	_____
4	220	_____	_____
5	300	_____	_____

2. Refer to the production table for jeans (Table 5.1). Suppose a firm had two sewing machines and could vary only the amount of labor input.
   (a) Graph the production function for jeans given the two sewing machines.
   (b) Compute the increase in total jeans output for 1, 2, 3, 4, 5, 6, and 7 workers used with the two sewing machines.
   (c) At what amount of labor input does the law of diminishing returns first become apparent?
3. Assume that the following costs are borne by a commercial fishing boat. Convert these costs into daily rates, using 30 days per month and 10 working hours per day. Then graph the fixed, variable, and total costs of fishing per day (in hours per day).

Item	Unit Cost	Usage
Fuel	$2 per gallon	4 gallons per hour
Bait	$5 per pound	1 pound per hour
Insurance	$1,800 per year	annual
Dock rent	$300 per month	monthly
License	$900 per year	annual
Radio	$720 per unit	annual
Crew	$10 per hour	3 crew per trip
Boat payments	$1,200 per month	monthly

Chapter 6

Competition

Catfish farmers in Mississippi are upset. During the last few years they have invested millions of dollars in converting cotton farms into breeding ponds for catfish. They now have 90,000 acres of ponds and supply over 80 percent of the nation's catfish. Unfortunately, catfish prices have been dropping. From January 1989 to January 1992, catfish prices fell 25 percent. Price declines have killed any hopes of making huge profits. Indeed, catfish prices are so low that many farmers are getting out of the business.

The dilemma the catfish farmers find themselves in is a familiar occurrence in competitive markets. When the profit prospects look good, everybody wants to get in on the act. As more and more firms start producing the good, however, prices and profits tumble. This helps explain why over 200,000 new firms are formed each year as well as why 50,000 others fail.

In this chapter we examine how supply decisions are made in competitive markets—markets in which all producers are relatively small and lack market power. Our focus on competition centers on the following questions:

- What are the unique characteristics of competitive markets?
- How do competitive firms maximize profits?
- How are the quantity and price of a good determined in competitive markets?

By answering these questions, we will develop more insight into supply decisions and thus the core issues of WHAT, HOW, and FOR WHOM goods and services are produced.

MARKET STRUCTURE

The quest for profits is the common denominator of business enterprises. But not all businesses have the same opportunity to pursue profits. Millions of firms, like Mississippi catfish farms, are very small and entirely at the mercy of the marketplace. A small decline in the market price of their product often spells financial ruin. Even when such firms make a profit,

119

they must always be aware of new competition, new products, or changes in technology.

Larger firms don't have to work quite so hard to maintain their standing. Huge corporations often have the power to raise prices, to change consumer tastes (through advertising), or even to prevent competitors from taking a slice of the profit pie. Such powerful firms can protect and perpetuate their profits. They are more likely to dominate markets than to be at their mercy.

Business firms may be neither giants nor dwarfs. Those are extremes of **market structure** that illustrate the range of power a firm might possess. Most real-world firms fall along a spectrum that stretches from the powerless to the powerful. At one end of the spectrum (Figure 6.1) we place perfectly **competitive firms**—firms that have no power over the price of goods they produce. Like the catfish farmers in the Delta, a perfectly competitive firm must take whatever price for its wares the market offers; it is a *price taker*. A market composed entirely of competitive firms—and without anyone dominating the demand side either—is referred to as a (perfectly) **competitive market**. *In a perfectly competitive market, no single producer or consumer has any control over the price or quantity of the product.*

At the other end of the spectrum of market structures are monopolies. A **monopoly** is a single firm that produces the entire supply of a particular good. As the sole supplier of a good, a monopoly has the power to set market prices, not simply respond to them. Such market power means that monopolies are price *setters*, not price takers.

Among the 20 million or so business enterprises in the United States, there are relatively few monopolies. Local phone companies, cable TV companies, and utility firms often have a monopoly in specific geographic areas. The National Football League also has a monopoly on professional football. The NFL owners know that if they raise ticket prices, fans won't go elsewhere to watch a football game. These situations are the exception to the rule, however. Typically, more than one firm supplies a particular product.

Consider the case of IBM. IBM is a megacorporation with over $80 billion in annual sales revenue and more than 300,000 employees. It is not a monopoly, however. Other firms produce computers that are virtually identical to IBM products. These "IBM clones" limit IBM's ability to set prices for its own output. In other words, other firms in the same market limit IBM's **market power.** IBM is not completely *powerless*, however; it is still large enough to have some direct influence on computer prices and output. Because it has some market power over computer prices, IBM is not a *perfectly* competitive firm.

> **market structure:** The number and relative size of firms in an industry.

> **competitive firm:** A firm without market power, with no ability to alter the market price of the goods it produces.

> **competitive market:** A market in which no buyer or seller has market power.

> **monopoly:** A firm that produces the entire market supply of a particular good or service.

> **market power:** The ability to alter the market price of a good or service.

FIGURE 6.1
Market Structures

The number and relative size of firms producing a good vary across industries. Market structures range from perfect competition to monopoly. Most real-world firms are along the continuum of *imperfect* competition. Market structure affects market outcomes, i.e., the price and quantity of goods supplied.

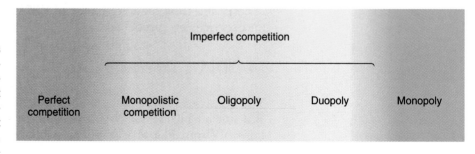

Economists have created categories to distinguish the degrees of competition in product markets. These various market structures are illustrated in Figure 6.1. At one end of the spectrum is perfect competition, where lots of small firms vie for consumer purchases. At the other extreme is monopoly, where only one firm supplies a particular product.

In between the extremes of monopoly (no competition) and perfect competition lie various forms of imperfect competition, including:

- **Duopoly:** Only two firms supply a particular product.
- **Oligopoly:** A few large firms supply all or most of a particular product.
- **Monopolistic competition:** Many firms supply essentially the same product, but each enjoys significant brand loyalty.

How a firm is classified across this spectrum depends not only on its size, but also on how many other firms produce identical or similar products. IBM, for example, would be classified in the oligopoly category for large business computers. IBM supplies nearly 70 percent of all business computers and confronts only a few rival producers. In the personal computer market, however, IBM has a small market share (about 10 percent) and faces dozens of rivals. In that market IBM would fit into the category of monopolistic competition. Gasoline stations, fast-food outlets, and even colleges are other examples of monopolistic competition: many firms are trying to "rise above the crowd," to get the consumer's attention (and purchases).

Market structure has important effects on the supply of goods. How much you pay for a product depends partly on how many firms offer it for sale. The quality of the product may also depend on the degree of competition in the marketplace. In this chapter we focus on supply behavior and market outcomes associated with only one market structure, that of perfect competition. In the next chapter we'll look at the other extreme of market structure, monopoly.

PERFECT COMPETITION

The most distinctive characteristic of a competitive industry is that the many individual firms that make up the industry are all price takers. *A perfectly competitive firm is one whose output is so small in relation to market volume that its output decisions have no perceptible impact on price.* A competitive firm can sell all its output at the prevailing market price. If it tries to charge a higher price, it will not sell anything, because consumers will shop elsewhere. In this sense, a perfectly competitive firm has no *market power*—no ability to control the market price for the good it sells.

At first glance, it might appear that all firms have market power. After all, who is to stop a producer from raising prices? The important concept here, however, is *market* price, that is, the price at which goods are actually sold. You might want to resell this textbook for $50. But you will discover that the bookstore will not buy it at that price. Anyone can change the *asking* price of a good, but actual sales will occur only at the market price. With so many other students offering to sell their books, the bookstore knows it does not have to pay the $50 you are asking. Because you do not have any market power, you have to accept the "going price" for used texts if you want to sell this book.

The same kind of powerlessness is characteristic of the small catfish farmer. Like any producer, the lone catfish farmer can increase or reduce his rate of output by making alternative production decisions. But his decision will not affect the market price of catfish.

Even a larger farmer who can alter his harvest by as much as 100,000 pounds of fish per year will not influence the market price of catfish. Why not? Because over 300 million pounds of catfish are brought to market every year, and another 100,000 pounds simply isn't going to be noticed. In other words, *the output of the lone farmer is so small relative to the market supply that it has no significant effect on the total quantity or price in the market.*

One can visualize the difference between competitive firms and firms with market power by considering what would happen to U.S. catfish supplies and prices if one of Farmer Hollingsworth's ponds ran out of oxygen and his 100,000 catfish died (see Headline). Then contrast this with the likely consequences for U.S. auto supplies and prices if the Ford Motor Company were to close down suddenly. The one event would go unnoticed by the public; the impact of the other would be dramatic.

The same kind of contrast is evident when an expansion of output is contemplated. Were Farmer Hollingsworth to double his production capacity (build another ten ponds), the added catfish output would not show up in commerce statistics. U.S. catfish production is calibrated in the hundreds of millions of pounds, and no one is going to notice another 100,000 fish. Were Ford, on the other hand, to double its production, the added output would not only be noted but would tend to depress automobile prices as Ford tried to unload its heavy inventories.

HEADLINE

COMPETITIVE MARKETS

Southern Farmers Hooked on New Cash Crop

Catfish are replacing crops and dairy farming as a cash industry in much of the South, particularly in Mississippi's Delta region, where 80 percent of farm-bred catfish are grown.

Production has skyrocketed in the USA from 16 million pounds in 1975 to an expected 340 million pounds this year.

The business is growing among farmers in Alabama, Arkansas and Louisiana.

Catfish farming is similar to other agriculture, experts say. One thing is the same: It takes money to get started.

"If you have a good row-crop farmer, you have a good catfish farmer," says James Hoffman of Farm Fresh Cat-

fish Co. in Hollandale, Miss. "But you can't take a poor row-crop farmer and make him a good catfish farmer."

Greensboro, Ala., catfish farmer Steve Hollingsworth says he spends $18,000 a week on feed for the 1 million catfish in his ponds.

"Each of the ponds has about 100,000 fish," he says. "You get about 60 cents per fish, so that's about $60,000."

The investment can be lost very quickly "if something's wrong in that pond," like an inadequate oxygen level, Hollingsworth says.

"You can be 15 minutes too late getting here, and all your fish are gone," he says.

—Mark Mayfield

Price Takers

The critical distinction between Ford and Farmer Hollingsworth is not in their motivation but in their ability to alter market outcomes. Both are out to make a buck and thus seek to produce the rate of output that maximizes profit. What makes Farmer Hollingsworth's situation different is the fact that his output decisions do not influence catfish prices. In this sense, he has one less problem to worry about. *A perfectly competitive firm confronts a horizontal demand curve for its own output.* However much Farmer Hollingsworth works his ponds to produce, he will have no influence on the price of catfish. All catfish look alike, so Farmer Hollingsworth's catfish will fetch the same price as everyone else's catfish. To maximize his profits, Farmer Hollingsworth can only strive to run an efficient operation and to make the right supply decisions. He is a *price taker*, taking the market price of catfish as a fact of life and doing the best he can within that constraint. Were he to attempt to enlarge his profits by raising his catfish prices above market levels, he would find himself without customers, because the consumers would go elsewhere to buy their catfish.

Ford Motor Company, on the other hand, can behave like a *price setter*. Instead of waiting to find out what the market price is and making appropriate output adjustments, Ford has the discretion to "announce" prices at the beginning of every model year. Fords are not exactly like Chevrolets or Toyotas in the minds of consumers. Because Fords are *differentiated*, Ford knows that sales will not fall to zero if its car prices are set a little higher than those of other car manufacturers. Ford confronts a downward-sloping rather than a perfectly horizontal demand curve.

Market Demand vs. Firm Demand

To appreciate the unique nature of perfect competition, *you must distinguish between the market demand curve and the demand curve confronting a particular firm.* Farmer Hollingsworth's small operation does not contradict the law of demand. The quantity of catfish purchased in the supermarket still depends on catfish prices. That is to say, the *market* demand curve for catfish is still downward-sloping, just as the market demand for cars is downward-sloping. Farmer Hollingsworth himself faces a horizontal demand curve only because his share of the market is so infinitesimal that changes in his output do not disturb the market equilibrium.

Collectively, though, individual farmers do count. If 10,000 small, competitive farmers were to expand their catfish production at the same time as Farmer Hollingsworth, the market equilibrium would be disturbed. That is to say, a competitive market composed of 10,000 individually powerless producers still sees a lot of action. The power here resides in the collective action of all the producers, however, and not in the individual action of any one. Were catfish production to increase so abruptly, the catfish could be sold only at lower prices, in accordance with the downward-sloping nature of the *market* demand curve. The distinction between the actions of a single producer and those of the market are illustrated in Figure 6.2. Notice that

• *The market demand curve for a product is always downward-sloping.*
• *The demand curve facing a perfectly competitive firm is horizontal.*

That horizontal demand curve is the distinguishing feature of *perfectly* competitive firms. If a firm can raise its price without losing *all* its customers, it is not a perfectly competitive firm.

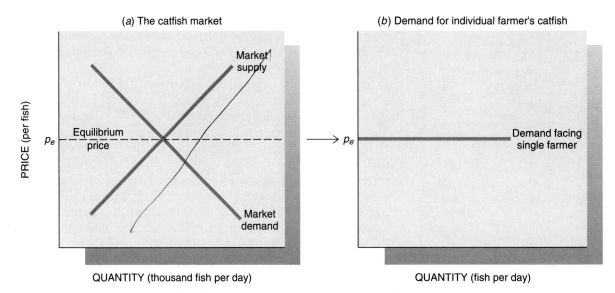

FIGURE 6.2
Market vs. Firm Demand

Consumer demand for any product is downward-sloping, as in the catfish market. The equilibrium price (p_e) of catfish is established by the intersection of *market* demand and *market* supply. This market-established price is the only one at which an individual farmer can sell catfish. If the farmer asks a higher price, no one will buy his catfish, since they can buy identical catfish from other farmers at p_e. But a farmer can sell all of his catfish at the equilibrium price. The lone farmer thus confronts a horizontal demand curve for his own output. (Notice the difference in market and individual farmer quantities.)

THE FIRM'S PRODUCTION DECISION

production decision: The selection of the short-run rate of output (with existing plant and equipment).

In view of the fact that a competitive firm can sell all of its output at the market price, it has only one supply decision to make—that is, how much to produce. Choosing a rate of output is a firm's **production decision.** Should it produce all the output it can? Or should it produce at less than its capacity output?

Output and Revenues

total revenue: The price of a product multiplied by the quantity sold in a given time period, $p \times q$.

The more output a competitive firm produces, the greater its revenues will be. **Total revenue** is the price of the good multiplied by the quantity sold:

- Total revenue = price × quantity

Since a competitive firm can sell all of its output at the market price, total revenue is a simple multiple of that price.

If a competitive firm wanted to maximize total revenue, its strategy would be obvious: it would simply produce as much output as possible.

Revenues vs. Profits

profit: The difference between total revenue and total cost.

We have already established, however, that business firms strive to maximize total *profits,* not total *revenues.* Total **profit** is the difference between total revenues and total costs. Hence a profit-maximizing firm must look not only at revenues but at costs as well. As output increases, total revenues go up, but profits may not. If costs rise too fast, profits may actually decline as output increases. This is a situation to be avoided.

We may embark on the search for maximizing profits with two clues:

- *Maximizing output or revenue is not the way to maximize profits.*
- *Total profits depend on how costs increase as output expands.*

With these clues, we may narrow the scope of our search for the profit maximizing rate of output.

PROFIT MAXIMIZATION

We can advance still further toward the goal of maximum profits by employing a rather primitive but quite practical maxim. This third clue tells us to produce an additional unit of output only if that unit brings in more revenue than it costs. A producer who follows this clue will move steadily closer to maximum profits. We shall explain this clue by looking first at the revenue side of production ("what it brings in"), then at the cost side ("what it costs").

Price

For a perfectly competitive firm, it is easy to determine how much revenue a unit of output will bring in. All we have to look at is price. *Since competitive firms are price takers, they must take whatever price the market has put on their product.* Thus a catfish farmer can readily determine the value of his fish by looking at the market price of catfish.

Marginal Cost

Knowing what the market price of catfish is leaves us just one step away from applying the simple rule for profit maximization. We already know what one more unit brings in (its price); all we need to do now is look at its cost.

The production process for catfish farming is fairly straightforward. The "factory" in this case is a pond; the rate of production is the number of fish harvested from the pond per hour. A farmer can alter the rate of production at will, up to the breeding capacity of the pond.

Assume that the *fixed* cost of the pond is $10 per hour. The fixed costs include the rental value of the pond and the cost of electricity for keeping the pond oxygenated so the fish can breathe. These fixed costs must be paid no matter how many fish the farmer harvests.

To harvest catfish from the pond, the farmer must incur additional costs. Labor is needed to net and sort the fish. The cost of labor is *variable*, depending on how much output the farmer decides to produce. If no fish are harvested, no variable costs are incurred.

marginal cost: The increase in total costs associated with a one-unit increase in production.

The **marginal costs** of harvesting refer to the additional costs incurred to harvest *one* more basket of fish. Generally, we expect marginal costs to rise as the rate of production increases. The law of diminishing returns applies to catfish farming as well. As more labor is hired, each worker has less space (pond area) and capital (access to nets, sorting trays) to work with. Accordingly, it takes a little more labor time (marginal cost) to harvest each additional fish.

Figure 6.3 illustrates these marginal costs. The unit of production used here is baskets of fish per hour. Notice how the MC rises as the rate of out-

FIGURE 6.3
The Costs of Catfish Production

Marginal cost is the increase in total cost associated with a one-unit increase in production. When production expands from 2 to 3 units per day, total costs increase by $9 (from $22 to $31 per day). The marginal cost of the third basket is therefore $9, as seen in row *D* of the table and point *D* in the graph.

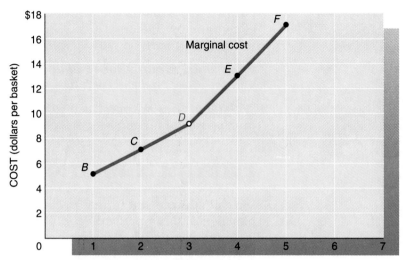

	Rate of Output (baskets per hour)	Total Cost (per hour)	Marginal Cost (per unit)	Average Cost (per unit)
A	0	$10	—	—
B	1	15	$ 5	$15.00
C	2	22	7	11.00
D	3	31	9	10.33
E	4	44	13	11.00
F	5	61	17	12.20

put increases. At the output rate of 4 baskets per hour (point *E*), marginal cost is $13. Hence the fourth basket increases total costs by $13. The fifth basket is even more expensive, with a marginal cost of $17.

Profit-Maximizing Rate of Output

We are now in a position to make a production decision. The rule about never producing anything that costs more than it brings in boils down to a comparison of *price* and marginal cost. We do not want to produce an additional unit of output if its MC exceeds its price. If MC exceeds price, we are spending more to produce that extra unit than we are getting back: total profits will decline if we produce it.

The opposite is true when price exceeds MC. If an extra unit brings in more revenue than it costs to produce, it is adding to total profit. Total profits must increase in this case. Hence a competitive firm wants to expand the rate of production whenever price exceeds MC.

Since we want to expand output when price exceeds MC and contract output if price is less than MC, the profit-maximizing rate of output is easily found. ***Short-run profits are maximized at the rate of output where price equals marginal cost.*** The **competitive profit-maximization rule** is summarized in Table 6.1.

Figure 6.4 illustrates the application of our profit-maximization rule in the production of catfish. We shall assume that the prevailing price of catfish is $13 a basket. At this price we can sell all the fish we can produce,

competitive profit-maximization rule: Produce at that rate of output where price equals marginal cost.

TABLE 6.1
Short-Run Profit-Maximization Rules for Competitive Firm

The relationship between price and marginal cost dictates short-run production decisions. For competitive firms, profits are maximized at that rate of output where price = MC.

If	Then
price > MC	increase output rate
price = MC	maintain output rate (profits maximized)
price < MC	decrease output rate

up to our short-run capacity. The fish cannot be sold at a higher price, because lots of farmers grow fish and sell them for $13. If we try to charge a higher price, consumers will buy their fish from other producers. Hence the demand curve facing this one firm is horizontal at the price of $13 a basket.

The costs of harvesting catfish were already examined in Figure 6.3. The key concept illustrated here is marginal cost. The MC curve slopes upward.

Also depicted in Figure 6.4 are the total revenues, costs, and profits of alternative production rates. Study the table first. Notice that the firm loses $10 per hour if it produces no fish (row *A*). At zero output, total revenue is zero ($p \times q = 0$). However, the firm must still contend with fixed costs

FIGURE 6.4
Maximization of Profits for Competitive Firm

A competitive firm maximizes total profit at the output rate where MC = *p*. If MC is less than price, the firm can increase profits by producing more. If MC exceeds price, the firm should reduce output. In this case, profit maximization occurs at an output of 4 baskets of fish per hour.

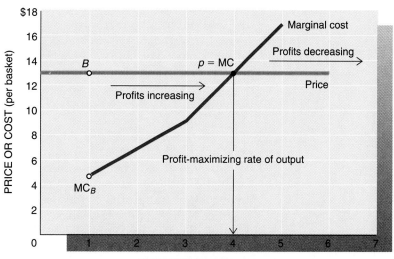

	(1) Number of Baskets (per hour)	(2) Price	(3) Total Revenue	(4) Total Cost	(5) Total Profit	(6) Price	(7) Marginal Cost
A	0	—	0	$10.00	−$10.00	—	—
B	1	$13.00	$13.00	15.00	− 2.00	$13.00	$ 5.00
C	2	13.00	26.00	22.00	+ 4.00	13.00	7.00
D	3	13.00	39.00	31.00	+ 8.00	13.00	9.00
E	4	13.00	52.00	44.00	+ 8.00	13.00	13.00
F	5	13.00	65.00	61.00	+ 4.00	13.00	17.00

of $10 per hour. Total profit—total revenue minus total cost—is therefore *minus* $10; the firm incurs a loss.

Row *B* of the table shows how this loss is reduced when 1 basket of fish is produced per hour. The production and sale of 1 basket per hour brings in $13 of total revenue (column 3). The total cost of producing 1 basket per hour is $15 (column 4). Hence the total loss associated with an output rate of 1 basket per hour is $2 (column 5). This may not be what we hoped for, but it is certainly better than the $10 loss incurred at zero output.

The superiority of producing 1 basket per hour rather than none is also evident in columns 6 and 7 of row *B*. The first basket produced fetches a price of $13. Its *marginal cost* is only $5. Hence it brings in more added revenue than it costs to produce. Under these circumstances—whenever price exceeds MC—output should definitely be expanded.

The excess of price over MC for the first unit of output is also illustrated by the graph in Figure 6.4. Point *B* ($13) lies above MC$_B$ ($5); the *difference* between these two points measures the contribution that the first basket of fish makes to the total profits of the firm. In this case, that contribution equals $13 − $5 = $8, and production losses are reduced by that amount when the rate of output is increased from zero to 1 basket per hour.

So long as price exceeds MC, further increases in the rate of output are desirable. Notice what happens to profits when the rate of output is increased from 1 to 2 baskets per hour (row *C*). The price of the second basket is $13; its MC is $7. Therefore it *adds* $6 to total profits. Instead of losing $2 per hour, the firm is now making a profit of $4 per hour. The second unit of output has improved the situation considerably.

The firm can make even more profits by expanding the rate of output further. Look what happens when the rate of output reaches 3 baskets per hour (row *D* of the table). The price of the third basket is $13; its marginal cost is $9. Therefore the third basket makes a $4 contribution to profits. By increasing its rate of output to 3 baskets per hour, the firm doubles its total profits.

This firm will never make huge profits. The fourth unit of output has a price of $13 and a MC of $13 as well. It does not contribute to total profits, nor does it subtract from them. The fourth unit of output represents the highest rate of output the firm desires. At the rate of output where price = MC, total profits of the firm are maximized.

Notice what happens if we expand output beyond 4 baskets per hour. The price of the fifth basket is still $13; its MC is $17. The fifth basket costs more than it brings in. If we produce that fifth basket, total profit will decline by $4. The fifth unit of output makes us worse off. This eventuality is evident in the graph of Figure 6.4: at the output rate of 5 baskets per hour, the MC curve lies above the price curve. The lesson here is clear: ***output should not be increased if MC exceeds price.***

The outcome of the production decision is illustrated in Figure 6.4 by the intersection of the price and MC curves. At this intersection, price equals MC and profits are maximized. If we produced less, we would be giving up potential profits. If we produced more, total profits would also fall.

Total Profit

To reach the right production decision, we need only compare price and marginal costs. Having found the desired rate of output, however, we may want to take a closer look at the profits we are accumulating. We could, of course, content ourselves with the statistics in the table of Figure 6.4. But a picture would be nice, too, especially if it reflected our success in production. Figure 6.5 provides such a picture.

Figure 6.5 takes advantage of the fact that total profit is equal to *average* profit per unit multiplied by the number of units produced. Profit *per unit*, in turn, is equal to price *minus* average total cost—that is

- Profit per unit = p − ATC

The price of catfish is illustrated in Figure 6.5 by the price line at $13. The average cost of producing catfish is illustrated by the ATC curve. Like the ATC curve we encountered in Chapter 5, this one has a U shape. Therefore, the *difference* between price and average cost—profit per unit—is illustrated by the vertical distance between the price and ATC curves. At 4 baskets of fish per hour, for example, profit per unit equals $13 − $11 = $2.

To compute *total* profits, we note that

- Total profits = profit per unit × quantity

$$= (p - \text{ATC}) \times q$$

In this case, the 4 baskets generate a profit of $2 each, for a *total* profit of $8 per hour. *Total* profits are illustrated in Figure 6.5 by the shaded rectangle. (Recall that the area of a rectangle is equal to its height [profit per unit] multiplied by its width [quantity sold].)

Profit per unit is not only used to compute total profits but is often of interest in its own right. Businesspeople like to cite statistics on "markups," which are a crude index to per-unit profits. However, ***the profit-maximizing producer never seeks to maximize per-unit profits.*** What counts is *total* profits, not the amount of profit per unit. This is the age-old problem of trying to sell ice cream for $5 a cone. You might be able to maximize profit per unit if you could sell 1 cone for $5, but you would make a lot more money if you sold 100 cones at a per-unit profit of only 50 cents each.

Similarly, ***the profit-maximizing producer has no particular desire to produce at that rate of output where ATC is at a minimum.*** Minimum ATC does represent least-cost production. But additional units of output, even though they raise average costs, will increase total profits. This is evident in Figure 6.5: price exceeds MC for some output to the right of min-

FIGURE 6.5
Illustrating Total Profit

Total profits can be computed as profit *per unit* (p − ATC) multiplied by the quantity sold. This is illustrated by the shaded rectangle. To find the profit-maximizing rate of output, we could use this graph or just the MC and price curves of Figure 6.4.

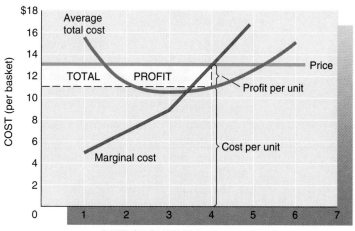

imum ATC (the bottom of the U). Therefore, total profits are increasing as we increase the rate of output beyond the point of minimum average costs. ***Total profits are maximized only where p = MC.***

SUPPLY BEHAVIOR

Our interest in the quest for maximum profits stemmed from our concern to explain the supply side of markets. What we are trying to do here is figure out how markets determine WHAT, HOW, and FOR WHOM. To do that, we need to know not only how demand curves are constructed but also how supply curves are derived.

A Firm's Supply

supply: The ability and willingness to sell (produce) specific quantities of a good at alternative prices in a given time period, *ceteris paribus*.

The profit-maximizing rule provides a basis for the short-run supply decisions of a competitive firm. The **supply** decision is how much output a firm should supply at various prices. We now know, however, that a competitive firm has no control over the price of its output. The only thing the competitive firm controls is its own rate of output. Hence to maximize profits ***competitive firms adjust the quantity supplied until MC = price.***

Suppose the price of catfish was only $9 per basket instead of $13. Would it still make sense to harvest 4 baskets per hour? No. Four baskets is the profit-maximizing rate of output only when the price of catfish is $13. At a price of $9 a basket, it would not make sense to produce 4 baskets, since the MC of the fourth basket ($13) would exceed its price. In this case, the most profitable rate of output would be only 3 baskets of fish per hour (see Figure 6.4).

The marginal cost curve thus tells us how much output a firm will supply at different prices. Once we know the price of catfish, we can look at the MC curve to determine exactly how many fish Farmer Hollingsworth will harvest. In other words, ***the marginal cost curve is the short-run supply curve for a competitive firm.***

If marginal costs determine the supply decisions of a firm, then anything that alters marginal cost will change supply behavior. The most important influences on marginal cost (and supply behavior) are

- ***The price of factor inputs***
- ***Technology***
- ***Expectations***

A catfish farmer will supply more fish at any given price if the price of feed declines. If fish can be bred faster because of advances in genetic engineering, supply will also increase (shift). Finally, if producers expect factor prices to rise or demand to diminish, they may be more willing to supply output now.

You can put the concept of marginal cost pricing to use the next time you buy a car. The car dealer wants to get a price that covers all his costs, including a share of the rent, electricity, and insurance (fixed costs). He might, however, be willing to sell the car for only its *marginal* cost—that is, the wholesale price he paid for the car plus a little labor time (variable costs). So long as the price exceeds marginal cost, the dealer is better off selling the car than not selling it.

Market Supply

| market supply: The total quantities of a good that sellers are willing and able to sell at alternative prices in a given time period, *ceteris paribus*. |

Up until now we have examined the supply behavior of a single competitive firm. As we observed, the production decision of a competitive firm is based on a comparison of price and the marginal cost of producing its output. The perfectly competitive firm has no power over the price at which its product sells; instead, the competitive firm is a price taker. It *responds* to the market price by producing that rate of output where marginal cost equals price.

But what about the **market supply** of catfish? We need a *market* supply curve to determine the *market* price the individual farmer will confront. In the previous discussion, we simply picked a price arbitrarily, at $13 per basket. Now, however, our objective is to find out where that market price comes from.

Like the market supply curves we first encountered in Chapter 3, the market supply of catfish is obtained by simple addition. All we have to do is add up the quantities each farmer stands ready to supply at a given price and we will know the total number of fish to be supplied to the market at that price. Figure 6.6 illustrates this summation. Notice that *the market supply curve is the sum of the marginal cost curves of all the firms*. Hence whatever determines the marginal cost of a typical firm will also de-

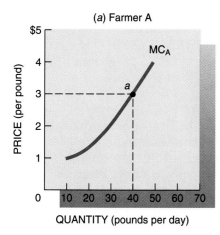

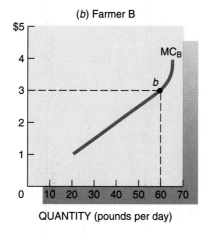

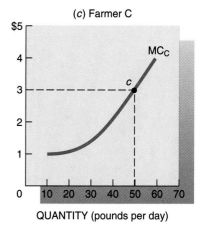

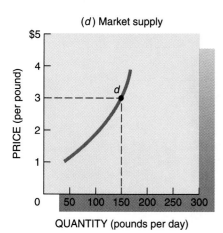

FIGURE 6.6
Competitive Market Supply

The portion of the MC curve that lies above ATC is a competitive firm's short-run supply curve. The curve MC_A tells us that Farmer A will produce 40 pounds of catfish per day if the market price is $3 per pound.

To determine the *market supply*, we add up the quantities supplied by each farmer. The total quantity supplied to the market here is 150 pounds per day ($= a + b + c$). Market supply depends on the number of firms and their respective marginal costs.

termine industry supply. Specifically, the ***market supply of a competitive industry is determined by***

- ***The price of factor inputs***
- ***Technology***
- ***Expectations***
- ***The number of firms in the industry***

INDUSTRY ENTRY AND EXIT

equilibrium price: The price at which the quantity of a good demanded in a given time period equals the quantity supplied.

These determinants of supply provide the basis for constructing a market supply curve. When combined with a market demand curve, this will permit us to identify the **equilibrium price**—that is, the price that matches the quantity demanded to the quantity supplied.

What is fascinating about competitive markets is not the equilibrium price that emerges but the way in which the price is established. The number of firms in a competitive industry isn't fixed. Quite the contrary. Additional firms will *enter* the industry when profits are plentiful. So, too, will firms *exit* the industry when profit opportunities look better elsewhere. These entry and exit flows give competitive markets a unique character that responds well to consumer demands.

Entry

Suppose that the equilibrium price in the catfish industry is $13. This short-run equilibrium is illustrated in Figure 6.7 by the point E_1 at the intersection of market demand and the market supply curve S_1. At that price, the typical catfish farmer would harvest 4 baskets of fish per hour and earn a profit of $8 per hour (Figure 6.5).

The profitable equilibrium at E_1 is not likely to last, however. Farmers still growing cotton or other crops will see the profits being made by catfish farmers and lust after them. They, too, will want to dig up their crops and replace them with catfish ponds. This is a serious problem for the catfish farmers in Mississippi. It is fairly inexpensive to get into the catfish

FIGURE 6.7
Market Entry

If more firms enter an industry, the market supply curve (S_1) shifts to the right (S_2). This creates a new equilibrium (E_2), where output is higher (q_2) and price is lower (p_2).

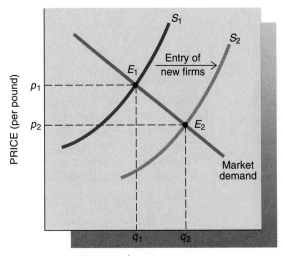

QUANTITY (thousands of pounds per day)

business. You can start with a pond, some breeding stock, and relatively little capital equipment. Accordingly, when catfish prices are high, lots of cotton farmers are ready and willing to bulldoze a couple of ponds and get into the catfish business. The entry of more farmers into the catfish industry increases the market supply and drives down catfish prices.

The impact of market entry on market outcomes is illustrated in Figure 6.7. The initial equilibrium at E_1 was determined by the supply behavior of existing producers. If those producers were earning a profit, however, other firms would likely enter the industry. When they do, the industry supply curve shifts to the right (S_2) and a new equilibrium is established at E_2. Notice that *industry output increases and price falls when firms enter an industry.*

Tendency toward Zero Profits

Whether or not more cotton farmers enter the catfish industry depends on the profit outlook they perceive. If the relationship between price and cost in catfish farming looks better than that in cotton, more farmers will flood their cotton fields. As they do, the market supply curve will continue shifting to the right, driving catfish prices down.

How far can catfish prices fall? *The force that drives catfish prices down is market entry.* New firms continue to enter the industry so long as profits exist. Hence the price of catfish will continue to fall until all profits disappear.

Notice in Figure 6.8 where this occurs. When price drops from p_1 to p_2, the typical firm reduces its output from q_1 to q_2. At the price p_2, however, the firm is still making a profit, since price exceeds average cost at the output q_2.

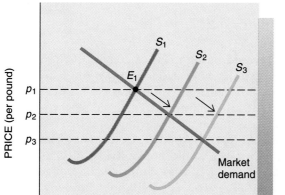

(*a*) Market entry pushes price down and . . .

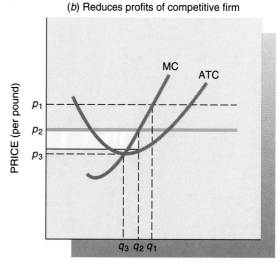

(*b*) Reduces profits of competitive firm

FIGURE 6.8
The Lure of Profits

If economic profits exist in an industry, more firms will want to enter it. As they do, the market supply curve will shift to the right and cause a drop in the market price (part *a*). The lower market price, in turn, will reduce the output and profits of the typical firm (part *b*). Once the market price is driven down to p_3, all profits disappear and entry ceases.

The persistence of profits lures still more firms into the industry. As they enter the industry, the market price of fish will be pushed ever lower (Figure 6.8a). When the price falls to p_3, the most profitable rate of output will be q_3 (where MC = p). But at that level, price no longer exceeds average cost. ***Once price falls to the level of minimum average cost, all profits disappear.*** This zero-profit outcome occurs at the bottom of the U-shaped ATC curve.

When profits vanish, market entry ceases. No more cotton farmers will switch to catfish farming once the price of catfish falls to the level of average total cost.

Exit

In the short run, catfish prices might actually fall *below* average total cost. In that event, the typical catfish farmer would be incurring an economic *loss*. Suddenly, fields of cotton would look a lot more enticing than ponds full of fish. Before long, some catfish farmers would start filling in their ponds and planting cotton again (see accompanying Headline). As they exited the catfish industry, the market supply curve would shift to the left and catfish prices would rise a bit. Eventually, price will rise to the level of average costs, at which point further exits will cease. Once entry and exit cease, the market price will stabilize.

Equilibrium

The lesson to be learned from catfish farming is straightforward:

- ***The existence of profits in a competitive industry induces entry.***
- ***The existence of losses in a competitive industry induces exits.***

Accordingly, we can anticipate that prices in a competitive market will continue to adjust until all entry and exit cease. At that point, the market will be in equilibrium. ***In competitive market equilibrium***

- ***Price equals minimum average cost.***
- ***Economic profit is eliminated.***

Catfish farmers would be happier, of course, if the price of catfish did not decline to the point where economic profits disappear. But how are they going to prevent it? Farmer Hollingsworth knows all about the law of demand and would like to get other farmers to slow production a little before all the profits disappear. But Farmer Hollingsworth is powerless to stop the forces of a competitive market. He cannot afford to reduce his own catfish production. Nobody would notice the resulting drop in market supplies, and catfish prices would continue to slide. The only one affected would be Farmer Hollingsworth, who would be denying himself the opportunity to share in the good fortunes of the catfish market while they lasted. As long as others are willing and able to enter the industry and increase output, Farmer Hollingsworth must do the same or deny himself even a small share of the available profits. Others will be willing to expand catfish production so long as catfish breed economic profits—that is, so long as the rate of return in catfish production is superior to that available elsewhere. They will be able to do so as long as it is easy to get into catfish production.

Farmer Hollingsworth's dilemma goes a long way toward explaining why catfish farming is not highly profitable. Every time the profit picture looks

HEADLINE

ENTRY AND EXIT

Too Many Plants Spoiling Catfish Price

A Decrease in Profit May Force Some Farmers and Processors Out of Business.

Mississippi's catfish industry is likely to lose farmers and processors before former levels of profitability return, experts said Tuesday.

"We've got to have less processing capacity. There are too many processing plants . . . cutting each other's prices in the marketplace," said Indianola farmer and processor Julian Allen.

Allen and others attending *The Catfish Journal's* Fish Processing and Feed Conference in Jackson lamented the recent drop in catfish prices to their lowest levels in four years. The U.S. Department of Agriculture reported that the average farm price in August was 60 cents per pound—21 percent lower than August 1990 and the worst since September 1987.

"This is almost the toughest time in the industry in 10 years. In 1981, we had $300-a-ton feed, 19-percent interest rates and 50-cent fish," said Allen, who runs South-Fresh Farms near Indianola. "It's not quite that bad today, but it's close."

Allen said he couldn't estimate numbers of farmers or processors who will shake out during the current turmoil, but predicted, "We'll see different ones. Some existing ones won't be running and new ones will be built."

Hugh Warren, executive vice president of the Indianola-based Catfish Farmers of America, said the strife over price "hurts all across the board—from the feed mills to the pond bank."

"It's like playing the stock market—if we knew the answer, we'd all be rich. The good thing is that sales are

Catfish Prices (Average price per pound paid to producers)

Sept. '90	76¢
Oct.	76¢
Nov.	75¢
Dec.	72¢
Jan. '91	69¢
Feb.	69¢
March	69¢
April	69¢
May	66¢
June	65¢
July	63¢
Aug.	60¢

up. But whenever an industry moves forward, it never wants to do it smoothly," Warren said.

—Mac Gordon

Reprinted by permission of *The Clarion-Ledger*, Jackson, Mississippi, October 2, 1991, p. 5B. Art adapted from U.S. Department of Agriculture.

good, everybody tries to get in on the action, a phenomenon that keeps catfish prices down close to the costs of production. This kind of pressure on prices and profits is a fundamental characteristic of competitive markets. *As long as it is easy for existing producers to expand production or for new firms to enter an industry, economic profits will not last long.* Industry output will expand, market prices will fall, and rates of profit will diminish. Thus the rate of profits in catfish farming is kept down by the fact that anyone with a pond and a couple of catfish can get into the business fairly easily. People will be tempted to enter the catfish business whenever profits are attractive.

Low Barriers to Entry

> **barriers to entry:** Obstacles that make it difficult or impossible for would-be producers to enter a particular market, e.g., patents.

New producers will be able to enter a profitable industry and help drive down prices and profits as long as there are no significant **barriers to entry.** Such barriers may include patents, control of essential factors of production, long-established consumer acceptance, and various forms of price control. All such barriers make it expensive, risky, or impossible for new firms to enter into production. In the absence of such barriers, new firms can enter an industry more readily and at less risk. Not surprisingly, firms already entrenched in a profitable industry do their best to keep newcomers out, by erecting barriers to entry. As we saw, there are few barriers to entering the catfish business.

Market Characteristics

This brief review of catfish economics illustrates a few general observations about the structure, behavior, and outcomes of a competitive market:

- *Many firms.* A competitive market will include a great many firms, none of which has a significant share of total output.
- *Identical products.* Products are homogeneous. One firm's product is virtually indistinguishable from any other firm's product.
- *MC = p.* All competitive firms will seek to expand output until marginal cost equals price.
- *Low barriers.* Barriers to enter the industry are low. If economic profits are available, more firms will enter the industry.
- *Zero economic profit.* The tendency of production and market supplies to expand when profit is high puts heavy pressure on prices and profits in competitive industries. Economic profit will approach zero in the long run as prices are driven down to the level of average production costs.
- *Perfect information.* All buyers and sellers are fully informed of market opportunities.

POLICY PERSPECTIVES

The Virtues of Competition

In Chapter 3 we noted that there is a comparatively strong case to be made for the market mechanism. In particular, we observed that the market mechanism permits individual consumers and producers to express their views about WHAT to produce, HOW to produce, and FOR WHOM to produce by "voting" for particular goods and services by way of market purchases and sales. If a great many people want and are willing to pay for a particular good, the market mechanism will assist in bringing about more of the desired production. If little of a particular good or service is desired, the market mechanism will signal this fact to producers and stimulate a reallocation of the economy's resources in another direction. How well this market mechanism works depends in part on how competitive markets are.

The Relentless Profit Squeeze

> **market mechanism:** The use of market prices and sales to signal desired outputs (or resource allocations).

The unrelenting squeeze on prices and profits that we have observed in the market is a fundamental characteristic of the competitive process. Indeed, the **market mechanism** works best under such circumstances. The existence of economic profits is an indication that consumers place a high value on a particular product and are willing to pay a comparatively high price to get it. The high price and profits signal this information to profit-hungry entrepreneurs, who eagerly come forward to satisfy consumer demands. Thus *high profits in a particular industry indicate that consumers want* *a different mix of output* (more of that industry's goods). The competitive squeeze on those same profits indicates that resources are being reallocated to produce that desired mix. In a competitive market, consumers get more of the goods they desire, and at a lower price.

When the competitive pressure on prices is carried to the limit, the products in question are also produced at the least possible cost, another dimension of economic efficiency. This was illustrated by the tendency of catfish prices to be driven down to the level of minimum average costs. Once the market equilibrium has been established, society is getting the most it can from its available (scarce) resources.

At the limit of the process, all economic profit is eliminated. This doesn't mean that producers are left empty-handed, however. To begin with, the zero profit limit is rarely, if ever, reached, because new products are continually being introduced, consumer demands change, and more efficient production processes are discovered. In fact, the competitive process creates strong pressures to pursue product and technological innovation. In a competitive market, the adage about the early bird getting the worm is particularly apt. As we observed in the catfish market, the first ones to perceive and respond to the potential profitability of catfish farming were the ones who made the greatest profits.

The sequence of events common to a competitive market situation includes the following:

- High prices and profits signal consumers' demand for more output.
- Economic profit attracts new suppliers.
- The market supply curve shifts to the right.
- Prices slide down the market demand curve.
- A new equilibrium is reached at which increased quantities of the desired product are produced and its price is lower. Average costs of production are at or near a minimum, much more of the product is supplied and consumed, and economic profit approaches zero.
- Throughout the process producers experience great pressure to keep ahead of the profit squeeze by reducing costs, a pressure that frequently results in product and technological innovation.

What is essential to note about the competitive process is that the potential threat of other firms to expand production or new firms to enter the industry keeps existing firms on their toes. Even the most successful firm cannot rest on its laurels for long. To stay in the game, competitive firms must continually improve technology, improve their product, and reduce costs.

The Social Value of Losses

Not all firms can maintain a competitive pace. Throughout the competitive process, many firms incur economic losses, shut down production, and exit the industry. These losses are a critical part of the market mechanism. *Economic losses are a signal to producers that they are not using society's scarce resources in the best way.* Consumers want those resources reallocated to other firms or industries that can better satisfy consumer demands.

Competitive Efficiency

In seeking to keep ahead of the game, competitive firms collectively move closer to society's goals, producing the level and mix of output consumers desire with the most efficient combination of resources. In this sense, a market composed of hundreds or even thousands of individually powerless firms is capable of maximizing consumer welfare. Two specific dimensions of competitive efficiency are noteworthy.

Minimum Average Cost of Production. Because competitive pressures squeeze profit margins, the price of a competitively produced good is driven down to its minimum average cost of production. This means that society is devoting the minimal amount of resources necessary to produce that good. In deciding how to produce, a competitive market tends, therefore, to promote maximum **efficiency.**

Marginal Cost Pricing. The second dimension of competitive efficiency relates to the *mix* of output. In choosing WHAT to produce, we know that the production of one good must be cut back if we are to get more of another good (as long as we are operating on or near the production-possibilities curve). The goods given up are, of course, the **opportunity cost** of getting what we want.

Rational choices about the mix of output require that we know how many resources are required to get one more computer (or anything else). The labor and materials used up in the production of computers cannot be used to produce harmonicas. Our measure of the amount of resources used to produce one more computer is its *marginal cost.* Thus rational decision making requires that we be able to choose among alternative goods and services on the basis of our desires and each good's marginal cost.

A competitive market provides us with the information necessary for making such choices. Why? Because competitive firms offer their goods for sale at the level of marginal costs. That is, they always strive to produce at the rate of output at which price equals marginal cost. Hence the price signal the consumer gets in the marketplace is an accurate reflection of opportunity cost. As such, it offers a reliable basis for making choices about the mix of output and attendant allocation of resources. In this sense, the **marginal cost pricing** characteristic of competitive markets permits society to fulfill its economic goals. The amount consumers are willing to pay for a good (its price) equals its opportunity cost (marginal cost).

efficiency (technical): Maximum output of a good from the resources used in production.

opportunity cost: The most desired goods or services that are forgone in order to obtain something else.

marginal cost pricing: The offer (supply) of goods at prices equal to their marginal cost.

SUMMARY

- Market structure affects the behavior of firms and thus market outcomes. Market structures range from perfect competition to monopoly.
- A perfectly competitive firm has no power to alter the market price of the goods it sells. The perfectly competitive firm confronts a horizontal demand curve for its own output even though the relevant *market* demand curve is negatively sloped.
- Profit maximization induces the competitive firm to produce at that rate of output where marginal cost equals price. This represents the short-term equilibrium of the firm.
- A competitive firm's supply curve is identical to its marginal cost curve. In the short run, the quantity supplied will rise or fall with price.
- The determinants of supply include the price of inputs, technology, and expectations. If any of these determinants change, the *firm's* supply curve

will shift. *Market* supply will shift if costs or the number of firms in the industry change.

- If short-term profits exist in a competitive industry, new firms will enter the market. The resulting shift of supply will drive market prices down the market demand curve. As prices fall, the profit of the industry and its constituent firms will be squeezed.
- The limit to the competitive price and profit squeeze is reached when price is driven down to the level of minimum average cost. Additional output and profit will be attained only if technology is improved (lowering costs) or if demand increases.
- If the market price falls below ATC, firms will exit an industry. Price will stabilize only when entry and exit cease (and zero profit prevails).
- The most distinctive thing about competitive markets is the persistent pressure they exert on prices and profits. The threat of competition is a tremendous incentive for producers to respond quickly to consumer demands and to seek more efficient means of production. In this sense, competitive markets do best what markets are supposed to do—efficiently allocate resources.

Terms to Remember

Define the following terms:

market structure	profit	equilibrium price
competitive firm	marginal cost	barriers to entry
competitive market	competitive profit-	market mechanism
monopoly	maximization rule	efficiency
market power	supply	opportunity cost
production decision	market supply	marginal cost pricing
total revenue		

Questions for Discussion

1. What industries do you regard as being highly competitive? Can you identify any barriers to entry in those industries?
2. According to the Headline on p. 122, by how much did catfish production increase between 1975 and 1989? Where did all these catfish come from? Can you illustrate this explanation with a graph?
3. If there were more bookstores around your campus, would textbook prices rise or fall? Why aren't there more bookstores?
4. Should a firm try to sell its output at the level of average total cost or at marginal cost? When might it be forced to alter its pricing?
5. How many fish should a commercial fisherman try to catch in a day? Should he catch as many as possible or return to dock before filling the boat with fish? Under what economic circumstances should he not even take the boat out?
6. Why would anyone want to enter a profitable industry knowing that profits would eventually be eliminated by competition?
7. What rate of output is appropriate for a "nonprofit" corporation (e.g., a university or hospital)?

Problems

1. Use Figure 6.5 to determine how many fish should be harvested at market prices of

    (*a*) $17   (*b*) $13   (*c*) $9

    How much profit does the farmer make at each of these prices?

2. Suppose the typical catfish farmer was incurring an economic loss at the prevailing price p_1. What forces would raise the price? What price would prevail in long-term equilibrium? Illustrate your answers with separate graphs for the catfish market and the typical farmer.
3. Suppose that the monthly market demand schedule for Frisbees is

Price	$8	$7	$6	$5	$4	$3	$2	$1
Quantity demanded	1,000	2,000	4,000	8,000	16,000	32,000	64,000	150,000

Suppose further that the marginal and average costs of Frisbee production for every competitive firm are

Rate of output	100	200	300	400	500	600
Marginal cost	$2.00	$3.00	$4.00	$5.00	$6.00	$7.00
Average cost	2.00	2.50	3.00	3.50	4.00	4.50

Finally, assume that the equilibrium market price is $6 per Frisbee.
 (a) Draw the cost curves of the typical firm and identify its profit-maximizing rate of output and its total profits.
 (b) Draw the market demand curve and identify market equilibrium.
 (c) How many (identical) firms are initially producing Frisbees?
 (d) How much profit is the typical firm making?
 (e) In view of the profits being made, more firms will want to get into Frisbee production. In the long run, these new firms will shift the market supply curve to the right and push price down to average total cost, thereby eliminating profits. At what equilibrium price are all profits eliminated? How many firms will be producing Frisbees at this price?

Chapter 7

Monopoly

In 1908 Ford produced the Model T, the car "designed for the common man." It was cheap, reliable, and as easy to drive as the horse and buggy it was replacing. Ford sold 10,000 Model T's in its first full year of production (1909). After that, sales more than doubled every year. In 1913, nearly 200,000 Model T's were sold and Ford was fast changing American patterns of consumption, travel, and living standards.

During this early development of the U.S. auto industry, Henry Ford dominated the field. There were other producers, but the Ford Motor Company was the only producer of an inexpensive "motorcar for the multitudes." In this situation, Henry Ford could dictate the price and the features of his cars. When he opened his new assembly line factory at Highland Park, he abruptly raised the Model T's price by $100—an increase of 12 percent—to help pay for the new plant. Then he decided to paint all Model T's black. When told of consumer complaints about the lack of colors, Ford advised one of his executives in 1913: "Give them any color they want so long as it's black."[1]

market power: The ability to alter the market price of a good or service.

Henry Ford had **market power.** He could dictate what color car Americans would buy. And he could raise the price of Model T's without fear of losing all his customers. Such power is alien to competitive firms. Competitive firms are always under pressure to reduce costs, improve quality, and cater to consumer preferences.

In this chapter we will continue to examine how market structure influences market outcomes. Specifically, we examine how a market controlled by a single producer—a monopoly—behaves. We are particularly interested in the following questions:

- What price will a monopolist charge for its output?
- How much will it produce?
- Are consumers better or worse off when only one firm controls an entire market?

[1]Charles E. Sorensen, *My Forty Years with Ford* (New York: W. W. Norton & Co., 1956), p. 127.

MONOPOLY STRUCTURE

The essence of market power is the ability to alter the price of a product. The catfish farmers of Chapter 6 had no such power. Because many other farms were producing and selling the same good, each catfish producer had to act as a *price taker*. Each farm could sell all the fish it harvested at the prevailing market price. If the farmer tried to charge a higher price for his catfish, the individual farmer would lose all his customers. This inability to set the price of their output is the most distinguishing characteristic of perfectly competitive firms.

Catfish don't, of course, violate the law of demand. Some people will, in fact, continue to buy catfish at higher prices. Likewise, the quantity demanded in the marketplace will increase if price falls. As tasty as catfish are, people are not willing to buy unlimited quantities of them at $13 per basket. The marginal utility of extra fish, in fact, diminishes very rapidly. To induce consumers to buy more fish, the price of fish must be reduced.

This seeming contradiction between the law of demand and the situation of the competitive firm was explained by the existence of two distinct demand curves. The "demand for catfish" refers to the **market demand** for that good; like all other consumer demand curves, this market demand curve is downward-sloping. The second demand curve was constructed to represent the situation confronting a *single firm* in the competitive catfish market; that demand curve was horizontal.

> **market demand:** The total quantities of a good or service people are willing and able to buy at alternative prices in a given time period; the sum of individual demands.

Monopoly = Industry

> **patent:** Government grant of exclusive ownership of an innovation.

> **monopoly:** A firm that produces the entire market supply of a particular good or service.

We now confront an entirely different market structure. Suppose that the entire output of catfish could be produced by a single large producer. Assume that Universal Fish actually has a patent on the oxygenating equipment needed to maintain commercial-sized fish ponds. A **patent** gives a firm the exclusive right to produce or license a product. With its patent, Universal Fish can deny other farmers access to oxygenating equipment and thus establish itself as the sole supplier of catfish. Such a firm is a **monopoly**—that is, a single firm that produces the entire market supply of a good.

In view of the fact that a monopoly has no direct competition, you'd hardly expect it to behave like a competitive firm. Competitive firms are always under pressure from other firms in the industry and the threat of additional market entry. A monopolist, however, owns the ballpark and can set the rules of the game. Is a monopoly going to charge the same price for fish as a competitive industry would? Not likely. As we'll see, a monopolist can use its market power to charge higher prices and retain larger profits.

The emergence of a monopoly obliterates the distinction between industry demand and the demand curve facing the firm. A monopoly *is* the industry. Hence there is only *one* demand curve to worry about, and that is the market (industry) demand curve. ***In monopoly situations the demand curve facing the firm is identical to the market demand curve for the product.***

Price vs. Marginal Revenue

Although monopolies simplify the geometry of the firm, they complicate the arithmetic of supply decisions. Competitive firms maximize profits by producing at that rate of output where *price* equals marginal cost. Monopolies do not maximize profits in the same way. They still heed the advice about never producing anything that costs more than it brings in. But as strange as it may seem, what is "brought in" from an additional sale is not the price in this case.

The contribution to total revenue of an additional unit of output is called **marginal revenue (MR).** To calculate marginal revenue, we compare the total revenues received before and after a one-unit increase in the rate of production; the difference between the two totals equals *marginal* revenue.

If every unit of output could be sold at the same price, marginal revenue would equal price. But what would the demand curve look like in such a case? It would have to be *horizontal,* indicating that consumers were prepared to buy everything produced at the existing price. As we have observed, however, a horizontal demand curve only applies for small competitive firms, firms that produce only a tiny fraction of total market output. ***For perfectly competitive firms, price equals marginal revenue.***

The situation in monopoly is different. The firm is so big that its output behavior affects market prices. Indeed, a monopolist can sell additional output only if it *reduces* prices. Universal Fish might be able to sell 1 ton of fish for $6,000. If it wants to sell 2 tons, however, it has to reduce the price per ton. Suppose it reduces the price to $5,000 per ton. In that case we observe that

- Total revenue = 2 tons × $5,000 = $10,000

By how much did total revenue *increase* when 2 tons were sold? Previously, the company sold 1 ton for $6,000. Now it sells 2 tons for $10,000. Hence, total revenue has *increased* by $4,000. This *change* in total revenue represents the *marginal* revenue of the second ton.

Notice in the calculation that marginal revenue ($4,000) is less than price ($5,000). This will always be the case when the demand curve facing the firm is downward-sloping. Since the demand curve facing a monopolist is always downward-sloping, we can conclude that ***marginal revenue is always less than price for a monopolist.***

Figure 7.1 provides a simple illustration of the relationship between price and marginal revenue. The demand curve and schedule represent the market demand for catfish and thus the sales opportunities for the Universal Fish monopoly. According to this information, Universal Fish can sell 1 basket of fish per hour at a price of $13. If the company wants to sell a larger quantity of fish, however, it has to reduce its price. According to the market demand curve shown here, the price must be lowered to $12 to sell 2 baskets per hour. This reduction in price is shown by a movement along the demand curve from point *A* to point *B*.

Our primary focus here is on marginal revenue. We want to show what happens to total revenue when unit sales increase by 1 basket per hour. To do this, we must compute the total revenue associated with each rate of output, then observe the changes that occur.

The calculations necessary for computing MR are summarized in Figure 7.1. Row *A* of the table indicates that the total revenue resulting from one sale per hour is $13. To increase sales, price must be reduced. Row *B* indicates that total revenues rise to only $24 per hour when catfish sales double. The *increase* in total revenues resulting from the added sale is thus $11. The marginal revenue of the second basket is therefore $11. This is illustrated in the last column of the table and by point *b* on the marginal revenue curve.

marginal revenue (MR): The change in total revenue that results from a one-unit increase in quantity sold.

FIGURE 7.1
Price Exceeds Marginal
Revenue in Monopoly

If a firm must lower its price to sell additional output, marginal revenue is less than price. If the firm wants to increase its sales from 1 to 2 baskets per hour, for example, price must be reduced from $13 to $12. The marginal revenue of the second basket is therefore only $11. This is indicated in row *B* of the table and by point *b* on the graph.

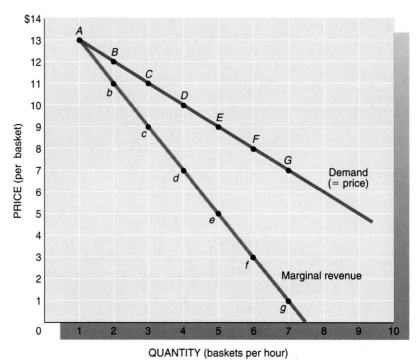

QUANTITY (baskets per hour)

	(1) Quantity	×	(2) Price	=	(3) Total Revenue	(4) Marginal Revenue
A	1		$13		$13	
B	2		12		24	$11
C	3		11		33	9
D	4		10		40	7
E	5		9		45	5
F	6		8		48	3
G	7		7		49	1

Notice that the MR of the second basket ($11) is *less* than its price ($12). This is because both baskets are being sold for $12 apiece. In effect, the firm is giving up the opportunity to sell only 1 basket per hour at $13 in order to sell a larger quantity at a lower price. In this sense, the firm is sacrificing $1 of potential revenue on the first basket of fish in order to increase *total* revenue. Marginal revenue measures the change in total revenue that results.

So long as the demand curve is downward-sloping, MR will always be less than price. Compare columns 2 and 4 of the table in Figure 7.1. At each rate of output in excess of one basket, marginal revenue is less than price. This is also evident in the graph: ***the MR curve lies below the demand (price) curve at every point but the first.***

MONOPOLY BEHAVIOR

Like all other producers, a monopolist is in business to maximize total profits. A monopolist does this a bit differently from a competitive firm, however.

Profit Maximization

The distinction between price and marginal revenue created by a downward-sloping demand curve requires us to adapt the profit-maximizing rule. To maximize profits, a monopolist must equate marginal cost ("what it costs") to marginal revenue ("what it brings in"). Hence *a monopolist maximizes profits at the rate of output where MR = MC*.

> **profit-maximization rule:** Produce at that rate of output where marginal revenue equals marginal cost.

Note that competitive firms actually do the same thing. In their case, MR and price are identical. Hence a competitive firm maximizes profits where MC = MR = *p*. Thus the general **profit-maximization rule (MR = MC)** applies to *all* firms; only those firms that are perfectly competitive use the special case of MC = *p* (= MR).

The Production Decision

> **production decision:** The selection of the short-run rate of output (with existing plant and equipment).

Figure 7.2 shows how a monopolist applies the profit-maximization rule to the **production decision.** The demand curve represents the market demand for catfish; the marginal revenue curve is derived from it, as shown in Figure 7.1. The marginal cost curve in Figure 7.2 represents the costs incurred by Universal Fish in supplying the market. Universal's objective is to select that one rate of output that maximizes total profit.

Competitive firms make the production decision by locating the intersection of marginal cost and price. A monopolist, however, looks for the rate of output where marginal cost equals marginal revenue. This is illustrated in Figure 7.2 by the intersection of the MR and MC curves (point *d*).

FIGURE 7.2
Profit Maximization

The most profitable rate of output is indicated by the intersection of marginal revenue and marginal cost (point *d*). In this case, marginal revenue and marginal cost intersect at an output of 4 baskets per hour. Point *D* indicates that consumers will pay $10 per basket for this much output. Total profits equal price ($10) minus average total cost ($8), multiplied by the quantity sold (4).

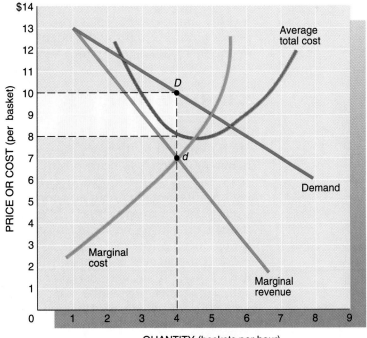

QUANTITY (baskets per hour)

Looking down from that intersection, we see that the associated rate of output is 4 baskets per hour. Thus 4 baskets is the profit-maximizing rate of output.

The Monopoly Price

How much should Universal Fish charge for these 4 baskets of fish? Naturally, the monopolist would like to charge a very high price. But its ability to charge a high price is limited by the demand curve. The demand curve always tells how much consumers are willing to pay for any given quantity. Hence once we have determined the quantity that is going to be supplied (4 baskets per hour), we can look at the demand curve to determine the price ($10 at point *D*) that consumers will pay for these catfish. That is to say,

- *The intersection of the marginal revenue and marginal cost curves (point d) establishes the profit-maximizing rate of output.*
- *The demand curve tells us the highest price consumers are willing to pay for that specific quantity of output (point D).*

If Universal Fish ignored these principles and tried to charge $13 per basket, consumers would buy only 1 basket, leaving it with 3 unsold baskets of fish. As the monopolist will soon learn, *only one price is compatible with the profit-maximizing rate of output.* In this case the price is $10. This price is found in Figure 7.2 by moving up from the quantity 4 until reaching the demand curve at point *D*. Point *D* tells us that consumers are able and willing to buy 4 baskets of fish per hour only at the price of $10 each. A monopolist that tries to charge more than $10 will not be able to sell all 4 baskets of fish. That could turn out to be a smelly and unprofitable situation.

Monopoly Profits

Also illustrated in Figure 7.2 are the total profits of the Universal Fish monopoly. To compute total profits we can first calculate profit per unit, that is, price minus *average* total cost. In this case, profit per unit is $2. Multiplying profit per unit by the quantity sold (4) gives us total profits of $8 per hour, as illustrated by the shaded rectangle.

BARRIERS TO ENTRY

The profits attained by Universal Fish as a result of its monopoly position are not the end of the story. As we observed earlier, the existence of economic profit tends to bring profit-hungry entrepreneurs swarming like locusts. Indeed, in the competitive catfish industry of Chapter 6, the lure of high profits brought about an enormous expansion in catfish farming and a steep decline in catfish prices. What, then, can we expect to happen in the catfish industry now that Universal has a monopoly position and is enjoying huge profits?

The consequences of monopoly for prices and output can be seen in Figure 7.3. In this case, we must compare monopoly behavior to that of a competitive *industry*. Remember that a monopoly is a single firm that comprises the entire industry. What we want to depict, then, is how a different market structure (perfect competition) would alter prices and the quantity supplied.

If a competitive industry were producing at point *D*, it, too, would be

FIGURE 7.3
Monopoly vs. Competitive Outcomes

A monopoly will produce at the rate of output where MR = MC. A competitive industry will produce where MC = p. Hence, a monopolist produces less (q = 4) than a competitive industry (q = 5). It also charges a higher price ($10 vs. $9).

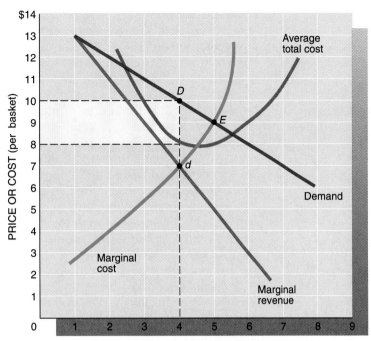

generating a profit with the costs shown in Figure 7.3. A competitive industry would not maintain that rate of output, however. All the firms in a competitive industry try to maximize profits by equating price and marginal cost. At point D, however, price exceeds marginal cost. Hence a competitive industry would quickly move from point D (the monopolist's equilibrium) to point E, where marginal cost and price are equal. At point E (the short-run competitive equilibrium), more fish are supplied, their price is lower, and industry profits are smaller.

Threat of Entry

At point E, catfish farming is still profitable, since price ($9) exceeds average cost ($8) at that rate of production. Although total profits at point E ($5 per hour) are less than at point D ($8 per hour), they are still attractive. These remaining profits will lure more entrepreneurs into a competitive industry. As more firms enter, the market supply curve will shift to the right, driving prices down further. Output will increase and prices will decline until all economic profit is eliminated and entry ceases (long-run competitive equilibrium).

Will this sequence of events occur in a monopoly? Absolutely not. Remember that Universal Fish is now assumed to have an exclusive patent on oxygenating equipment and can use this patent as an impassable barrier to entry. Consequently, would-be competitors can swarm around Universal's profits until their wings drop off; Universal is not about to let them in on the spoils. Universal Fish has the power and the incentive to maintain production and price at point D in Figure 7.3. In the absence of competition, monopoly outcomes won't budge. We conclude, therefore, that *a monopoly attains higher prices and profits by restricting output*.

The secret to a monopoly's success lies in its **barriers to entry.** So long

barriers to entry: Obstacles that make it difficult or impossible for would-be producers to enter a particular market, e.g, patents.

as entry barriers exist, a monopoly can control (restrict) the quantity of goods supplied. The barrier to entry in this catfish saga is the patent on oxygenating equipment. Without access to that technology, would-be catfish farmers must continue to farm cotton.

Polaroid vs. Kodak

A patent was also the source of monopoly power in the battle between Polaroid and Eastman Kodak. Edwin Land invented the instant-development camera in 1947 and got a patent on his invention. Over the subsequent 29 years, the company he founded was the sole supplier of instant-photography cameras and racked up billions of dollars in profits. Along the way, the Polaroid Corporation acquired still more patents to protect Dr. Land's original invention and subsequent improvements.

Polaroid's huge profits were too great a prize to ignore. In 1976, the Eastman Kodak Company decided to enter the market with an instant camera of its own. The availability of a second camera quickly depressed camera prices and squeezed Polaroid's profits.

Polaroid cried foul and went to court to challenge Kodak's entry into the instant-photography market. Polaroid claimed that Kodak had infringed on Polaroid's patent rights and was producing cameras illegally. Kodak responded that it had developed its cameras independently and used no processes protected by Polaroid's patents.

HEADLINE

BARRIERS TO ENTRY

Making a Mint on Mario

Judging by the size of the shipments unloaded on the docks of Seattle, the recession hasn't quite found Nintendo Co., the tireless Japanese video game maker that runs the U.S. market as a virtual private mint. . . .

Nintendo holds a perch that most companies only dream of. It created a product line of vast appeal—nearly one-third of all American homes today have video games—yet it has managed to guard the underlying technology so closely that people who want it generally can get it from only one source.

With this dominance has come enormous profitability. Japanese newspaper Nihon Keizai Shimbun has forecast profits of $1.2 billion this fiscal year for Nintendo, which employs only about 3,000 people worldwide. That sum would place it ahead of Japanese industrial powerhouses Hitachi Ltd. and Nippon Steel Corp. . . .

Nintendo has done one key thing differently than its predecessors. In the first video game boom, independent software companies were free to write games for player units made by other companies; Nintendo insisted—largely successfully—on controlling who creates games and what types are created, and forced licensees to use it to manufacture the cartridges that store the games.

To enforce its control, it placed special electronic chips in its machines to block the playing of games not licensed by Nintendo. While a few software companies managed to crack the code and write Nintendo-compatible games on their own, most took the license route. . . .

But Nintendo's marketing practices also have run afoul of the Federal Trade Commission and many state governments. The FTC alleged earlier this year that Nintendo threatened to withhold products from retailers who sold at a discount. Nintendo denies wrongdoing but promised not to engage in the future in the type of activity described by the FTC. In addition to paying nearly $5 million in fines and costs in connection with price-fixing charges, it agreed to distribute $25 million in $5 discount coupons to customers, redeemable against the future purchase of Nintendo products.

—John Burgess

The Washington Post, December 15, 1991, p. H1. © 1991, The Washington Post. Reprinted with permission.

HEADLINE

ANTITRUST

Topps Gum Strikes Out on Baseball Card Game

PHILADELPHIA (UPI)—In July 1980, Topps Chewing Gum Inc. lost its 14-year monopoly of the bubblegum baseball card industry and was ordered to pay triple damages of $3 to a Philadelphia competitor.

Fleer Corp. of Philadelphia filed a lawsuit in 1975 against Topps of Brooklyn, which since 1966 had signed exclusive contracts with virtually every major and minor league baseball player to appear on 2½-by-3½ cards tucked in with a sheet of pink bubble gum.

U.S. District Judge Clarence Newcomer ruled that Topps and the Major League Baseball Players' Association unfairly edged Fleer out of the market.

But he balked at what he called "guesswork" at determining the extent of Fleer's losses. Newcomer awarded Fleer a nominal $1 damage award, which under antitrust laws is tripled to $3. . . .

Topps sold over $7 million worth of baseball cards that year.

After the courts broke Topps's monopoly, several competitors leaped into the market. By 1993, Topps was selling only 1 of every 5 baseball card sold.

The Washington Post, July 5, 1980. Reprinted with the permission of United Press International, Inc. And *USA Today*, May 20, 1993. Copyright 1993, USA TODAY. Reprinted with permission.

The ensuing legal battle lasted fourteen years. In the end, a federal judge concluded that Kodak had violated Polaroid's patent rights. Kodak not only stopped producing instant cameras but also offered to repurchase all of the 16 million cameras it had sold (for which film would no longer be available).

In addition to restoring Polaroid's monopoly, the court ordered Kodak to pay Polaroid for its lost monopoly profits. The court essentially looked at Figure 7.3 and figured out how much profit Polaroid would have made had it enjoyed an undisturbed monopoly in the instant-photography market. Prices would have been higher, output lower, and profits greater. Using such reasoning, the judge determined that Polaroid's profits would have been $909.5 million higher if Kodak had never entered the market—*twice* as high as the profits actually earned. Kodak had to repay Polaroid these lost profits in 1990.

The accompanying Headlines illustrate other barriers to entry that have been used to protect monopolies. Nintendo kept rivals at bay by prohibiting Nintendo game developers from designing games for anyone else. Topps Chewing Gum maintained a fourteen-year monopoly on baseball cards by signing players to exclusive contracts. The former Soviet Union used more draconian methods to maintain its sable monopoly.

WHAT, HOW, FOR WHOM

Competition vs. Monopoly

The different behavior of the catfish market under competitive and monopoly conditions illustrates basic features of market structures. We may summarize the sequence of events that occurs in each type of market structure as follows:

COMPETITIVE INDUSTRY

- High prices and profits signal consumers' demand for more output.
- The high profits attract new suppliers.
- Production and supplies expand.
- Prices slide down the market demand curve.
- A new equilibrium is established wherein more of the desired product is produced, its price falls, average costs of production approach their minimum, and economic profits approach zero.
- Price equals marginal cost throughout the process.
- Throughout the process, there is great pressure to keep ahead of the profit squeeze by reducing costs or improving product quality.

MONOPOLY INDUSTRY

- High prices and profits signal consumers' demand for more output.
- Barriers to entry are erected to exclude potential competition.
- Production and supplies are constrained.
- Prices don't move down the market demand curve.
- No new equilibrium is established; average costs are not necessarily at or near a minimum, and economic profits are at a maximum.
- Price exceeds marginal cost at all times.
- There is no squeeze on profits and thus no pressure to reduce costs or improve product quality.

HEADLINE

PROTECTING A MONOPOLY

Foxy Soviets Pelt the West

Sable Monopoly Traps Hard Currency, Coats Capitalists

LENINGRAD—Crown sable from the eastern Siberian region of Barguzin, star of the Soviet fur collection, went on sale just as a deep freeze gripped this former imperial city.

It was a good day to sell furs and on that day late last month, the first in the 99th Leningrad fur auction, the Soviet Union collected a cool $30 million from merchants of high fashion gathered from around the capitalist world.

Fur is one of the Soviet Union's best known consumer goods exports. It is also bait for a country eager to trap hard currency: last year, the Soviet Union earned $100 million in fur sales.

In the case of sable, the Soviet Union has something no one else has—in capitalist lingo, a monopoly.

Ivan the Terrible is said to have made the sale of live sables abroad a crime punishable by death. Peter the Great on his travels in the West is said to have carried along trunks of sable skins to use as currency.

In the best-selling novel *Gorky Park*, popular among fur traders, it was the Soviet sable monopoly that was the key to the tangled tale of murderous intrigue.

There is another story, origin and veracity unknown, that an American once traded a rare North American species to the Soviets in exchange for two live Russian sables—only to find when he got home that they had been sterilized.

This year Neiman-Marcus bought about 3,000 sable skins, the highest priced at $560 for a pelt that could fit on a big cat. The skins must be carefully matched for texture and colors to make a coat. At least 50 pelts go into a street-length coat.

David Wolfe, Neiman-Marcus senior vice president, estimated that this year, the firm bought enough for about 10 top-quality coats, after the mixing and matching is done. The rest will go into sable jackets and trimmings, and any small pieces left on the cutting room floor will be swept up and sold in bags to be patched together elsewhere.

The careful selection process explains the final price for a sable coat: about $100,000 and up for the best.

—Celestine Bohlen

The Washington Post, February 5, 1985, p. A10. ©1985, The Washington Post. Reprinted with permission.

WHAT Gets Produced

To the extent that monopolies behave as we have discussed, they alter our output of goods and services in two specific ways. You remember that competitive industries tend, in the long run, to produce at minimum average costs. Competitive industries also pursue cost reductions and product improvements relentlessly. These pressures tend to expand our production possibilities. No such forces are at work in the monopoly we have discussed here. Hence there is a basic tendency for monopolies to inhibit economic growth.

> **marginal cost pricing:** The offer (supply) of goods at prices equal to their marginal cost.

Another important feature of competitive markets is their tendency toward **marginal cost pricing.** Marginal cost pricing is important to consumers because it permits rational choices among alternative goods and services. In particular, it informs consumers of the true opportunity costs of various goods, thereby allowing them to choose the mix of output that delivers the most utility with available resources. In our monopoly example, however, consumers end up getting fewer catfish than they would like, while the economy continues to produce cotton and other goods that are less desired. Thus the mix of output shifted away from catfish when Universal took over the industry. The presence of monopoly therefore alters society's answer to the question of WHAT to produce.

FOR WHOM

Monopoly also changes the answer to the FOR WHOM question. The reduced supply and higher price of catfish imply that some people will have to eat canned tuna instead of breaded catfish. The monopolist's restricted output will also reduce job opportunities in the Delta, leaving some families with less income. The monopolist will end up with fat profits and thus greater access to all goods and services.

HOW

Finally, monopoly may also alter the HOW response. Competitive firms are likely to seek out new ways of breeding, harvesting, and distributing catfish. A monopoly, however, can continue to make profits from existing equipment and technology. Accordingly, monopolies tend to inhibit technology—how things are produced—by keeping potential competition out of the market.

POLICY PERSPECTIVES

Pros and Cons of Monopoly

Despite the strong and general case to be made against monopoly, it is conceivable that monopolies could also benefit society. One of the arguments made for concentrations of market power is that monopolies have greater ability to pursue research and development. Another is that the lure of monopoly power creates a tremendous incentive for invention and innovation. A third argument in defense of monopoly is that large companies can produce goods more efficiently than smaller firms. Finally, it is argued that even monopolies have to worry about *potential* competition and will behave accordingly. We must pause to reflect, then, on whether and how market power might be of some benefit.

Research and Development

The argument that monopolies are in a position to undertake valuable research and development rests on two facts. First, such firms are sheltered from the constant pressure of competition. Second, they have the resources (monopoly profits) with which to carry out expensive R&D functions. The manager of a perfectly competitive firm, by contrast, has to worry about day-to-day production decisions and profit margins. As a result, she is unable to take the longer view necessary for significant research and development and could not afford to pursue such a view even if she could see it. Thus, it is contended, market power is desirable because of the research and development opportunities it creates.

The basic problem with the R&D argument is that it says nothing about *incentives*. Although monopolists have a clear advantage in pursuing research and development activities, they have no clear incentive to do so. They can continue to make substantial profits just by maintaining market power. Research and development are not necessarily required for profitable survival. In fact, research and development that tend to make existing products or plant and equipment obsolete run counter to a monopolist's vested interest and so may actually be suppressed. Brian Maxwell thought this is why the giant food manufacturers spurned his idea for PowerBars (see Headline). In contrast, a perfectly competitive firm cannot continue to make significant profits unless it stays ahead of the competition. This pressure constitutes a significant incentive to discover new products or new and cheaper ways of producing old products.

Entrepreneurial Incentives

The second defense of market power is that monopoly profits act as a tremendous incentive for entrepreneurial activity. As we observed in Chapter 6, every business is out to make a buck, and it is the quest for profits that keeps industries running. Thus, it is argued, even greater profit prizes will stimulate more entrepreneurial activity. Little Horatio Algers will work harder and longer if they can dream of one day possessing a whole monopoly.

HEADLINE

R & D INCENTIVES

PowerBar: A Marathon Man's Idea Hits Big

Are big-company research departments the place to look for new product ideas? Not likely, says Brian Maxwell, inventor of the PowerBar. In 1986, Maxwell wrote to Quaker Oats Company about an "energy bar" he had developed. How did they respond? "We have our own R and D department, thank you very much, please leave us alone," Maxwell recalls them saying. They already had plenty of products to sell.

Now Maxwell is having the last laugh. A world-class marathoner, Maxwell got the idea for a high-energy, low-fat snack after low blood sugar caused him to tire and narrowly lose a race. After three years of testing and tasting—and a mere $75,000 investment—Maxwell perfected the PowerBar. When the big companies refused to license it, he marketed it himself. In 1994, his company sold $30 million worth of PowerBars and other companies—including Quaker Oats—were scrambling to catch up with his innovation.

"A Marathon Man with Marketing Power," *Business Week*, November 7, 1994, pp. 54–56. Reprinted from November 7, 1994, issue of *Business Week* by special permission, copyright © 1994 by McGraw-Hill, Inc.

The incentive argument for market power is enticing but not entirely convincing. After all, an innovator can make substantial profits in a competitive market, as it typically takes a considerable amount of time for the competition to catch up. Recall that the early birds did get the worm in the catfish industry in Chapter 6 even though profit margins were later squeezed. The same thing happened in the energy-bar market: Brian Maxwell made a bundle (see Headline) even though other firms later developed competing products. Hence it is not evident that the profit incentives available in a competitive industry are at all inadequate.

Economies of Scale

economies of scale: Reductions in minimum average costs that come about through increases in the size (scale) of plant and equipment.

A third defense of market power is the most convincing and also the simplest. A large firm, it is argued, can produce goods at a lower unit (average) cost than a small firm. That is, there are **economies of scale.** Thus if we desire to produce goods in the most efficient way—with the least amount of resources per unit of output—we should encourage and maintain large firms. By increasing efficiency through economies of scale, large firms expand society's production possibilities.

Consider once again the comparison we made earlier between Universal Fish and the competitive catfish industry. We explicitly assumed that Universal confronted the same production costs as the competitive industry. Thus Universal was not able to produce catfish any more cheaply than the competitive counterpart, and we concerned ourselves only with the different production decisions made by competitive and monopolistic firms.

It is conceivable that Universal Fish might use its size to achieve greater efficiency. Perhaps the firm could build one enormous pond and centralize all breeding, harvesting, and distributing activities. If successful, this centralization might reduce production costs, making Universal more efficient than a competitive industry composed of thousands of small farms (ponds).

Even though large firms may be able to achieve greater efficiencies than smaller firms, there is no assurance that they actually will. Increasing the size (scale) of a plant may actually reduce operating efficiency. Workers may feel alienated in a massive firm and perform below their potential. Centralization might also increase managerial "red tape" and increase costs. In evaluating the economies-of-scale argument for market power, then, we must recognize that efficiency and size do not necessarily go hand in hand. Only when there is clear evidence of economies of scale is this argument for industry concentration persuasive.

natural monopoly: An industry in which one firm can achieve economies of scale over the entire range of market supply.

Natural Monopolies. There is a special case where the economies-of-scale argument is very persuasive. In this case—called **natural monopoly**—a single firm can produce the entire market supply more efficiently than any large number of (smaller) firms. As the size (scale) of the one firm increases, its average costs continue to fall. These economies of scale give the one large producer a decided advantage over would-be rivals. Hence economies of scale act as a "natural" barrier to entry.

Telephone, cable, and utility services are classic examples of natural monopoly. It is much cheaper to install one system of cable or phone lines than a maze of competing ones. Accordingly, a single telephone or utility company can supply the market more efficiently than a large number of competing firms.

Although natural monopolies are economically desirable, they may be abused. We must ask whether and to what extent consumers are reaping some benefit from the efficiency a natural monopoly makes possible. Do consumers end up with lower prices, expanded output, and better service? Or does the monopoly tend to keep much of the benefits for itself, in the form of higher profits, wages, and more comfortable offices? Typically, federal, state, and local governments are responsible for regulating natural monopolies to ensure that the benefits of increased efficiency are shared with consumers.

Contestable Markets

contestable market: An imperfectly competitive industry subject to potential entry if prices or profits increase.

Governmental regulators are not necessarily the only force keeping monopolists in line. Even though a firm may produce the entire supply of a particular product at present, it may face *potential* competition from other firms. Potential rivals may be sitting on the sidelines, watching how well the monopoly fares. If it does too well, these rivals may enter the industry, undermining the monopoly structure and profits. In such **contestable markets,** monopoly behavior may be restrained by potential competition.

How "contestable" a market is depends not so much on its structure as on entry barriers. If entry barriers are insurmountable, would-be competitors are locked out of the market. But if entry barriers are modest, they will be surmounted when the lure of monopoly profits is irresistible. Foreign rivals already producing the same goods are particularly likely to enter domestic markets when monopoly prices and profits are high (see accompanying Headline).

Structure vs. Behavior. From the perspective of contestable markets, the whole case against monopoly is misconceived. Market *structure* per se is

HEADLINE

POTENTIAL COMPETITION

Foreign Automakers Invade Detroit's Home Turf

In 1983, the "Big Three" U.S. car makers, although technically not a monopoly, together produced over 95 percent of all American-made cars. But General Motors, Ford, and Chrysler still faced stiff competition. Foreign producers were selling over 2 million cars to U.S. consumers and millions more in foreign markets coveted by the Big Three. Competition accelerated even further when foreign producers started building factories in the United States (1978) and confronted the Big Three in their own backyard. By 1992, foreign firms were producing one out of every six cars made in America.

The experience of the auto industry underscores the importance of global markets in restraining monopoly power. As long as foreign producers are able to supply products to U.S. consumers—and even to build factories in the United States—domestic monopolies are unable to exploit their market power to the fullest. Attempts to

increase monopoly prices or profits may attract more foreign rivals. This potential competition may force monopolies to behave more like competitive producers—holding prices and costs down and seeking technological improvements.

From this perspective, the question for antitrust policy is not whether a monopoly exists but whether the market power is "contestable." Can potential producers (foreign or domestic) enter the industry if prices or profits increase? In other words, are the barriers to entry surmountable? If so, monopoly *structure* may not necessarily result in monopoly *behavior.*

As a practical matter, antitrust experts have tried to measure how "contestable" markets are. The basic measuring rod is the size of the monopoly price increase that would lure rival producers into the market. If only a small price increase would prompt new entrants into the market, then that monopoly market is highly "contestable."

not a problem: what counts is market *behavior*. If potential rivals force a monopolist to behave like a competitive firm, then monopoly imposes no cost on consumers or on society at large.

The experience with the Model T Ford illustrates the basic notion of contestable markets. At the time Henry Ford decided to increase the price of the Model T and paint them all black, the Ford Motor Company enjoyed a virtual monopoly on mass-produced cars. But potential rivals saw the profitability of offering additional colors and features (e.g., self-starter, left-hand drive). When they began producing cars in volume, Ford's market power was greatly reduced. In 1926, the Ford Motor Company tried to regain its dominant position by again supplying cars in colors other than black. By that time, however, consumers had more choices. Ford ceased production of the Model T in May 1927.

The experience with the Model T suggests that potential competition can force a monopoly to change its ways. Critics point out, however, that even contestable markets don't force a monopolist to act exactly like a competitive firm. There will always be a gap between competitive outcomes and those monopoly outcomes likely to entice new entry. That gap can cost consumers a lot. The absence of *existing* rivals is also likely to inhibit product and productivity improvements. From 1913 to 1926, all Model T's were black, and consumers had few alternatives. Ford changed its behavior only after *potential* competition became *actual* competition. Even after 1927, when the Ford Motor Company could no longer act like a monopolist, it still didn't price its cars at marginal cost.

SUMMARY

- Market power is the ability to influence the market price of goods and services. In product markets, such power usually resides on the supply side of the market, as consumers are too numerous and too independent to have any individual influence on the shape of the market demand curve.
- The extreme case of market power is monopoly, a situation in which only one firm produces the entire supply of a particular product and thus has an immediate impact on the quantity supplied to the market and the market price.
- The distinguishing feature of any firm with market power is the fact that the demand curve it faces is downward-sloping. In the case of monopoly, the demand curve facing the firm and the market demand curve are identical.
- The downward-sloping demand curve facing a monopolist creates a divergence between marginal revenue and price. To sell larger quantities of output, the monopolist must lower product prices. A firm without market power has no such problem.
- A monopolist will produce at the rate of output at which marginal revenue equals marginal cost. Because marginal revenue is always less than price for a monopoly, the monopolist will produce less output than will a competitive industry confronting the same market demand and cost opportunities. That reduced rate of output will be sold at higher prices, in accordance with the (downward-sloping) market demand curve.

- A monopoly will attain a higher level of profit than a competitive industry because of its ability to equate industry (i.e., its own) marginal revenues and costs. By contrast, a competitive industry ends up equating marginal costs and price, because its individual firms have no control over the market supply curve.
- Because the higher profits attained by a monopoly will attract envious entrepreneurs, barriers to entry are needed to prohibit other firms from expanding market supplies. Patents are one such barrier to entry.
- The defense of market power rests on (1) the alleged ability of large firms to pursue long-term research and development, (2) the incentives implicit in the chance to attain market power, (3) the efficiency that larger firms may attain, and (4) the contestability of even monopolized markets. The first two arguments are weakened by the fact that competitive firms are under much greater pressure to innovate and can stay ahead of the profit game if they do so. The contestability defense at best concedes some amount of monopoly exploitation.
- A natural monopoly exists when one firm can produce the output of the entire industry more efficiently than can a number of smaller firms. This advantage is attained from economies of scale. Large firms are not necessarily more efficient, however, because either constant returns to scale or diseconomies of scale may prevail.

Terms to Remember

Define the following terms:

market power	marginal revenue (MR)	marginal cost pricing
market demand	profit-maximization rule	economies of scale
patent	production decision	natural monopoly
monopoly	barriers to entry	contestable market

Questions for Discussion

1. If you owned the only bookstore on or near campus, what would you charge for this textbook? How much would you pay students for their used books?
2. Is single ownership of a whole industry necessary to exercise monopoly power? How might an industry with several firms achieve the same result? Can you think of any examples?
3. In addition to higher profits, what other benefits accrue to a firm with monopoly power?
4. Why don't monopolists try to establish "the highest price possible," as many people allege? What would happen to sales? To profits?
5. What circumstances might cause a monopolist to charge less than the profit-maximizing price?
6. What are the entry barriers that protected the firms discussed in the Headlines on pp. 150–152? Were these barriers insurmountable?
7. Why might Quaker Oats Company have rejected the idea for PowerBars? (See Headline on p. 154.)

Problems

1. Suppose the following data represent the market demand for catfish. Use this information to graph the demand and marginal revenue curves.

Price (per unit)	$20	19	18	17	16	15	14	13	12	11
Quantity demanded (units per day)	10	11	12	13	14	15	16	17	18	19

2. Assume that the following marginal costs exist in catfish production. Add these costs to the graph from problem 1 and identify

   (*a*) The monopolist's profit-maximizing rate of output
   (*b*) The profit-maximizing output of a competitive industry

Quantity produced (units per day)	10	11	12	13	14	15	16	17	18	19	20
Marginal cost (per unit)		3	5	7	9	12	15	18	21	25	29	33

3. Use Figure 7.2 to answer the following questions:

   (*a*) What rate of output maximizes total revenue?
   (*b*) What is marginal revenue at that rate of output? What is price?
   (*c*) What rate of output maximizes total profit?
   (*d*) What is MR at that rate of output? What is price?

Chapter 8

The Labor Market

In 1994, the chairman of General Motors was paid over $2 million for his services. The president of the United States was paid $200,000. And the secretary who typed the manuscript of this book was paid $17,000. What accounts for these tremendous disparities in earnings?

And why is it that the average college graduate earns over $35,000 a year while the average high school graduate earns less than $25,000? Are such disparities simply a reward for enduring four years of college, or do they reflect real differences in talent? Are you really learning anything that makes you that much more valuable than a high school graduate? For that matter, what are you worth? Not in metaphysical terms, but in terms of the wages that you would get paid in the marketplace.

If we are to explain why some people earn a great deal of income while others earn very little, we will have to consider both the *supply* and the *demand* for labor. In this regard, the following questions arise:

- How do people decide how much time to spend working?
- What determines the wage rate an employer is willing to pay?
- Why are some workers paid so much and others so little?

To answer these questions, we need to examine the behavior of labor *markets*.

LABOR SUPPLY

The following two ads appeared in the campus newspaper of a well-known university:

Will do ANYTHING for money: able-bodied liberal-minded male needs money, will work to get it. Have car. Call Tom 555-0989.

Computer Processing: Computer sciences graduate, knowledge of Windows and O/S systems; all major software. Looking for part-time position on or off campus. Please call Cindy, 555-0211, 9–5.

Although placed by individuals of very different talents, the ads clearly expressed Tom's and Cindy's willingness to work. Although we don't know how much money they were asking for their respective talents, or whether they ever found jobs, we can be sure that they were prepared to take a job at some wage rate. Otherwise, they would not have paid for the ads in the "Jobs Wanted" column of their campus newspaper.

The advertised willingness to work expressed by Tom and Cindy represents a **supply of labor.** They are offering to sell their time and talents to anyone who is willing to pay the right price. Their explicit offers are similar to those of anyone who looks for a job. Job seekers who check the current job openings at the student employment office or send résumés to potential employers are demonstrating a willingness to accept employment—that is, to *supply* labor. The 25,000 Muscovites who applied for jobs at Russia's first McDonald's were also offering to supply labor (see Headline).

> **labor supply:** The willingness and ability to work specific amounts of time at alternative wage rates in a given time period, *ceteris paribus*.

Our first concern in this chapter is to explain these labor-supply decisions. In general, we expect that the quantity of labor supplied depends on the wage rate. Specifically, we anticipate that the quantity of labor supplied—the number of hours people are willing to work—will increase as wage rates rise (see Figure 8.1).

But how do people decide how many hours to supply at any given wage rate? Do people try to maximize their income? If they did, we would all be holding three jobs and sleeping on the commuter bus. Few of us actually live this way. Hence, we must have other goals than simply maximizing our incomes.

Income vs. Leisure

The most visible benefit obtained from working is a paycheck. In general, the fatter the paycheck—the greater the wage rate offered—the more willing a person is to go to work.

As important as paychecks are, however, people recognize that working entails real sacrifices. Every hour we spend working implies one less hour

HEADLINE

LABOR SUPPLY

In Moscow, 25,000 Apply for 630 Jobs at McDonald's

More than 25,000 Muscovites have dreams of flipping burgers beneath the golden arches as a member of the worldwide Big Mac and French fry brigade, eager to share in the West's most greasy rite of passage.

The flood of job-seekers started almost immediately after a Moscow newspaper advertisement was published last month. More than 1,000 applications for the 630 available crew spots came the first day, said George Cohon, deputy chairman of Moscow McDonald's. More than 3,100 interviews have been conducted, seven days a week, with such criteria as whether applicants are legal Moscow residents.

Many job seekers are housewives and students from the prestigious Moscow University, and more than 20 percent speak two languages. Hiring is almost complete now, said Cohon, with only a few spots left to be filled. . . .

The Pushkin Square outlet, the biggest McDonald's in the world, will serve 15,000 diners a day, with 700 seats inside and 200 outside. . . .

Part-time Soviet workers make about 1½ rubles per hour, said Cohon, which is $2.50 at the commercial rate. But workers will also be rewarded every few months for productivity.

—Kara Swisher

The Washington Post, December 14, 1989, p. E1. © 1989, The Washington Post. Reprinted with permission.

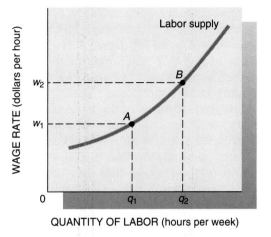

FIGURE 8.1
The Supply of Labor

The quantity of any good or service offered for sale typically increases as its price rises. Labor supply responds in the same way. At the wage rate w_1, the quantity of labor supplied is q_1 (point A). At the higher wage w_2, workers are willing to work more hours per week, that is, to supply a larger quantity of labor (q_2).

---

opportunity cost: The most desired goods or services that are forgone in order to obtain something else.

available for other pursuits. If we go to work, we have less time to watch TV, go to a soccer game, or simply enjoy a nice day. In other words, there is a real **opportunity cost** associated with working. Generally, we say that *the opportunity cost of working is the amount of leisure time that must be given up in the process.*

Because both leisure and income are valued, we confront a tradeoff when deciding whether to go to work. Going to work implies more income but less leisure. Staying home has the opposite consequences.

The inevitable tradeoff between labor and leisure explains the shape of individual labor-supply curves. As we work more hours, our leisure time becomes more scarce—and thus more valuable. We become increasingly reluctant to give up any remaining leisure time as it gets ever scarcer. People who work all week long are reluctant to go to work on Saturday. It's not that they are physically exhausted. It's just that they want some time to enjoy the fruits of their labor. As the accompanying Headline reveals, most American workers feel they've found a nice balance between work and leisure: Only 17 percent of the workforce would like to give up more leisure

---

HEADLINE

INCOME VS. LEISURE

Compensation and Contentment

The following responses were given in a public-opinion poll:

Question: Now I want to ask you a question about work and free time: Which of the following would you choose?

The American Enterprise, January/February 1995, p. 106.

Would choose . . .	Percent
Fewer hours on the job, more free time, less income	14%
More hours on the job, less free time, more income	17
Same hours on the job, same amount of free time, your current income	61

for more income. Accordingly, we require "overtime" pay or similar inducements to get us to work still more hours. In other words, *as the opportunity cost of job time increases*, *we require correspondingly higher rates of pay.* We will supply additional labor—work more hours—only if higher wage rates are offered; this is the message conveyed by the upward-sloping labor-supply curve.

The upward slope of the labor-supply curve is reinforced with the changing value of income. Our primary motive for working is the income a job provides. Those first few dollars are really precious, especially if you have bills to pay and no other source of support. As you work and earn more, however, you discover that your most urgent needs have been satisfied. You have food, shelter, some new clothes, and perhaps even a little entertainment. You may still want more things, but your consumption desires aren't so urgent. You'd like more income, but you aren't quite so desperate to get it. In other words, *the marginal utility of income declines as you earn more.* Accordingly, the wages offered for more work lose some of their allure. You may not be willing to work more hours unless offered a higher wage rate.

The upward slope of an individual's labor-supply curve is thus a reflection of two phenomena:

- The increasing opportunity cost of labor
- The decreasing marginal utility of income as a person works more hours

Money isn't necessarily the only thing that motivates people to work, of course. People *do* turn down higher-paying jobs in favor of lower-wage jobs that they like. Many mothers forgo high-wage "career" jobs in order to have more flexible hours and time at home. Volunteers offer their services just for the sense of contributing to their communities; no paycheck is required. Even MBA graduates say they are motivated more by the "challenge" of high-paying jobs rather than the money. When push comes to shove, however, money almost always makes a difference: people *do* supply more labor when offered higher wages.

Market Supply

> **market supply of labor:** The total quantity of labor that workers are willing and able to supply at alternative wage rates in a given time period, *ceteris paribus.*

The **market supply of labor** refers to all of the hours people are willing to work at various wages. It, too, is upward-sloping. As wage rates rise, not only do existing workers offer to work longer hours but other workers are drawn into the labor market as well. If jobs are plentiful and wages high, many students leave school and start working. Likewise, many homemakers decide that work outside the home is too hard to resist. As the flow of labor-market entrants increases, the total quantity of labor supplied to the market goes up.

LABOR DEMAND

> **demand for labor:** The quantities of labor employers are willing and able to hire at alternative wage rates in a given time period, *ceteris paribus.*

Regardless of how many people are *willing* to work, it is up to employers to decide how many people will *actually* work. Employers must be willing and able to hire workers if people are going to hold jobs and earn some income. That is to say, there must be a **demand for labor.**

The demand for labor is often visible in the help-wanted section of the newspaper. The accompanying Headline shows some of the job vacancies advertised in Auckland, New Zealand. The employers who paid for these

HEADLINE

LABOR DEMAND

Situations Vacant

BUSHMAN Skilled chainsaw operators or knuckle boom loader operator . . . work in West Auckland area.
CYCLE MECHANIC Looking for a top person to run our workshop. Excellent remuneration.
DEEP SEA Skipper, first mate, plus deck hands.

ESCORTS New escort agency requires sophisticated escorts.
RECEPTIONIST Data entry, word processing and a host of exciting activities. Immediate start.

New Zealand Herald, January 7, 1995, p. 23. Reprinted with permission of the *New Zealand Herald.*

ads were willing and able to hire a certain number of workers at specific wage rates. How did they decide what to pay or how many people to hire?

Derived Demand

> **derived demand:** The demand for labor and other factors of production results from (depends on) the demand for final goods and services produced by these factors.

In earlier chapters we emphasized that employers are profit maximizers. Their primary motivation for going into business is to make as much income as possible. In their quest for maximum profits, firms attempt to identify the rate of output at which marginal revenue equals marginal cost. Once they have identified the profit-maximizing rate of output, firms enter factor markets to purchase the required amounts of labor, equipment, and other resources. Thus *the quantity of resources purchased by a business depends on the firm's expected sales and output.* In this sense, we say that the demand for factors of production, including labor, is a **derived demand;** it is derived from the demand for goods and services.

Consider the plight of strawberry pickers. Strawberry pickers are paid very low wages and are employed only part of the year. But their plight cannot be blamed on the greed of the strawberry growers. Strawberry growers, like most producers, would love to sell more strawberries at higher prices. If they did, there is a strong possibility that the growers would hire more pickers and even pay them a higher wage rate. But the growers must contend with the market demand for strawberries. Growers have discovered that consumers are not willing to buy more strawberries at higher prices. As a consequence, the growers cannot afford to hire more pickers or pay them higher wages. In contrast, producers of computers are always looking for more workers and offer very high wages to get them.

Table 8.1 lists other occupations likely to experience unusually high or low demand in the next few years. As more Americans live longer, the demand for in-home health care continues to expand. With that increased demand for services comes a greater *derived* demand for health-care workers. By contrast, the demand for sewing-machine operators is declining as Americans buy more imported clothing.

The principle of derived demand suggests that if customers really want to improve the lot of strawberry pickers, they should eat more strawberries. An increase in the demand for strawberries will motivate growers to plant more berries and hire more labor to pick them. Until then, the plight of the pickers is not likely to improve.

TABLE 8.1
Shifting Demands for Labor

Wage and job prospects depend on changes in the demand for labor. The U.S. Department of Labor foresees major increases in the demand for computer technicians, medical aides, and paralegals. Conversely, an actual decline in the demand for college professors is anticipated, as college enrollments decline. Things look even worse for directory assistance operators, farmers, and bank tellers. These figures show projected job growth for the fastest and slowest growing occupations.

Occupation	Projected Growth of Jobs, 1992–2005
In increasing demand	
Home-health aides	138%
Computer systems analysts	112
Paralegals	86
Medical assistants	71
Corrections officers and jailers	70
Child-care workers	66
Travel agents	66
Flight attendants	51
In decreasing demand	
Directory assistance operators	−51
Sewing machine operators	−29
Meter readers, utilities	−25
Farmers	−21
Textile machine operators	−18
Bank tellers	− 4

Source: *Monthly Labor Review*, November 1993, pp. 58–86.

The number of strawberry pickers hired by the growers is not completely determined by the demand for strawberries. On the contrary, the number of pickers will also depend on the wage rate of pickers. That is to say, ***the quantity of labor demanded will depend on its price (the wage rate).*** In general, we expect that strawberry growers will be *willing to hire* more pickers at low wages than at high wages. Hence the demand for labor looks very much like the demand for any good or service (see Figure 8.2).

Marginal Physical Product

> **marginal physical product (MPP):** The change in total output associated with one additional unit of input.

The downward slope of the labor-demand curve is explained by the relationship between total *output* and the number of workers employed. A strawberry grower hires pickers to harvest more berries. Hence the value of another picker depends on how many berries he or she can pick.

Suppose for the moment that Marvin, a college dropout with three summers of experience as a canoe instructor, can pick 5 boxes per hour. These 5 boxes represent Marvin's **marginal physical product (MPP)**—in other

FIGURE 8.2
The Demand for Labor

The higher the wage rate, the smaller the quantity of labor demanded (*ceteris paribus*). At the wage rate W_1, only L_1 of labor is demanded. If the wage rate falls to W_2, a larger quantity of labor (L_2) will be demanded. The labor demand curve obeys the law of demand.

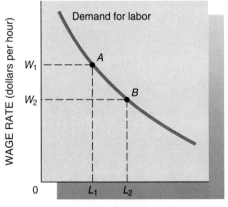

words, the *addition* to total output that will occur if the grower hires Marvin for an hour. That is

$$\bullet \quad \text{Marginal physical product} = \frac{\text{change in total output}}{\text{change in quantity of labor}}$$

Marginal physical product establishes an *upper limit* to the grower's willingness to pay. Clearly the grower can't afford to pay Marvin more than 5 boxes of strawberries for an hour's work; the grower will not pay Marvin more than he produces.

Marginal Revenue Product

Most strawberry pickers don't want to be paid in strawberries, of course. At the end of a day in the fields, the last thing a picker wants to see is another strawberry. Marvin, like the rest of the pickers, wants to be paid in cash. To find out how much cash he might be paid, all we need to know is what a box of strawberries is worth. This is easy to determine. The market value of a box of strawberries is simply the price at which the grower can sell it. Thus Marvin's contribution to output can be measured in either marginal physical product (5 boxes per hour) or the dollar value of that product.

The dollar value of a worker's contribution to output is called **marginal revenue product (MRP).** Marginal revenue product is the *change* in total revenue that occurs when more labor is hired—that is,

> **marginal revenue product (MRP):** The change in total revenue associated with one additional unit of input.

$$\bullet \quad \text{Marginal revenue product} = \frac{\text{change in total revenue}}{\text{change in quantity of labor}}$$

If the grower can sell strawberries for $2 a box, Marvin's marginal revenue product is simply 5 boxes per hour × $2 per box, or $10 per hour. In compliance with the rule about not paying anybody more than he or she contributes, the profit-maximizing grower should be willing to pay Marvin up to $10 an hour. Thus *marginal revenue product sets an upper limit to the wage rate an employer will pay.*

But what about a lower limit? Suppose that the pickers aren't organized and that Marvin is desperate for money. Under such circumstances, he might be willing to work—to supply labor—for only $3 an hour.

Should the grower hire Marvin for such a low wage? The profit-maximizing answer is obvious. If Marvin's marginal revenue product is $10 an hour and his wages are only $3 an hour, the grower will be eager to hire him. The difference between Marvin's marginal revenue product ($10) and his wage ($3) implies additional profits of $7 an hour. In fact, the grower will be so elated by the economics of this situation that he will want to hire everybody he can find who is willing to work for $3 an hour. After all, if the grower can make $7 an hour by hiring Marvin, why not hire 1,000 pickers and accumulate profits at an even faster rate?

The Law of Diminishing Returns

The exploitive possibilities suggested by Marvin's picking are clearly attractive; however, they merit some careful consideration. It isn't at all clear, for example, how the grower could squeeze 1,000 workers onto one acre of land and have any room left over for strawberry plants. There must be some limit to the profit-making potential of this situation.

A few moments' reflection on the absurdity of trying to employ 1,000 people to pick one acre of strawberries should be convincing evidence of the limits to profits here. You don't need two years of business school to recognize this. But some economics may help explain exactly why the grower's eagerness to hire additional pickers will begin to fade long before 1,000 are hired. The magic concept here is *marginal productivity*.

Diminishing MPP. The decision to hire Marvin originated in his marginal physical product—that is, the 5 boxes of strawberries he can pick in an hour's time. To assess the profitability of hiring additional pickers, we again have to consider what will happen to total output as additional labor is employed. To do so we need to keep track of marginal physical product.

Figure 8.3 provides a summary of the increases in strawberry output as additional pickers are hired. We start with Marvin, who picks 5 boxes of strawberries per hour. Total output and his marginal physical product are identical, because he is initially the only picker employed. When the grower hires George, Marvin's old college roommate, we observe the total output increases to 10 boxes per hour. This figure represents another increase of 5 boxes per hour. Accordingly, we may conclude that George's *marginal physical product* is 5 boxes per hour, the same as Marvin's. Naturally, the grower will want to hire George and continue looking for more pickers.

As more workers are hired, total strawberry output continues to increase, but not nearly as fast. Although the later hires work just as hard, the limited availability of land and capital constrain their marginal physical product. One problem is the number of boxes. There are only a dozen boxes, and the additional pickers often have to wait for an empty box. The time spent waiting depresses marginal physical product. The worst problem is space: as additional workers are crowded onto the one-acre patch, they begin to get in one another's way. The picking process is slowed, and marginal physical product is further depressed. Note that the MPP of the fifth picker is 2 boxes per hour, while the MPP of the sixth picker is only 1 box per hour. By the time we get to the seventh picker, marginal physical product actually falls to zero, as no further increases in total strawberry output take place.

Things get even worse if the grower hires still more pickers. If 8 pickers are employed, total output actually *declines*, because the pickers can no longer work efficiently under such crowded conditions. Hence the MPP of the eighth worker is *negative*, no matter how ambitious or hardworking this person may be. Figure 8.3 illustrates this decline in marginal physical product.

Our observations on strawberry production apply to most industries. Indeed, diminishing returns are evident in even the simplest production processes. Suppose you ask a friend to help you with your homework. A little help may go a long way toward improving your grade. Does that mean that your grade improvement will *double* if you get *two* friends to help? What if you get five friends to help? Suddenly, everyone's partying and your homework performance deteriorates. In general, ***the marginal physical product of labor declines as the quantity of labor employed increases.***

law of diminishing returns: The marginal physical product of a variable factor declines as more of it is employed with a given quantity of other (fixed) inputs.

You may recognize the **law of diminishing returns** at work here. Marginal productivity declines as more people must share limited facilities. Typically, diminishing returns result from the fact that an increasing number of workers leaves each worker with less land and capital to work with.

Diminishing MRP. As marginal *physical* product diminishes, so does marginal *revenue* product (MRP). As noted earlier, marginal revenue product is the increase in the *value* of total output associated with an added unit of labor (or other input). In our example, it refers to the increase in strawberry revenues associated with one additional picker.

FIGURE 8.3
Diminishing Marginal Physical Product

The marginal physical product of labor is the increase in total production that results when one additional worker is hired. Marginal physical product tends to fall as additional workers are hired in any given production process. This decline occurs because each worker has increasingly less of other factors (e.g., land) with which to work.

When the second worker (*George*) is hired, total output increases from 5 to 10 boxes per hour. Hence the second worker's MPP equals 5 boxes per hour. Thereafter, capital and land constraints diminish marginal physical product.

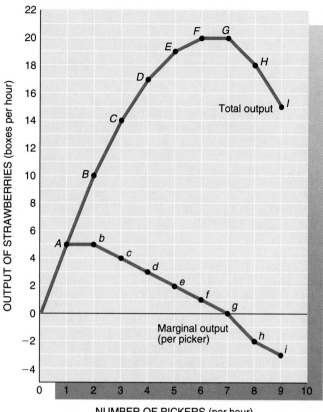

	Number of Pickers (per hour)	Total Strawberry Output (boxes per hour)	Marginal Physical Product (boxes per hour)
A	1 (Marvin)	5	5
B	2 (George)	10	5
C	3	14	4
D	4	17	3
E	5	19	2
F	6	20	1
G	7	20	0
H	8	18	−2
I	9	15	−3

The decline in marginal revenue product mirrors the drop in marginal physical product. Recall that a box of strawberries sells for $2. With this price and the output statistics of Figure 8.3, we can readily calculate marginal revenue product, as summarized in Table 8.2. As the growth of output diminishes, so does marginal revenue product. Marvin's marginal revenue product of $10 an hour has fallen to $4 by the time 4 pickers are employed and reaches zero when 7 pickers are employed.[1]

[1]Marginal revenue product would fall even faster if the price of strawberries declined as increasing quantities were supplied. We are assuming that the grower's output does not influence the market price of strawberries and, hence, that the grower is a *competitive* producer.

TABLE 8.2
Diminishing Marginal Revenue Product

Marginal revenue product (MRP) measures the change in total revenue that occurs when one additional worker is hired. At constant product prices, MRP equals MPP × price. Hence MRP declines along with MPP.

Number of Pickers (per hour)	Total Strawberry Output (boxes per hour)	×	Price of Strawberries (per box)	=	Total Strawberry Revenue (per hour)	Marginal Revenue Product
0	0		$2		0	—
1 (Marvin)	5		2		$10	$10
2 (George)	10		2		20	10
3	14		2		28	8
4	17		2		34	6
5	19		2		38	4
6	20		2		40	2
7	20		2		40	0
8	18		2		36	−4
9	15		2		30	−6

THE HIRING DECISION

The tendency of marginal revenue product to diminish will clearly cool the strawberry grower's eagerness to hire 1,000 pickers. We still don't know, however, how many pickers will be hired.

The Firm's Demand for Labor

Figure 8.4 provides the answer. We already know that the grower is eager to hire pickers whose marginal revenue product exceeds their wage. Suppose the going wage for strawberry pickers is $4 an hour. At that wage, the grower will certainly want to hire at least 1 picker, because the MRP of the first picker is $10 an hour (point *A* in Figure 8.4). A second worker will be hired as well, because that picker's MRP (point *B* in Figure 8.4) also exceeds the going wage rate. In fact, *the grower will continue hiring pickers until the MRP has declined to the level of the market wage rate.* Fig-

FIGURE 8.4
The Marginal Revenue Product Curve Is the Labor-Demand Curve

An employer is willing to pay a worker no more than his or her marginal revenue product. In this case, a grower would gladly hire a second worker, because that worker's MRP (point *B*) exceeds the wage rate ($4). The sixth worker will not be hired at that wage rate, however, since his MRP (at point *D*) is less than $4. The MRP curve is the labor-demand curve.

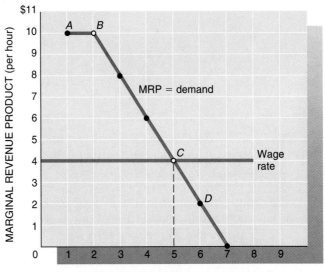

ure 8.4 indicates that this intersection (point *C*) occurs after 5 pickers are employed. Hence we can conclude that the grower will be willing to hire—will *demand*—5 pickers if wages are $4 an hour.

The folly of hiring more than 5 pickers is also apparent in Figure 8.4. The marginal revenue product of the sixth worker is only $2 an hour (point *D*). Hiring a sixth picker will cost more in wages than the picker brings in as revenue. The *maximum* number of pickers the grower will employ at prevailing wages is *5* (point *C*).

The law of diminishing returns also implies that all of the 5 pickers will be paid the same wage. Once 5 pickers are employed, we cannot say that any single picker is responsible for the observed decline in marginal revenue product. Marginal revenue product of labor diminishes because each worker has less capital and land to work with, not because the last worker hired is less able than the others. Accordingly, the "fifth" picker cannot be identified as any particular individual. Once 5 pickers are hired, Marvin's MRP is no higher than any other picker's. ***Each (identical) worker is worth no more than the marginal revenue product of the last worker hired, and all workers are paid the same wage rate.***

The principles of marginal revenue product apply to lawyers as well as strawberry pickers. Law school graduates now earn starting salaries of over $65,000 a year. As the accompanying Headline explains, these salaries are more than justified by the additional fees that law school graduates generate for the firms that hire them.

HEADLINE

MARGINAL REVENUE PRODUCT

Where the Really Big Money Is

New Lawyers Get $65,000 a Year;
Investment Bankers Pocket $100,000

Perry Mason didn't have it as good, and he rarely lost a case. Salaries for new lawyers are reaching a stratosphere once the exclusive province of masters of business administration. Blue-chip New York firms are paying more than $65,000 this year to lure 24-year-olds straight from the classroom, with some firms paying a $10,000-to-$20,000 bonus for working a year or two as a judge's clerk.

Call it Economics 101: Demand for well-trained but untried attorneys apparently outstrips the supply of top-ranking graduates of elite schools. Another reason for the escalating salaries is fear of massive defections to investment banks—where first-year earnings can reach six figures. Median investment-banking base salary for 1986 Harvard Business School graduates is $50,000 plus a $3,000-to-$90,000 bonus.

When the investment banks aren't being blamed for the high salaries, the target is Cravath, Swaine & Moore, one of the nation's most prestigious law firms. It raised pay for its 42 new associates $12,000 to $65,300 this year, including a $1,000-a-month housing allowance for all associates. Paul, Weiss, Rifkind, Wharton & Garrison followed suit with $65,000. Not to be outdone, Shearman & Sterling bid $67,000, and, though it won't say so, Sullivan & Cromwell reportedly upped the ante to $70,000.

Are the new lawyers worth it? "In terms of motivation, dedication and ability to quickly pick up the necessary skills, we're looking at the same kind of justification as businesses hiring M.B.A.'s from the top schools," says Shearman & Sterling partner Arthur Field. At a major firm, a new associate who bills for 2,100 hours of service a year at $75 an hour would generate $157,500 for the firm.

—Beth Brophy

U.S. News & World Report, June 16, 1986. Copyright © June 16, 1986. U.S. News & World Report.

Whatever the explanation for the disparity between the incomes of lawyers and strawberry pickers, the enormous gap between them seems awfully unfair. Can't the employment or wages of pickers be increased?

Changes in Wage Rates

Suppose the government were to set a minimum wage for strawberry pickers at $6 an hour. At first glance this action would appear to increase the wages of pickers, who have been earning only $4 an hour. This is not all good news for the strawberry pickers, however. ***There is a tradeoff between wage rates and the number of workers demanded.*** If wage rates go up, growers will hire fewer pickers.

Figure 8.5 illustrates this tradeoff. The grower's earlier decision to hire 5 pickers was based on a wage of $4 an hour (point *C*). If the wage jumps to $6 an hour, it no longer makes economic sense to keep 5 pickers employed. The MRP of the fifth worker is only $4 an hour (point *B*). The grower will respond to higher wage rates by moving up the labor-demand curve to point *A*. At point *A*, only 4 pickers are hired and MRP again equals the wage rate.

Changes in Productivity

The downward slope of the labor-demand curve does not doom strawberry pickers to low wages. It does emphasize, however, the inevitable link between workers' productivity and wages. ***To get higher wages without sacrificing jobs, labor productivity (MRP) must increase.***

Suppose that Marvin and his friends enroll in a local agricultural extension course and learn new methods of strawberry picking. With these new methods, the marginal physical product of each picker increases by 1 box per hour. With the price of strawberries still at $2 a box, this productivity improvement implies an increase in marginal *revenue* product of $2 per worker. This change causes a rightward *shift* of the labor-demand (MRP) curve, as in Figure 8.6.

Notice how the improvement in productivity has altered the value of strawberry pickers. The MRP of the fifth picker is now $5 an hour (point

FIGURE 8.5
Wages vs. Jobs

The downward slope of the labor-demand curve implies a tradeoff between wage rates and jobs. If the wage rate jumps from $4 to $6 an hour, the number of employed workers drops from 5 per hour (point *C*) to 4 (point *A*).

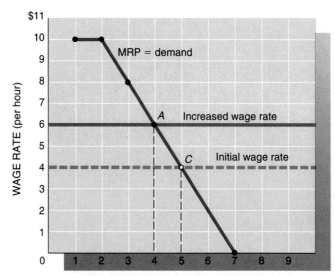

QUANTITY OF LABOR DEMANDED (pickers per hour)

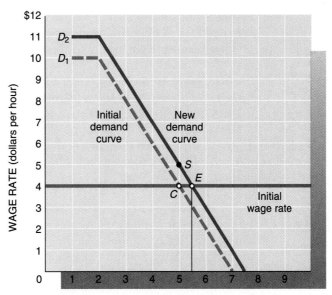

FIGURE 8.6
Increased Productivity

Wage and employment decisions depend on marginal revenue product. If productivity improves, the labor-demand curve shifts to the right (e.g., from D_1 to D_2), raising the MRP of all workers. The grower can now afford to pay higher wages (point S) or hire more workers (point E).

S) rather than $4 (point B). Hence the grower can now afford to pay higher wages. Or the grower could employ more pickers than before, moving from point C to point E. ***Increased productivity thus implies that workers can get higher wages without sacrificing jobs or more employment without lowering wages.*** Historically, increased productivity has been the most important source of rising wages and living standards.

Changes in Price

An increase in the price of strawberries would also help the pickers. Marginal revenue product reflects the interaction of productivity and product prices. If strawberry prices were to double, strawberry pickers would become twice as valuable, even without an increase in physical productivity. Such a change in product prices depends, however, on changes in the market supply and demand for strawberries.

MARKET EQUILIBRIUM

The principles that guide the hiring decisions of a single strawberry grower can be extended to the entire labor market. This suggests that the *market* demand for labor depends on

- The number of employers
- The marginal revenue product of labor in each firm and industry

Increases in either the demand for final products or the productivity of labor will tend to increase the demand for labor.

On the supply side of the labor market we have already observed that the market supply of labor depends on

- The number of workers
- Each worker's willingness to work at alternative wage rates

The supply decisions of each worker are in turn a reflection of tastes, income, wealth, expectations, other prices, and taxes.

Equilibrium Wage

> **equilibrium wage:** The wage at which the quantity of labor supplied in a given time period equals the quantity of labor demanded.

Figure 8.7 brings these market forces together. ***The intersection of the market supply and demand curves establishes the* equilibrium wage.** In our previous example we assumed that the prevailing wage was $4 an hour. In reality, the market wage will be w_e, as illustrated in Figure 8.7. ***The equilibrium wage is the only wage at which the quantity of labor supplied equals the quantity of labor demanded.*** Everyone who is willing and able to work for this wage will find a job.

Many people may be unhappy with the equilibrium wage. Employers may grumble that wages are too high. Workers may complain that wages are too low. Nevertheless, the equilibrium wage is the only one that clears the market.

Legal Minimum Wages

What Figure 8.7 illustrates is the *equilibrium* wage that would result from the free interplay of *market* demand and supply. Few governments are willing to leave wage setting entirely to market forces, however. The U.S. government decreed in 1938 that no worker could be paid less than 25 cents per hour. Since then, the U.S. Congress has repeatedly raised the minimum wage, and President Clinton proposed to increase it further to $5.15 by 1996 (see Headline).

Figure 8.8 illustrates the consequences of this minimum-wage legislation. The legislated minimum wage lies above the equilibrium wage w_e (as it must, to be meaningful). The higher wage floor forces employers up the market demand curve, reducing the number of workers demanded from q_e (point E) to q_d (point D). This is the same employer response we observed in the strawberry patch when pickers' wages were artificially inflated.

Note in Figure 8.8 what happens on the *supply* side as well. The higher minimum wage attracts more people into the labor market. The number of workers willing to work jumps from q_e (point E) to q_s (point S). Everybody wants one of those better-paying jobs.

There aren't enough jobs to go around, however. The number of jobs available at the minimum wage is only q_d; the number of job seekers at that wage is q_s. With more job seekers than jobs, unemployment results. We have a market surplus here equal to q_s minus q_d. Those workers are unemployed.

FIGURE 8.7
Equilibrium Wage

The intersection of *market* supply and demand determines the equilibrium wage in a competitive labor market. All of the firms in the industry can then hire as much labor as they want at that equilibrium wage. Likewise, anyone who is willing and able to work for the wage w_e will be able to find a job.

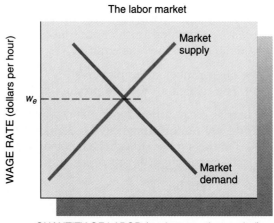

The labor market

QUANTITY OF LABOR (workers per time period)

HEADLINE

DISEQUILIBRIUM WAGES

Clinton Proposes $5.15 Minimum Wage

The federally mandated minimum wage started out at 25 cents an hour in 1938. Since then, Congress has raised the minimum repeatedly, reaching $4.25 in 1991 (see table).

In February 1995, President Clinton proposed another wage hike to $5.15 an hour in two annual 45-cent installments. Declaring that "we must reward work," Clinton pointed out that no worker could support a family with a full-time job paying only $4.25 an hour. Critics responded, however, that most minimum-wage workers—especially teenagers—live in middle-class households and do not have families to support. Furthermore, a higher minimum would cost jobs. As many as 40,000 to 100,000 jobs would be lost as a result of the higher wage floor. Republican Majority Leader Richard Armey,

a former economics professor, vowed to oppose another wage hike "with every fiber of my being."

Minimum-Wage History

Oct. '38	$0.25	May '74	$2.00
Oct. '39	0.30	Jan. '75	2.10
Oct. '45	0.40	Jan. '76	2.30
Jan. '50	0.75	Jan. '78	2.65
Mar. '56	1.00	Jan. '79	2.90
Sept. '61	1.15	Jan. '80	3.10
Sept. '63	1.25	Jan. '81	3.35
Feb. '67	1.40	Apr. '90	3.80
Feb. '68	1.60	Apr. '91	4.25

Compiled from articles in *The Washington Post*, February 3, 1995, and *Time*, February 6, 1995.

Legal minimum wages, then, have two distinct effects. They increase the wages of some workers who keep their jobs. But minimum-wage laws also *reduce* the number of jobs available. Accordingly, some workers end up better off, while others end up worse off. Those most likely to end up worse off are teenagers and other inexperienced workers whose marginal revenue product is below the legal minimum. They will have the hardest time finding a job when a wage floor is enacted.

Labor Unions

Labor unions are another force that attempts to set aside equilibrium wages. The workers in a particular industry may not be satisfied with the equilib-

FIGURE 8.8
Minimum-Wage Effects

A minimum wage increases the quantity of labor supplied but reduces the quantity demanded. Some workers end up with higher wages, but others ($q_s - q_d$) remain or become jobless.

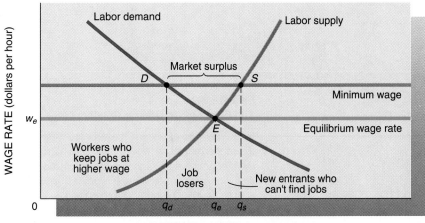

rium wage. They may decide to take *collective* action to get a higher wage. To do so, they form a labor union and bargain collectively with employers.

The formation of a labor union does not set aside the principles of supply and demand. The equilibrium wage remains at w_e, the intersection of labor supply and demand curves (see Figure 8.9a). If the union were successful in negotiating a higher wage (w_u in the figure), a labor-market surplus would appear ($l_3 - l_2$ in Figure 8.9a). These jobless workers would compete for the union jobs, putting downward pressure on the union-negotiated wage. Hence **to get and maintain an above-equilibrium wage, a union must exclude some workers from the market.** Effective forms of exclusion include union membership, required apprenticeship programs, and employment agreements negotiated with employers.

What happens to the excluded workers? In the case of a national minimum wage (Figure 8.8), the surplus workers remain unemployed. A union, however, sets above-equilibrium wages in only one industry or craft. Accordingly, there are lots of other potential jobs for the excluded nonunion workers. Their wages will suffer, however. As workers excluded from the unionized market (Figure 8.9a) stream into the nonunionized market (Figure 8.9b), they shift the nonunionized labor supply to the right. This influx of workers depresses nonunion wages, dropping them from w_e to w_n.

Although the theoretical impact of union exclusionism on relative wages is clear, empirical estimates of that impact are fairly rare. We do know that union wages in general are significantly higher than nonunion wages ($14.76 versus $11.70 per hour in 1994). But part of this differential is due to the

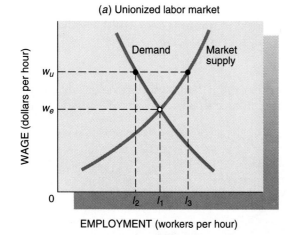 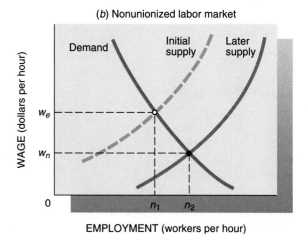

FIGURE 8.9
The Effect of Unions on Relative Wages

In the absence of unions, the average wage rate would be equal to w_e. As unions take control of the market, however, they seek to raise wage rates to w_u. The higher wage reduces the amount of employment in the unionized market from l_1 to l_2. The workers displaced from the unionized market will seek work in the nonunionized market, thereby shifting the nonunion supply curve to the right. The result will be a reduction of wage rates (to w_n) in the nonunionized market. Thus union wages end up higher than nonunion wages.

fact that unions are more common in industries that have always been more capital-intensive and paid relatively high wages. When comparisons are made within particular industries or sectors, the differential narrows considerably. Nevertheless, there is a general consensus that unions have managed to increase their relative wages from 15 to 20 percent.

POLICY PERSPECTIVES

Capping CEO Pay

In 1991 the chairman of the Coca-Cola Company received nearly $88 million in compensation. When challenged to defend his pay, Coke's CEO said he had earned every penny of it by enhancing the value of the company's stock (see Headline).

Critics of CEO pay don't accept this explanation. They make three points. First, the rise in the price of Coke's *stock* is not a measure of marginal revenue product. Only part of the increase in share prices was due to the company's performance; the rest was due to a general upswing in the stock market. Second, the revenues of the Coca-Cola Company probably wouldn't have been $88 million less in the absence of Mr. Goizueta. Hence his marginal revenue product was less than $88 million. Finally, Mr. Goizueta probably would have worked just as hard for, say, just $40 million or so. Therefore, his actual pay was more than required to elicit the desired supply response.

Critics conclude that many CEO paychecks are out of line with realities of supply and demand. They want corporations to reduce CEO pay and revise the process used for setting CEO pay levels.

IN THE NEWS

MEASURING MRP

Coke Chief: I'm Worth $88M

Stock Gains Justify Pay, Goizueta Says

Coca-Cola Chairman Roberto Goizueta told shareholders at Wednesday's annual meeting that he deserved last year's pay package of nearly $88 million—and they appeared to agree.

At the meeting, Coke said first-quarter net earnings rose 19% to $383 million, 58 cents a share, from $321 million, 48 cents a share, a year earlier.

Goizueta reminded the 4,000 shareholders meeting in Atlanta that three years ago, they overwhelmingly approved an executive incentive plan that resulted in his restricted stock award last year.

The award is 1 million Coke shares, worth about $83 million. But Goizueta, 60, can't sell the stock if he retires from the company before 1996. He also received nearly $5 million in salary and bonuses.

Goizueta said Coke's performance justified his pay. He pointed out that the stock has risen nearly 14-fold the past 10 years, outperforming the other 29 stocks in the Dow Jones industrial average. Goizueta, born in Cuba, became chairman and chief executive in 1981.

Goizueta said he views his stock "as my stake in our company—a stake the value of which I will work hard to increase in the future."

USA Today, April 16, 1992, p. 2B. Copyright 1992, USA TODAY. Reprinted with permission.

Unmeasured MRP

One of the difficulties in determining the appropriate level of CEO pay is the elusiveness of marginal revenue product. It is easy to measure the MRP of a strawberry picker or even a truck driver who delivers Coke. But a corporate CEO's contributions are less well-defined. A CEO is supposed to provide strategic leadership and a sense of mission. These are critical to a corporation's success but hard to quantify.

Congress confronts the same problem in setting the president's pay. We noted earlier that the president of the United States is paid $200,000 a year. Can we argue that this salary represents his marginal revenue product? For that matter, how would one begin to measure the MRP of the president? The wage we pay the president of the United States is less a reflection of his contribution to total output than a matter of custom. His salary also reflects the price voters believe is required to induce competent individuals to forsake private-sector jobs and assume the responsibilities of the presidency. In this sense, the wage paid to the president and other public officials is set by their **opportunity wage**—that is, the wage they could earn in private industry.

> **opportunity wage:** The highest wage an individual would earn in his or her best alternative job.

The same kinds of considerations influence the wages of college professors. The marginal revenue product of a college professor is not easy to measure. Is it the number of students he or she teaches, the amount of knowledge conveyed, or something else? Confronted with such problems, most universities tend to pay college professors according to their opportunity wage—that is, the amount the professors could earn elsewhere.

Opportunity wages also help explain the difference between the wage of the chairman of Coca-Cola and the workers who drive Coke trucks. The lower wage of drivers reflects not only their marginal revenue product at Coca-Cola, but also the fact that they are not trained for many other jobs. That is to say, their opportunity wages are low. By contrast, Coke's CEO has impressive managerial skills that are in demand by many corporations; his opportunity wages are high.

Opportunity wages help explain CEO pay but don't fully justify such high pay levels. If Coke's CEO pay is justified by opportunity wages, that means that another company would be willing to pay him that much. But what would justify such high pay at another company? Would his MRP be any easier to measure? Maybe *all* CEO paychecks have been inflated.

Critics of CEO pay conclude that the process of setting CEO pay levels should be changed. All too often, executive pay scales are set by self-serving committees comprised of executives of the same or similar corporations. Critics want a more independent assessment of pay scales, with non-affiliated experts and stockholder representatives. Some critics want to go a step further and set mandatory "caps" on CEO pay. President Clinton rejected legislated caps but proposed limiting the tax deductibility of CEO pay. According to Clinton's proposal, any CEO pay in excess of $1 million a year could not be treated as a business expense but would instead have to be paid out of after-tax profits. This change would put more pressure on corporations to examine the rationale for multi-million-dollar paychecks.

If markets work efficiently, such government intervention should not be necessary. Corporations that pay their CEOs excessively will end up with smaller profits than companies who pay market-based wages. Over time, "lean" companies will be more competitive than "fat" companies, and excessive pay scales will be eliminated. Proposals for CEO pay caps imply that CEO labor markets aren't efficient or that the adjustment process is too slow.

SUMMARY

- The motivation to work arises from a variety of social, psychological, and economic forces. People need income to pay their bills, but they also need to feel they have a role in society's efforts, and to attain a sense of achievement. As a consequence, people are willing to work—to supply labor.
- There is an opportunity cost involved in working—namely, the amount of leisure one sacrifices. People willingly give up additional leisure only if offered higher wages. Hence the labor supply curve is upward sloping.
- A firm's demand for labor reflects labor's marginal revenue product. The greater the marginal revenue product of labor, the larger the quantity of labor a firm is willing to hire at any given wage.
- The marginal revenue product of labor also establishes a limit to the wage rate that firms willingly pay. A profit-maximizing employer will not pay a worker more than the value of what the worker produces.
- The marginal revenue product of labor tends to diminish as additional workers are employed on a particular job (the law of diminishing returns). This decline occurs because additional workers have to share existing land and capital, leaving each worker with less land and capital to work with. The decline in MRP gives labor-demand curves their downward slope.
- The equilibrium wage is determined by the intersection of labor supply and demand curves. Attempts to set above-equilibrium wages cause labor surpluses by reducing the jobs available and increasing the number of job seekers.
- Labor unions attain above-equilibrium wages by excluding some workers from a particular industry or craft. The excluded workers increase the labor supply in the nonunion market, depressing wages there.
- Differences in marginal revenue product are an important explanation of wage inequalities. But the difficulty of measuring MRP in many instances leaves many wage rates to be determined by custom, power, discrimination, or opportunity wages.

Terms to Remember

Define the following terms:

labor supply	marginal physical product	law of diminishing
opportunity cost	(MPP)	returns
market supply of labor	marginal revenue product	equilibrium wage
demand for labor	(MRP)	opportunity wage
derived demand		

Questions for Discussion

1. Why are you doing this homework? What are you giving up? What utility do you expect to gain?
2. Would you continue to work after winning a lottery prize of $50,000 a year for life? Would you change schools, jobs, or career objectives? What factors besides income influence work decisions?
3. Is this course increasing your marginal productivity? If so, in what way?
4. Suppose George is making $13 an hour installing transistorized digital chips in electronic calculators. Would your offer to work for $8 an hour get you the job? Why might a profit-maximizing employer turn down your generous offer?

5. Should the minimum wage be increased? What are the arguments for and against a higher wage floor?
6. Explain why marginal physical product would diminish as
   (a) More secretaries are hired in an office
   (b) More professors are hired in the economics department
   (c) More construction workers are hired to build a school
7. Why are professors of computer science paid more than professors of English literature?

Problems

1. The following table depicts the number of grapes that can be picked in an hour with varying amounts of labor:

Number of pickers (per hour)	1	2	3	4	5	6	7	8
Output of grapes (in flats)	20	38	53	64	71	74	74	70

   Use this information to graph the total and marginal physical product of grape pickers.
2. Assuming that the price of grapes is $1.25 per flat, use the data in problem 1 to graph the marginal revenue product of grape pickers.
   How many pickers will be hired if the going wage rate is $10 per hour?
3. In Figure 8.8,
   (a) How many workers lose their jobs when the minimum wage is enacted?
   (b) How many workers are unemployed at the minimum wage?
   (c) What accounts for the difference between the answers to (a) and (b)?
4. Reread the Headline about law school graduates, "Where the Really Big Money Is," on page 171.
   (a) At Shearman & Sterling, the marginal revenue product of a new associate who bills for 2,100 hours of service a year at $75 an hour is $157,500. What is the difference between the marginal revenue product of a new law school graduate and the salary he or she receives from that firm?
   (b) Given similar differences at other law firms, are the salaries of law school graduates likely to rise even higher than is reported in the Headline? Why?
   (c) The article provides information on earnings in investment banking. What, is the article suggesting, is the opportunity wage of a law school graduate?
   (d) How might the marginal revenue product of law school graduates eventually be brought into line with their equilibrium salary?

Chapter 9

Government Intervention

The market has a keen ear for private wants, but a deaf ear for public needs.
—Robert Heilbroner

Markets work. The interaction of supply and demand in product markets *does* generate goods and services. Likewise, the interaction of supply and demand in labor markets *does* yield jobs, wages, and a distribution of income. As we have observed, the market is capable of determining WHAT goods to produce, HOW, and FOR WHOM.

But are the market's answers good enough? Is the mix of output produced by unregulated markets the best mix possible? Will producers choose the production process that strikes a desirable balance between production and the environment? Will the market-generated distribution of income be fair enough?

We have already seen that the market's answers might not be the best. Monopoly power might constrain the mix of output, raise product prices, and grab too large a share of total income. Such situations call for antitrust action to regulate or dismantle market power. Other circumstances may also prevent the market from offering up the optimal mix of output, method of production, or distribution of income. Whenever that happens, government intervention may be needed to ensure better answers to the WHAT, HOW, and FOR WHOM questions.

The purpose of this chapter is to identify the circumstances when government intervention is desirable. To this end, we try to answer the following questions:

- Under what circumstances do markets fail?
- How can government intervention help?
- How much government intervention is desirable?

As we'll see, there is substantial agreement about how and when markets fail to give us the best WHAT, HOW, and FOR WHOM answers. There is much less agreement about whether government intervention improves the situation. Indeed, an overwhelming majority of Americans are ambivalent about government intervention. They want the government to "fix" the mix of output, to protect the environment, and to ensure an adequate level of income for everyone. But voters are equally quick to blame government meddling for many of our economic woes.

MARKET FAILURE

We can visualize the potential for government intervention by focusing on the WHAT question. Our goal here is to produce the best possible mix of output with our existing resources. We illustrated this goal earlier with production-possibilities curves. Figure 9.1 assumes that of all the possible combinations of output we could produce, the unique combination at point X represents the most desirable, that is, the **optimal mix of output.**

> **optimal mix of output:** The most desirable combination of output attainable with existing resources, technology, and social values.

The Nature of Market Failure

> **market mechanism:** The use of market prices and sales to signal desired outputs (or resource allocations).

We have observed how the market mechanism can help us find this desired mix of output. The **market mechanism** moves resources from one industry to another in response to consumer demands. If we demand more computers—offer to buy more at a given price—more resources (labor) will be allocated to computer manufacturing. Similarly, a fall in demand will encourage producers to stop making computers and offer their services in another industry. Changes in market prices direct resources from one industry to another, moving us along the perimeter of the production-possibilities curve.

The Big Question is whether the mix of output selected by the market mechanism is the one most desired by society. If so, we don't need government intervention to change the mix of output. If not, we may need government intervention to guide the "invisible hand" of the market.

FIGURE 9.1
Market Failure

We can produce any mix of output on the production-possibilities curve. Our goal is to produce the optimal (best possible) mix of output, as represented by point X. Market forces, however, may produce another combination, like point M. In that case, the market fails—it produces a suboptimal mix of output.

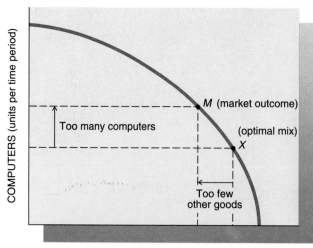

market failure: An imperfection in the market mechanism that prevents optimal outcomes.

We use the term **market failure** to refer to less than perfect (suboptimal) outcomes. If the invisible hand of the marketplace produces a mix of output that is different from the one society most desires, then it has failed. *Market failure implies that the forces of supply and demand have not led us to the best point on the production-possibilities curve.* Such a failure is illustrated by point *M* in Figure 9.1. Point *M* is assumed to be the mix of output generated by market forces. Notice that the market mix (*M*) does not represent the optimal mix, which is assumed to be at point *X*. The market in this case *fails;* we get the wrong answer to the WHAT question. Specifically, too many computers are produced at point *M* and too few of other goods. We would be better off with a slightly different mix of output.

Market failure opens the door for government intervention. If the market can't do the job, we need some form of *nonmarket* force to get the right answers. In terms of Figure 9.1, we need something to change the mix of output—to move us from point *M* (the market mix of output) to point *X* (the optimal mix of output). Accordingly, *market failure establishes a basis for government intervention.* We look to the government to push market outcomes closer to the ideal.

Sources of Market Failure

Because market failure is the justification of government intervention, we need to know how and when market failure occurs. *There are four specific sources of market failure:*

- *Public goods*
- *Externalities*
- *Market power*
- *Equity*

We will examine the nature of these problems, then see why government intervention is called for in each case.

PUBLIC GOODS

The market mechanism has the unique capability to signal consumer demands for various goods and services. By offering to pay higher or lower prices for some goods, we express our collective answer to the question of WHAT to produce. However, the market mechanism works efficiently only if the benefits of consuming a particular good or service are available only to the individuals who purchase that product.

Consider doughnuts, for example. When you eat a doughnut, you get the satisfaction from its taste and your fuller stomach—that is, you derive a private benefit. No one else reaps any significant benefit from your consumption of a doughnut: the doughnut you purchase in the market is yours alone to consume. Accordingly, your decision to purchase the doughnut will be determined by your anticipated satisfaction as well as your income and opportunity costs.

Joint Consumption

Most of the goods and services produced in the public sector are different from doughnuts—and not just because doughnuts look, taste, and smell different from nuclear submarines. When you buy a doughnut, you effectively exclude others from consumption of that product. If Dunkin' Donuts sells a particular pastry to you, it cannot supply the same pastry to some-one else. If you devour it, no one else can. In this sense, the transaction and product are completely private.

The same exclusiveness is not characteristic of national defense. If you buy a nuclear submarine to patrol the Pacific Ocean, there is no way you can exclude your neighbors from the protection your submarine provides. Either the submarine deters would-be attackers or it doesn't. In the former case, both you and your neighbors survive happily ever after; in the latter case, we are all blown away together. In that sense, you and your neigh-bors either consume or don't consume the benefits of nuclear submarine defenses *jointly*. There is no such thing as exclusive consumption here. The consumption of nuclear defenses is a communal feat, no matter who pays for them. Accordingly, national defense is regarded as a **public good** or product, in the sense that *consumption of a public good by one person does not preclude consumption of the same good by another person.* By contrast, a doughnut is a **private good** because if I eat it, nobody else can consume it.

public good: A good or service whose consumption by one per-son does not exclude consump-tion by others.

private good: A good or service whose consumption by one per-son excludes consumption by others.

The Free-Rider Dilemma

free rider: An individual who reaps direct benefits from some-one else's purchase (consump-tion) of a public good.

The "communal" nature of public goods leads to a real dilemma. If you and I will *both* benefit from nuclear defenses, which one of us should buy the nuclear submarine? I would prefer, of course, that *you* buy it, thereby pro-viding me with protection at no direct cost. Hence I may profess no desire for nuclear subs, secretly hoping to take a **free ride** on your market pur-chase. Unfortunately, you, too, have an incentive to conceal your desire for national defenses. As a consequence, neither one of us may step forward to demand nuclear subs in the marketplace. We will both end up defense-less.

Flood control is also a public good. No one in the valley wants to be flooded out. But each landowner knows that a flood-control dam will pro-tect *all* the landowners, regardless of who pays. Either the entire valley is protected or no one is. Accordingly, individual farmers and landowners may say they don't *want* a dam and aren't willing to *pay* for it. Everyone is wait-ing and hoping that someone else will pay for flood control. In other words, everyone wants a *free ride*. Thus, if we leave it to market forces, no one will *demand* flood control and everyone in the valley will be washed away.

The difference between public goods and private goods rests on *techni-cal* considerations, not political philosophy. The central question is whether we have the technical capability to exclude nonpayers. In the case of na-tional defense or flood control, we simply don't have that capability. Even city streets have the characteristics of public goods. Although we could the-oretically restrict the use of streets to those who paid to use them, a toll gate on every corner would be exceedingly expensive and impractical. Here, again, joint or public consumption appears to be the only feasible alterna-tive.

To the list of public goods we could add the administration of justice, the regulation of commerce, and the conduct of foreign relations. These ser-vices—which cost tens of *billions* of dollars and employ thousands of work-ers—provide benefits to everyone, no matter who pays for them. More im-portantly, there is no evident way to exclude *nonpayers* from the benefits of these services.

The free riders associated with public goods upset the customary prac-tice of paying for what you get. If I can get all the streets, defenses, and laws I desire without paying for them, I am not about to complain. I am perfectly happy to let you pay for the services while all of us consume them. Of course, you may feel the same way. Why should you pay for these services if you can consume just as much of them when your neighbors foot the whole bill? It might seem selfish not to pay your share of the cost of providing public goods. But you would be better off in a material sense if you spent your income on doughnuts, letting others pick up the tab for public services.

Because the familiar link between paying and consuming is broken, public goods cannot be peddled in the supermarket. People are reluctant to buy what they can get free. This is a perfectly rational response for a consumer who has limited income to spend. Hence *if public goods were marketed like private goods, everyone would wait for someone else to pay.* The end result might be a total lack of public services. This is the kind of dilemma Robert Heilbroner had in mind when he spoke of the market's "deaf ear" (see quote at the beginning of this chapter).

The production-possibilities curve in Figure 9.2 illustrates the dilemma created by public goods. Suppose that point *A* represents the optimal mix of private and public goods. It is the mix of goods and services we would select if everyone's preferences were known and reflected in production decisions. The market mechanism will not lead us to point *A*, however, because the demand for public goods will be hidden. If we rely on the market, nearly everyone will withhold demand for public goods, waiting for a "free ride" to point *A*. As a result, we will get a smaller quantity of public goods than we really want. The market mechanism will leave us at a mix of output like that at point *B*, with few, if any, public goods. Since point *A* is assumed to be optimal, point *B* must be *suboptimal* (inferior to point *A*). The market fails: we cannot rely on the market mechanism to allocate resources to the production of public goods, no matter how much they might be desired.

Note that we are using "public good" in a different way than most people use it. To most people, the term "public good" refers to any good or service the government produces. In economics, however, the meaning is much more restrictive. *The distinction between public goods and private goods*

FIGURE 9.2
Underproduction of Public Goods

Suppose point *A* represents the optimal mix of output, i.e., the mix of private and public goods that maximizes society's welfare. Because consumers will not demand purely public goods in the marketplace, the price mechanism will not allocate so many resources to the production of public goods. Instead, the market will tend to produce a mix of output like point *B*, which includes fewer public goods and more private goods than is optimal.

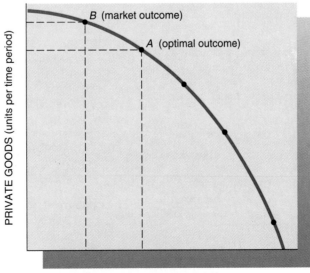

PUBLIC GOODS (units per time period)

is based on the nature of the goods, not who produces them. The term "public good" refers only to those goods and services that are consumed jointly, both by those who pay for them and by those who don't. Public goods can be produced by either the government or the private sector. Private goods can be produced in either sector as well.

The existence of public goods creates a dilemma. The problem is that *the market tends to underproduce public goods and overproduce private goods.* If we want more public goods, we need a *nonmarket* force—government intervention—to get them. The government will have to force people to pay taxes, then use the tax revenues to pay for the production of defense, flood control, and other public goods.

EXTERNALITIES

The free-rider problem associated with public goods provides one justification for government intervention into the market's decision about WHAT to produce. It is not the only justification, however. Further grounds for intervention arise from the tendency of costs or benefits of some market activities to "spill over" onto third parties.

Your demand for a good reflects the amount of satisfaction you expect from its consumption. The price you are willing and able to pay for it acts as a market signal to producers of your preferences. Often, however, your consumption may affect others. The purchase of cigarettes, for example, expresses a smoker's demand for that good. But others may suffer from that consumption. In this case, smoke literally spills over onto other consumers, causing them discomfort and possibly even ill health (see Headline). Yet their loss is not reflected in the market—the harm caused to nonsmokers is *external* to the market price of cigarettes.

HEADLINE

EXTERNALITIES

Passive Smoke Deadly

Secondhand cigarette smoke will be classified as a cause of cancer in a government report to be published later this summer.

Estimates of the number of lung-cancer cases caused by passive smoke also will be reported.

Wednesday, the *Los Angeles Times* reported that an Environmental Protection Agency study says "passive smoking" causes more than 3,000 lung-cancer cases annually.

Bob Axelrad, director of EPA's indoor air division, could not comment on the *Times* story because the report—based on 24 epidemiological studies—is preliminary and could be toned down. It:

- Assesses the risks of passive smoking.

- Offers workplace guidelines to cut hazards.

The report will be available for review at the end of May, says Axelrad.

Reports by the surgeon general and National Academy of Sciences in 1986 linked passive smoke to lung cancer; up to 46,000 non-smokers a year may die, a 1988 study said.

EPA scientists have estimated the risk of indoor pollution from tobacco smoke is twice as great as the danger from radon.

—Dan Sperling

USA Today, May 10, 1990, p. 1. Copyright 1990, USA TODAY. Reprinted with permission.

externalities: Costs (or benefits) of a market activity borne by a third party; the difference between the social and private costs (benefits) of a market activity.

The term **externalities** refers to all costs or benefits of a market activity borne by a third party, that is, by someone other than the immediate producer or consumer. Whenever externalities are present, the preferences expressed in the marketplace will not be a complete measure of a good's value to society. As a consequence, the market will fail to produce the right mix of output. Specifically, *the market will underproduce goods that yield external benefits and overproduce those that generate external costs.* Government intervention may be needed to move the mix of output closer to society's optimal point.

Externalities also exist in production. A steel plant that burns high-sulfur coal tends to destroy the surrounding environment. Yet the damage inflicted on neighboring people, vegetation, and buildings is external to the cost calculations of the firm. Because the cost of such pollution is not reflected in the price of steel, the firm will tend to produce more steel (and pollution) than is socially desirable. To reduce this imbalance, the government has to step in and somehow change market outcomes.

Production Decisions

For a sense of how markets fail to deal with externalities, consider again how the basic production decision is made. As we observed in earlier chapters, the choice of an output rate is based on comparisons of marginal costs and marginal revenues. What kinds of decisions are made when some of the costs are borne by someone else?

Suppose you're operating an electric power plant. Power plants are major sources of air pollution and responsible for nearly all thermal water pollution. Hence your position immediately puts you on the most-wanted list of pollution offenders. But suppose you bear society no grudges and would truly like to help eliminate pollution. Let's consider the alternatives.

Figure 9.3a depicts the marginal and average total costs (MC and ATC) associated with the production of electricity. By equating marginal cost (MC) to price (= marginal revenue, MR), we observe (point A) that profit maximization occurs at an output of 1,000 kilowatt-hours per day. Total profits are illustrated by the shaded rectangle between the price line and the average total cost (ATC) curve.

The profits illustrated in Figure 9.3a are achieved in part by use of the cheapest available fuel under the boilers (which create the steam that rotates the generators). Unfortunately, the cheapest fuel is high-sulfur coal, a major source of air pollution. Other fuels (e.g., low-sulfur coal, fuel oil) pollute less but cost more. Were you to switch to one of them, the ATC and MC curves would both shift upward, as in Figure 9.3b. Under these conditions, the most profitable rate of output would be less than before (point B), and total profits would decline (note the smaller profit rectangle in Figure 9.3b). Thus pollution abatement can be achieved, but only at significant cost to the plant.

The same kind of cost considerations lead the plant to engage in thermal pollution of adjacent waterways. Cool water must be run through an electric utility plant to keep the turbines from overheating. And once the water runs through the plant, it is too hot to recirculate. Hence it must be either dumped back into the adjacent river or cooled off by being circulated through cooling towers. As you might expect, it is cheaper simply to dump the hot water in the river. The fish don't like it, but they don't have to pay the construction costs associated with cooling towers. Were you to get on the environmental bandwagon and build those towers, your production

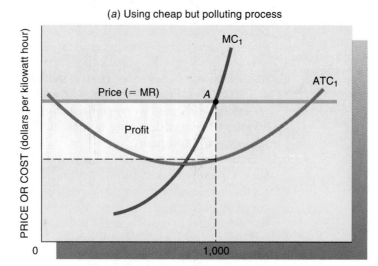

(a) Using cheap but polluting process

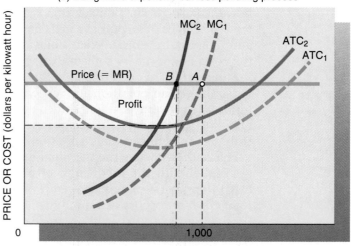

(b) Using more expensive but less polluting process

FIGURE 9.3
Profit Maximization in Electric Power Production

Production processes that control pollution may be more expensive than those that do not. If they are, the MC and ATC curves will shift upward (to MC_2 and ATC_2). At the new profit-maximizing rate of output (point B), output and total profit shrink. Hence a producer has an incentive to continue polluting, using cheaper technology.

costs would rise, just as they did in Figure 9.3b. The fish would benefit, but at your expense.

The big question here is whether you and your fellow stockholders would be willing to incur higher costs in order to cut down on pollution. Eliminating either the air pollution or the water pollution emanating from the electric plant will cost a lot of money; eliminating both will cost much more. And to whose benefit? To the people who live downstream and downwind? We don't expect profit-maximizing producers to take such concerns into account. The behavior of profit maximizers is guided by comparisons of revenues and costs, not by philanthropy, aesthetic concerns, or the welfare of fish.

The moral of this story—and the critical factor in pollution behavior—is that people tend to maximize their personal welfare, balancing *private* benefits against *private* costs. For the electric power plant, this means making production decisions on the basis of revenues received and costs incurred.

"Where there's smoke, there's money."

Drawing by Joe Mirachi; © 1985 The New Yorker Magazine, Inc.

The fact that the power plant imposes costs on others, in the form of air and water pollution, is irrelevant to its profit-maximizing decision. Those costs are *external* to the firm and do not appear on its profit-and-loss statement. Those external costs are no less real, but they are incurred by society at large rather than by the firm.

Whenever external costs exist, a private firm will not allocate its resources and operate its plant in such a way as to maximize social welfare. In effect, society is permitting the power plant the free use of valued resources—clean air and clean water. Thus the power plant has a tremendous incentive to substitute those resources for others (such as high-priced fuel or cooling towers) in the production process. The inefficiency of such an arrangement is obvious when we recall that the function of markets is to allocate scarce resources in accordance with consumers' expressed demands. Yet here we are, proclaiming a high value for clean air and clean water and encouraging the power plant to use up both resources by offering them at zero cost to the firm.

Social vs. Private Costs

social costs: The full resource costs of an economic activity, including externalities.

private costs: The costs of an economic activity directly borne by the immediate producer or consumer (excluding externalities).

The inefficiency of this market arrangement can be expressed in terms of a distinction between social costs and private costs. **Social costs** are the total costs of all the resources that are used in a particular production activity. On the other hand, **private costs** are the resource costs that are incurred by the specific producer.

Ideally, a producer's private costs will encompass all the attendant social costs, and production decisions will be consistent with our social welfare. Unfortunately, this happy identity does not always exist, as our experience with the power plant illustrates. *When social costs differ from private costs, external costs exist. In fact, external costs are equal to the difference between the social and private costs*—that is

- External costs = social costs − private costs

When external costs are present, the market mechanism will not allocate resources efficiently. This is another case of market failure. The price signal confronting producers is flawed. By not conveying the full (social) cost of scarce resources, the market encourages excessive pollution. We end up with a suboptimal mix of output and the wrong production processes. Our collective social welfare would be greater with different market behavior and a cleaner environment.

The nature and consequences of this market failure are illustrated in Figure 9.4, which again depicts the cost situation confronting the electric power plant. Notice that we use two different marginal cost curves this time. The lower one, the *private* MC curve, reflects the private costs incurred by the power plant when it operates on a profit-maximization basis, using high-sulfur coal and no cooling towers. It is identical to the MC curve of Figure 9.3*a*. We now know, however, that such operations impose external costs on others in the form of air and water pollution. Hence social costs are higher than private costs, as reflected in the *social* MC curve. To maximize social welfare, we would equate social marginal costs with marginal revenue (point *A* in Figure 9.4) and thus produce at the output level q_s. The private profit maximizer, however, equates *private* marginal costs and marginal revenue (point *B*) and thus ends up producing at q_p, making more profit but also causing more pollution. As a general rule, *if pollution costs are external, firms will produce too much of a polluting good.*

Consumption Decisions

A divergence between private and social costs can also be observed in many consumption activities. A consumer tends to maximize personal welfare. We buy and use more of those goods and services that yield the highest satisfaction (marginal utility) per dollar expended. By implication (and the law of demand), we tend to use more of a product if we can get it at a discount—that is, pay less than the full price. Unfortunately, the "discount" often takes the form of an external cost imposed on neighbors and friends.

Automobile driving illustrates the problem. The amount of driving one

**FIGURE 9.4
Market Failure**

Social costs exceed private costs by the amount of external costs (externalities). Production decisions based on private costs alone will lead us to point *B*, where private MC = MR. At point *B*, the rate of output is q_p.

To maximize social welfare, we equate *social* MC and MR, as at point *A*. Only q_s of output is socially desirable. The failure of the market to convey the full costs of production keeps us from attaining this outcome.

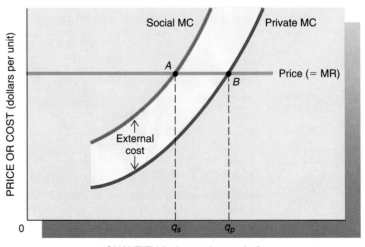

does is influenced by the price of a car and the marginal costs of driving it. As was convincingly illustrated during the energy crisis of the 1970s, people buy smaller cars and drive less when the attendant marginal costs (for instance, gasoline prices) increase substantially. But automobile use involves not only *private costs* but *external costs* as well. Auto emissions (carbon monoxide, hydrocarbons, and nitrogen oxides) are an all-too-evident example. In effect, automobile drivers have been able to use a valued resource, clean air, at no cost to themselves. Naturally, they tended to use more of that resource than they otherwise would, thus lowering their private marginal costs and driving and polluting more. Few motorists saw any personal benefit in installing exhaust-control devices, because the quality of the air they breathed would be little affected by their own efforts. Low private costs led to excessive pollution when high social costs were dictating cleaner air.

A divergence between social and private costs can be observed even in the simplest of consumer activities, such as throwing an empty soda can out the window of your car. To hang onto the soda can and later dispose of it in a trash barrel involves personal effort and thus private marginal costs. To throw it out the window not only is more exciting but effectively transfers the burden of disposal costs to someone else. Thus private costs can be distinguished from social costs. The resulting externality ends up as roadside litter.

The same kind of divergence between private and social costs helps to explain why people abandon old cars in the street rather than haul them to scrap yards. It also explains why people use vacant lots as open dumps. In all of these cases, **the polluter benefits by substituting external costs for private costs.** In other words, market incentives encourage environmental damage.

Policy Options

The failure of the market to include environmental costs in production and consumption decisions creates a basis for government intervention. Our goal in this case is to discourage production and consumption activities that impose high external costs on society. We can do this in one of two ways:

- *Alter market incentives*
- *Bypass market incentives*

Emission Fees. Insofar as market incentives are concerned, the key to environmental protection is to eliminate the divergence between private costs and social costs. The opportunity to shift some costs onto others lies at the heart of the pollution problem. If we could somehow compel producers to *internalize* all costs—pay for both private and previously external costs—the divergence would disappear, along with the incentive to pollute. Thus we have to find a way to make polluters pay for their pollution.

One possibility is to establish a system of **emission charges,** direct costs attached to the act of polluting. Suppose that we let you keep your power plant and permit you to operate it according to profit-maximizing principles. The only difference is that we no longer agree to supply you with clean air and cool water at zero cost. From now on, we will charge you for these scarce resources. We might, say, charge you 2 cents for every gram of noxious emission you discharge into the air. In addition we might charge you

> **emission charge:** A fee imposed on polluters, based on the quantity of pollution.

3 cents for every gallon of water you use, heat, and discharge back into the river.

Confronted with such emission charges, you would have to alter your production decision. ***An emission charge increases private marginal cost and thus encourages lower output.*** Figure 9.5 illustrates this effect.

Once an emission fee is in place, a producer may also reevaluate the production process. Consider again the choice of fuels to be used in our fictional power plant. We earlier chose high-sulfur coal, for the very good reason that it was the cheapest fuel available. Now, however, there is an additional cost attached to burning such fuel, in the form of an emission charge on noxious pollutants. This higher marginal cost might prompt a switch to less polluting fuels. The actual response of producers will depend on the relative costs involved. If emission charges are too low, it may be more profitable to continue burning and polluting with high-sulfur coal and simply pay a nominal fee. This is a simple pricing problem. The government could set the emission price higher, prompting the desired behavioral responses.

What works on producers will also sway consumers. Surely you've heard of deposits on returnable bottles. At one time the deposits were imposed by the beverage producer to encourage you to bring the bottle back so it could be used again. But producers discovered that such deposits discouraged sales and yielded very little cost savings. The economics of returnable bottles were further undermined by the advent of metal cans and, later, plastic bottles. Thirty years ago, virtually all soft drinks and most beer came in returnable bottles. Today, returnable bottles are rarely used. One result is the inclusion of over 30 billion bottles and 60 billion cans in our solid-waste-disposal problem.

We could reduce this solid-waste problem by imposing a deposit on all beverage containers. This would internalize pollution costs for the consumer and render the throwing of a soda can out the window equivalent to throwing away money. Some people would still find the thrill worthwhile, but they would be followed around by others who attached more value to money. The state of Oregon imposed a 5-cent deposit on beverage containers in 1972 and soon thereafter discovered that beverage-container

FIGURE 9.5
Emission Fees

Emission charges can be used to close the gap between marginal social costs and marginal private costs. Faced with an emission charge of t, a private producer will reduce output from q_0 to q_1. Emission charges may also induce different investment decisions.

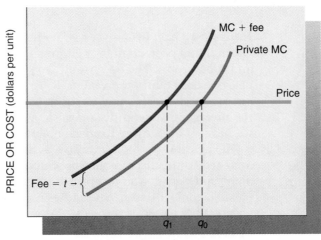

litter in Oregon declined by 81 percent! Since that time, other states and communities have also imposed mandatory deposits as a mechanism for eliminating the distinction between social and private costs.

Regulation. Although emission fees can be used to alter market outcomes, the incentive approach is not the only policy option. Direct regulation has been a frequently used alternative. The federal government began regulating auto emissions in 1968 and got tough under the provisions of the Clean Air Act of 1970. The act required auto manufacturers to reduce hydrocarbon, carbon monoxide, and nitrogen oxide emissions by 90 percent within six years of the act's passage. Although the timetable for reducing pollutants was later extended, the act did stimulate auto manufacturers to reduce auto emissions dramatically: by 1990, new cars were emitting only 4 percent as much pollution as 1970 models.

Regulatory standards may specify not only the required reduction in emissions, but also the *process* by which those reductions are to be achieved. Clean air legislation mandated not only fewer auto emissions but also specific processes (e.g., catalytic converters, lead-free gasoline) for attaining them. Specific processes and technologies are also required for toxic waste disposal and water treatment. Laws requiring the sorting and recycling of trash (see Headline) are also examples of process regulation.

Although such hands-on regulation can be effective, this policy option also entails risks. By requiring all market participants to follow specific rules, the regulations may impose excessive costs on some activities and too low a constraint on others. Some communities may not need the level of sewage treatment the federal government prescribes. Individual households may not generate enough trash to make sorting and separate pickups economically sound. Some producers may have better or cheaper ways of attaining environmental standards. **Excessive process regulation may raise the costs of environmental protection** and discourage cost-saving innovation. There is also the risk of regulated processes becoming entrenched long after they are obsolete.

Regulation also entails compliance and enforcement costs. Government agencies must monitor market behavior to assure that regulations are ad-

HEADLINE

BYPASSING THE MARKET

Los Angeles Requires Recycling, Trash Separation

LOS ANGELES—The City Council has unanimously approved mandatory trash separation and recycling in a $160 million program to halve the amount of garbage deposited in the city's rapidly filling landfills.

While about 1,000 U.S. cities, including Washington, D.C., have some kind of recycling program, the Los An-

geles effort will be among the nation's largest, along with those in New York City and statewide in New Jersey.

The plan will require all 720,000 single-family households in the city to separate glass and plastic bottles, aluminum cans and newspaper into different containers for collection. The city eventually will sell reusable materials to recyclers.

The Washington Post, December 22, 1989, p. A14. © 1989, The Washington Post. Reprinted with permission.

hered to. Market participants must learn about the regulations, implement them, and usually complete some compliance paperwork. All of these activities require scarce resources (labor) that could be used to produce other goods and services. Accordingly, regulations must not only be well designed, but also be beneficial enough to justify their opportunity costs.

MARKET POWER

In the case of both public goods and externalities, the market fails to achieve the optimal mix of output because the price signal is flawed. The price consumers are willing and able to pay for a specific good does not reflect all the benefits or cost of producing that good.

The market may fail, however, even when the price signals are accurate. The *response* to price signals, rather than the signals themselves, may be flawed.

Restricted Supply

Market power is often the cause of a flawed response. Suppose there were only one airline company in the world. This single seller of airline travel would be a monopoly—that is, the only producer in that industry. As a monopolist, the airline could charge extremely high prices without worrying that travelers would flock to a competing airline. At the same time, the high prices paid by consumers would express the importance of that service to society. Ideally, such prices would act as a signal to producers to build and fly more planes—to change the mix of output. But a monopolist does not have to cater to every consumer whim. It can limit airline travel and thus obstruct our efforts to achieve an optimal mix of output.

> **market power:** The ability to alter the market price of a good or service.

Monopoly is the most severe form of **market power.** More generally, market power refers to any situation where a single producer or consumer has the ability to alter the market price of a specific product. If the publisher (McGraw-Hill) charges a high price for this book, you will have to pay the tab. McGraw-Hill has market power because there are relatively few economics textbooks and your professor has required you to use this one. You don't have power in the textbook market because your decision to buy or not will not alter the market price of this text. You are only one of the million students who are taking an introductory economics course this year.

The market power McGraw-Hill possesses is derived from the copyright on this text. No matter how profitable textbook sales might be, no one else is permitted to produce or sell this particular text. Patents are another common source of market power, because they also preclude others from making or selling a specific product. Market power may also result from control of resources, restrictive production agreements, or efficiencies of large-scale production.

Whatever the source of market power, the direct consequence is that one or more producers attain discretionary power over the market's response to price signals. They may use that discretion to enrich themselves rather than to move the economy toward the optimal mix of output. In this case, the market will again fail to deliver the most desired goods and services.

Antitrust Policy

The most obvious course for government intervention in this case is to prevent or dismantle concentrations of market power. That is the essential pur-

antitrust: Government intervention to alter market structure or prevent abuse of market power.

pose of **antitrust** policy. The legal foundations of federal antitrust activity are contained in three laws:

- **The Sherman Act (1890).** The Sherman Act prohibits "conspiracies in restraint of trade," including mergers, contracts, or acquisitions that threaten to monopolize an industry. Firms that violate the Sherman Act are subject to fines of up to $1 million, and their executives may be subject to imprisonment. In addition, consumers who are damaged—for example, via high prices—by a "conspiracy in restraint of trade" may recover treble damages. With this act as its principal "trust-busting" weapon, the U.S. Department of Justice has blocked attempted mergers and acquisitions, forced changes in price or output behavior, required large companies to sell some of their assets, and even sent corporate executives to jail for "conspiracies in restraint of trade."
- **The Clayton Act (1914).** The Clayton Act of 1914 was passed to outlaw specific antitrust behavior not covered by the Sherman Act. The principal aim of the act was to prevent the development of monopolies. To this end the Clayton Act prohibits price discrimination, exclusive dealing agreements, certain types of mergers, and interlocking boards of directors among competing firms.
- **The Federal Trade Commission Act (1914).** The increased antitrust responsibilities of the federal government created the need for an agency that could study industry structures and behavior so as to identify anticompetitive practices. The Federal Trade Commission was created for this purpose in 1914.

In the early 1900s this antitrust legislation was used to break up the monopolies that dominated the steel and tobacco industries. In the 1980s the same legislation was used to dismantle AT&T's near monopoly of telephone service. The court forced AT&T to sell off its local telephone service companies (the "Baby Bells") and allow competitors more access to long-distance service. The resulting competition pushed prices down and spawned a new wave of telephone technology and services.

Although antitrust policy has produced some impressive results, its potential is limited. There are over 20 million businesses in the United States and the "trust busters" can watch only so many. Even when they decide to take action, there is no guarantee of success. In 1969, for example, the U.S. Justice Department filed suit against IBM, accusing it of unfairly dominating the mainframe computer business. Over the next thirteen years, IBM submitted *66 million* pages of documents in its own defense. Finally, in 1982, the Justice Department dropped the case, having concluded that IBM's size and behavior did not preclude effective competition in the computer industry. By then, all of the government's lawyers who had originally prepared the IBM case had left the Justice Department.

Even with unlimited resources, antitrust policy entails difficult decisions. What, for example, constitutes a "monopoly" in the real world? Must a company produce 100 percent of a particular good to be a threat to consumer welfare? How about 99 percent? Or even 75 percent?

And what specific monopolistic practices should be prohibited? Should we be looking for specific evidence of "price gouging"? Or should we focus on barriers to entry and unfair market practices?

These kinds of questions determine how and when antitrust laws will be enforced. Just the threat of enforcement, however, may help push market outcomes in the desired direction.

EQUITY

Public goods, externalities, and market power all cause resource misallocations. Where these phenomena exist, the market mechanism will fail to produce the optimal mix of output.

Beyond the question of WHAT to produce, we are also concerned about FOR WHOM output is to be produced. Is the distribution of goods and services generated by the marketplace "fair"? If the market fails to reflect our notions of equity, government intervention may be needed to redistribute income.

In general, the market mechanism tends to answer the basic question of FOR WHOM to produce by distributing a larger share of total output to those with the most income. Although this result may be efficient, it is not necessarily equitable. Individuals who are aged or disabled, for example, may be unable to earn much income yet still be regarded as "worthy" recipients of goods and services. In such cases, we may want to change the market's answer to the basic question of FOR WHOM goods are produced. Instead of relying exclusively on the market mechanism to determine people's income, we provide income transfers. **Transfer payments** are income payments for which no goods or services are exchanged. They are used to bolster the incomes of those for whom the market itself provides too little.

transfer payments: Payments to individuals for which no current goods or services are exchanged, e.g., Social Security, welfare, unemployment benefits.

To some extent, government intervention in the distribution of income can also be explained by the theory of public goods. If the public sector did not provide help to the aged, the disabled, the unemployed, and the needy, what would they do? Some might find a little extra work, but many would starve, even die. Others would resort to private solicitations or criminal activities to fend off hunger or death. This would mean more homeless people and muggers on the streets. In nearly all cases, the general public would be beset with much of the burden and consequences of poverty and disability, either directly or through pangs of conscience. Because the sight or knowledge of hungry or sick neighbors is something most people seek to avoid, the elimination of poverty creates some satisfaction for a great many people.

But even if the elimination of poverty were a common objective, it could be accomplished by individual action. If I contributed heavily to the needy, then you and I would both be relieved of the burden of the poor. We could both walk the streets with less fear and better consciences. Hence you could benefit from my expenditure, just as was possible in the case of national defense. In this sense, the relief of misery is a *public* good. Were I the only taxpayer to benefit substantially from the reduction of poverty, then charity would be a private affair. As long as income support substantially benefits the public at large, then income redistribution is a *public* good, for which public funding is appropriate. This is the *economic* rationale for public income-redistribution activities. To this rationale one can add such moral arguments as seem appropriate.

MACRO INSTABILITY

The micro failures of the marketplace imply that we are at the wrong point on the production-possibilities curve or inequitably distributing the output produced. There is another basic question we have swept under the rug, however. How do we get to the production-possibilities curve in the first place? To reach the curve, we must utilize all available resources and technology. Can we be confident that the invisible hand of the marketplace will use all of our resources? Or will some people remain unemployed—that is, willing to work, but unable to find a job?

And what about prices? Price signals are a critical feature of the market mechanism. But the validity of those signals depends on some stable measure of value. What good is a doubling of salary when the price of everything you buy doubles as well? Generally, rising prices will enrich people who own property and impoverish people who rent. That is why we strive to avoid inflation—a situation where the *average* price level is increasing.

Historically, the marketplace has been wracked with bouts of both unemployment and inflation. These experiences have prompted calls for government intervention at the macro level. ***The goal of macro intervention is to foster economic growth—to get us on the production-possibilities curve (full employment), to maintain a stable price level (price stability), and increase our capacity to produce (growth).*** The means for achieving this goal are examined in the macro section of this course.

POLICY PERSPECTIVES

A New "Contract for America"?

The potential micro and macro failures of the marketplace provide specific justifications for government intervention. The question then turns to how well the activities of the public sector correspond to these implied mandates. Just because some intervention is justified doesn't mean that any and all government activity is desirable. Should there be some limits to the size and scope of government intervention? Is the public sector now too big?

These questions took on a new urgency in the 1994 congressional elections. President Clinton was widely regarded as a champion of big government. He wanted the government to play a larger role in the provision of health care, skills training, environmental protection, income security, and business investment. To pay for this expansion of government activity, President Clinton convinced the Democrat-controlled Congress to raise taxes and reduce military spending.

In 1994, the Republican party made the size and scope of government intervention a central campaign issue. They argued that the government had gone too far in regulating the economy—that **government failure,** not market failure, was the principal problem. They offered a "Contract with America" that promised less government intervention in the WHAT, HOW, and FOR WHOM questions.

The Republican electoral victory in 1994 seemed to reflect a widespread perception that the government had, in fact, gone too far in regulating the economy. Within weeks of the election, President Clinton responded by dramatically altering his policy blueprint. He proposed substantial reductions in major federal agencies [e.g., Departments of Transportation, Housing and Urban Development (HUD), Energy]. He also proposed to reverse earlier tax increases by offering tax cuts for middle-class families with children and education expenses. These proposals would tend to shrink the size of the public sector and expand the size of the private sector.

government failure: Government intervention that fails to improve economic outcomes.

Opportunity Cost

> **opportunity cost:** The most desired goods or services that are forgone in order to obtain something else.

At the heart of any decision to expand or contract the public sector is a perception of how well the government is performing. If government agencies are doing a poor job of providing desired services, there is clear justification for trimming their sails. Even when they are doing a *good* job, however, there still may be a case for reducing their size and scope. The core economic issue is not whether the government is using scarce resources well but whether it is using resources *better* than the private sector would.

The key concept here is **opportunity cost.** The more police officers or schoolteachers employed by the public sector, the fewer workers available to private producers and consumers. Similarly, the more typewriters, pencils, and paper consumed by government agencies, the fewer accessible to individuals and private companies. In other words, *everything the public sector does involves an opportunity cost.*

When assessing government's role in the economy, then, *we must consider not only what governments do but also what we give up to allow them to do it.* The theory of public goods tells us only what activities are appropriate for government, not the proper *level* of such activity. National defense is clearly a proper function of the public sector. Not so clear, however, is how much government should spend on tanks and aircraft carriers. The same is true of environmental protection or law enforcement.

The concept of opportunity costs puts a new perspective on the whole question of government size. Before we can decide how big is "too big," we must decide what we are willing to give up to support the public sector. A military force of 2 million men and women is "too big" from an economic perspective only if we value the forgone private production and consumption more highly than we value added strength of our defenses. The government has gone "too far" if the highway it builds is less desired than the park and homes it implicitly replaced. In these and all cases, the assessment of bigness must come back to a comparison of what is given up with what is received. The assessment of government failure thus comes back to points on the production-possibilities curve. Has the government moved us closer to the optimal mix of output or not?

This is a tough question to answer in the abstract. We can, however, use the concept of opportunity cost to assess the effectiveness of specific government interventions. From this perspective, *additional public-sector activity is desirable only if the benefits from that activity exceed its opportunity costs.* In other words, we compare the benefits of a public project to the value of the private goods given up to produce it. By performing this calculation repeatedly along the perimeter of the production-possibilities curve, we could locate the optimal mix of output—the point at which no further increase in public-sector spending activity is desirable.

This same principle can be used to decide *which* goods to produce within the public sector. A public project is desirable only to the extent that it promises to yield some benefits (or utility). But all public projects involve some costs. Hence a project should be pursued only if it can deliver a satisfactory *ratio* of benefits to costs. Otherwise we would not be making very good use of our limited resources. In general, we would want to pursue those projects with the highest benefit-cost ratio. They will maximize the amount of utility we get from the resources we devote to the public sector.

Although the principles of cost-benefit analysis are simple enough, they are deceptive. How are we to measure the potential benefits of improved police services, for example? Should we estimate the number of robberies and murders prevented, calculate the worth of each, and add up the benefits? And how are we supposed to calculate the worth of a saved life? By a person's earnings? Value of assets? Number of friends? And what about the increased sense of security people have when they know the police are patrolling in their neighborhood? Should this be included in the benefit calculation? Some people will attach great value to this service; others will attach little. Whose values should we use?

When we are dealing with (private) market goods and services, we can gauge the benefits of production by the amount of money consumers are willing to pay for some particular output. In the case of public goods, however, we must make crude and highly subjective estimates of the benefits yielded by a particular output. Accordingly, cost-benefit analyses are valuable only to the extent that they are based on broadly accepted perceptions of benefits (or costs). In practice, consensus on the value of benefits is hard to reach, and locating the optimal mix of output entails political as well as economic judgments.

The same problems arise in evaluating the government's efforts to redistribute incomes. Government transfer payments now go to retired workers, disabled persons, veterans, farmers, sick people, students, pregnant women, unemployed persons, poor people, and a long list of other recipients. To pay for all these transfers, the government must raise tax revenues. With so many people paying taxes and receiving transfer payments, the net effects on the distribution of income are not easy to figure out. Yet we cannot determine whether this government intervention is "worth it" until we know how the FOR WHOM answer was changed and what the tax-and-transfer effort cost us. Here again, there is at least a possibility of government failure.

SUMMARY

- Government intervention in the marketplace is justified by a variety of market failures.
- The micro failures of the market originate in public goods, externalities, market power, and an inequitable distribution of income. These flaws deter the market from achieving the optimal mix of output or distribution of income.
- Public goods are those that cannot be consumed exclusively; they are jointly consumed regardless of who pays. Because everyone seeks a free ride, no one demands public goods in the marketplace.
- Externalities are costs (or benefits) of a market transaction borne by a third party. Externalities create a divergence between social and private costs, causing suboptimal market outcomes.
- Market power enables a producer to thwart market signals and maintain a suboptimal mix of output. Antitrust policy seeks to prevent or restrict market power.
- The market-generated distribution of income may be regarded as unfair. This equity concern may prompt the government to intervene with taxes and transfer payments.
- The macro failures of the marketplace are reflected in unemployment and inflation. Government intervention is intended to achieve full employment and price stability.
- Government failure occurs when intervention moves us away from rather than toward the optimal mix of output (or income). Failure may result

from outright waste (operational inefficiency) or from a misallocation of resources. All government activity must be evaluated in terms of its opportunity cost, that is, the *private* goods and services forgone to make resources available to the public sector.

Terms to Remember

Define the following terms:

optimal mix of output	free rider	market power
market mechanism	externalities	antitrust
market failure	social costs	transfer payments
public good	private costs	government failure
private good	emission charge	opportunity cost

Questions for Discussion

1. Why should taxpayers subsidize public colleges and universities? What benefits do they receive from someone else's education?
2. If you abhor tennis, should you be forced to pay local taxes that are used to build and maintain public tennis courts? If you don't like national defense, should you be able to withhold the part of your taxes that pays for it? What would happen if everyone followed this rationale?
3. Could local fire departments be privately operated, with services sold directly to customers? What problems would be involved in such a system?
4. Identify specific government activities that are justified by different micro failures.
5. Why would auto manufacturers resist exhaust-control devices? How would their costs, sales, and profits be affected?
6. Does anyone have an incentive to maintain auto-exhaust-control devices in good working order? How can we ensure that they will be maintained?
7. Suppose we established a $10,000 fine for water pollution. Would some companies still find that polluting was economical? Under what conditions?
8. What economic costs are imposed by mandatory sorting of trash? Are these costs justified?
9. Should we eliminate all pollution? What would such an effort cost?
10. Four companies produce virtually all breakfast cereals. How might this concentration of market power affect market outcomes? What should the government do, if anything?
11. The government now spends close to $300 billion a year on Social Security benefits. Why don't we leave it to individuals to save for their own retirement?

Problems

1. Suppose the following data represent the prices that each of three consumers is willing to pay for a good.

Quantity	Consumer A	Consumer B	Consumer C
1	$50	$40	$30
2	30	20	20
3	20	15	10

(a) Construct the market demand curve for this good.

(b) If this good were priced in the market at $40, how many units would be demanded?

(c) Now suppose that this is a public good, in the sense that all consumers receive satisfaction from the good even if only one person buys it. Construct the social demand curve for this good.

(d) Based on the social demand curve, how many units of this good are demanded by society at a price of $40?

(e) What is the evidence of market failure in this case?

2. The following cost schedule depicts the private and social costs associated with the daily production of apacum, a highly toxic fertilizer. The sales price of apacum is $18 per ton.

Output (in tons)	0	1	2	3	4	5	6	7	8
Total private cost	$5	7	13	23	37	55	77	103	133
Total social cost	$7	13	31	61	103	157	223	301	391

Using the schedule

(a) Graph the private and social marginal costs associated with apacum production.

(b) Identify the profit-maximizing private and social rates of output and associated profits.

(c) On the basis of these curves, identify the pollution fee (fine) we would have to charge per unit in order to persuade the producer to produce the socially optimal rate of output.

3. If a new home can be constructed for $75,000, what is the opportunity cost of federal defense spending, measured in terms of private housing? (Assume a defense budget of $260 billion per year.)

SECTION III

MACROECONOMICS

Macroeconomics focuses on the performance of the entire economy rather than on the behavior of individual participants (a micro concern). The central concerns of macro policy are the rate of output, the level of prices, economic growth, and our trade and payments balances with the rest of the world.

Chapter 10

The Business Cycle

In 1929, it looked as though the sun would never set on the American economy. For eight years in a row, the U.S. economy has been expanding rapidly. During the "Roaring Twenties" the typical American family drove its first car, bought its first radio, and went to the movies for the first time. With factories running at capacity, virtually anyone who wanted to work readily found a job.

Under these circumstances everyone was optimistic. In his Acceptance Address of November 1928, president-elect Herbert Hoover echoed this optimism, by declaring: "We in America today are nearer to the final triumph over poverty than ever before in the history of any land. . . . We shall soon with the help of God be in sight of the day when poverty will be banished from this nation."

The booming stock market seemed to confirm this optimistic outlook. Between 1921 and 1927, the stock market's value more than doubled, adding billions of dollars to the wealth of American households and businesses. The stock-market boom accelerated in 1927, causing stock prices to double again in less than two years. The roaring stock market made it look easy to get rich in America.

The party ended abruptly on October 24, 1929. On what came to be known as Black Thursday, the stock market crashed. In a few hours, the market value of U.S. corporations fell abruptly, in the most frenzied selling ever seen (see Headline). The next day President Hoover tried to assure America's stockholders that the economy was "on a sound and prosperous basis." But despite his assurances and the efforts of leading bankers to stem the decline, the stock market continued to plummet. The following Tuesday (October 29) the pace of selling quickened. By the end of the year, over $40 billion of wealth had vanished in the Great Crash. Rich men became paupers overnight; ordinary families lost their savings, their homes, and even their lives.

HEADLINE

THE CRASH OF 1929

Market in Panic as Stocks Are Dumped in 12,894,600 Share Day; Bankers Halt It

Effect Is Felt on the Curb and Throughout Nation—Financial District Goes Wild

The stock markets of the country tottered on the brink of panic yesterday as a prosperous people, gone suddenly hysterical with fear, attempted simultaneously to sell a record-breaking volume of securities for whatever they would bring.

The result was a financial nightmare, comparable to nothing ever before experienced in Wall Street. It rocked the financial district to its foundations, hopelessly overwhelmed its mechanical facilities, chilled its blood with terror.

In a society built largely on confidence, with real wealth expressed more or less inaccurately by pieces of paper, the entire fabric of economic stability threatened to come toppling down.

Into the frantic hands of a thousand brokers on the floor of the New York Stock Exchange poured the selling orders of the world. It was sell, sell, sell—hour after desperate hour until 1:30 P.M.

—Laurence Stern

The World, October 25, 1929.

The devastation was not confined to Wall Street. The financial flames engulfed the farms, the banks, and industry. Between 1930 and 1935, millions of rural families lost their farms. Automobile production fell from 4.5 million cars in 1929 to only 1.1 million in 1932. So many banks were forced to close that newly elected President Roosevelt had to declare a "bank holiday" in March 1933 to stem the outflow of cash to anxious depositors.

Throughout these years, the ranks of the unemployed continued to swell. In October 1929, only 3 percent of the work force was unemployed. A year later over 9 percent of the work force was unemployed, and millions of additional workers were getting by on lower wages and shorter hours. Still, things got worse. By 1933 over one-fourth of the labor force was unable to find work. People slept in the streets, scavenged for food, and sold apples on Wall Street.

The Great Depression seemed to last forever. In 1933 President Roosevelt lamented that one-third of the nation was ill-clothed, ill-housed, and ill-fed. Thousands of unemployed workers marched to the Capitol to demand jobs and aid. In 1938, nine years after Black Thursday, nearly 20 percent of the work force was still unemployed.

The Great Depression shook not only the foundations of the world economy but also the self-confidence of the economics profession. No one had predicted the depression and few could explain it. How could the economy perform so poorly for so long? What could the government do to prevent such a catastrophe? Suddenly, there were more questions than answers.

macroeconomics: The study of aggregate economic behavior, of the economy as a whole.

The scramble for answers became the springboard for modern **macroeconomics,** the study of aggregate economic behavior. The basic purpose of macroeconomic theory is to *explain* the **business cycle**—to identify the forces that cause the overall economy to expand or contract. Macro *policy* tries to *control* the business cycle, using the insights of macro theory.

business cycle: Alternating periods of economic growth and contraction.

In this chapter we focus on the nature of the business cycle and the related problems of unemployment and inflation. Our goal is to acquire a sense of why the business cycle is so feared. To address these concerns we need to know

- What are business cycles?
- What damage does unemployment cause?
- Who is hurt by inflation?

As we answer these questions, we will get a sense of why people worry so much about the macro economy and why they demand that "Washington" do something about it.

HISTORICAL CYCLES

The central concern of macroeconomics is the business cycle—that is, alternating periods of economic expansion and contraction. These upswings and downswings of the economy are gauged in terms of changes in total output. An economic upswing, or expansion, refers to an increase in the volume of goods and services produced. An economic downswing, or contraction, occurs when the total volume of production declines.

Figure 10.1 depicts the basic features of a business cycle. The cycle looks like a roller coaster, climbing steeply, then dropping from its peak. Once the trough is reached, the upswing starts again.

In reality, business cycles are not as regular or as predictable as Figure 10.1 suggests. The U.S. economy has experienced recurrent upswings and downswings, but of widely varying length, intensity, and frequency.

Real GDP

real GDP: The inflation-adjusted value of GDP; the value of output measured in constant prices.

Actual business cycles are measured by changes in **real GDP**—that is, the market value of all the goods and services produced within a nation's borders, with market values measured in *constant* prices (the prices of a specific base year). From one year to the next, all prices might double, thus doubling the *value* of output. But the *volume* (quantity) of output is what determines how well we are fed, clothed, and housed. The physical volume of output also determines how many jobs will be available. Accordingly, we distin-

FIGURE 10.1
The Business Cycle

The model business cycle resembles a roller coaster. Output first climbs to a peak, then decreases. After hitting a trough, the economy recovers, with real GDP again increasing.

A central concern of macroeconomic theory is to determine whether a recurring business cycle exists, and if so, what forces cause it.

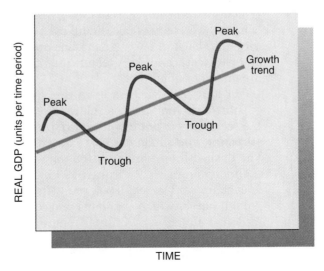

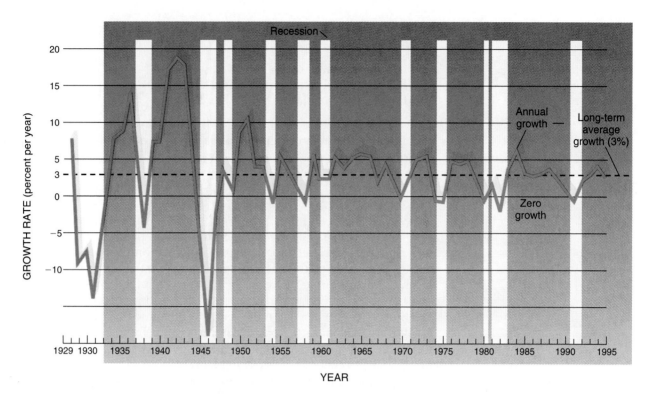

FIGURE 10.2
The Business Cycle in U.S. History

From 1929 to 1995, real GDP increased at an average rate of 3 percent a year. But annual growth rates have departed widely from that average. Years of above-average growth seem to alternate with years of sluggish growth and years in which total output actually *declines*. Such *recessions* occurred in 1980, 1981–82, and again in 1990–91.

Source: *Economic Report of the President*, 1995.

guish changes in the value of output from changes in the quantity of output. The yardstick of *real* GDP does this by valuing output at constant prices. *Changes in real GDP refer to changes in the volume (quantity) of output.*

From a distance, America's economic track record looks like a steady growth path. From 1929 to today, real GDP has more than sextupled. That is to say, we are now producing over six times as many goods and services as we did back in 1929. Americans now consume a greater variety of goods and services, and in greater quantities, than earlier generations ever dreamed possible.

Our long-term success in raising living standards is clouded by a spate of short-term macro setbacks. On closer inspection, *the growth path of the U.S. economy is not a smooth, rising trend but, instead, a series of steps, stumbles, and setbacks.* This short-run instability is evident in Figure 10.2. The dashed line represents the long-term *average* growth rate of the U.S. economy. From 1929 through 1995, the U.S. economy expanded at an average rate of 3 percent per year. Also shown in the figure is the annual growth curve, which indicates *year-to-year* variations in real GDP growth. Although annual growth rates tend to stay relatively close to the long-term average rate of 3 percent, there are significant departures. There are many economic "booms," with growth rates in excess of 5 percent. There are also several economic "busts," when the economic growth curve fell below zero and total output actually *decreased* from one year to the next.

The Great Depression

The most prolonged departure from our long-term growth path occurred during the Great Depression. Between 1929 and 1933, total U.S. output steadily declined. Real GDP fell nearly 30 percent in those four years. Industrial output declined even further, as investments in new plant and equipment virtually ceased. Economies around the world came to a grinding halt (see Headline).

The U.S. economy started to grow again in 1934, but the rate of expansion was modest. Millions of people remained out of work. In 1936–37, the situation worsened again, and total output once more declined. As a consequence, the rate of total output in 1939 was virtually identical to that in 1929. Because of continuing population growth, GDP per capita was actually *lower* in 1939 than it had been in 1929. American families had a *lower* standard of living in 1939 than they had enjoyed ten years earlier.

World War II

World War II greatly increased the demand for goods and services and ended the Great Depression. During the war years, output grew at unprecedented rates—almost 19 percent in a single year (1942). Virtually everyone was employed, either in the armed forces or in the factories. Throughout the war, our productive capacity was strained to the limit.

Recent Recessions

recession: A decline in total output (real GDP) for two or more consecutive quarters.

In the postwar years the U.S. economy resumed a pattern of alternating growth and contraction. The contracting periods are called recessions. Specifically, the term **recession** refers to a decline in real GDP that continues for at least two successive quarters. As Table 10.1 indicates, there have been ten recessions since 1944. The most severe recession occurred immediately after World War II ended, when sudden cutbacks in defense production caused sharp declines in output (−38%). That first postwar recession lasted only eight months, however, and raised the rate of unemployment to only 4.3 percent. By contrast, the recession of 1981–82 was much longer (sixteen months) and pushed the national unemployment rate

HEADLINE

WORLDWIDE LOSSES

Depression Slams World Economies

The Great Depression was not confined to the U.S. economy. Most other countries suffered substantial losses of output and employment, over a period of many years. Between 1929 and 1932, industrial production around the world fell 37 percent. The United States and Germany suffered the largest losses, while Spain and the Scandinavian countries lost only modest amounts of output. For specific countries, the decline in output is shown in the accompanying table.

Some countries escaped the ravages of the Great Depression altogether. The Soviet Union, largely insulated from Western economic structures, was in the midst of Stalin's forced industrialization drive during the

Country	Percentage Decline In Output
Chile	−22%
France	−31
Germany	−47
Great Britain	−17
Japan	− 2
Norway	− 7
Spain	−12
United States	−46

1930s. China and Japan were also relatively isolated from world trade and finance, and so suffered less damage from the depression.

TABLE 10.1
Business Slumps, 1929–92

The U.S. economy has experienced twelve business slumps since 1929. None of the post–World War II recessions has come close to the severity of the Great Depression of the 1930s. Recent slumps have averaged ten months in length (versus ten *years* for the 1930s depression).

Dates	Duration (months)	Percentage Decline in Output	Peak Unemployment Rate
Aug. '29–Mar. '33	43	53.4%	24.9%
May '37–June '38	13	32.4	20.0
Feb. '45–Oct. '45	8	38.3	4.3
Nov. '48–Oct. '49	11	9.9	7.9
July '53–May '54	10	10.0	6.1
Aug. '57–Apr. '58	8	14.3	7.5
Apr. '60–Feb. '61	10	7.2	7.1
Dec. '69–Nov. '70	11	8.1	6.1
Nov. '73–Mar. '75	16	14.7	9.0
Jan. '80–July '80	6	8.7	7.6
July '81–Nov. '82	16	12.3	10.8
July '90–Feb. '91	8	2.2	6.5

to 10.8 percent. That was the highest unemployment rate since the Great Depression of the 1930s.

From November 1982 until November 1989, the U.S. economy enjoyed an unusually long and robust expansion. In the process, nearly 20 million jobs were created and total output increased by over 30 percent. Once again, however, the economy ran out of steam. The expansion slowed in the winter of 1990 and then slid into another recession in July of that year. Yet another upswing began eight months later. Although the recovery started slowly, it picked up steam in 1993 and 1994. By 1995, economists were worried that the economy might not have enough resources available to sustain such above-average growth rates.

UNEMPLOYMENT

The most visible consequence of a recession is a decline in output. Indeed, recessions are *defined* in terms of declines in real GDP. But *people,* not just output, suffer in recessions. When output declines, *jobs* are eliminated. In the 1990–91 recession over 2 million American workers lost their jobs. Other

ROB ROGERS reprinted by permission of UFS, Inc.

would-be workers—including graduating students—had great difficulty finding jobs. These are the human dimensions of a recession (see Headline).

The Labor Force

labor force: All persons over age sixteen who are either working for pay or actively seeking paid employment.

Our concern about the human side of recession doesn't mean that we believe *everyone* should have a job. We do, however, strive to ensure that jobs are available for all individuals who *want* to work. This requires us to distinguish the general population from the smaller number of individuals who are ready and willing to work, that is, those who are in the **labor force.** The *labor force consists of everyone over the age of sixteen who is actually working plus all those who are not working but are actively seeking employment.* As Figure 10.3 shows, only about half of the population participates in the labor market. The rest of the population ("nonparticipants") are too young, in school, retired, sick or disabled, institutionalized, or attending to household needs.

Note that our definition of labor-force participation excludes most household and volunteer activities. A woman who chooses to devote her energies to household responsibilities or to unpaid charity work is not counted as part of the labor force, no matter how hard she works. Because she is neither in paid employment nor seeking such employment in the marketplace, she is regarded as outside the labor market (a "nonparticipant"). But if she decides to seek a paid job outside the home and engages in an active job search, we would say that she is "entering the labor force." Students, too, are typically out of the labor force until they leave school and actively look for work, either during summer vacations or after graduation.

unemployment rate: The proportion of the labor force that is unemployed.

The Unemployment Rate. The widely reported **unemployment rate** is based only on the job status of labor-force participants. The rate is calculated as:

$$\text{Unemployment rate} = \frac{\text{number of unemployed people}}{\text{size of the labor force}}$$

HEADLINE

UNEMPLOYMENT BENEFITS

Unemployment Benefits Not for Everyone

In 1994, nearly 8 million people collected unemployment benefits averaging $182 per week. But don't rush to the state unemployment office yet—not all unemployed people are eligible. To qualify for weekly unemployment benefits you must have worked a substantial length of time and earned some minimum amount of wages, both determined by your state. Furthermore, you must have a "good" reason for having lost your last job. Most states will not provide benefits to students (or their professors!) during summer vacations, to professional athletes in the off-season, or to individuals who quit their last jobs.

If you qualify for benefits, the amount of benefits you receive each week will depend on your previous wages. In most states the benefits are equal to about one-half of the previous weekly wage, up to a state-determined maximum. The average benefit in 1994 ranged from $118 per week in Louisiana to a high of $266 in Hawaii.

Unemployment benefits are financed by a tax on employers and can continue for as long as twenty-six weeks. During periods of high unemployment, the duration of benefit eligibility may be extended another thirteen weeks or more, as Congress did in 1991.

U.S. Bureau of Labor Statistics.

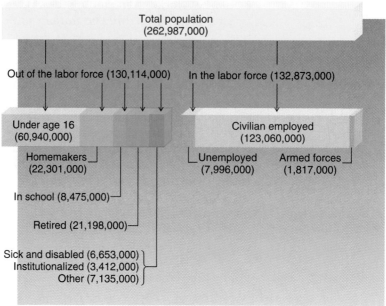

FIGURE 10.3
The Civilian Labor Force, 1994

Only half of the total U.S. population participates in the civilian labor force. The rest of the population is too young, in school, at home, retired, or otherwise unavailable.

Unemployment statistics count only those participants who are not currently working and actively seeking paid employment. Nonparticipants are neither employed nor actively seeking employment.

Source: U.S. Department of Labor.

---

unemployment: The inability of labor-force participants to find jobs.

To be counted as *unemployed,* a person must not only be jobless but also actively looking for work. A full-time student, for example, may be jobless but would not be counted as unemployed. Likewise, a full-time homemaker who is not looking for paid employment outside the home would not be included in our measure of **unemployment.**

Figure 10.3 indicates that nearly 8 million Americans were counted as unemployed in 1994. The civilian labor force (excluding the armed forces) at that time included 131 million individuals. Accordingly, the civilian unemployment *rate* was

$$\text{Civilian unemployment rate, in 1994} = \frac{8 \text{ million unemployed}}{131 \text{ million in labor force}} = 6.1\%$$

As Figure 10.4 illustrates, the unemployment rate in 1994 was below that of 1992 and 1993, and far below the experience of 1982.

The unemployment rate is based on monthly household surveys conducted by the U.S. Census Bureau. The monthly reports are watched closely as an indicator of how well the economy is performing. They are also an index of human misery. People who lose their jobs experience not only a sudden loss of income but also losses of security and self-confidence. Extended periods of unemployment may undermine families as well as finances. An unemployed person's health may suffer too. Thomas Cottle, a lecturer at Harvard Medical School, stated the case more bluntly: "I'm now convinced that unemployment is *the* killer disease in this country—responsible for wife beating, infertility, and even tooth decay." The accompanying Headline documents some of the symptoms on which such diagnoses are based; notice how death rates increase when the economy slumps.

Full Employment

The potentially disastrous consequences of prolonged unemployment would seem to merit a national commitment to guaranteeing every labor-force participant a job. This is not necessarily a desirable goal, however. There are several good reasons for pursuing *low,* but not *zero,* unemployment.

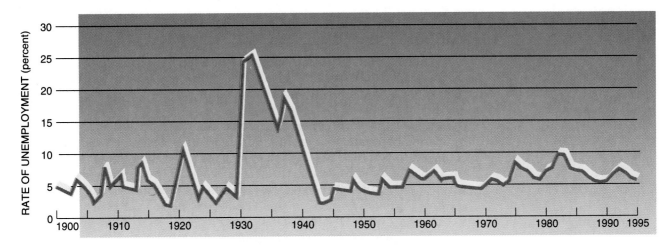

FIGURE 10.4
The Unemployment Record

Unemployment rates reached record heights during the Great Depression. The postwar record is much better than the prewar record, even though "full employment" has been infrequent.

Source: U.S. Department of Labor.

Seasonal Unemployment. Seasonal variations in employment conditions are one persistent source of unemployment. Some joblessness is virtually inevitable as long as we continue to grow crops, build houses, or go skiing at certain seasons of the year. At the end of each of these "seasons," thousands of workers must go searching for new jobs, experiencing some seasonal unemployment in the process.

HEADLINE

SOCIAL COSTS

Recession's Cost: Lives

The economy may be killing us.

A study out today says a poor economy in 30 selected cities is responsible for:

- 6.7% more murders—730 a year.
- 3.1% more deaths from stroke—1,386 annually.
- 5.6% more fatal heart disease—17,654 a year.

Another report blames the recession for 1,170 more suicides in the USA—up 3.9%.

The middle class was hurting before the recession, says University of Utah economist Mary Merva.

"We were already pushed to the limit," says Merva, who co-authored a study of unemployment in 30 big cities with 80 million people from 1976 to 1990.

"This could be the straw that breaks our back."

The study found that a 1 percentage point rise in unemployment meant more crime:

- Violent, up 3.4%.
- Non-violent, up 2.4%.

"Stress can be directed inward, like smoking, drinking or having higher blood pressure," Merva says, "or outward like beating your wife, abusing your child."

Johns Hopkins University economist Harvey Brenner, author of a similar report, says a troubled economy breeds a sick society.

"Health and social well-being of the country is directly affected by the behavior of the economy," he says.

"When national economic decisions are made, health concerns should have a seat at the table."

—Robert Davis

USA Today, October 16, 1992, p. A1. Copyright 1992, USA TODAY. Reprinted with permission.

Seasonal fluctuations also arise on the supply side of the labor market. Teenage unemployment rates, for example, rise sharply in the summer as students look for temporary jobs. To avoid such unemployment completely, we would either have to keep everyone in school or ensure that all students went immediately from the classroom to the workroom. Neither alternative is likely, much less desirable.

Frictional Unemployment. There are other reasons for accepting a certain amount of unemployment. Many workers have sound financial or personal reasons for leaving one job to look for another. In the process of moving from one job to another, a person may well miss a few days or even weeks of work without any serious personal or social consequences. On the contrary, people who spend more time looking for work may find *better* jobs. If they do find higher-paying jobs as a result of more extensive job searching, they will be better off. The economy will also benefit if they end up in more productive jobs.

The same is true of students first entering the labor market. It is not likely that you will find a job the moment you leave school. Nor should you take any job just because it's available. If you spend some time looking for work, you are more likely to find a job you like. The job-search period gives you an opportunity to find out what kinds of jobs are available, what skills they require, and what they pay. Accordingly, a brief period of job search for persons entering the labor market may benefit both the individual involved and the larger economy. The unemployment associated with these kinds of job search is referred to as *frictional* unemployment.

Structural Unemployment. For many job seekers, the period between jobs may drag on for months or even years because they do not have the skills that employers require. In the early 1980s, the steel and auto industries "downsized," eliminating over half a million jobs. The displaced workers had years of work experience. But their specific skills were no longer in demand. They were *structurally* unemployed. The same kind of structural displacement hit the defense industry in the 1990s. Cutbacks in national defense spending forced weapons manufacturers, aerospace firms, and electronics companies to reduce output and lay off thousands of workers. The displaced workers soon discovered that their highly developed skills were not immediately applicable in nondefense industries.

Teenagers—especially minority youth in inner cities—suffer similar structural problems. They simply don't have the work skills that today's jobs require. When such structural unemployment exists, more job creation alone won't necessarily reduce unemployment. On the contrary, more job demand might simply push wages higher for workers already employed.

Cyclical Unemployment. There are still other forms of unemployment. Of special significance is *cyclical* unemployment—joblessness that occurs when there are simply not enough jobs to go around. Cyclical unemployment exists when the number of workers demanded falls short of the number of persons in the labor force. This is not a case of mobility between jobs (frictional unemployment) or even of job seekers' skills (structural unemployment). Rather, it is simply an inadequate level of demand for goods and services and thus for labor.

The Great Depression is the most striking example of cyclical unemployment. The dramatic increase in unemployment rates that began in 1930 (see Figure 10.4) was not due to any increase in "friction" or sudden decline in workers' skills. Instead, the high rates of unemployment that persisted for a *decade* were due to a sudden decline in the market demand for goods and services. How do we know? Just notice what happened to our unemployment rate when the demand for military goods and services increased in 1941!

The Policy Goal. In later chapters we will examine the causes of cyclical unemployment and explore some potential policy responses. At this point, however, we are just establishing some perspective on the goal of full employment. In general, we can say that our goal is to avoid as much cyclical and structural unemployment as possible. We are also concerned about inflation, however. This requires us to leave a little slack in the economy to absorb price pressures. This implies that we are willing to accept some cyclical and structural unemployment. But how much? In practice, an unemployment rate of between 4 and 6 percent has been viewed as an acceptable compromise. In 1990, the Bush administration decided that 5 percent unemployment was a reasonable approximation to **full employment.** The economy approached that goal in early 1990, but unemployment rates then rose when the economy slipped into the 1990–91 recession. After rising to a peak of 7.6 percent in June 1992, the unemployment rate again headed south. When the unemployment rate got below 5.5 percent, President Clinton's advisers concluded that the economy was again approaching "full employment."

> **full employment:** The lowest rate of unemployment compatible with price stability; variously estimated at between 4 and 6 percent unemployment.

INFLATION

What worries presidential advisers when unemployment rates decline is the threat of inflation. When the economy expands too fast, prices start rising. The ensuing inflation pinches family pocketbooks, upsets financial markets, and ignites a storm of political protest. Runaway inflations have crushed whole economies and toppled governments. In Germany, prices rose more than twenty-five-fold in only one month during the *hyperinflation* of 1922–23. As the accompanying Headline describes, those runaway prices forced people to change their market behavior radically. After the Soviet Union collapsed in 1989, Russia also experienced price increases that exceeded 2,000 percent a year. Such uncontrolled inflation sent consumers scrambling for goods that became increasingly hard to find at "reasonable" prices. To avoid that kind of economic disruption, every American president since Franklin Roosevelt has expressed a determination to keep prices from rising.

Relative vs. Average Prices

> **inflation:** An increase in the average level of prices of goods and services.

Although most people worry about inflation, few understand it. Most people associate **inflation** with price increases on specific goods and services. The economy is not necessarily experiencing an inflation, however, every time the price of a cup of coffee goes up. We must be careful to distinguish the phenomenon of inflation from price increases for specific goods. *Inflation is an increase in the average level of prices, not a change in any specific price.*

Suppose you wanted to know the average price of fruit in the supermarket. Surely you would not have much success in seeking out an aver-

HEADLINE

HYPERINFLATION

Inflation and the Weimar Republic

At the beginning of 1921 in Germany, the cost-of-living index was 18 times higher than its 1913 prewar base, while wholesale prices had mushroomed by 4,400%. Neither of these increases are negligible, but inflation and war have always been bedfellows. Normally, however, war ends and inflation recedes. By the end of 1921, it seemed that way; prices rose more modestly. Then, in 1922, inflation erupted.

Zenith of German Hyperinflation

Wholesale prices rose fortyfold, an increase nearly as large as during the prior eight years, while retail prices rose even more rapidly. The hyperinflation reached its zenith during 1923. Between May and June 1923, consumer prices more than quadrupled; between July and August, they rose more than 15 times; in the next month, over 25 times; and between September and October, by ten times the previous month's increase.

The German economy was thoroughly disrupted. Businessmen soon discovered the impossibility of rational economic planning. Profits fell as employees demanded frequent wage adjustments. Workers were often paid daily and sometimes two or three times a day, so that they could buy goods in the morning before the inevitable afternoon price increase. The work ethic suffered; wage earners were both more reluctant to work

and less devoted to their jobs. Bankers were on the phone hour after hour, quoting the value of the mark in dollars, as calls continuously came in from merchants who needed the exchange rate to adjust their mark prices.

In an age that preceded the credit card, businessmen traveling around the country found themselves borrowing funds from their customers each stage of the way. The cash they'd allocated for the entire trip barely sufficed to pay the way to the next stop. Speculation began to dominate production.

As a result of the decline in profitability, in the ability to plan ahead, and the concern with speculation rather than production, unemployment rose, increasing by 600% between Sept. 1 and Dec. 15, 1923. And, as the hyperinflation intensified, people found goods unobtainable.

Hyperinflation crushed the middle class. Those thrifty Germans who had placed their savings in corporate or government bonds saw their lifetime efforts come to naught. Debtors sought out creditors to pay them in valueless currency. The debts of German government and industry disappeared. Farmers, too, profited, for, like farmers elsewhere, they were debtors. Nevertheless, the hyperinflation left a traumatic imprint on the German people, a legacy which colors their governmental policy to this day.

—Jonas Prager

age fruit—nobody would be quite sure what you had in mind. You might have some success, however, if you sought out the prices of apples, oranges, cherries, and peaches. Knowing the price of each kind of fruit, you could then compute the average price of fruit. The resultant figure would not refer to any particular product but would convey a sense of how much a typical basket of fruit might cost. By repeating these calculations every day, you could then determine whether fruit prices, *on average*, were changing. On occasion, you might even notice that apple prices rose while orange prices fell, leaving the *average* price of fruit unchanged.

The same kinds of calculations are made to measure inflation in the entire economy. We first determine the average price of all output—the average price level—then look for changes in that average. A rise in the average price level is referred to as inflation.

The average price level may fall as well as rise. A decline in average prices—a **deflation**—occurs when price decreases on some goods and services outweigh price increases on all others. Although we have not experienced any general deflation since 1940, general price declines were frequent in earlier periods.

deflation: A decrease in the average level of prices of goods and services.

relative price: The price of one good in comparison with the price of other goods.

Because inflation and deflation are measured in terms of average price levels, it is possible for individual prices to rise or fall continuously without changing the average price level. We already noted, for example, that the price of apples can rise without increasing the average price of fruit, so long as the price of some other fruit (e.g., oranges) falls. In such circumstances, **relative prices** are changing, but not average prices. An increase in the relative price of apples, for example, simply means that apples have become more expensive in comparison with other fruits (or any other goods or services).

Changes in relative prices may occur in a period of stable average prices, or in periods of inflation or deflation. In fact, in an economy as vast as ours—where literally millions of goods and services are exchanged in the factor and product markets—relative prices are always changing. Indeed, relative price changes are an essential ingredient of the market mechanism. If the relative price of apples increases, that is a signal to farmers that they should grow more apples and less of other fruits.

A general inflation—an increase in the *average* price level—does not perform this same market function. If all prices rise at the same rate, price increases for specific goods are of little value as market signals. In less extreme cases, when most but not all prices are rising, changes in relative prices do occur but are not so immediately apparent.

Redistributions

The distinction between relative and average prices helps us determine who is hurt by inflation—and who is helped. Popular opinion notwithstanding, it is simply not true that everyone is worse off when prices rise. ***Although inflation makes some people worse off, it makes other people better off.*** Some people even get rich when prices rise! These redistributions occur because people buy different combinations of goods and services, own different assets, and sell distinct goods or services (including labor). The impact of inflation on individuals, therefore, depends on how the prices of the goods and services each person buys or sells actually change. In this sense, ***inflation acts just like a tax, taking income or wealth from some people and giving it to others.*** This "tax" is levied through changes in prices, changes in incomes, and changes in wealth.

Price Effects. Price changes are the most familiar of inflation's pains. If you have been paying tuition, you know how the pain feels. In the last few years the average cost of tuition has increased rapidly. In 1975, the average tuition at public colleges and universities was $400 per year. In 1991, in-state tuition was over $2,000 (see Headline). At private universities, tuition has increased eightfold in the last ten years, to over $12,000. You don't need a whole course in economics to figure out the implications of these tuition hikes. To stay in college, you (or your parents) must forgo increasing amounts of other goods and services. You end up being worse off, since you cannot buy as many goods and services as you were able to buy before tuition went up.

nominal income: The amount of money income received in a given time period, measured in current dollars.

The effect of tuition increases on your economic welfare is reflected in the distinction between nominal income and real income. **Nominal income** is the amount of money you receive in a particular time period; it is measured in current dollars. **Real income,** by contrast, is the purchasing power of that money, as measured by the quantity of goods and services your dollars will buy. If the number of dollars you receive every year is always the same, your *nominal income* doesn't change, but your *real income* will rise or fall with price changes.

real income: Income in constant dollars; nominal income adjusted for inflation.

HEADLINE

PRICE EFFECTS

Inflation 101

Public college tuition for state residents jumped 13.6 percent in 1991, to an average of $2,019 a year. Here's the range:

Largest increases	1991 increase	Average tuition
N.Y.	53%	$2,511
Mass.	37%	$3,359
Ore.	33%	$2,487
Calif.	28%	$1,498
Smallest increases		
La.	1%	$1,557
Ariz.	3%	$1,549
Hawaii	3%	$1,159
Ga.	4%	$1,703

U.S. News & World Report, Feb. 3, 1992, p. 63—Basic data: American Association of State Colleges and Universities. Compiled by Constance Johnson and Greg Ferguson. Copyright, Feb. 3, 1992, *U.S. News & World Report.*

Suppose you had an income of $6,000 a year while you're in school. Out of that $6,000 you must pay for your tuition, room and board, books, and everything else. The budget for your first year at school might look like this:

FIRST YEAR'S BUDGET

Nominal income	$6,000
Consumption	
Tuition	$3,000
Room and board	2,000
Books	300
Everything else	700
Total	$6,000

After paying for all your essential expenses, you have $700 to spend on clothes, entertainment, or anything else you want.

Now suppose tuition increases to $3,500 in your second year, while all other prices remain the same. What will happen to your nominal income? Nothing. You will still be getting $6,000 a year. Your *real* income, however, will suffer. This is evident in the second year's budget:

SECOND YEAR'S BUDGET

Nominal income	$6,000
Consumption	
Tuition	$3,500
Room and board	2,000
Books	300
Everything else	200
Total	$6,000

You now have to use more of your income to pay tuition. This means you have less income to spend on other things. You will have to cut back somewhere. After paying for room, board, books, and the increased tuition, only $200 is left for "everything else." This is $500 less than in the prior year's budget. That means fewer pizzas, movies, dates, or anything you'd like to buy. The pain of higher tuition will soon be evident; your *nominal income* hasn't changed, but your *real income* has.

Although tuition hikes reduce the real income of students and their families, nonstudents are not hurt by such price increases. A nonstudent with $6,000 of nominal income could continue to buy the same goods and services she was buying before tuition went up. In fact, if tuition *doubled*, nonstudents really wouldn't care. They could continue to buy the same bundle of goods and services they had been buying all along. Tuition increases reduce the real incomes only of people who go to college.

There are two basic lessons about inflation to be learned from this sad story:

- *Not all prices rise at the same rate during an inflation.* In our example, tuition increased substantially while other prices remained steady. Hence the "average" rate of price increase was not representative of any particular good or service. Typically, some prices rise very rapidly, others only modestly, and still others not at all. Table 10.2 illustrates some recent variations in price changes. The average rate of inflation (2.7 percent in 1994) disguised very steep price hikes for coffee, lettuce, and college tuition.

TABLE 10.2
Not All Prices Rise at the Same Rate

The average rate of inflation conceals substantial differences in the price changes of specific goods and services. The impact of inflation on individuals depends in part on which goods and services are consumed. People who buy goods whose prices are rising fastest lose more real income. In 1994, college students and coffee drinkers were particularly hard hit by inflation.

Item	Price Change in 1994 (percent)	Item	Price Change in 1994 (percent)
Food		Other	
Lettuce	+79.8	College tuition	+ 6.3
Coffee	+55.4	Funerals	+ 5.8
Bananas	+12.1	Newspapers	+ 5.0
Eggs	+ 0.3	Cable TV	− 2.6
Pork chops	− 4.8	Computers	− 9.1
Transportation		Women's dresses	−11.1
Used cars	+ 8.8		
New cars	+ 3.2		
Gasoline	+ 6.4	Average inflation rate	+ 2.7
Air fares	− 9.5		

Source: U.S. Bureau of Labor Statistics

● *Not everyone suffers equally from inflation.* This follows from our first observation. Those people who consume the goods and services that are rising faster in price bear a greater burden of inflation; their real incomes fall more. In 1994, people who consumed lettuce or coffee suffered the most from changing prices. Other consumers bore a lesser burden, or even none at all, depending on how fast the prices rose for the goods they enjoyed.

We conclude, then, that the price increases associated with inflation redistribute real income. In the example we have discussed, college students end up with fewer goods and services than they had before. Other consumers can continue to purchase at least as many goods as before, perhaps even more. Thus output is effectively *redistributed* from college students to others. Naturally, most college students aren't very happy with this outcome. Fortunately for you, inflation doesn't always work out this way.

Income Effects. The redistributive effects of inflation are not limited to changes in prices. Changes in prices automatically influence nominal incomes also.

If the price of tuition does in fact rise faster than all other prices, we can safely make three predictions:

● The *real income* of college students will fall relative to that of nonstudents (assuming constant nominal incomes).
● The *real income* of nonstudents will rise relative to that of students (assuming constant nominal incomes).
● The *nominal income* of colleges and universities will rise.

This last prediction simply reminds us that someone always pockets higher prices. *What looks like a price to a buyer looks like income to a seller.* If students all pay higher tuition, the university will take in more income. To the extent that the nominal incomes of colleges and universities increase faster than average prices, they actually *benefit* from inflation. That is to say, they end up being able to buy *more* goods and services (including faculty, buildings, and library books) after a period of inflation than they could before. Their real income rises. Whether one likes this outcome depends on whether anyone in the family works for the university or sells it goods and services.

On average, people's incomes do keep pace with inflation. Again, this is a direct consequence of the circular flow: what one person pays out someone else takes in. *If prices are rising, incomes must be rising, too.* Notice in Figure 10.5 that average wages have pretty much risen in step with prices. From this perspective, it makes no sense to say that "inflation hurts everybody." On *average*, at least, we are no worse off when prices rise, since our (average) incomes increase at the same time.

No one is exactly "average," of course. In reality, some people's incomes rise faster than inflation while others' increase more slowly. Hence the redistributive effects of inflation also originate in varying rates of growth in nominal income. If everyone's income increased at the rate of inflation, inflation would not have such a large redistributive effect. In reality, however, nominal incomes increase at very different rates.

Wealth Effects. The same kind of redistribution occurs between those who hold some form of wealth and those who do not. Suppose that on January 1 you deposit $100 in a savings account, where it earns 5 percent interest until you withdraw it on December 31. At the end of the year you will have

FIGURE 10.5
Nominal Wages and Prices

Inflation implies not only higher prices but higher wages as well. What is a price to one person is income to someone else. Hence inflation cannot make *everyone* worse off. This graph confirms that average wages have risen along with average prices. When nominal wages rise faster than prices, *real* wages are increasing. Higher real wages reflect higher productivity (more output per worker).

Source: *Economic Report of the President*, 1995.

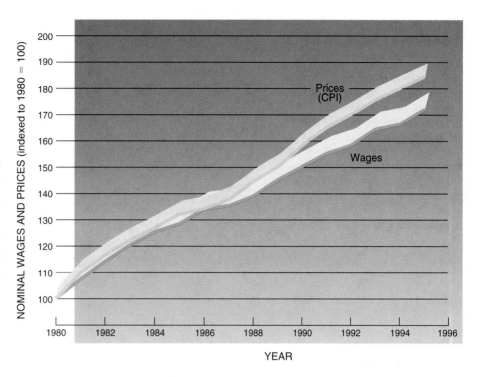

more nominal wealth ($105) than you started with ($100). But what if all prices have doubled in the meantime? At the end of the year, your accumulated savings ($105) buys less than it would have at the start of the year. In other words, inflation in this case reduces the *real* value of your savings. You end up with fewer goods and services than those individuals who spent all their income earlier in the year! Table 10.3 shows how different rates of inflation alter the real value of money hidden under the mattress for ten years.

Table 10.4 shows how the value of various assets actually changed in the 1980s. Between 1984 and 1994, the average price level rose by 42 percent. The price of stocks increased much faster, however, while the price of gold fell. Hence people who held their wealth in the form of stocks rather than gold came out ahead. Both stockholders and gold collectors did better than investors in oil or silver, however.

TABLE 10.3
Inflation's Impact, 1995–2005

In the 1980s, the U.S. rate of inflation ranged from a low of 1 percent to a high of 13 percent. Does a range of 12 percentage points really make much difference? One way to find out is to see how a specific sum of money will shrink in real value in the 1990s.

Here's what would happen to the *real* value of $1,000 from January 1, 1995, to January 1, 2005, at different inflation rates. At 2 percent inflation, $1,000 held for ten years would be worth $820. At 10 percent inflation that same $1,000 would buy only $386 worth of goods in the year 2005.

	Annual Inflation Rate				
Year	2 Percent	4 Percent	6 Percent	8 Percent	10 Percent
1995	$1,000	$1,000	$1,000	$1,000	$1,000
1996	980	962	943	926	909
1997	961	925	890	857	826
1998	942	889	840	794	751
1999	924	855	792	735	683
2000	906	822	747	681	621
2001	888	790	705	630	564
2002	871	760	665	584	513
2003	853	731	627	540	467
2004	837	703	592	500	424
2005	820	676	558	463	386

TABLE 10.4
The Real Story of Wealth

Households hold their wealth in many different forms. As the value of various assets changes, so does a person's wealth. Between 1984 and 1994, prices rose an average of 42 percent. But the prices of stocks, bonds, and diamonds rose even faster. People who held these assets gained in *real* (inflation-adjusted) wealth. Home prices also rose but by just a bit more than average prices. Hence, the *real* value of homes changed little.

Asset	Percentage Change in Value, 1984–94
Stocks	322
Bonds	273
Diamonds	75
Housing	49
Average price of goods	42
Gold	−2
U.S. farmland	−7
Stamps	−9
Silver	−61
Gold	−66

Source: Salomon Brothers, Inc.

Robin Hood? By altering relative prices, incomes, and the real value of wealth, then, inflation turns out to be a mechanism for redistributing incomes. ***The redistributive mechanics of inflation include***

- ***Price effects.*** People who prefer goods and services that are increasing in price least quickly end up with a larger share of real income.
- ***Income effects.*** People whose nominal incomes rise faster than the rate of inflation end up with a larger share of total income.
- ***Wealth effects.*** People who own assets that are increasing in real value end up better off than others.

On the other hand, people whose nominal incomes do not keep pace with inflation end up with smaller shares of total output. The same thing is true of those who enjoy goods that are rising fastest in price or who hold assets that are declining in real value. In this sense, ***inflation acts just like a tax, taking income or wealth from one group and giving it to another.*** But we have no assurance that this particular tax will behave like Robin Hood,

"DO I HAVE YOUR ASSURANCE THAT PRICES WILL NOT BE INCREASED BEFORE WE ARE SERVED?"

From *The Wall Street Journal*—by permission. Cartoon Features Syndicate.

taking from the rich and giving to the poor. It may do just the opposite. Not knowing who will win or lose the inflation sweepstakes may make everyone fear rising price levels.

Uncertainty

The uncertainties of inflation may also cause people to change their consumption, saving, or investment behavior. When average prices are changing rapidly, economic decisions become increasingly difficult. Should you commit yourself to four years of college, for example, if you are not certain that you or your parents will be able to afford the full costs? In a period of stable prices you can at least be fairly certain of what a college education will cost over a period of years. But if prices are rising, you can no longer be sure how large the bill will be. Under such circumstances, many individuals may decide not to enter college rather than risk the possibility of being driven out later by rising costs.

The uncertainties created by changing price levels affect production decisions as well. Imagine a firm that is considering building a new factory. Typically the construction of a factory takes two years or more, including planning, site selection, and actual construction. If construction costs or prices change rapidly during this period, the firm may find that it is unable to complete the factory or to operate it profitably. Confronted with this added uncertainty, the firm may decide to do without a new plant, or at least to postpone its construction until a period of stable prices returns.

Inflation need not always lead to a cutback in consumption and production. On the contrary, the uncertainties generated by inflation may just as easily induce people to buy *more* goods and services now, before prices rise further. In their haste to beat inflation, however, consumers and producers may make foolish decisions, buying goods or services that they will later decide they don't really need or want.

Measuring Inflation

In view of the potential consequences of inflation, the measurement of inflation serves two purposes: to gauge the average rate of inflation and to identify its principal victims. Until we know how fast prices are rising and which groups are suffering the greatest loss of real income, we can hardly begin to design appropriate public policies.

> **Consumer Price Index (CPI):** A measure (index) of changes in the average price of consumer goods and services.

Consumer Price Index. The most frequently cited measure of inflation is the **Consumer Price Index (CPI).** As its name suggests, the CPI is a mechanism for measuring changes in the average price of consumer goods and services. It is analogous to the fruit price index we discussed earlier. The CPI does not refer to the price of any particular good but, rather, to the average price of all consumer goods.

By itself, the "average price" of consumer goods is not a very useful number. Once we know the average price of consumer goods, however, we are able to observe whether that average rises—that is, whether inflation is occurring. By observing the extent to which prices increase, we can calculate the **inflation rate,** that is, the annual percentage increase in the average price level.

> **inflation rate:** The annual rate of increase in the average price level.

To compute the CPI, the Bureau of Labor Statistics periodically surveys families to determine what goods and services consumers actually buy. The Bureau of Labor Statistics then goes shopping in various cities across the country, recording the prices of 184 items that make up the typical market basket. This shopping survey is undertaken every month, in 85 areas and at a variety of stores in each area.

As a result of its surveys, the Bureau of Labor Statistics can tell us what's happening to consumer prices. Suppose, for example, that the market basket cost $100 in 1995, and that one year later the same basket of goods and services cost $110. On the basis of those two shopping trips, we could conclude that consumer prices had risen by 10 percent in one year—that is, that the rate of inflation was 10 percent per annum.

In practice, the CPI is usually expressed in terms of what the market basket cost in 1982–84. For example, the CPI stood at 150 in January 1995. In other words, it cost $150 in 1995 to buy the same market basket that cost only $100 in the base period (1982–84). Thus prices had increased by an average of 50 percent over that period. Each month the Bureau of Labor Statistics updates the CPI, telling us how the current cost of that same basket compares to its cost in 1982–84.

Price Stability

In view of the inequities, anxieties, and real losses caused by inflation, it is not surprising that price stability is a major goal of economic policy. As we observed at the beginning of this chapter, every American president since Franklin Roosevelt has decreed price stability to be a foremost policy goal. Unfortunately, few presidents (or their advisers) have stated exactly what they mean by "price stability." Do they mean *no* change in the average price level? Or is some upward creep in the CPI consistent with the notion of price stability?

price stability: The absence of significant changes in the average price level; officially defined as a rate of inflation of less than 3 percent.

The Policy Goal. An explicit numerical goal for **price stability** was established for the first time in the Full Employment and Balanced Growth Act of 1978. According to that act, the goal of economic policy is to hold the rate of inflation under 3 percent.

Why did Congress choose 3 percent inflation rather than zero inflation as the benchmark for price stability? Two considerations were important. First, Congress recognized that efforts to maintain absolutely stable prices (zero inflation) might threaten full employment. Recall that our goal of "full employment" is defined as the lowest rate of unemployment *consistent with stable prices*. The same kind of thinking is apparent here. The amount of inflation regarded as tolerable depends in part on how anti-inflation strategies affect unemployment. If policies that promise zero inflation raise unemployment rates too high, people may prefer to accept a little inflation. After reviewing our experiences with both unemployment and inflation, Congress concluded that 3 percent inflation was a "safe" target.

The second argument for setting our price-stability goal above zero inflation relates to our measurement capabilities. Although the Consumer Price Index is very thorough, it is not a perfect measure of inflation. In essence, the CPI simply monitors the price of specific goods over time. Over time, however, the goods themselves change, too. Old products become better as a result of *quality improvements*. A television set costs more today than it did in 1955, but today's TV also delivers a bigger, clearer picture—and in color! Hence increases in the price of television sets tend to exaggerate the true rate of inflation: part of the higher price represents more product.

The same kind of quality changes distort our view of how car prices have changed. Car purchases are a major item in the average household's budget. Accordingly, changes in auto prices have a substantial effect on the CPI. Since 1958, the average price of a new car has risen from $2,867 to nearly $20,000. But today's cars aren't really comparable to those of 1958. Since that time, the quality of cars has been improved with electronic ignitions, emergency flashers, rear-window defrosters, crash-resistant bodies, air bags, antilock brakes, remote-control mirrors, seatbelts, variable-speed windshield wipers, radial tires, a doubling of fuel mileage, and a 100-fold decrease in exhaust pollutants. Accordingly, the six-fold increase in average car prices since 1958 greatly overstates the true rate of inflation.

The problem of measuring quality improvements is even more apparent in the case of new products. The computers and word processors found in many offices and homes today did not exist when the Census Bureau conducted its 1972–73 survey of consumer expenditure. The 1982–84 survey included these new products, but the CPI itself was not revised until 1987. In the intervening years, the real incomes of consumers were affected by these and other goods the CPI did not include. The same thing is happening now: new products and continuing quality improvements are enriching our consumption, even though they are not reflected in the CPI. Hence there is a significant (though unmeasured) element of error in the CPI insofar as it is intended to gauge changes in the average prices paid by consumers. The goal of 3 percent inflation allows for such errors.

SUMMARY

- The long-term growth rate of the U.S. economy is approximately 3 percent a year. But output doesn't increase 3 percent every year. In some years real GDP grows much faster; in other years growth is slower. Sometimes total output actually declines.
- These short-run variations in GDP growth are the focus of macroeconomics. Macro theory tries to explain the alternating periods of growth and contraction that characterize the business cycle; macro policy attempts to control the cycle.
- To understand unemployment, we need to distinguish the labor force from the larger population. Only people who are working (employed) or spend some time looking for a job (unemployed) are participants in the labor force. People who are neither working nor looking for work are outside the labor force.
- The most visible loss imposed by unemployment is reduced output of goods and services. Those individuals actually out of work suffer lost income, heightened insecurity, and even reduced longevity.
- There are four types of unemployment: seasonal, frictional, structural, and cyclical. Because some seasonal and frictional unemployment is inevitable, and even desirable, full employment is not defined as zero unemployment. These considerations, plus fear of inflation, result in full employment being defined as an unemployment rate of about 5.5 percent.
- Inflation is an increase in the average price level. Typically it is measured by changes in a price index such as the Consumer Price Index (CPI).
- Inflation redistributes income by altering relative prices, incomes, and wealth. Because not all prices rise at the same rate and because not all people buy (and sell) the same goods or hold the same assets, inflation does not affect everyone equally. Some individuals actually gain from inflation, whereas others suffer a drop in real income.
- Inflation threatens to reduce total output because it increases uncertainties about the future and thereby inhibits consumption and production decisions. Fear of rising prices can also stimulate spending, forcing the government to take restraining action that threatens full employment.

- The U.S. goal of price stability is defined as an inflation rate of less than 3 percent per year. This goal recognizes potential conflicts between zero inflation and full employment, as well as the difficulties of measuring quality improvements and new products.

Terms to Remember

Define the following terms:

macroeconomics	unemployment rate	nominal income
business cycle	full employment	real income
real GDP	inflation	Consumer Price Index
recession	deflation	inflation rate
labor force	relative price	price stability
unemployment		

Questions for Discussion

1. If business cycles were really inevitable, what purpose would macro policy serve?
2. Could we ever achieve an unemployment rate *below* "full employment"? What problems might we encounter if we did?
3. Have you ever had difficulty finding a job? Why didn't you get one right away? What kind of unemployment did you experience?
4. Can you identify any groups of people who are particularly helped or hurt by inflation? Explain.
5. Would it be advantageous to borrow money if you expected prices to rise? Why, or why not? Provide a numerical example.
6. Why did the Great Depression last so long? What happened to all the jobs?

Problems

1. Suppose the following data describe a nation's population:

	Year 1	Year 2
Population	200 million	203 million
Labor force	120 million	125 million
Unemployment rate	6 percent	6 percent

   (*a*) How many people are unemployed in each year?
   (*b*) How many people are employed in each year?
   (*c*) Compute the employment rate (i.e., number employed ÷ *population*) in each year.
   (*d*) How can the employment rate rise when the *unemployment* rate is constant?
2. What would the *real* value be in ten years of $500 you hid under your mattress if the inflation rate is
   (*a*) 4%
   (*b*) 8%
   (Hint: Table 10.3 provides clues.)
3. Suppose you will have an annual nominal income of $40,000 for the next five years, without any increases. However, the inflation rate is 5 percent.
   (*a*) Find the real value of your $40,000 salary for each of the next 5 years.

(b) Suppose your boss agrees to raise your $40,000 salary by 5 percent for each of the next five years. Given the 5 percent inflation rate for each of those five years, what is the real value of your salary for each year?

4. The following table lists the prices of a small market basket purchased in both 1990 and 1995. Assuming that this basket of goods is representative of all goods and services

   (a) Compute the cost of the market basket in 1990.
   (b) Compute the cost of the market basket in 1995.
   (c) By how much has the average price level risen between 1990 and 1995?
   (d) The average household's nominal income increased from $35,000 to $45,000 between 1990 and 1995. What happened to its real income?

Item	Quantity	Price (per unit) 1990	Price (per unit) 1995
Coffee	20 pounds	$ 3	$ 4
Tuition	1 year	4,000	7,000
Pizza	100 pizzas	8	10
VCR rental	75 days	15	10
Vacation	2 weeks	300	500

Chapter 11

Aggregate Supply and Demand

The uneven growth record of the U.S. economy reinforces the notion of a recurring business cycle. But the historical record raises more questions than it answers. Are business cycles really inevitable? At first blush, the historical string of recessions suggests they are. A closer look, however, indicates that the magnitude of recessions has diminished greatly. None of the post–World War II recessions has come close to the depths or duration of the Great Depression. This suggests that modern economic policy has had some success in taming, if not eliminating, the business cycle. Perhaps better economic policies might eliminate the threats of unemployment and inflation altogether.

The central focus of **macroeconomics** is on these very questions, that is, what causes business cycles and what, if anything, the government can do about them. Can government intervention prevent or correct market excesses? Or is government intervention likely to make things worse?

To answer these questions, we need a "model" of how the economy works. The model must provide a reasonably clear view of how the various pieces of the economy interact. Such a model will allow us not only to see how the macro economy "works" but also to pinpoint potential causes of macro failure.

In developing a macro model, the following questions must be answered:

* What are the major elements of a macro model?
* How do the forces of supply and demand fit into such a model?
* How does the model reflect major debates in macro theory and policy?

A basic macro model can be very useful. It can help explain the continuing debates about the causes of business cycles. A macro model can also be used to identify policy options for government intervention.

macroeconomics: The study of aggregate economic behavior, of the economy as a whole.

231

A MACRO VIEW

Macro Outcomes

Figure 11.1 provides a broad view of the macro economy. The primary outcomes of the macro economy are arrayed on the right side of the figure. These basic *macro outcomes include*

- *Output:* total volume of goods and services produced (real GDP)
- *Jobs:* levels of employment and unemployment
- *Prices:* average price of goods and services
- *Growth:* year-to-year expansion in production capacity
- *International balances:* international value of the dollar; trade and payments balances with other countries

These macro outcomes define our nation's economic welfare. That is to say, we measure our economic well-being in terms of the volume of output produced, the number of jobs created, price stability, and the rate of economic expansion. We also seek to maintain a certain balance in our international trade and financial relations. The performance of the economy is rated by the "scores" on these five macro outcomes.

Macro Determinants

Figure 11.1 also provides an overview of the separate forces that affect macro outcomes. Three very broad forces are depicted. These *determinants of macro performance include*

- *Internal market forces:* population growth, spending behavior, invention and innovation, and the like
- *External shocks:* wars, natural disasters, trade disruptions, and so on

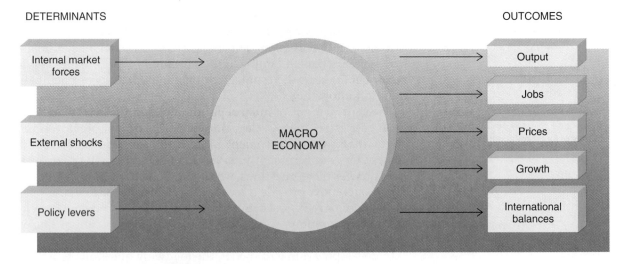

FIGURE 11.1
The Macro Economy

The primary outcomes of the macro economy are output of goods and services, jobs, prices, economic growth, and international balances (trade, currency). These outcomes result from the interplay of international market forces (e.g., population growth, innovation, spending patterns), external shocks (e.g., wars, weather, trade disruptions), and policy levers (e.g., tax and budget decisions).

- *Policy levers:* tax policy, government spending, changes in the availability of money, and regulation, for example

In the absence of external shocks or government policy, an economy would still function—it would still produce output, create jobs, develop prices, and maybe even grow. The U.S. economy operated this way for much of its history. Even today, many less developed countries and areas operate in relative isolation from government and international events. In these situations, macro outcomes depend exclusively on internal market forces.

STABLE OR UNSTABLE?

The central concern of macroeconomic theory is whether the internal forces of the marketplace will generate desired outcomes. Will the market mechanism assure us full employment? Will the market itself maintain price stability? Or will the market *fail*, subjecting us to recurring bouts of unemployment, inflation, and declining output?

Classical Theory

Prior to the 1930s, macro economists thought there could never be a Great Depression. The economic thinkers of the time asserted that the economy was inherently stable. During the nineteenth century and the first thirty years of the twentieth century, the U.S. economy had experienced some bad years—years in which the nation's output declined and unemployment increased. But most of these episodes were relatively short-lived. The dominant feature of the industrial era was growth—an expanding economy, with more output, more jobs, and higher incomes nearly every year.

In this environment, Classical economists, as they later became known, propounded an optimistic view of the macro economy. *According to the Classical view, the economy "self-adjusts" to deviations from its long-term growth trend.* Producers might occasionally reduce their output and throw people out of work. But these dislocations would cause little damage. If output declined and people lost their jobs, the internal forces of the marketplace would quickly restore prosperity. Economic downturns were viewed as temporary setbacks, not permanent problems.

The cornerstones of Classical optimism were flexible prices and flexible wages. If producers were unable to sell all their output at current prices, they had two choices. They could reduce the rate of output and throw some people out of work. Or they could reduce the price of their output, thereby stimulating an increase in the quantity demanded. According to the law of demand, price reductions cause an increase in unit sales. If prices fall far enough, all the output produced can be sold. Thus flexible prices—prices that would drop when consumer demand slowed—virtually guaranteed that all output could be sold. No one would have to lose a job because of weak consumer demand.

Flexible prices had their counterpart in factor markets. If some workers were temporarily out of work, they would compete for jobs by offering their services at lower wages. As wage rates declined, producers would find it profitable to hire more workers. Ultimately, flexible wages would ensure that everyone who wanted a job would have a job.

Say's Law: Supply creates its own demand.

These optimistic views of the macro economy were summarized in Say's Law. **Say's Law**—named after the nineteenth-century economist Jean-

Baptiste Say—decreed that "supply creates its own demand." Whatever was produced would be sold. All workers who sought employment would be hired. Unsold goods and unemployed labor could emerge in this Classical system. But both would disappear as soon as people had time to adjust prices and wages. There could be no Great Depression—no protracted macro failure—in this Classical view of the world. Indeed, internal market forces (e.g., flexible prices and wages) could even provide an automatic adjustment to external shocks (e.g., wars, droughts, trade disruptions) that threatened to destabilize the economy. The Classical economists saw no need for the box labeled "policy levers" in Figure 11.1; government intervention in the macro economy was unnecessary.

The Great Depression was a stunning blow to Classical economists. At the onset of the depression, Classical economists assured everyone that the setbacks in production and employment were temporary and would soon vanish. Andrew Mellon, secretary of the U.S. Treasury, expressed this optimistic view in January 1930, just a few months after the stock-market crash. Assessing the prospects for the year ahead, he said: "I see nothing . . . in the present situation that is either menacing or warrants pessimism. . . . I have every confidence that there will be a revival of activity in the spring and that during the coming year the country will make steady progress."[1] Merrill Lynch, one of the nation's largest brokerage houses, was urging people to buy stocks. But the depression deepened. Indeed, unemployment grew and persisted, *despite* falling prices and wages (see Figure 11.2). The Classical self-adjustment mechanism simply did not work.

[1] David A. Shannon, *The Great Depression* (Englewood Cliffs, N.J.: Prentice Hall, 1960), p. 4.

FIGURE 11.2
Inflation and Unemployment, 1900–1940

In the early twentieth century, prices responded to both upward and downward changes in aggregate demand. Periods of high unemployment also tended to be brief. In the 1930s, however, unemployment rates rose to unprecedented heights and stayed high for a decade. Falling wages and prices did not restore full employment. This macro failure prompted calls for new theories and policies to control the business cycle.

Source: U.S. Bureau of the Census, *Historical Statistics of the United States*, 1957.

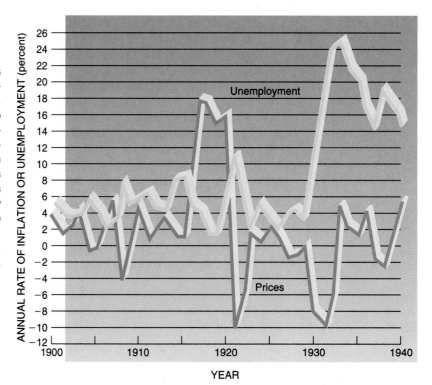

The Keynesian Revolution

The Great Depression destroyed the credibility of Classical economic theory. As John Maynard Keynes wrote in 1935, Classical economists

> were apparently unmoved by the lack of correspondence between the results of their theory and the facts of observation:—a discrepancy which the ordinary man has not failed to observe. . . .
>
> The celebrated optimism of [Classical] economic theory . . . is . . . to be traced, I think, to their having neglected to take account of the drag on prosperity which can be exercised by an insufficiency of effective demand. For there would obviously be a natural tendency towards the optimum employment of resources in a Society which was functioning after the manner of the classical postulates. It may well be that the classical theory represents the way in which we should like our Economy to behave. But to assume that it actually does so is to assume our difficulties away.[2]

Keynes went on to develop an alternative view of the macro economy. Whereas the Classical economists viewed the economy as inherently stable, *Keynes asserted that the private economy was inherently unstable.* Small disturbances in output, prices, or unemployment were likely to be magnified, not muted, by the invisible hand of the marketplace. The Great Depression was not a unique event, Keynes argued, but a calamity that would recur if we relied on the market mechanism to self-adjust. Macro failure was the rule, not the exception, for a purely private economy.

In Keynes's view, the inherent instability of the marketplace required government intervention. When the economy falters, we cannot afford to wait for some assumed self-adjustment mechanism. We must instead intervene to protect jobs and income. Keynes concluded that "policy levers" (see Figure 11.1) were both effective and necessary. Without such intervention, he believed, the economy was doomed to bouts of repeated macro failure.

Modern economists hesitate to give policy intervention that great a role. Nearly all economists recognize that policy intervention affects macro outcomes. But there are great arguments about just how effective any policy lever is. A vocal minority of economists even echoes the Classical notion that policy intervention may be either ineffective or, worse still, inherently destabilizing.

THE AGGREGATE SUPPLY–DEMAND MODEL

These persistent debates can best be understood in the familiar framework of supply and demand—the most commonly used tools in an economist's toolbox. All of the macro outcomes depicted in Figure 11.1 are the result of market transactions—an interaction between supply and demand. Hence *any influence on macro outcomes must be transmitted through supply or demand.* In other words, if the forces depicted on the left side of Figure 11.1 affect neither supply nor demand, they will have no impact on macro outcomes. This makes our job easier. We can resolve the question about macro stability by focusing on the forces that shape supply and demand in the macro economy.

---

[2] John Maynard Keynes, *The General Theory of Employment, Interest and Money* (London: Macmillan, 1936), pp. 33–34.

Aggregate Demand

> **aggregate demand:** The total quantity of output demanded at alternative price levels in a given time period, *ceteris paribus*.

> **real GDP:** The inflation-adjusted value of GDP; the value of output measured in constant prices.

Economists use the term "aggregate demand" to refer to the collective behavior of all buyers in the marketplace. Specifically, **aggregate demand** refers to the various quantities of output that all market participants are willing and able to buy at alternative price levels in a given period. Our view here encompasses the collective demand for *all* goods and services, rather than the demand for any single good.

To understand the concept of aggregate demand better, imagine that everyone is paid on the same day. With their income in hand, people then enter the product market. The question is: How much will people buy?

To answer this question, we have to know something about prices. If goods and services are cheap, people will be able to buy more with their given income. On the other hand, high prices will limit both the ability and willingness to purchase goods and services. Note that we are talking here about the average price level, not the price of any single good.

This simple relationship between average prices and real spending is illustrated in Figure 11.3. On the horizontal axis we depict the various quantities of output that might be purchased. We are referring here to **real GDP**, an inflation-adjusted measure of physical output.

On the vertical axis we measure prices. Specifically, Figure 11.3 depicts alternative levels of *average* prices. As we move up the vertical axis, the average price level rises; as we move down, the average price level falls.

The aggregate demand curve in Figure 11.3 has a familiar shape. The message of this downward-sloping macro curve is a bit different, however. ***The aggregate demand curve illustrates how the volume of purchases varies with average prices.*** The downward slope of the aggregate demand curve suggests that with a given (constant) level of income, people will buy more goods and services at lower prices. The curve doesn't tell us *which* goods and services people will buy; it simply indicates the total volume (quantity) of their intended purchases.

At first blush, a downward-sloping demand curve hardly seems remarkable. But because *aggregate* demand refers to the total volume of spending, Figure 11.3 requires a distinctly macro explanation. That explanation includes three separate phenomena:

FIGURE 11.3
Aggregate Demand

Aggregate demand refers to the total output demanded at alternative price levels (*ceteris paribus*). The vertical axis here measures the average level of all prices, rather than the price of a single good. Likewise, the horizontal axis refers to the real value of all goods, not the quantity of only one product.

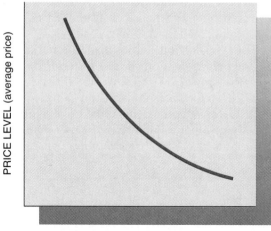

PRICE LEVEL (average price)

REAL OUTPUT (quantity per year)

- *Real balances effect:* The most obvious explanation for the downward slope of the aggregate demand curve is that cheaper prices make dollars more valuable. That is to say, *the real value of money is measured by how many goods and services each dollar will buy.* In this respect, lower prices make you "richer": the cash balances you hold in your pocket, in your bank account, or under your pillow are worth more when the price level falls. With a given cash balance, you can suddenly buy more goods. Lower prices also increase the value of other dollar-denominated assets (e.g., bonds), thus increasing the wealth of consumers. As their wealth increases, consumers feel less need to save and are likely to buy a greater quantity of goods and services. Thus the aggregate demand curve slopes downward to the right.
- *Foreign trade effect:* The downward slope of the aggregate demand curve is reinforced by changes in imports and exports. Consumers have the option of buying either domestic or foreign goods. A decisive factor in choosing between imported or domestic goods is their relative price. When the prices of imported goods rise, U.S. consumers tend to buy more American-made products. Conversely, higher prices for domestic output induce U.S. consumers to substitute imports for home-grown products. The quantity of domestic goods demanded declines when the domestic price level rises. Foreign consumers, too, have less incentive to buy American-made products (our exports) when U.S. prices rise. These changes in imports and exports contribute to the downward slope of the aggregate demand curve.
- *Interest-rate effect:* Changes in the price level also affect the amount of money people need to borrow, and so tend to affect interest rates. At lower price levels, consumer borrowing needs are smaller. As the demand for loans diminishes, interest rates tend to decline as well. This "cheaper" money stimulates more borrowing and loan-financed purchases.

The combined forces of these real-balances, foreign-trade, and interest-rate effects give the aggregate demand curve its downward slope. People buy a larger volume of output when the price level falls (*ceteris paribus*).

Aggregate Supply

While lower price levels tend to increase the volume of output demanded, they have the opposite effect on the aggregate quantity supplied. Prices determine how much income producers receive for their efforts. If the price level falls, producers as a group are being squeezed. In the short run, producers are saddled with some relatively constant costs like rent, interest payments, negotiated wages, and inputs already contracted for. If output prices fall, producers will be hard-pressed to pay these costs, much less earn a profit. Their response will be to reduce the rate of output.

Rising output prices have the opposite effect. Because many costs are relatively constant in the short run, higher prices for goods and services tend to widen profit margins. As profit margins widen, producers will want to produce and sell more goods. Thus **we expect the rate of output to increase when the price level rises**. This expectation is reflected in the upward slope of the aggregate supply curve in Figure 11.4. **Aggregate supply** reflects the various quantities of real output that firms are willing and able to produce at alternative price levels, in a given time period.

The upward slope of the aggregate supply curve is also explained by rising costs. To increase the rate of output, producers must acquire more re-

aggregate supply: The total quantity of output producers are willing and able to supply at alternative price levels in a given time period, *ceteris paribus.*

FIGURE 11.4
Aggregate Supply

Aggregate supply refers to the total volume of output producers are willing and able to bring to the market at alternative price levels (*ceteris paribus*). The upward slope of the aggregate supply curve reflects the fact that profit margins widen when output prices rise (especially when short-run costs are constant). Producers respond to wider profit margins by supplying more output.

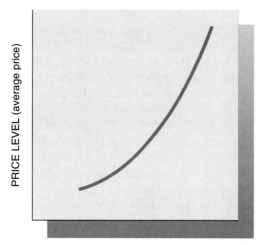

sources (e.g., labor) and use existing plant and equipment more intensively. These greater strains on our productive capacity tend to raise production costs. Producers must therefore charge higher prices to recover the higher costs that accompany increased capacity utilization. Again, this results in an upward-sloping aggregate supply curve, as seen in Figure 11.4.

Macro Equilibrium

What we end up with here is two rather conventional-looking supply and demand curves. But these particular curves have special significance. Instead of describing the behavior of buyers and sellers in a single market, *aggregate supply and demand curves summarize the market activity of the whole (macro) economy.* These curves tell us what *total* amount of goods and services will be supplied or demanded at various price levels.

These graphic summaries of buyer and seller behavior provide some initial clues as to how macro outcomes are determined. The most important clue is point E in Figure 11.5, where the aggregate demand and supply curves intersect. This is the only point at which the behavior of buyers and sellers is compatible. We know from the aggregate demand curve that peo-

FIGURE 11.5
Macro Equilibrium

The aggregate demand and supply curves intersect at only one point (E). At that point, the price (P_E) and output (Q_E) combination is compatible with both buyers' and sellers' intentions. The economy will gravitate to those equilibrium price (P_E) and output (Q_E) levels. At any other price level (e.g., P_1), the behavior of buyers and sellers is incompatible.

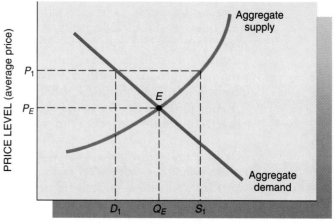

ple are willing and able to buy the quantity Q_E when prices are equal to P_E. From the aggregate supply curve we know that businesses are prepared to sell the quantity Q_E at the price level P_E. Hence buyers and sellers are willing to trade exactly the same quantity (Q_E) at that price level. We call this situation **macro equilibrium**—the unique combination of prices and output that is compatible with both buyers' and sellers' intentions.

> **equilibrium (macro):** The combination of price level and real output that is compatible with both aggregate demand and aggregate supply.

To appreciate the significance of macro equilibrium, suppose that another price or output level existed. Imagine, for example, that prices were higher, at the level P_1 in Figure 11.5. How much output would people want to buy at that price level? How much would business want to produce and sell?

The aggregate demand curve tells us that people would want to buy only the quantity D_1 at the higher price level P_1. In contrast, business firms would want to sell a larger quantity, S_1. This is a *disequilibrium* situation, in which the intentions of buyers and sellers are incompatible. The aggregate quantity supplied (S_1) exceeds the aggregate quantity demanded (D_1). Accordingly, a lot of goods will remain unsold at price level P_1.

To sell these goods, producers will have to reduce their prices. As the prices drop, producers will decrease the volume of goods sent to market. At the same time, the quantities that consumers seek will increase. This adjustment process will continue until point E is reached and the quantities demanded and supplied are equal. At that point, the lower price level P_E will prevail.

The same kind of adjustment process would occur if a lower price level first existed. At lower prices, the aggregate quantity demanded would exceed the aggregate quantity supplied. The resulting shortages would permit sellers to raise their prices. As they did so, the aggregate quantity demanded would decrease, and the aggregate quantity supplied would increase. Eventually, we would return to point E, where the aggregate quantities demanded and supplied are equal.

Equilibrium is unique; it is the only price–output combination that is mutually compatible with aggregate supply and demand. In terms of graphs, it is the only place the aggregate supply and demand curves intersect. At point E there is no reason for the level of output or prices to change. The behavior of buyers and sellers is compatible. By contrast, any other level of output or prices creates a disequilibrium that requires market adjustments. All other price and output combinations, therefore, are unstable. They will not last. Eventually, the economy will return to point E.

MACRO FAILURE

There are ***two potential problems with the macro equilibrium*** depicted in Figure 11.5:

- *Undesirability:* The price–output relationship at equilibrium may not satisfy our macroeconomic goals.
- *Instability:* Even if the designated macro equilibrium is optimal, it may be displaced by macro disturbances.

Undesirable Outcomes

The macro equilibrium depicted in Figure 11.5 is simply the intersection of two curves. All we know for sure is that people want to buy the same quantity that businesses want to sell at the price level P_E. This quantity (Q_E)

may be more or less than our full-employment capacity. This contingency is illustrated in Figure 11.6. The output level Q_F represents the quantity of output that could be produced if the labor force were fully employed. At macro equilibrium, however, only the quantity Q_E is being produced. The economy is not fully utilizing its production possibilities.

The shortfall in equilibrium output illustrated in Figure 11.6 implies that the economy will be burdened with cyclical **unemployment.** Full employment is attained only if we produce at Q_F. Market forces, however, lead us to the lower rate of output at Q_E. Some workers can't find jobs.

> **unemployment:** The inability of labor-force participants to find jobs.

Similar problems may arise from the equilibrium price level. Suppose that P^* represents the most desired price level. In Figure 11.6 we see that the equilibrium price level P_E exceeds P^*. If market behavior determines prices, the price level will rise above the desired level. The resulting increase in average prices is what we call **inflation.**

> **inflation:** An increase in the average level of prices of goods and services.

It could be argued, of course, that our apparent macro failures are simply an artifact. We could have drawn our aggregate supply and demand curves to intersect at point F in Figure 11.6. At that intersection we would be assured of both price stability and full employment. Why didn't we draw them there, rather than intersecting at point E?

On the graph we can draw curves anywhere we want. In the real world, however, only one set of curves will correctly express buyers' and sellers' behavior. We must emphasize here that these "correct" curves may *not* intersect at point F, thus denying us price stability, full employment, or both. That is the kind of economic outcome illustrated in Figure 11.6.

Unstable Outcomes

Figure 11.6 is only the beginning of our macro worries. Suppose, just suppose, that the aggregate supply and demand curves actually intersected in the perfect spot. That is to say, imagine that macro equilibrium yielded the optimal levels of both employment and prices, thus satisfying our two foremost macroeconomic goals. If this happened, could we settle back and stop fretting about the state of the economy?

Unhappily, even a "perfect" macro equilibrium doesn't ensure a happy

FIGURE 11.6
An Undesired Equilibrium

Equilibrium establishes only the levels of prices and output that are compatible with both buyers' and sellers' intentions. These outcomes may not satisfy our policy goals. In this case, the equilibrium price level is too high (above P^*) and the equilibrium output rate falls short of full-employment GDP (Q_F).

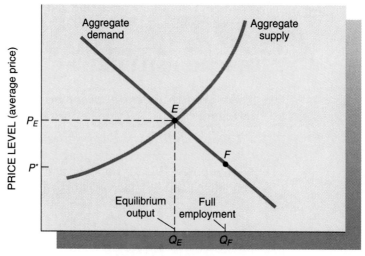

ending. The aggregate supply and demand curves that momentarily bring us macro bliss are not necessarily permanent. They can *shift*—and they will, whenever the behavior of buyers and sellers changes.

When Iraq invaded Kuwait in August 1990, the price of oil shot up. This oil price hike directly increased the cost of production in a wide range of U.S. industries, making producers less willing and able to supply goods at prevailing prices. Thus the aggregate supply curve *shifted to the left*, as in Figure 11.7*a*.

The impact of a leftward supply shift on the economy is evident. Whereas macro equilibrium was originally located at the optimal point *F*, the new equilibrium is located at point *G*. At point *G*, less output is produced and prices are higher. Full employment and price stability have vanished before our eyes.

A shift of the aggregate demand curve could do similar damage. Suppose American consumers suddenly acquired a greater yen for Japanese products. If they spent more of their income on imports, they would be less able and willing to buy American products. This change in consumer behavior would be reflected in a leftward shift of the aggregate demand curve for domestic goods, as in Figure 11.7*b*. The resulting disturbance would knock the economy out of its equilibrium at point *F*, leaving us at point *H*, with less output at home.

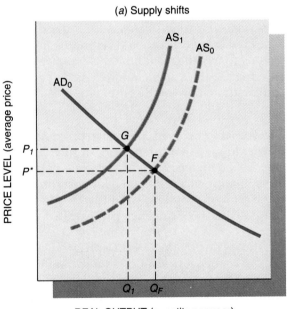

(*a*) Supply shifts

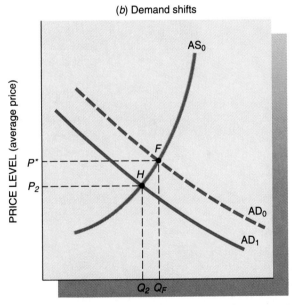

(*b*) Demand shifts

FIGURE 11.7
Macro Disturbances

(*a*) A decrease (leftward shift) of the aggregate supply (AS) curve tends to reduce real GDP and raise average prices. When supply shifts from AS_0 to AS_1, the equilibrium moves from *F* to *G*. Such a supply shift may result from higher import prices, changes in tax policy, or other events.

(*b*) A decrease (leftward shift) in aggregate demand (AD) tends to reduce output and price levels. A fall in demand may be due to increased taste for imports, changes in expectations, higher taxes, or other events.

The situation gets even crazier when the aggregate supply and demand curves shift repeatedly in different directions. A leftward shift of the aggregate demand curve can cause a recession, as the rate of output falls. A later rightward shift of the aggregate demand curve can cause a recovery, with real GDP (and employment) again increasing. Shifts of the aggregate supply curve can cause similar upswings and downswings. Thus **business cycles *result from recurrent shifts of the aggregate supply and demand curves.***

| **business cycle:** Alternating periods of economic growth and contraction. |

COMPETING THEORIES

Figures 11.6 and 11.7 hardly inspire optimism about the macro economy. Figure 11.6 suggests that the odds of the market generating an equilibrium at full employment and price stability are about the same as finding a needle in a haystack. Figure 11.7 suggests that if we are lucky enough to find the needle, we will probably drop it again. From this perspective, it appears that our worries about the business cycle are well founded.

The Classical economists had no such worries. As we saw earlier, they believed that the economy would gravitate toward full employment. Keynes, on the other hand, worried that the macro equilibrium might start out badly and get worse in the absence of government intervention.

Aggregate supply and demand curves provide a convenient framework for comparing these and other theories on how the economy works. Essentially, *macro controversies focus on the shape of aggregate supply and demand curves and the potential to shift them.* With the right shape—or the correct shift—any desired equilibrium could be attained. As we will see, there are differing views as to whether and how this happy outcome might come about. These differing views can be classified as demand-side explanations, supply-side explanations, or some combination of the two.

Demand-Side Theories

Keynesian Theory. Keynesian theory is the most prominent of the demand-side theories. Keynes argued that a deficiency of spending would tend to depress an economy. This deficiency might originate in consumer saving, inadequate business investment, or insufficient government spending. Whatever its origins, the lack of spending would leave goods unsold and production capacity unused. This contingency is illustrated by point E_1 in Figure 11.8a.

Keynes developed his theory during the Great Depression, when the economy seemed to be stuck at a very low level of equilibrium output, far below full employment GDP. The only way to end the depression, he argued, was for someone to start demanding more goods. He advocated a big increase in government spending to start the economy moving toward full employment.

Keynesian economists also advocate tax cuts to stimulate consumer spending. With more after-tax dollars in their pockets, consumers are likely to spend more. Hence *Keynesian theory urges increased government spending or tax cuts as mechanisms for increasing (shifting) aggregate demand.* If too much aggregate demand were pushing the price level up, Keynes advocated moving these policy levers in the opposite direction.

Monetary Theories. Another demand-side theory emphasizes the role of money in financing aggregate demand. Money and credit affect the ability and willingness of people to buy goods and services. Accordingly, if the right

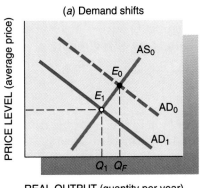
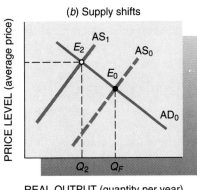
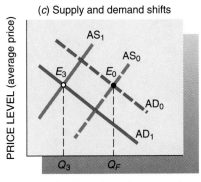

FIGURE 11.8
Origins of a Recession

Unemployment can result from several kinds of market phenomena, including

  (*a*) Total output will fall if aggregate demand (AD) declines. The shift from AD_0 to AD_1 changes equilibrium from point E_0 to E_1.

  (*b*) Unemployment can also emerge if aggregate supply (AS) declines, as the shift from AS_0 to AS_1 shows.

  (*c*) If aggregate demand and aggregate supply both decline, output and employment also fall.

amount of money is not available, aggregate demand may be too small. High interest rates might also dissuade people from buying enough goods and services to assure full employment. In such situations, an increase in the money supply or a reduction in interest rates might be the best way to shift the aggregate demand curve into the desired position.

Monetary theories thus focus on the control of money and interest rates as mechanisms for shifting the aggregate demand curve.

Supply-Side Theories

Figure 11.8*b* illustrates an entirely different explanation of the business cycle. Notice that the aggregate *supply* curve is on the move in Figure 11.8*b*. The initial equilibrium is again at point E_0. This time, however, aggregate demand remains stationary, while aggregate supply shifts. The resulting decline of aggregate supply causes output and employment to decline (to Q_2 from Q_F).

Figure 11.8*b* tells us that aggregate supply may be responsible for downturns as well. Our failure to achieve full employment may result from the unwillingness of producers to provide more goods at existing prices. That unwillingness may originate in simple greed, in rising costs, in resource shortages, or in government taxes and regulation. Whatever the cause, if the aggregate supply curve is AS_1 rather than AS_0, full employment will not be achieved with the demand AD_0. To get more output, the supply curve must shift back to AS_0. The mechanisms for shifting the aggregate supply curve in the desired direction are the focus of supply-side theories.

Eclectic Explanations

Not everyone blames either the demand side or the supply side exclusively. The various macro theories tell us that both supply and demand can cause us to achieve or miss our policy goals. These theories also demonstrate how various shifts of the aggregate supply and demand curves can achieve any specific output or price level. Figure 11.8c illustrates how undesirable macro outcomes can be caused by shifts of both aggregate curves. Eclectic explanations of the business cycle draw from both sides of the market.

POLICY OPTIONS

Aggregate supply and demand curves not only help illustrate the causes of the business cycle; they also imply a fairly straightforward set of policy options. Essentially, *the government has three policy options:*

- *Shift the aggregate demand curve.* Find and use policy tools that stimulate or restrain total spending.
- *Shift the aggregate supply curve.* Find and implement policy levers that reduce the costs of production or otherwise stimulate more output at every price level.
- *Do nothing.* If we can't identify or control the determinants of aggregate supply or demand, then we shouldn't interfere with the market.

Historically, all three approaches have been adopted.

The "Classical" approach to economic policy embraced the "do nothing" perspective. Prior to the Great Depression, most economists were convinced that the economy would self-adjust to full employment. If the initial equilibrium rate of output was too low, the resulting imbalances would alter prices and wages, inducing changes in market behavior. The aggregate supply and demand curves would "naturally" shift, until they reached the intersection at point E_0 where full employment (Q_F) prevails.

Recent versions of the Classical theory—dubbed the New Classical Economics—stress not only the market's "natural" ability to self-adjust to *long-run* equilibrium, but also the inability of the government to improve *short-run* market outcomes. New Classical Economists point to the increasing ability of market participants to anticipate government policies—and to take defensive actions that thwart them.

Fiscal Policy

fiscal policy: The use of government taxes and spending to alter macroeconomic outcomes.

The Great Depression cast serious doubt on the Classical self-adjustment concept. According to Keynes's view, the economy would *not* self-adjust. Rather, it might stagnate at point E_1 until aggregate demand was forcibly shifted. An increase in government spending on goods and services might provide the necessary shift. Or a cut in taxes might be used to stimulate greater consumer and investor spending. These budgetary tools are the hallmark of fiscal policy. Specifically, **fiscal policy** is the use of government tax and spending powers to alter economic outcomes.

Fiscal policy is an integral feature of modern economic policy. Every year the president and the Congress debate the budget. They argue about whether the economy needs to be stimulated or restrained. They then argue about the level of spending or taxes required to ensure the desired outcome. This is the heart of fiscal policy.

Monetary Policy

monetary policy: The use of money and credit controls to influence macroeconomic activity.

The government budget doesn't get all the action. As suggested earlier, the amount of money in circulation may also affect macro equilibrium. If so, then the policy arsenal must include some levers to control the money supply. These are the province of monetary policy. **Monetary policy** refers to the use of money and interest rates to alter economic outcomes.

The Federal Reserve (the "Fed") has direct control over monetary policy. The Fed is an independent regulatory body, charged with maintaining an "appropriate" supply of money. In practice, the Fed increases or decreases the money supply in accordance with its views of macro equilibrium.

Supply-Side Policy

> **supply-side policy:** The use of tax rates, (de)regulation, and other mechanisms to increase the ability and willingness to produce goods and services.

Fiscal and monetary policies focus on the demand side of the market. Both policies are motivated by the conviction that appropriate shifts of the aggregate demand curve can bring about desired changes in output or price levels. **Supply-side policies** offer an alternative; they seek to shift the aggregate supply curve.

There are scores of supply-side levers. The most familiar are the tax cuts implemented by the Reagan administration in 1981. These tax cuts were designed to increase *supply*, not just demand (as traditional fiscal policy does). By reducing tax rates on wages and profits, the Reagan tax cuts sought to increase the willingness to supply goods at any given price level. The promise of greater after-tax income was the key incentive for the supply shift.

Republicans used a similar argument in 1994 to reduce the tax on capital gains (profits from the sale of acquired property). Lower capital-gains tax rates, they argued, would encourage people to invest more in factories, equipment, and office buildings. As investment increased, so would the capacity to supply goods and services. As the accompanying Headline suggests, this particular supply-side mechanism is popular among business people and investors.

Other supply-side levers are less well recognized but nevertheless important. Your economics class is an example. The concepts and skills you learn here should increase your productive capabilities. This expands the econ-

HEADLINE

SUPPLY-SIDE POLICY

A Tax Cut for Capital Gains

Few policy proposals put as warm a glow in the hearts of American business leaders, entrepreneurs, and investors as the idea of cutting the tax rates on capital gains. Lower capital gains taxes reduce the cost of capital because they increase its after-tax return. From this flow all kinds of beneficent effects, including increased national output, more investment, higher asset prices—and, of course, larger profits for investors. James L. Mann, chief executive officer of SunGard Data Systems, a computer service firm with 1994 revenues of $440 million, speaks for the consensus in corporate America when he says, "It's good for the economy, good for my business, and good for me." The view from Wall Street is just as unequivocal. Bullish as his company's trademark Texas longhorns, Merrill Lynch's chief investment strategist Charles Clough states, "Past capital gains cuts have led to investment booms, and presumably there'd be nothing different this time."

What is very different from even a few months ago is the political landscape. As the smoke clears from the battle that was Election Day 1994, congressional Republicans sound like the 19th-century Senator who declared that "to the victor belong the spoils." Cutting the capital gains tax rate is high on their agenda. They fought bloodily and vainly for it during their years in the political wilderness. In the Contract With America, the party platform that served them so well last fall, they promised to lower the top rate from 28% to 19.8% and index future gains against inflation so that you'd pay tax only on your real ones.

—Rob Norton

Fortune, February 6, 1995, p. 117. © 1995 Time Inc. All rights reserved.

omy's capacity. With a more educated work force, a greater supply of goods and services can be produced at any given price level. Hence government subsidies to higher education might be viewed as part of supply-side policy. Government support for employment and training programs also shifts the aggregate supply curve to the right.

Government regulation is another staple of supply-side policy. Regulations that slow innovation or raise the cost of doing business reduce aggregate supply. Removing unnecessary "red tape" can facilitate more output and reduce inflationary pressures.

POLICY PERSPECTIVES

The Changing Choice of Policy Levers, 1960–95

The various policy levers in our basic macro model have all been used at one time or another. The "do nothing" approach prevailed until the Great Depression. Since that devastating experience, more active policy roles have predominated.

Fiscal policy dominated economic debate in the 1960s. When the economy responded vigorously to tax cuts and increased government spending, it appeared that fiscal policy might be the answer to our macro problems. Many economists even began to assert that they could "fine-tune" the economy—generate very specific changes in macro equilibrium with appropriate tax and spending policies.

The promise of fiscal policy was tarnished by our failure to control inflation in the late 1960s. It was further compromised by the simultaneous outbreak of both inflation and unemployment in the 1970s. This new macro failure appeared to be chronic, immune to the cures proposed by fiscal policy. Solutions to our macro problems were sought elsewhere.

Monetary policy was next in the limelight. The "flaw" in fiscal policy, it was argued, originated in its neglect of monetary constraints. More government spending, for example, might require so much of the available money supply that private spending would be "crowded out." To ensure a net boost in aggregate demand, more money would be needed, thus requiring action by the Fed.

In the late 1970s the Fed dominated macro policy. It was hoped that appropriate changes in the money supply would foster greater macro stability. Reduced inflation and lower interest rates were the immediate objectives. Both were to be accomplished by placing greater restraints on the supply of money. Full employment was also anticipated, as investment and consumption spending responded positively to lower, and more predictable, interest and inflation rates.

The heavy reliance on monetary policy lasted only a short time. When the economy skidded into yet another recession, the search for effective policy tools resumed.

Supply-side policies became important in 1980. In his 1980 presidential campaign, Ronald Reagan asserted that supply-side tax cuts, deregulation of markets, and other supply-focused policies would reduce both inflation and unemployment. According to Figure 11.8c such an outcome appeared at least plausible. A rightward shift of the aggregate supply curve does reduce both prices and unemployment. Although the Reagan administration later embraced an eclectic mix of fiscal, monetary, and supply-side policies, its initial supply-side emphasis was very distinctive.

The Bush administration pursued a less activist approach. George Bush initially resisted tax increases, but later accepted them as part of a budget compromise that also reduced government spending. When the economy slid into recession in 1990, President Bush maintained a hands-off policy. Like Classical economists, Bush kept assuring the public that the economy would "come around" on its own. Not until the 1992 elections approached did he propose more active intervention. By then it was too late for him, however. Voters were swayed by Bill Clinton's promises to use tax cuts and increased government spending (fiscal policy) to create "jobs, jobs, jobs."

After he was elected, President Clinton reversed policy direction. Rather than delivering the promised tax cuts, Clinton pushed a tax *increase* through Congress. He also pared the size of his planned spending increases. This fiscal-policy retreat cleared the field for the reemergence of monetary policy as the decisive policy lever.

The Republican victories in the 1994 elections forced President Clinton to do another fiscal-policy U-turn. The Republicans' "Contract with America" promised both tax cuts for the average family (fiscal policy) and reduced taxation of capital gains (supply-side policy). Confronted with the electoral popularity of these proposals, President Clinton moved quickly after the November 1994 elections to resurrect his 1992 tax-cut promise. He also shifted gears on spending, proposing new cuts in government programs. That mix of tax cuts and spending reductions, he argued, would keep the economy on track while changing the relative size of the public and private sectors. The job of fighting inflation was left up to the Fed's monetary policy.

SUMMARY

- The primary outcomes of the macro economy are output, prices, jobs, and international balances. These outcomes result from the interplay of internal market forces, external shocks, and policy levers.
- All of the influences on macro outcomes are transmitted through aggregate supply or aggregate demand. Aggregate supply and demand determine the equilibrium rate of output and prices. The economy will gravitate to that unique combination of output and price levels.
- Macro equilibrium may not be consistent with our nation's employment or price goals. Macro failure occurs when the economy's equilibrium is not optimal.
- Macro equilibrium may be disturbed by changes in aggregate supply (AS) or aggregate demand (AD). Such changes are illustrated by shifts of the AS and AD curves, and they lead to a new equilibrium. Recurring AS and AD shifts cause business cycles.
- Competing economic theories try to explain the shape and shifts of the aggregate supply and demand curves, thereby explaining the business cycle. Specific theories tend to emphasize demand or supply influences.
- Macro policy options range from doing nothing (the Classical approach) to various strategies for shifting either the aggregate demand curve or the aggregate supply curve.
- Fiscal policy uses government tax and spending powers to alter aggregate demand. Monetary policy uses money and credit availability for the same purpose.

- Supply-side policies include all interventions that shift the aggregate supply curve. Examples include tax incentives, (de)regulation, and resource development.

Terms to Remember

Define the following terms:

macroeconomics	aggregate supply	aggregate supply
Say's Law	equilibrium (macro)	fiscal policy
aggregate demand	unemployment	monetary policy
real GDP	inflation	supply-side policy

Questions for Discussion

1. If all wages and prices both fell by 20 percent, would you be better or worse off? Could you buy more goods?
2. Why might consumers suddenly demand fewer goods at current prices? How would this change affect aggregate demand?
3. What would a *horizontal* aggregate supply curve imply about producer behavior? How about a vertical AS curve?
4. If equilibrium is compatible with both buyers' and sellers' intentions, how can it be undesirable?
5. The stock-market crash of October 1987 greatly reduced the wealth of the average American household. How might this have affected aggregate demand? Aggregate supply?
6. President Bush maintained a "hands-off" policy during the 1990–91 recession. How did he expect the economy to recover on its own?
7. How might an income-tax cut alter the behavior of consumers? Of business investors?
8. Why would anyone expect an increase in business investment if the tax on capital gains were reduced (Headline, p. 245)? Why would anyone object to such a tax cut?

Problems

1. Draw a conventional aggregate demand curve on a graph. Then add three different aggregate supply curves, labeled
    S_1: Horizontal curve
    S_2: Upward-sloping curve
    S_3: Vertical curve
   all intersecting the AD curve at the same point.
   If AD were to increase (shift to the right), which AS curve would lead to
    (*a*) The biggest increase in output?
    (*b*) The largest jump in prices?
    (*c*) The least inflation?
2. The following schedule provides information with which to draw both an aggregate demand curve and an aggregate supply curve. Both curves are assumed to be straight lines.

Average Price (dollars per unit)	Quantity Demanded (units per year)	Quantity Supplied (units per year)
$1,000	0	1,000
100	900	100

    (*a*) At what price level does equilibrium occur?

    (*b*) What curve would have shifted if a new equilibrium were to occur at an output level of 700 and a price level of $700?

    (*c*) What curve would have shifted if a new equilibrium were to occur at an output level of 700 and a price level of $500?

    (*d*) What curve would have shifted if a new equilibrium were to occur at an output level of 700 and a price level of $300?

    (*e*) Compared to the initial equilibrium (a), how have the outcomes in (b), (c), and (d) changed price levels or output?

3. Suppose business investment amounts to $500 billion a year and generates capital gains of $50 billion a year. If the level of investment remained unchanged, how much of those gains would investors get to keep after paying taxes before and after the tax cut discussed in the Headline on page 245? What would happen to tax receipts? How much more investment would be needed after the tax cut to restore tax receipts to their pre-tax level?

Chapter 12

Fiscal Policy

During the Great Depression of the 1930s, as many as 13 million Americans were out of work. They were capable people and eager to work. But no one would hire them. As sympathetic as employers might have been, they simply could not use any more workers. Consumers were not buying the goods and services already being produced. Employers were more likely to cut back production and lay off still more workers than to hire any new ones. As a consequence, an "army of the unemployed" was created in 1929 and continued to grow for nearly a decade. It was not until the outbreak of World War II that enough jobs could be found for the unemployed, and most of these "jobs" were in the armed forces.

The Great Depression was the springboard for the Keynesian approach to economic policy. John Maynard Keynes concluded that the ranks of unemployed persons were growing because of problems on the *demand* side of product markets. People simply were not able and willing to buy all the goods and services the economy was capable of producing. As a consequence, producers had no incentive to increase output or to hire more labor. So long as the demand for goods and services was inadequate, unemployment was inevitable.

Keynes sought to explain how a deficiency of demand could arise, then to show how and why the government had to intervene. Keynes was convinced that government intervention was necessary to ensure optimal macro outcomes. This Keynesian conclusion provided the foundation for government intervention in the macro economy. Keynes's focus was on **fiscal policy,** that is, the government's use of its tax and spending powers to alter macro outcomes. He urged policymakers to use these powers to minimize the swings of the business cycle.

> **fiscal policy:** The use of government taxes and spending to alter macroeconomic outcomes.

In this chapter, we take a closer look at what Keynes intended. We focus on the following questions:

- Why did Keynes think the market was inherently unstable?
- How can fiscal policy help stabilize the economy?
- How will the use of fiscal policy affect the government's budget deficit?

COMPONENTS OF AGGREGATE DEMAND

> **aggregate demand:** The total quantity of output demanded at alternative price levels in a given time period, *ceteris paribus*.

The premise of fiscal policy is that the **aggregate demand** for goods and services will not be compatible with economic stability. Recessions occur when aggregate demand declines; recessions persist when aggregate demand remains below the economy's capacity to produce. Inflation results from similar imbalances. If aggregate demand increases faster than output, average prices rise. Prices will keep rising until aggregate demand is compatible with the rate of production.

But why do such macro failures occur? Why shouldn't aggregate demand reflect the economy's full employment potential?

Aggregate demand lumps together the spending behavior of all market participants. To determine whether we are likely to have the right amount of aggregate demand, we need to take a closer look at its ingredients. Who buys the goods and services on which output decisions and jobs depend?

The *four major components of aggregate demand are*

C:	*consumption*
I:	*investment*
G:	*government spending*
X − M:	*net exports (exports minus imports)*

Consumption

> **consumption:** Expenditure by consumers on final goods and services.

Consumption refers to all household expenditures on goods and services—everything from groceries to college tuition. Just look around and you can see the trappings of our consumer-oriented economy. In the aggregate, consumption spending accounts for approximately two-thirds of total spending in the U.S. economy (Figure 12.1).

Because consumer spending looms so large in aggregate demand, any change in consumer behavior can have a profound impact on employment

FIGURE 12.1
Components of Aggregate Demand

In 1994, the output of the U.S. economy was $6.7 trillion. Two-thirds of that output consisted of consumer goods and services. The government sector (federal, state, and local) demanded 17 percent of total output. Investment spending took another 15 percent. Finally, because imports exceeded exports, the impact of net exports on aggregate demand was negative.

Source: *Economic Report of the President*, 1995.

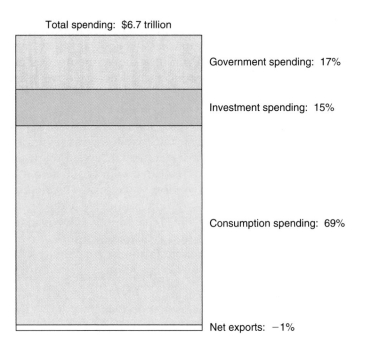

Total spending: $6.7 trillion

Government spending: 17%

Investment spending: 15%

Consumption spending: 69%

Net exports: −1%

and prices. Economists try to anticipate such changes by studying consumer behavior. Clues to consumer behavior are often found in surveys of consumer confidence and expenditure plans. If consumer confidence is rising, consumer *spending* may increase. When consumer confidence jumped in late 1992 (see Headline), economists predicted a stronger economy (they were right).

Investment

investment: Expenditures on (production of) new plant and equipment (capital) in a given time period, plus changes in business inventories.

Investment refers to spending by business on new plant and equipment. When a corporation decides to build a new factory, the resulting expenditure adds to aggregate demand. When farmers decide to replace their old tractors, their purchases also increase total spending on goods and services.

Changes in business inventory are also counted as "investment." Retail stores stock their shelves with goods bought from other firms. Although they hope to resell these goods later, the inventory buildup reflects a demand for goods and services. If companies allow their inventories to shrink, then inventory investment would be negative. During the Great Depression not only was inventory investment negative but spending on plant and equipment also plummeted. As a result, total business investment plunged by 70 percent between 1929 and 1933. This plunge in investment spending wracked aggregate demand and eliminated millions of jobs.

Government Spending

Government spending is a third source of aggregate demand. The federal government currently spends over $1.6 trillion a year, and state and local governments collectively spend just as much. Not all of that spending gets counted as part of aggregate demand, however. Aggregate demand refers

HEADLINE

EXPECTATIONS

Consumers' Confidence up Sharply

Consumers may be sending glad tidings for a healthier economy in the New Year.

The Conference Board, a research group, said Tuesday its consumer confidence index leaped to 78.3 in December, from 65.6 last month.

Economists hope consumers aren't just experiencing a temporary mood swing because a solid recovery depends on their increased spending.

That accounts for about two-thirds of all economic activity.

But for now, at least, other signs also are encouraging:

• Retailers enjoyed a holiday shopping "bonanza not equaled since 1983," says the Johnson Redbook, a newsletter that tracks retail sales.

Its estimate: retail revenue the four weeks before Christmas was 10.4% above 1991.

Other analysts expect the increase to be somewhat lower.

• Sales of existing homes rose last month to the highest level in six years, says the National Association of Realtors.

Housing, like consumer confidence, is a key measure of economic strength.

The economy may not be "in great shape, but it is moving forward," says Mark Zandi, an economist with Regional Financial Associates.

—Bill Montague

USA Today, December 30, 1992, p. 1A. Copyright 1992, USA TODAY. Reprinted with permission.

to spending on goods and services. Much of what the government spends, however, are merely *income transfers*—payments to individuals for which no services are exchanged. Uncle Sam, for example, mails out over $300 billion a year in Social Security checks. This doesn't represent a demand for goods and services. That money will become part of aggregate demand only when the Social Security recipients spend their transfer income.

Only that portion of government budgets that gets spent on goods and services represents part of aggregate demand. Aggregate demand includes federal, state, and local spending on highways, schools, police, national defense, and all other goods and services the public sector provides. Such spending now accounts for nearly one-fifth of aggregate demand.

Net Exports

> **net exports:** Exports minus imports $(X - M)$.

The fourth component of aggregate demand, **net exports,** is the difference between export and import spending. The demand of foreigners for American-made goods and services shows up as exported goods. At the same time, Americans spend some of their income on goods imported from other countries. The difference between export and import demands represents the *net* demand for domestic output.

In 1994, net exports were negative. This means that Americans were buying more goods from abroad than foreigners were buying from us. The net effect of trade was thus to reduce domestic aggregate demand. That is why net exports is a negative amount in Figure 12.1.

Equilibrium

The four components of aggregate demand combine to determine the shape and position of the aggregate demand curve. Notice that *aggregate demand is not a single number but instead a schedule of planned purchases.* The quantity of output market participants desire to purchase depends in part on the price level.

Suppose the existing price level is P_1, as seen in Figure 12.2, and that the curve AS represents aggregate supply. Full employment is represented by the output level Q_F. What we want to know is whether aggregate demand will be just enough to assure both price stability and full employment. This

FIGURE 12.2
The Desired Equilibrium

The goal of fiscal policy is to achieve price stability and full employment, the desired equilibrium represented by point *a*. This equilibrium will occur only if aggregate demand is equal to AD*. Less demand (e.g., AD₁) will cause unemployment; more demand (e.g., AD₂) will cause inflation.

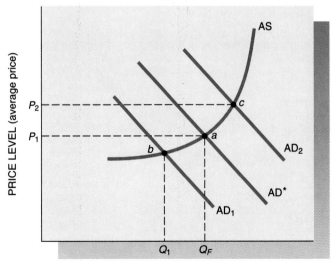

PRICE LEVEL (average price)

REAL OUTPUT (quantity per year)

equilibrium (macro): The combination of price level and real output that is compatible with both aggregate demand and aggregate supply.

happy **equilibrium** occurs only if the aggregate demand curve intersects the aggregate supply curve at point *a*. The curve AD* achieves this goal.

Aggregate demand may turn out to be less than perfect, however. If $C + I + G + (X - M)$ at the price level P_1 does not add up to the desired rate of aggregate demand, full employment will not be attained. This is the problem illustrated by the curve AD_1. In this case, aggregate demand falls short, leaving some potential output unsold at the undesired equilibrium point *b*.

The curve AD_2 illustrates a situation of excessive aggregate demand. The combined expenditure plans of market participants exceed the economy's full-employment output. The resulting scramble for available goods and services pushes prices up to the level P_2. This inflationary equilibrium is illustrated by point *c*.

THE NATURE OF FISCAL POLICY

Clearly, we will fulfill our macroeconomic goals only if we get the right amount of aggregate demand (the curve AD* in Figure 12.2). But what are the chances of such a fortunate event? Keynes asserted that the odds were stacked against such an outcome. Indeed, Keynes concluded that *it would be a minor miracle if C + I + G + (X − M) added up to exactly the right amount of aggregate demand.* Consumers, investors, and foreigners all make independent decisions on how much to spend. Why should those separate decisions result in just enough demand to assure full employment and price stability? It is far more likely that the level of aggregate demand will turn out to be wrong. In these circumstances, government spending must be the safety valve that expands or contracts aggregate demand as needed. *The use of government spending and taxes to adjust aggregate demand is the essence of fiscal policy.* Figure 12.3 puts fiscal policy into the framework of our basic macro model.

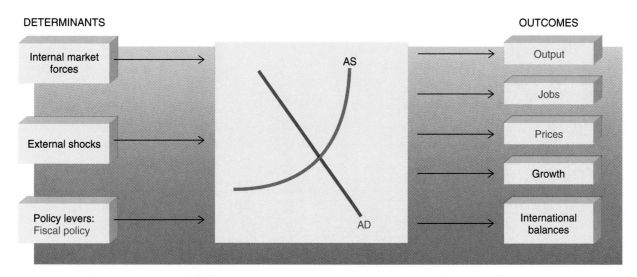

FIGURE 12.3
Fiscal Policy

Fiscal policy refers to the use of the government tax and spending powers to alter macro outcomes. Fiscal policy works principally through shifts of the aggregate demand curve.

FISCAL STIMULUS

Suppose that aggregate demand has fallen short of our goals and unemployment rates are high. This scenario is illustrated again in Figure 12.4, this time with some numbers added. Full employment is reached when $6 trillion of output is demanded at current price levels, as indicated by Q_F. The quantity of output demanded at current price levels, however, is only $5.6 trillion ($Q_1$). Thus $400 billion worth of production capacity remains idle.

The goal here is to *shift* the aggregate demand curve to the right. Such a shift will occur if people are willing to buy more output at current prices. In this case, spending has to increase by $400 billion per year. How can fiscal policy make this happen?

More Government Spending

The simplest solution to the demand shortfall would be to increase government spending. If the government were to step up its purchases of tanks, highways, schools, and other goods, the increased spending would add directly to aggregate demand. This would shift the aggregate demand curve rightward, moving us closer to full employment. Hence **increased government spending is a form of fiscal-policy stimulus.**

Multiplier Effects. It isn't necessary for the federal government to fill the entire gap between desired and current spending. In fact, if government spending did increase by $400 billion, aggregate demand would shift *beyond* point *a* in Figure 12.4. In that case we would quickly move from a situation of *inadequate* aggregate demand (AD₁) to a situation of *excessive* aggregate demand.

The solution to this apparent riddle lies in the circular flow of income. According to the circular flow, **an increase in spending results in increased incomes.** When the government increases its spending, it creates additional income for market participants. The recipients of this income will in turn spend it. Hence each dollar gets spent and respent several times. As a result, every dollar of government spending has a *multiplied* impact on aggregate demand.

FIGURE 12.4
Deficient Demand

The aggregate demand curve AD₁ results in only $5.6 trillion of final sales at current price levels (P_1). This is well short of full employment (Q_F), which occurs at $6.0 trillion of output. The fiscal-policy goal is to shift the AD curve until it passes through point *a*.

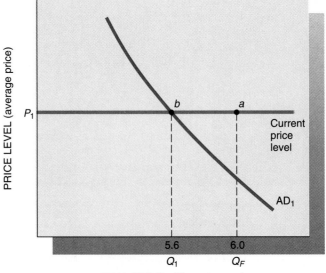

Suppose that the government decided to spend an additional $100 billion per year on a fleet of cruise missiles. This $100 billion of new defense expenditure would add directly to aggregate demand. But that is only the beginning of a very long story. The people who build cruise missiles will be on the receiving end of a lot of income. Their fatter paychecks, dividends, and profits will enable them to increase their own spending.

What *will* the aerospace workers do with all that income? They have only two choices: ***all income is either spent or saved.*** Hence every dollar of income must go to consumer spending or to **saving.** From a macroeconomic perspective, the only important decision the aerospace workers have to make is what percentage of income to spend and what percentage to save (i.e., not spend). Any additional consumption spending contributes directly to aggregate demand. That portion of income that is saved (not spent) goes under the mattress or into banks or other financial institutions.

Suppose aerospace workers decide to spend 75 percent of any extra income they get and to save the rest (25 percent). We call these percentages the marginal propensity to consume and the marginal propensity to save, respectively. The **marginal propensity to consume (MPC)** is the fraction of additional income people spend. The **marginal propensity to save (MPS)** is the fraction of new income that is saved.

Figure 12.5 illustrates how the spending and saving decisions are connected. In this case we have assumed that the MPC equals 0.75. Hence, 75 cents out of any extra dollar gets spent. By definition, the remaining 25 cents gets saved. The MPC and MPS tell us how the aerospace workers will behave when their incomes rise.

According to these behavioral patterns, the aerospace workers will use their additional $100 billion of income as follows:

$$\text{Increased consumption} = \text{MPC} \times \text{additional income}$$
$$= 0.75 \times \$100 \text{ billion}$$
$$= \$75 \text{ billion}$$

$$\text{Increased saving} = \text{MPS} \times \text{additional income}$$
$$= 0.25 \times \$100 \text{ billion}$$
$$= \$25 \text{ billion}$$

Thus all of the new income is either spent ($75 billion) or saved ($25 billion).

Our focus here is on the increased consumption of the aerospace workers. This $75 billion of new consumption adds directly to aggregate demand.

saving: Income minus consumption; that part of disposable income not spent.

marginal propensity to consume (MPC): The fraction of each additional (marginal) dollar of disposable income spent on consumption.

marginal propensity to save (MPS): The fraction of each additional (marginal) dollar of disposable income not spent on consumption; 1 − MPC.

FIGURE 12.5
MPC and MPS

The marginal propensity to consume (MPC) tells us what portion of an extra dollar of income will be spent. The remaining portion will be saved. The MPC and MPS help us predict consumer behavior.

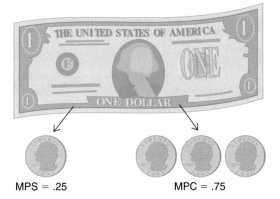

MPS = .25   MPC = .75

Hence aggregate demand has now been increased *twice:* first by the government expenditure on missiles ($100 billion) and then by the additional consumption of aerospace workers ($75 billion). Thus aggregate demand has increased by $175 billion as a consequence of the stepped-up defense expenditure. ***The fiscal stimulus to aggregate demand includes both the initial increase in government spending and all subsequent increases in consumer spending triggered by the government outlays***. That combined stimulus is already up to $175 billion.

The stimulus of new government spending doesn't stop with the aerospace workers. Table 12.1 tells the rest of the story. Suppose the aerospace workers spend their $75 billion on new boats. This increases the income of boat builders. They, too, are then in a position to increase *their* spending.

Suppose the boat builders also have a marginal propensity to consume of 0.75. They will then spend 75 percent of their new income ($75 billion). This will add another $56.25 billion to consumption demand.

Notice in Table 12.1 what is happening to cumulative spending as the multiplier process continues. When the boat builders go on a spending spree, there is a cumulative increase in spending:

Cycle 1: Government expenditure on cruise missiles	$100.00 billion
Cycle 2: Aerospace workers' purchase of boats	75.00 billion
Cycle 3: Boat builders' expenditure on beer	56.25 billion
Cumulative increase in spending after three cycles	$231.25 billion

TABLE 12.1
The Multiplier Process at Work

Purchasing power is passed from hand to hand in the circular flow. The *cumulative* change in total expenditure that results from a new injection of spending into the circular flow depends on the MPC and the number of spending cycles that occur. The limit to multiplier effects is established by the ratio 1/(1 − MPC). In this case, MPC = 0.75, so the multiplier equals 4. That is to say, total spending will ultimately rise by $400 billion per year as a result of an increase in *G* of $100 billion per year.

Spending Cycles	Change in Spending During Cycle (billions per year)	Cumulative Increase in Spending (billions per year)
First cycle: government buys $100 billion worth of missiles	$100.00	$100.00
Second cycle: missile workers have more income, buy new boats (MPC = 0.75)	75.00	175.00
Third cycle: boat builders have more income, spend it on beer (0.75 × $75)	56.25	231.25
Fourth cycle: bartenders and brewery workers have more income ($56.25 billion), spend it on new cars (0.75 × $56.25)	42.19	273.44
Fifth cycle: auto workers have more income, spend it on clothes (0.75 × $42.19)	31.64	305.08
Sixth cycle: apparel workers have more income, spend it on movies and entertainment (0.75 × $31.64)	23.73	328.81
⋮	⋮	⋮
*N*th cycle and beyond		400.00

As a result of the circular flow of spending and income, the impact of the initial government expenditure has already more than doubled.

Table 12.1 follows the multiplier process to its logical end. Each successive cycle entails less new income and smaller increments to spending. Ultimately, the changes get so small that they are not even noticeable. By that time, however, the *cumulative* change in spending is huge. The cumulative change in spending is $400 billion: $100 billion of initial government expenditure and an additional $300 billion of consumption induced by multiplier effects. Thus *the demand stimulus initiated by increased government spending is a multiple of the initial expenditure.*

To compute the cumulative change in spending, we need not examine each cycle of the multiplier process. There is a shortcut. The entire sequence of multiplier cycles is summarized in a single number, aptly named the *multiplier*. The **multiplier** tells us how much *total* spending will change in response to an initial spending stimulus. The multiplier is computed as

> **multiplier:** The multiple by which an initial change in aggregate spending will alter total expenditure after an infinite number of spending cycles; $1/(1 - MPC)$.

$$\bullet \ \text{Multiplier} = \frac{1}{1 - MPC}$$

In our case, where $MPC = 0.75$, the multiplier is

$$\text{Multiplier} = \frac{1}{1 - MPC}$$

$$= \frac{1}{1 - 0.75} = \frac{1}{0.25} = 4$$

Using this multiplier we can confirm the conclusion of Table 12.1 by observing that

$$\bullet \ \begin{array}{l} \text{Total change} \\ \text{in spending} \end{array} = \text{multiplier} \times \begin{array}{l} \text{initial change in} \\ \text{government spending} \end{array}$$

$$= \frac{1}{1 - MPC} \times \$100 \text{ billion per year}$$

$$= \frac{1}{1 - 0.75} \times \$100 \text{ billion per year}$$

$$= 4 \times \$100 \text{ billion per year}$$

$$= \$400 \text{ billion per year}$$

The impact of the multiplier is illustrated in Figure 12.6. The AD_1 curve represents the inadequate aggregate demand that caused the initial unemployment problem (Figure 12.4). When the government increases its defense spending, the aggregate demand curve shifts rightward by $100 billion to AD_2. This increase in defense expenditure sparks a consumption spree, shifting aggregate demand further, to AD_3. This combination of increased government spending and induced consumption is sufficient to restore full employment.

The multiplier packs a lot of punch. *Every dollar of fiscal stimulus has a multiplied impact on aggregate demand.* This makes fiscal policy easier. The multiplier also makes fiscal policy riskier, however, by exaggerating any intervention mistakes.

FIGURE 12.6
Multiplier Effects

A $100 billion increase in government spending shifts the aggregate demand curve to the right by a like amount (i.e., AD_1 to AD_2). Aggregate demand gets another boost from the additional consumption induced by multiplier effects. In this case, an MPC of 0.75 results in $300 billion of additional consumption.

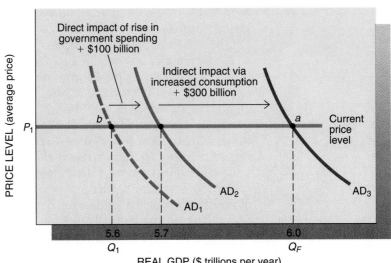

Tax Cuts

disposable income: After-tax income of consumers.

Although government spending is capable of moving the economy to its full-employment potential, increased G is not the only way to get there. The stimulus required to raise output and employment levels from Q_1 to Q_F could originate in C or I as well as from G. It could also come from abroad, in the form of increased demand for our exports. In other words, any Big Spender would help, whether from the public sector or the private sector. Of course, the reason we are initially at Q_1 instead of Q_F in Figure 12.6 is that consumers and investors have chosen not to spend as much as is required for full employment.

Consumer and investor decisions are subject to change. Moreover, fiscal policy can help stimulate such changes. Congress not only buys goods and services but also levies taxes. By lowering taxes, the government increases the **disposable income** of the private sector. This was the objective of President Clinton's proposal to allow families a tax credit for their children (see Headline). By putting $36 billion more after-tax income into the hands of consumers, Clinton hoped to stimulate (shift) the consumption component of aggregate demand.

Taxes and Consumption. A tax cut directly increases the disposable income of consumers. The question, here, however, is how a tax cut affects *spending*. Remember that our goal is to increase (shift) aggregate demand. This will not happen unless consumers respond to a tax cut by increasing their expenditure on goods and services. Will they?

So long as the marginal propensity to consume is greater than zero, we can count on consumers to spend some of the tax cut. If the MPC is 0.75, consumers will spend 75 cents out of every tax-cut dollar. In other words

$$\bullet \quad \frac{\text{Initial increase}}{\text{in consumption}} = \text{MPC} \times \text{tax cut}$$

If taxes were cut by $100 billion, the resulting consumption spree would amount to

$$\frac{\text{Initial increase}}{\text{in consumption}} = 0.75 \times \$100 \text{ billion}$$

$$= \$75 \text{ billion}$$

HEADLINE

FISCAL STIMULUS

A $500 Tax Credit for Children

Clinton has proposed a $500 tax credit for each child 12 and under. The full credit would go to families with $60,000 or less in adjusted gross income. Families with $60,000 to $75,000 adjusted gross income would get a partial credit. Above $75,000, no credit. Adjusted gross income is total income, minus a few items, such as individual retirement account contributions.

Clinton proposed starting with a $200 per-child credit in the 1995 tax year. So taxpayers wouldn't feel any benefit until they file their 1995 tax return in 1996. The credit would increase every year to the maximum $500 in 1998. Clinton aides say, however, that the phase-in dates could change.

Tax credits are a good deal. They are subtracted directly from the tax you owe. That's far better than a deduction, which is subtracted from adjusted gross income. If you are in the 28% tax bracket, you need a $1,786 deduction to cut your taxes $500. . .

The Clinton child-care proposal would cost the government about $36 billion.

USA Today, December 19, 1994, p. 3B. Copyright 1989, USA TODAY. Reprinted by permission.

Hence ***the effect of a tax cut that increases disposable incomes is to stimulate consumer spending***. A tax cut, therefore, shifts the aggregate demand curve to the right.

The initial consumption spree induced by a tax cut starts the multiplier process in motion. The new consumer spending creates additional income for producers and workers, who will then use the additional income to increase their own consumption. This will propel us along the multiplier path already depicted in Table 12.1. The cumulative change in total spending will be

$$\bullet \quad \text{Cumulative change in spending} = \text{multiplier} \times \text{initial change in consumption}$$

In this case, the cumulative change is

$$\text{Cumulative change in spending} = \frac{1}{1 - \text{MPC}} \times \$75 \text{ billion}$$

$$= 4 \times \$75 \text{ billion}$$

$$= \$300 \text{ billion}$$

Here again we see that the multiplier increases the impact of a tax cut on aggregate demand. ***The cumulative increase in aggregate demand is a multiple of the initial tax cut.*** Thus the multiplier makes both increased government spending and tax cuts very powerful policy levers.

Taxes and Investment. A tax cut may also be an effective mechanism for increasing investment spending. Investment decisions are guided by expectations of future profit, particularly after-tax profits. If a cut in corporate taxes raises potential after-tax profits, it should encourage additional investment. Once an increase in the rate of investment spending enters the circular flow, it has a multiplier effect on total spending like that which follows an initial change in consumer spending. Thus tax cuts for consumers or investors provide an alternative to increased government spending as a mechanism for stimulating aggregate spending.

Tax cuts designed to stimulate C and I have been used frequently. In 1963, President John F. Kennedy announced his intention to reduce taxes in order to stimulate the economy, citing the fact that the marginal propensity to consume for the average American family at that time appeared to be exceptionally high. His successor, Lyndon Johnson, concurred with Kennedy's reasoning. Johnson agreed to "shift emphasis sharply from expanding federal expenditure to boosting private consumer demand and business investment." He proceeded to cut personal and corporate taxes $11 billion. President Johnson proclaimed that "the $11 billion tax cut will challenge American businessmen, investors, and consumers to put their enlarged incomes to work in the private economy to expand output, investment, and jobs." He added, "I am confident that our private decision makers will rise to this challenge." They apparently did, because $C + I$ increased $33 billion in 1963 and another $46 billion in 1965 (in part as a result of multiplier effects, of course).

The largest tax cut in history was initiated by President Ronald Reagan in 1981. The Reagan administration persuaded Congress to cut personal taxes $250 billion over a three-year period and to cut business taxes another $70 billion. The resulting increase in disposable income stimulated consumer spending and helped push the economy out of the 1981–82 recession. When the economy slowed down in 1989–90, President George Bush proposed cutting the capital gains tax. His principal argument for this tax cut was its potential to stimulate investment.

President Clinton used the same Keynesian argument when he ran for president in 1992. With the economy still far short of its productive capacity (Q_F), he called for more fiscal stimulus. To create that stimulus, he promised both to cut taxes and to increase government spending.

Inflation Worries

After he was elected, President Clinton changed his mind about the need for fiscal stimulus. Rather than delivering the middle-class tax cut he had promised, Clinton instead decided to *raise* taxes. This abrupt policy U-turn was motivated in part by the recognition of how powerful the multiplier is. The economy was already expanding when Clinton was elected and the multiplier was at work. As each successive spending cycle developed, the economy would move closer to full employment. Any *new* fiscal stimulus would accelerate that movement. As a result, the economy might end up expanding so fast that it would overshoot the full-employment goal.

If too much fiscal stimulus were enacted, the resultant pressure might force prices higher. In other words, a tax cut in 1993 carried the risk of causing inflation. This risk was illustrated in Figure 12.2. As aggregate demand increases from AD_1 to AD^*, the price level creeps up. If aggregate demand increases further to AD_2, the price level jumps. In this case, fiscal stimulus designed to achieve full employment creates an inflation problem.

FISCAL RESTRAINT

The threat of inflation suggests that fiscal *restraint* may be an appropriate policy strategy at times. If excessive aggregate demand is causing prices to rise, the goal of fiscal policy will be to reduce aggregate demand, not stimulate it (see Figure 12.7).

The means available to the federal government for restraining aggregate demand emerge again from both sides of the budget. The difference here

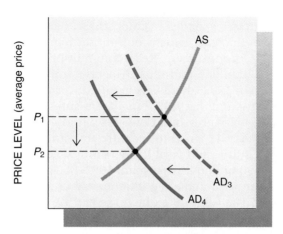

FIGURE 12.7
Fiscal Restraint

Fiscal restraint is used to reduce inflationary pressures. The strategy is to shift the aggregate demand curve to the left with budget cuts or tax hikes.

is that we use the budget tools in reverse. We now want to *reduce* government spending or *increase* taxes.

Budget Cuts

Cutbacks in government spending directly reduce aggregate demand. Their impact is much larger than their apparent size, however, due to the multiplier.

Suppose the government cut military spending by $100 billion. This would throw a lot of aerospace employees out of work. Thousands of workers would get smaller paychecks, or perhaps none at all. These workers would be forced to cut back on their own spending, thereby reducing the consumption component of aggregate demand. Hence aggregate demand would take two hits: first a cut in government spending, then induced cutbacks in consumer spending. The multiplier process works in both directions.

The marginal propensity to consume again reveals the power of the multiplier process. If the MPC is 0.75, the consumption of aerospace workers will drop by $75 billion when the government cutbacks reduce their income by $100 billion. (The rest of the income loss will be covered by a reduction in savings balances.)

From this point on the story should sound familiar. As detailed in Table 12.1, the $100 billion government cutback will ultimately reduce consumer spending by $300 billion. The *total* drop in spending is thus $400 billion. Like their mirror image, **government cutbacks have a multiplied effect on aggregate demand.** The total impact is equal to

$$\bullet \quad \begin{array}{c} \text{Cumulative reduction} \\ \text{in spending} \end{array} = \text{multiplier} \times \text{initial budget cut}$$

Tax Hikes

Tax increases can also be used to shift the aggregate demand curve to the left. The direct effect of a tax increase is a reduction in disposable income. People will pay the higher taxes by reducing their consumption and depleting their savings. The reduced consumption results in less aggregate demand. As consumers "tighten their belts," they set off the multiplier process, leading to a much larger cumulative shift of aggregate demand.

Tax increases have been used to "cool" the economy on several occasions. In 1968, for example, the economy was rapidly approaching full employment and Vietnam War expenditures were helping to drive up prices. Congress responded by imposing a 10 percent surtax (temporary additional tax) on income, which took more than $10 billion in purchasing power away from consumers. Resultant multiplier effects reduced spending in 1969 over $20 billion and thus helped restrain price pressures.

In 1982, there was great concern that the 1981 tax cuts had been excessive and that inflationary pressures were building up. To reduce that inflationary pressure, Congress withdrew some of its earlier tax cuts, especially those designed to increase investment spending. The net effect of the Tax Equity and Fiscal Responsibility Act of 1982 was to increase taxes roughly $90 billion for the years 1983–85. This shifted the aggregate demand curve leftward, reducing inflationary pressures (see Figure 12.7).

The Clinton tax increase of 1993 also restrained aggregate demand. The initial fiscal restraint from the tax increase and spending slowdown amounted to roughly $40 billion. This helped to slow the rate of economic growth and to keep inflation in check. The tax increases did nothing for President Clinton's popularity, however. After the Republican election victories in November 1994, President Clinton again decided that tax cuts were needed.

Fiscal Guidelines

The basic rules for fiscal policy are so simple that they can be summarized in a small table. The policy goal is to match aggregate demand with the full-employment potential of the economy. The fiscal mechanism for attaining that goal is the government budget. By changing taxes or government spending, the government can shift the aggregate demand curve. If successful, such shifts can produce an equilibrium that is consistent with our macro goals. Table 12.2 summarizes the guidelines laid down by John Maynard Keynes for attaining fiscal-policy success.

TABLE 12.2
Fiscal Policy Guidelines

The Keynesian emphasis on aggregate demand results in simple guidelines for fiscal policy: reduce aggregate demand to fight inflation; increase aggregate demand to fight unemployment.

Problem	Solution	Method
Unemployment (recession)	Increase aggregate demand	Increase government spending Cut taxes
Inflation	Reduce aggregate demand	Cut government spending Raise taxes

POLICY PERSPECTIVES

Unbalanced Budgets

The primary lever of fiscal policy is the federal government's budget. As we have observed, changes in either federal taxes or outlays are the mechanism for shifting the aggregate demand curve. The use of this mechanism has a troubling implication: ***The use of the budget to manage aggregate demand implies that the budget will often be unbalanced.*** In the face of a recession, for example, the government has sound reasons both to cut taxes and to increase its own spending. By reducing tax revenues and increasing expenditures simultaneously, however, the federal government will throw its budget out of balance.

Budget Deficit. When government expenditures exceed tax revenues, a **budget deficit** exists. The deficit is measured by the difference between expenditures and receipts:

$$\text{Budget deficit} = \text{government spending} - \text{tax revenues}$$

where spending exceeds revenues. In 1995, the federal budget deficit was approximately $200 billion. To pay for such deficit spending, the government must borrow money, either directly from the private sector or from the banking sector.

Budget Surplus. In theory, government revenues may also exceed government spending, giving rise to a **budget surplus.** If the government had more revenue than expenditure, it could use the surplus to pay off debts incurred in earlier deficit years. Back in 1836, the federal government simply distributed its budget surplus to the states, as it had no accumulated debt of its own. That was the last time the U.S. government was completely out of debt.

A River of Red Ink. The last year in which the federal government even had a budget surplus was 1969. Since then, the federal budget has been "in the red" (deficit) every year. As Figure 12.8 reveals, the deficits of the 1980s and 1990s have routinely been measured in the range of $150 billion to $200 billion per year, far above earlier levels.

To Balance or Not to Balance?

The red ink that has flowed from the federal budget has raised a chorus of protests. People say they want Uncle Sam to balance his budget, just like individual consumers must. John Maynard Keynes called that notion poppycock. From a Keynesian perspective, budget deficits and surpluses are a routine feature of fiscal policy. The appropriateness of any given deficit or surplus depends on the need for more or less spending injections. ***In Keynes's view, a balanced budget would be appropriate only if the resulting aggregate demand were consistent with full-employment equilibrium.*** If this condition was not met, an unbalanced budget would be appropriate. The size of the desired deficit or surplus would depend on the extent of required stimulus or restraint.

Although the theory of unbalanced budgets is clear, budget policy has not been so convincing. The string of deficits depicted in Figure 12.8 certainly casts doubt on the allegiance to fiscal guidelines (Table 12.2). Has the economy really needed the constant stimulus of widening deficits? Or have politicians found it too difficult to raise taxes or cut spending when fiscal restraint was called for?

Concern over the *politics* of the budget has led many critics to demand that the federal government be *required* to balance the budget every year. In 1995, there was even widespread support for the idea of amending the U.S. Constitution to require a balanced budget. However, forcing the government to balance the budget every year would undermine the *economic* function of the budget. The ability to shift aggregate demand with changes in government spending and taxes is a basic lever of macroeconomic policy. Dismantling that lever would weaken the government's ability to stabilize the economy. The challenge is to use the fiscal policy lever wisely.

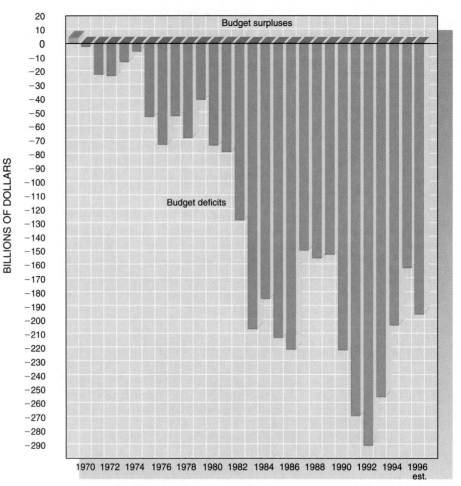

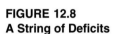
BILLIONS OF DOLLARS

YEAR

FIGURE 12.8
A String of Deficits

The federal government has not achieved an annual budget surplus since 1969. In the early 1980s, federal deficits increased dramatically. They soared further in the early 1990s as a result of a prolonged recession, high interest payments, bank bailouts, and the continued expansion of government programs.

Source: Office of Management and Budget.

SUMMARY

- The Keynesian explanation of macro instability requires government intervention to shift the aggregate demand curve to the desired rate of output. The government can do this by balancing aggregate spending with the economy's full-employment potential.
- To boost aggregate demand, the government may either increase its own spending or cut taxes. To restrain aggregate demand, the government may reduce its own spending or raise taxes.
- Any change in government spending or taxes will have a multiplied impact on aggregate demand. The additional impact comes from changes in consumption caused by changes in disposable income.
- The marginal propensity to consume tells how changes in disposable income affect consumer spending. The MPC is the fraction of each additional dollar spent (i.e., not saved).
- The size of the multiplier depends on the marginal propensity to consume. The higher the MPC, the larger the multiplier, where the multiplier = 1/(1 − MPC).

- Fiscal stimulus carries the risk of inflation. Keynes dismissed this threat with a horizontal AS curve. The threat is real, however, if the AS curve is upward sloping.
- A balanced budget is appropriate only if the resulting aggregate demand is compatible with full employment and price stability. Otherwise, *unbalanced* budgets (deficits or surpluses) are appropriate.

Terms to Remember

Define the following terms:

fiscal policy	saving	disposable income
aggregate demand	marginal propensity to	budget deficit
consumption	consume (MPC)	budget surplus
investment	marginal propensity to	
net exports	save (MPS)	
equilibrium (macro)	multiplier	

Questions for Discussion

1. How long does it take you to spend any income you receive? What happens to the dollars you spend?
2. What is your MPC? Would a welfare recipient and a millionaire have the same MPC? What determines a person's MPC?
3. What do people do with that fraction of their income they save?
4. How long does the multiplier process take? How many cycles are likely to occur in a year's time? How will this alter the impact of fiscal policy?
5. Do fiscal-policy makers really need to know the magnitudes of the MPC and multipliers? Could they get along as well without such information?
6. If the guidelines for fiscal policy (Table 12.2) are so simple, why does the economy ever suffer from unemployment or inflation?
7. Would a constitutional amendment that would require the federal government to balance its budget (incur no deficits) be desirable? Explain.

Problems

1. (*a*) The multiplier process depicted in Table 12.1 is based on an MPC of 0.75. Recompute the first five cycles using an MPC of 0.50.
   (*b*) What is the value of the multiplier in this case?
   (*c*) What is the multiplier when the MPC is (1) 0.80 and (2) 0.90?
2. Suppose the government increases education spending by $20 billion. How much additional *consumption* will this increase cause?
3. By how much would taxes be reduced by President Clinton's child tax-credit proposal (see Headline, p. 261)? If the marginal propensity to save is .20,
   (*a*) How much of the tax cut will consumers spend?
   (*b*) By how much will aggregate demand increase as this additional consumption works its way through the economy?

Chapter 13

Money and Banks

Sophocles, the ancient Greek playwright, had very strong opinions about the role of money. As he saw it, "Of evils upon earth, the worst is money. It is money that sacks cities, and drives men forth from hearth and home; warps and seduces native intelligence, and breeds a habit of dishonesty."

In modern times, people may still be seduced by the lure of money and fashion their lives around its pursuit. Nevertheless, it is hard to imagine an economy functioning without money. Money affects not only morals and ideals but also the way an economy works.

The purpose of this and the following chapter is to examine the role of money in the economy today. We begin with a very simple question:

- What is money?

As we shall discover, money isn't exactly what you think it is. Once we have established the characteristics of money, we go on to ask:

- Where does money come from?
- What role do banks play in the macro economy?

In the next chapter we look at how the Federal Reserve System controls the supply of money and thereby affects macroeconomic outcomes. We will then have a second policy lever in our basic macro model.

THE USES OF MONEY

To appreciate the significance of money for a modern economy, imagine for a moment that there were no such thing as money. How would you get something for breakfast? If you wanted eggs for breakfast, you would have to tend your own chickens or go see Farmer Brown. But how would you pay Farmer Brown for his eggs? Without money, you would have to offer

barter: The direct exchange of one good for another, without the use of money.

him goods or services that he could use. In other words, you would have to engage in primitive **barter**—the direct exchange of one good for another—in order to get eggs for breakfast. You would get those eggs only if Farmer Brown happened to want the particular goods or services you had to offer and if the two of you could agree on the terms of the exchange.

The use of money greatly simplifies market transactions. It's a lot easier to exchange money for eggs at the supermarket than to go into the country and cut hay or lay sod every time you crave some eggs. Our ability to use money in market transactions, however, depends on the grocer's willingness to accept money as a *medium of exchange*. The grocer sells eggs for money only because he can use the same money to pay his help and buy the goods he himself desires. He, too, can exchange money for goods and services. Accordingly, money plays an essential role in facilitating the continuous series of exchanges that characterize a market economy.

Money has other desirable features. The grocer who accepts your money in exchange for a carton of eggs doesn't have to spend his income immediately. On the contrary, he can hold onto the money for a few days or months, without worrying about its spoiling. Hence money is also a useful *store of value,* that is, a mechanism for transforming current income into future purchases. Finally, common use of money serves as a *standard of value* for comparing the market worth of different goods. A dozen eggs is more valuable than a dozen onions if it costs more at the supermarket.

We may identify, then, several essential characteristics of what we call money. Specifically, ***anything that serves all of the following purposes can be thought of as money:***

- ***Medium of exchange:*** is accepted as payment for goods and services (and debts)
- ***Store of value:*** can be held for future purchases
- ***Standard of value:*** serves as a yardstick for measuring the prices of goods and services

The great virtue of money is that it facilitates market exchanges and specialization in production. In fact, efficient division of labor requires a system whereby people can exchange the things they produce for the things they desire. Money makes this system of exchange possible.

Many Types of "Money"

Although markets cannot function without money, they can get along without *dollars*. U.S. dollars are just one example of money. In the early days of Colonial America, there were no U.S. dollars. People used Indian wampum, then tobacco, grain, fish, and furs as mediums of exchange. Throughout the colonies, gunpowder and bullets were frequently used for small change. These forms of money weren't as convenient as U.S. dollars, but they did the job. So long as they served as a medium of exchange, a store of value, and a standard of value, they were properly regarded as money.

The first paper money issued by the U.S. federal government consisted of $10 million worth of "greenbacks," printed in 1861 to finance the Civil War. The Confederate states also issued paper money to finance their side of the Civil War. Confederate dollars became worthless, however, when the South lost and people no longer accepted Confederate currency in exchange for goods and services.

When communism collapsed in Eastern Europe, similar problems arose. In Poland, the zloty was shunned as a form of money in the early 1980s.

HEADLINE

BARTER

The Worthless Ruble

At the beginning of 1992, citizens of the former Soviet Union held over 800 billion rubles. They didn't want to hold so many rubles, but they had little choice. Consumers simply couldn't spend the rubles they earned. Shelves in state stores were barren of consumer goods. Everything from sugar and vodka to meat and apartments was rationed. Consumers could buy only so much of these goods, regardless of how many rubles they had to spend. Even then, they had to stand in line for hours for the opportunity to buy their permitted ration—and hope it was available.

One reason the shelves were empty is that producers did not want to sell their output for rubles. If producers sold output through official state stores, they were paid very low prices set by the government. Even the much higher ruble prices available in the newly freed "open" market weren't that attractive. What would a potato farmer want with more rubles anyway? He would just end up with more unwanted rubles that no one else accepted in trade. He was better off keeping his potatoes. At least they had *value* in the marketplace.

As the value of the ruble plummeted, Soviet producers and consumers turned to barter. Workers who helped harvest potatoes took payment in potatoes. Farmers traded potatoes for machinery, cigarettes, gasoline, and vodka. Consumers hoarded all the goods they could acquire, believing that sugar, flour, matches, and soap were better stores of value than rubles. These goods were also more readily accepted in market exchanges. As barter replaced ruble transactions, production and distribution systems crumbled, accelerating the disintegration of the Soviet economy (and political union).

Poles preferred to use cigarettes and vodka as mediums of exchange and stores of value. So much Polish currency (zlotys) was available that its value was suspect. The same problem undermined the value of the Russian ruble in the 1990s. Russian consumers preferred to hold and use American dollars rather than the rubles that few people would accept in payment for goods and services (see Headline). Cigarettes, vodka, and even potatoes were a better form of money than Russian rubles.

THE MONEY SUPPLY

Cash vs. "Money"

In the U.S. economy today, such unusual forms of money are rarely used. Nevertheless, the concept of money includes more than the dollar bills and coins in your pocket or purse. Most people realize this when they offer to pay for goods with a check or ATM card rather than cash. The "money" you have in a checking account can be used to buy goods and services or to pay debts, or it can be retained for future use. In these respects, your checking account balance is as much a part of your "money" as are the coins and dollars in your pocket or purse. In fact, if everyone accepted your checks (and if the checks could also operate vending machines and pay telephones), there would be no need to carry cash.

There is nothing unique about cash, then, insofar as the market is concerned. ***Checking accounts can and do perform the same market functions as cash.*** Accordingly, we must include checking account balances in our concept of **money**. The essence of money is not its taste, color, or feel but, rather, its ability to purchase goods and services.

money: Anything generally accepted as a medium of exchange.

Transactions Accounts

To determine how much money is available to purchase goods and services, we need to do more than count up all our coins and currency—we must also include our checking account balances. All kinds of checking accounts (e.g., NOW, credit union share drafts, debit accounts) are available at financial institutions today. And all "checking" accounts have a common feature: they permit depositors to spend their deposit balances easily, without making a special trip to the bank to withdraw funds. All you need is a checkbook or ATM card.

transactions account: A bank account that permits direct payment to a third party (e.g., with a check).

Because all such checking-account balances can be used directly in market transactions (without a trip to the bank), they are collectively referred to as "transactions accounts." The distinguishing feature of all **transactions accounts** is that they permit direct payment to a third party, without requiring a trip to the bank to make a special withdrawal. The payment itself may be in the form of a check, a debit-card transfer, or an automatic payment transfer. In all such cases, ***the balance in your transactions account substitutes for cash, and is, therefore, a form of money.***

Basic Money Supply

money supply (M1): Currency held by the public, plus balances in transactions accounts.

Because all transactions accounts can be spent as readily as cash, they are counted as part of our money supply. Adding transactions-account balances to the quantity of coins and currency held by the public gives us one measure of the amount of money available—that is, the basic **money supply.** The basic money supply is typically referred to by the abbreviation **M1.**

Figure 13.1 illustrates the actual composition of our money supply. The first component of M1 is the cash people hold (currency in circulation outside of commercial banks). Clearly, ***cash is a small part of the money supply; most money consists of balances in transactions accounts.*** This really should not come as too much of a surprise. People generally prefer to use checks rather than cash for large market transactions (see Headline). Checks turn out to be more convenient than cash, because they eliminate trips to the bank. Checks are also safer: lost or stolen cash is gone forever; checkbooks are easily replaced, at little or no cost.

Credit cards are another popular medium of exchange. As the Headline reveals, people use credit cards for about one-third of all purchases over

FIGURE 13.1
Composition of the Basic Money Supply (M1)

The money supply (M1) includes all cash held by the public plus balances people hold in transactions accounts (e.g., checking, NOW, ATS, and credit union share-draft accounts). Cash is a relatively small part of our money supply.

Source: Federal Reserve Board of Governors, February 1995.

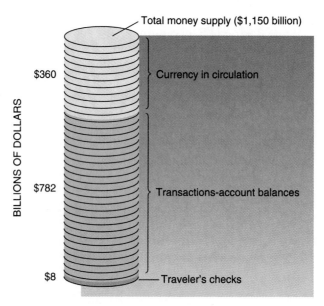

HEADLINE

MEDIUMS OF EXCHANGE

Purchase Plans

People use cash for 70 percent of small (under $50) pur-
chases. Most larger purchases are made with a check or credit card (which is itself later paid off with a check).

Size of Purchase	Method of Payment			
	Cash	**Check**	**Credit Card**	**Other**
$1–$50	70%	24%	5%	1%
$51–$100	35	42	21	2
$101–$250	22	43	32	2
Above $250	18	42	34	3

Note: Numbers may not total 100 percent because of no response or rounding.

Source: Consumer survey reported in *The Wall Street Journal*, November 23, 1987, p. 29. Reprinted by permission of *The Wall Street Journal*, © 1987 Dow Jones & Company, Inc. All Rights Reserved Worldwide.

$100. This use is not sufficient, however, to qualify credit cards as a form of "money." Credit card balances must be paid by check or cash. Hence credit cards are simply a payment *service*, not a final form of payment (credit card companies charge fees and interest for this service). The cards themselves are not a store of value, in contrast to cash or bank account balances.

The last component of our basic money supply consists of traveler's checks issued by nonbank firms (e.g., American Express). These, too, can be used directly in market transactions, just like good old-fashioned cash.

"Near Money"

Transactions accounts are not the only substitute for cash. Even a conventional savings account can be used to finance market purchases. This use of a savings account may require a trip to the bank for a special withdrawal. But that is not too great a barrier to consumer spending. Many savings banks make that trip unnecessary by offering computerized withdrawals and transfers from their savings accounts, some even at supermarket service desks or cash machines. Others offer to pay your bills if you phone in instructions.

Not all savings accounts are so easily spendable. Certificates of deposit, for example, require a minimum balance to be kept in the bank for a specified number of months or years; early withdrawal results in a loss of interest. Funds held in certificates of deposit cannot be transferred automatically to a checking account (like passbook savings balances) or to a third party (like NOW-account balances). As a result, certificates of deposit are seldom used for everyday market purchases. Nevertheless, such accounts still function like "near money" in the sense that savers can go to the bank and withdraw cash if they really want to buy something.

Another popular way of holding money is to buy shares of money-market mutual funds. Deposits into money-market mutual funds are pooled and used to purchase interest-bearing securities (e.g., Treasury bills). The resultant interest payments are typically higher than those paid by banks. Moreover, money-market funds can often be withdrawn immediately, just like those in transactions accounts. When interest rates are high, deposits move out of regular transactions accounts into these money-market mutual funds in order to earn a higher return.

Additional measures of the money supply (M2, M3, etc.) have been constructed to account for the possibility of using money-market mutual funds and various other deposits to finance everyday spending. At the core of all such measures, however, are cash and transactions-account balances, the key elements of the basic money supply (M1). Accordingly, we will limit our discussion to just M1.

Aggregate Demand

> **aggregate demand:** The total quantity of output demanded at alternative price levels in a given time period, *ceteris paribus*.

Our concern about the specific nature of money stems from our broader interest in macro outcomes. As we have observed, total output, employment, and prices are all affected by changes in **aggregate demand.** How much money people have may be one of the determinants of their spending behavior. Accordingly, it is important to know what "money" is and where it comes from.

CREATION OF MONEY

When people ponder where money comes from, they often have a simple answer: "the government prints it." They may even have toured the Bureau of Engraving and Printing in Washington, D.C., and seen dollar bills running off the printing presses. Or maybe they visited the U.S. Mint in Denver or Philadelphia and saw coins being stamped.

There is something wrong with this explanation of the origin of money, however. Figure 13.1 provides a clue. Notice again that currency and coins account for less than a third of the basic money supply. So we need to look elsewhere for the origins of money. Specifically, where do all the transactions accounts come from? How do people acquire transactions deposits (checking-account balances, NOW balances, etc.)? How does the total amount of such deposits—and, therefore, the money supply of the economy—change?

Deposit Creation

Many people assume that all transactions-account balances come from cash deposits. But this is not the case. Most deposits into transactions accounts are checks or computer transfers; hard cash is seldom used. When people get paid, for example, they typically deposit their paychecks at the bank. Some employers even arrange automatic payroll deposits, thereby eliminating the need to go to the bank at all. The employee never sees or deposits cash in these cases (see cartoon).

If checks are used to make deposits, then the supply of checks provides an initial clue about where money comes from. Anyone can buy blank checks and sign them, of course. But banks won't cash checks without some assurance that there are funds in a bank to make the check good. Banks, in fact, "hold" checks for a few days to confirm the existence of sufficient

FRANK & ERNEST reprinted by permission of Newspaper Enterprise Association.

account balances to cover the check. Likewise, retailers won't accept checks unless they get some deposit confirmation or personal identification. The constraint on check writing, then, is not the supply of paper, but the availability of transactions-account balances.

Like a good detective novel, the search for the origins of money seems to be going in a circle. It appears that transactions-account deposits come from transactions-account balances. This seeming riddle suggests that money creates money. But it offers no clue to us to how the money got there in the first place. Who created the first transactions-account balance? What was used as a deposit?

The solution to this mystery is totally unexpected: banks themselves create money. They don't print dollar bills. But they do make loans. The loans become transactions-account balances, and therefore part of the money supply. This is the answer to the apparent riddle. Quite simply, ***in making a loan, a bank effectively creates money, because transactions-account balances are counted as part of the money supply.*** And you are free to spend that money, just as if you had earned it yourself.

To understand where money comes from, then, we must recognize two basic principles:

- Transactions-account balances are the largest portion of our money supply.
- Banks create transactions-account balances by making loans.

In the following two sections we shall examine this process of creating money—**deposit creation**—more closely.

deposit creation: The creation of transactions deposits by bank lending.

A Monopoly Bank

Suppose, to keep things simple, that there is only one bank in town, University Bank, and no one regulates bank behavior. Imagine also that you have been saving some of your income by putting loose change into a piggy bank. Now, after months of saving, you break the bank and discover that your thrift has yielded $100. You immediately deposit this money in a new checking account at University Bank.

Your initial deposit will have no immediate effect on the money supply (M1). The coins in your piggy bank were already counted as part of the money supply, because they represented cash held by the public. ***When you deposit cash or coins in a bank, you are changing the composition of the money supply, not its size.*** The public (you) now holds $100 less of coins but $100 more of transactions deposits. Accordingly, no money is lost or created by the demise of your piggy bank (the initial deposit).

University Bank is not in business just for your convenience. On the contrary, it is in business to earn a profit. To earn a profit on your deposit, University Bank will have to put your money to work. This means using your deposit as the basis for making a loan to someone who is willing to pay the bank interest for use of money.

Typically, a bank does not have much difficulty finding someone who wants to borrow money. Many firms and individuals have expenditure desires that exceed their current money balances. These market participants are eager to borrow whatever funds banks are willing to lend. The question is, how much money can a bank lend? Can it lend your entire deposit? Or must University Bank keep some of your coins in reserve, in case you want to withdraw them? The answer may surprise you.

An Initial Loan. Suppose that University Bank decided to lend the entire $100 to Campus Radio. Campus Radio wants to buy a new antenna but doesn't have any money in its own checking account. To acquire the antenna, Campus Radio must take out a loan. It finds a willing creditor at University Bank.

When University Bank agrees to lend Campus Radio $100, it does so by crediting the account of Campus Radio. Instead of giving Campus Radio $100 cash, University Bank simply adds $100 to Campus Radio's checking-account balance. That is to say, the loan is made with a simple bookkeeping entry.

This simple bookkeeping procedure has important implications. When University Bank lends $100 to the Campus Radio account, it "creates" money. Keep in mind that transactions deposits are counted as part of the money supply. Moreover, Campus Radio can use this new money to purchase its desired antenna, without worrying that its check will bounce.

Or can it? Once University Bank grants a loan to Campus Radio, both you and Campus Radio have $100 in your checking accounts to spend. But the bank is holding only $100 of **reserves** (your coins). In other words, the increased checking-account balance obtained by Campus Radio does not limit your ability to write checks. There has been a net *increase* in the value of transactions deposits, but no increase in bank reserves.

bank reserves: Assets held by a bank to fulfill its deposit obligations.

Using the Loan. What happens if Campus Radio actually spends the $100 on a new antenna? Won't this "use up" all the reserves held by the bank, and endanger your check-writing privileges? The answer is no.

Consider what happens when Atlas Antenna receives the check from Campus Radio. What will Atlas do with the check? Atlas could go to University Bank and exchange the check for $100 of cash (your coins). But Atlas probably doesn't have any immediate need for cash. Atlas may prefer to deposit the check in its own checking account at University Bank (still the only bank in town). In this way, Atlas not only avoids the necessity of going to the bank (it can deposit the check by mail), but also keeps its money in a safe place. Should Atlas later want to spend the money, it can simply write a check. In the meantime, the bank continues to hold its entire reserves (your coins) and both you and Atlas have $100 to spend.

Fractional Reserves. Notice what has happened here. The money supply has increased by $100 as a result of deposit creation (the loan to Campus

Radio). Moreover, the bank has been able to support $200 of transaction deposits (your account and either the Campus Radio or Atlas account) with only $100 of reserves (your coins). In other words, *bank reserves are only a fraction of total transactions deposits*. In this case, University Bank's reserves (your $100 in coins) are only 50 percent of total deposits. Thus the bank's **reserve ratio** is 50 percent—that is

reserve ratio: The ratio of a bank's reserves to its total transactions deposits.

$$\bullet \quad \frac{\text{Reserve}}{\text{ratio}} = \frac{\text{bank reserves}}{\text{total deposits}}$$

The ability of University Bank to hold reserves that are only a fraction of total deposits results from two facts: (1) people use checks for most transactions, and (2) there is no other bank. Accordingly, reserves are rarely withdrawn from this monopoly bank. In fact, if people *never* withdrew their deposits and *all* transactions accounts were held at University Bank, University Bank would not really need any reserves. In this most unusual case, University Bank could continue to make as many loans as it wanted. Every loan it made would increase the supply of money.

Reserve Requirements

In reality, many banks are available, and people both withdraw cash from their accounts and write checks to people who have accounts in other banks. In addition, bank lending practices are regulated by the Federal Reserve System. *The Federal Reserve System requires banks to maintain some minimum reserve ratio.* This reserve requirement directly limits the ability of banks to grant new loans.

The potential impact of Federal Reserve requirements on bank lending can be readily seen. Suppose that the Federal Reserve had imposed a minimum reserve requirement of 75 percent on University Bank. Such a requirement would have prohibited University Bank from lending $100 to Campus Radio. That loan would have resulted in $200 of deposits, supported by only $100 of reserves. The actual ratio of reserves to deposits would have been 50 percent ($100 of reserves ÷ $200 of deposits). That would have violated the Fed's assumed 75 percent reserve requirement. A 75 percent reserve requirement means that University Bank must hold at all times **required reserves** equal to 75 percent of *total* deposits, including those created through loans.

required reserves: The minimum amount of reserves a bank is required to hold by government regulation; equal to required reserve ratio times transactions deposits.

The bank's dilemma is evident in the following equation:

$$\bullet \quad \frac{\text{Required}}{\text{reserves}} = \frac{\text{minimum reserve}}{\text{ratio}} \times \frac{\text{total}}{\text{deposits}}$$

To support $200 of total deposits, University Bank would need to satisfy this equation:

$$\frac{\text{Required}}{\text{reserves}} = 0.75 \times \$200 = \$150$$

But the bank has only $100 of reserves (your coins) and so would violate the reserve requirement if it increased total deposits to $200 by lending $100 to Campus Radio.

University Bank can still issue a loan to Campus Radio. But the loan must be less than $100 in order to keep the bank within the limits of the required reserve formula. Thus *a minimum reserve requirement directly limits deposit-creation possibilities*.

Assets		Liabilities	
Required reserves (@ .75 of deposits)	$90	Your account balance	$100
Excess reserves	10	Borrower's account balance	20
Total reserves	$100	Total deposits	$120
Loans	20		
Total assets	$120		

Excess Reserves

> **excess reserves:** Bank reserves in excess of required reserves.

Banks will sometimes hold reserves in excess of the minimum required by the Fed. Such reserves are called **excess reserves** and calculated as

$$\frac{\text{Excess}}{\text{reserves}} = \frac{\text{total}}{\text{reserves}} - \frac{\text{required}}{\text{reserves}}$$

Suppose again that your bank holds the $100 in coins that you deposited and confronts a 75 percent reserve requirement. In this case, however, we will assume it lends only $20. Now what does its reserve position look like?

On the liabilities side of the ledger, the bank now has $120 of new deposits, as depicted in Table 13.1. One hundred dollars of that total was deposited by you and a $20 balance was created by the bank when it made a loan.

How many reserves is the bank supposed to hold to support these deposits? If the required reserve ratio is 75 percent, it has

$$\frac{\text{Required}}{\text{reserves}} = 0.75 \times \$120 = \$90$$

By assumption, however, the bank is holding more reserves than that. It therefore has

$$\frac{\text{Excess}}{\text{reserves}} = \frac{\text{total reserves}}{\text{of } \$100} - \frac{\text{required reserves}}{\text{of } \$90} = \$10$$

This bank has not fully utilized its lending capacity. *So long as a bank has excess reserves it can make more loans.* If it does, the nation's money supply will increase further.

A Multibank World

In reality, there is more than one bank in town. Hence, any loan University Bank makes may end up as a deposit in another bank rather than at its own. This complicates the arithmetic of deposit creation but doesn't change its basic character. Indeed, the existence of a multibank system makes the money-creation process even more powerful.

In a multibank world, *the key issue is not how much excess reserves any specific bank holds but how much excess reserves exist in the entire banking system.* If excess reserves exist anywhere in the system, then some banks still have unused lending authority.

THE MONEY MULTIPLIER

Excess reserves are the sources of bank lending authority. If there are no excess reserves in the banking system, banks can't make any more loans.

Although an *absence* of excess reserves precludes further lending activity, the *amount* of excess reserves doesn't define the limit to further loans. This surprising conclusion emerges from the way a multibank system works. Consider again what happens when someone borrows all of a bank's excess reserves. In Table 13.1 we assumed that University Bank had $10 of remaining excess reserves. If someone borrows that much money from University Bank, those excess reserves will be depleted. The money won't disappear, however. Once the borrower *spends* the money, someone else will *receive* $10. If that person deposits the $10 elsewhere, then another bank will acquire a new deposit.

If another bank gets a new deposit, both its required reserves and its excess reserves increase as well. We're talking about a $10 deposit. If the Federal Reserve minimum is 75 percent (as in Table 13.1), then *required* reserves increase by $7.50. The remaining $2.50, therefore, represents *excess* reserves. This second bank can now make additional loans in the amount of $2.50.

Perhaps you are beginning to get a sense that the process of deposit creation will not come to an end quickly. On the contrary, it can continue indefinitely as deposits move from bank to bank, creating some excess reserves with every move. This process is very much like the income multiplier, which creates additional income every time income is spent. People often refer to deposit creation as the money multiplier process, with the **money multiplier** expressed as the reciprocal of the required reserve ratio. That is

money multiplier: The number of deposit (loan) dollars that the banking system can create from $1 of excess reserves; equal to 1 ÷ required reserve ratio.

$$\bullet \quad \frac{\text{Money}}{\text{multiplier}} = \frac{1}{\text{required reserve ratio}}$$

The money-multiplier process is illustrated in Figure 13.2. When a new deposit enters the banking system, it creates both excess and required reserves. The required reserves represent leakage from the flow of money, since they cannot be used to create new loans. Excess reserves, on the other hand, can be used for new loans. Once those loans are made, they typically become transactions deposits elsewhere in the banking system. Then some additional leakage into required reserves occurs, and further loans are made. The process continues until all excess reserves have leaked into required reserves. Once excess reserves have all disappeared, the total value of new loans will equal initial excess reserves multiplied by the money multiplier.

Limits to Deposit Creation

The potential of the money multiplier to create loans is summarized by the equation

$$\bullet \quad \begin{matrix}\text{Excess}\\ \text{reserves}\\ \text{of banking}\\ \text{system}\end{matrix} \times \begin{matrix}\text{money}\\ \text{multiplier}\end{matrix} = \begin{matrix}\text{potential}\\ \text{deposit creation}\end{matrix}$$

FIGURE 13.2
The Money-Multiplier Process

Part of every new bank deposit leaks into required reserves. The rest—excess reserves—can be used to make loans. These loans, in turn, become deposits elsewhere. The process of money creation continues until all available reserves are required.

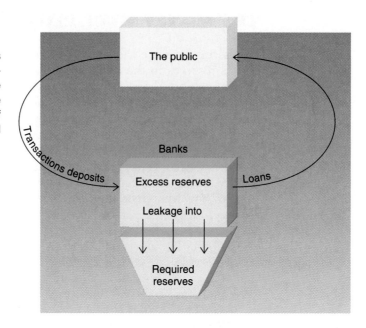

Notice how the money multiplier worked in our previous example. The value of the money multiplier was equal to 1.33, since we assumed that the required reserve ratio was 0.75. At the time we observed what was going on (Table 13.1), the bank had $10 in excess reserves. According to the money multiplier, then, the deposit-creation potential of the banking system was

$$\underset{(\$10)}{\text{Excess reserves}} \times \underset{(1.33)}{\text{money multiplier}} = \underset{\text{creation (\$13.30)}}{\text{potential deposit}}$$

If all the banks fully utilize their excess reserves at each step of the money-multiplier process, the banking system can make additional loans in the amount of $13.30.

Excess Reserves as Lending Power

While you are reviewing Table 13.1, notice the critical role that excess reserves play in the process of deposit creation. A bank can make loans only if it has excess reserves. Without excess reserves, all of a bank's reserves are required, and no further liabilities (transactions deposits) can be created with new loans. On the other hand, a bank with excess reserves can make additional loans. In fact,

- *Each bank may lend an amount equal to its excess reserves and no more.*

As such loans enter the circular flow and become deposits elsewhere, they create new excess reserves and further lending capacity. As a consequence,

- *The entire banking system can increase the volume of loans by the amount of excess reserves multiplied by the money multiplier.*

By keeping track of excess reserves, then, we can gauge the lending capacity of any bank or, with the aid of the money multiplier, the entire banking system.

POLICY PERSPECTIVES

The Macro Role of Banks

The bookkeeping details of bank deposits and loans are complex and often frustrating. But they do demonstrate convincingly that banks can create money. This implies that banks have some direct influence on economic activity, because all of our market transactions involve the use of money. The purpose of this final section is to see how the banking system fits into our macro model.

Financing Aggregate Demand

What we have demonstrated in this chapter is that banks perform two essential functions:

- Banks transfer money from savers to spenders by lending funds (reserves) held on deposit.
- The banking system creates additional money by making loans in excess of total reserves.

In performing these two functions, banks change the size of the money supply—that is, the amount of purchasing power available for buying goods and services. In the process, the banking system may alter aggregate demand. The loans banks offer to their customers will be used to purchase new cars, homes, business equipment, and other output. All of these purchases will add to aggregate demand. Hence ***increases in the money supply tend to increase aggregate demand.***

When banks curtail their lending activity, the opposite occurs. People can't get the loans or credit they need to finance desired consumption or investment. As a result, ***aggregate demand declines when the money supply shrinks.***

The central role of the banking system in the economy is emphasized in Figure 13.3. In this depiction of the circular flow, income flows from product markets through business firms to factor markets and returns to consumers in the form of disposable income. Consumers spend most of their income but also save (don't spend) some of it. This consumer saving could pose a problem for the economy if no one else were to step up and buy the goods and services consumers leave unsold.

The banking system is the key link between consumer savings and the demand originating in other sectors of the economy. To see how important that link is, imagine that *all* consumer saving was deposited in piggy banks rather than depository institutions (banks) and that no one used checks. Under these circumstances, banks could not transfer money from savers to spenders by holding deposits and making loans. The banks could not create the money needed to boost aggregate demand.

In reality, a substantial portion of consumer saving *is* deposited in banks. These and other bank deposits can be used as the basis of loans, thereby returning purchasing power to the circular flow. In fact, the primary economic function of banks is not to store money but to transfer purchasing power from savers to spenders. They do so by lending money to businesses for new plant and equipment, to consumers for new homes or cars, and to government entities that desire greater purchasing power. Moreover, because the banking system can make *multiple* loans from available reserves, banks don't have to receive all consumer saving in order to carry out their function. On the contrary, ***the banking system can create any desired level of money supply if allowed to expand or reduce loan activity at will.***

FIGURE 13.3
Banks in the Circular Flow

Banks help to transfer income from savers to spenders. They do this by using their deposits to make loans to business firms and consumers who desire to spend more money than they have. By lending money, banks help to maintain any desired rate of aggregate spending.

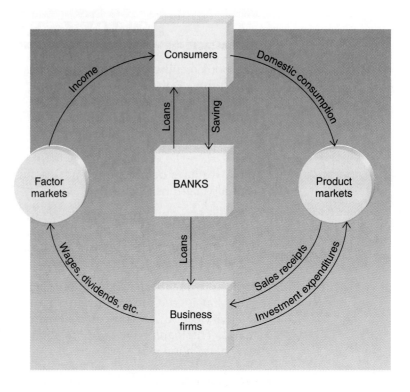

Constraints on Lending Activity

There are four major constraints on deposit creation. The first of these constraints is the willingness of consumers and businesses to continue using and accepting checks rather than cash in the marketplace. If people preferred to hold cash rather than checkbooks, banks would not be able to acquire or maintain the reserves that are the foundation of bank lending activity.

The second constraint on deposit creation is the willingness of consumers, businesses, and governments to borrow the money that banks make available. If no one wanted to borrow any money, deposit creation would never begin. By the same reasoning, if all excess reserves are not borrowed (lent), deposit creation will not live up to its theoretical potential.

The banks themselves may not be willing to satisfy all credit demands. This was the case in the 1930s when the banks declined to use their excess reserves for loans they perceived to be too risky. In the recession of 1990–91 many banks again closed their loan windows. A sharp downturn in real estate prices left many borrowers unable to repay prior loans. This forced many banks to foreclose on bad loans. In the process, they got stuck with unsalable property and huge losses. Hundreds of banks were forced to close or restructure. These and other banks were unable or unwilling to make new loans until they acquired greater reserves. The resulting "credit crunch" constrained aggregate demand and prolonged the recession.

The last and most important constraint on deposit creation is the Federal Reserve System. In the absence of government regulation, individual banks would have tremendous power over the money supply and therewith all macroeconomic outcomes. The government limits this power by regulating bank lending practices. The levers of Federal Reserve policy are examined in the next chapter.

SUMMARY

- In a market economy, money serves a critical function in facilitating exchanges and specialization, thus permitting increased output. "Money" in this context may refer to anything that serves as a medium of exchange, store of value, and standard of value.
- The most common measure of the money supply (M1) includes both cash and balances people hold in transactions accounts (e.g., checking, NOW, and ATS accounts).
- Banks have the power to create money simply by making loans. In making loans, banks create new transactions deposits, which become part of the money supply.
- The ability of banks to make loans—create money—depends on their reserves. Only if a bank has excess reserves—reserves greater than those required by federal regulation—can it make new loans.
- As loans are spent, they create deposits elsewhere, making it possible for other banks to make additional loans. The money multiplier (1 ÷ required reserve ratio) indicates the total value of deposits that can be created by the banking system from excess reserves.
- The role of banks in creating money includes the transfer of money from savers to spenders as well as deposit creation in excess of deposit balances. Taken together, these two functions give banks direct control over the amount of purchasing power available in the marketplace.
- The deposit-creation potential of the banking system is limited by government regulation. It is also limited by the willingness of market participants to hold deposits or borrow money. At times, banks themselves may be unwilling to use all their lending ability.

Terms to Remember

Define the following terms:

barter	aggregate demand	required reserves
money	deposit creation	excess reserves
transactions account	bank reserves	money multiplier
money supply (M1)	reserve ratio	

Questions for Discussion

1. Do cigarettes and vodka satisfy the three conditions for "money" (see Headline on p. 271).
2. Why aren't credit cards counted as "money"?
3. Does money have any intrinsic value? If not, why are people willing to accept money in exchange for goods and services?
4. Have you ever borrowed money to buy a car, pay tuition, or for any other purpose? In what form did you receive the money? How did your loan affect the money supply? Aggregate demand?
5. Does the fact that your bank keeps only a fraction of your account balance in reserve make you uncomfortable? Why don't people rush to the bank and retrieve their money? What would happen if they did?
6. If people never withdrew cash from banks, how much money could the banking system potentially create? Could this really happen? What might limit deposit creation in this case?
7. If all banks heeded Shakespeare's admonition "Neither a borrower nor a lender be," what would happen to the supply of money?

Problems

1. What percentage of your monthly spending do you pay with (*a*) cash, (*b*) check, (*c*) credit card, or (*d*) automatic transfers? How do you pay off the credit card balance? How does your use of cash compare with the composition of the money supply (Figure 13.1)?

2. Suppose that an Irish Sweepstakes winner deposits $10 million in cash into her transactions account at the Bank of America. Assume a reserve requirement of 25 percent and no excess reserves in the banking system prior to this deposit. Show the changes on the Bank of America balance sheet when the $10 million is initially deposited.

3. In December 1994, a man in Ohio decided to deposit all of the *8 million* pennies he had been saving for nearly 65 years. (His deposit weighed over 48,000 pounds!) With a reserve requirement of 20 percent, how did his deposit change the lending capacity of
   (*a*) his bank?
   (*b*) the banking system?

Chapter 14

Monetary Policy

We have seen how money is created. We have also gotten a few clues about how the government limits money creation and thus influences aggregate demand. The intent of this chapter is to examine the mechanics of government control more closely. The basic issues to be addressed are

- How does the government control the amount of money in the economy?
- How does the money supply affect macroeconomic outcomes?

Most people have a ready answer for the first question. The popular view is that the government controls the amount of money in the economy by printing more or fewer dollar bills. But we have already observed that the concept of "money" is not so simple. **Banks, not the printing presses, create most of our money.** In making loans, banks create transactions deposits that are counted as part of the money supply (M1).

Because bank lending activities are the primary source of money, the government must regulate bank lending if it wants to control the amount of money in the economy. That is exactly what the Federal Reserve System does. The Federal Reserve System—the "Fed"—not only limits the volume of loans that the banking system can get from any given level of reserves; it can also alter the amount of reserves in the banking system.

monetary policy: The use of money and credit controls to influence macroeconomic activity.

The Federal Reserve System's control over the supply of money is the key mechanism of **monetary policy.** The potential of this policy lever to alter macro outcomes is illustrated in Figure 14.1. By making more or less money available, the Fed can shift aggregate demand. The resulting shifts can alter the rate of output, the price level, and the number of available jobs.

Vladimir Lenin, the first communist leader of the Soviet Union, was impressed by the potential of monetary policy. When the Communist party was still consolidating its power after the 1917 revolution and civil war, Lenin introduced a new currency—the *chervonets*. His aim was to replace the czarist ruble and hundreds of regional currencies with the chervonets. A single currency would help integrate the many different republics into the new Soviet Union. As he saw it, monetary policy was an important *po-*

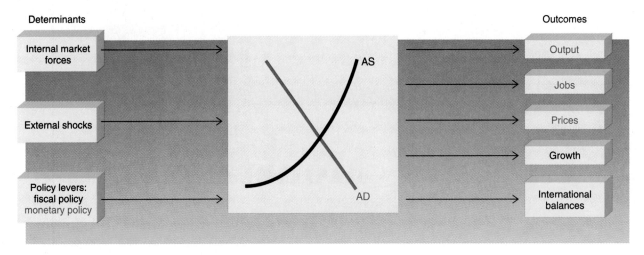

FIGURE 14.1
Monetary Policy

Monetary policy tries to alter macro outcomes by managing the amount of money available in the economy. By changing the money supply and/or interest rates, monetary policy seeks to shift aggregate demand.

litical tool, as well as an economic one. A common currency would increase interregional trade and strengthen the power of the state.

Lenin also saw the destructive potential of monetary policy. Indeed, he argued that the best way to destroy a society is to destroy its money. If a society's money became valueless, it would no longer be accepted in exchange for goods and services in product markets. As a consequence, people would resort to barter, and the economy's efficiency would be severely impaired. Ironically, the dismantling of the Soviet Union itself was accelerated by an excess supply of money and a breakdown in market transactions.

All countries have learned the importance of controlling the amount of money. Although not always successful, every country uses monetary policy to influence macroeconomic outcomes.

THE FEDERAL RESERVE SYSTEM

Control of the money supply in the United States starts with the Fed. The Fed is actually a system of regional banks and central controls, headed by a chairman of the board.

Federal Reserve Banks

The core of the Federal Reserve System consists of twelve Federal Reserve banks, located in the various regions of the country. Each of these banks acts as a central banker for the private banks in its region. In this role, the Fed banks perform many critical services, including the following:

- *Clearing checks between private banks.* Suppose the Bank of America in San Francisco receives a deposit from one of its customers in the form of a share draft written on the New York State Employees Credit Union. The Bank of America doesn't have to go to New York to collect the cash or other reserves that support that draft. Instead, the Bank of America can deposit the draft (check) at its account with the Federal Reserve Bank of San Francisco. The Fed then collects from the Credit Union. This vital clearinghouse service saves the Bank of America and other private banks a great deal of time and expense. In view of the fact that over 65 *billion* checks are written every year, this clearinghouse service is an important feature of the Federal Reserve System.

- *Holding bank reserves.* Notice that the clearinghouse service of the Fed was facilitated by the fact that the Bank of America (and the New York Employees Credit Union) had their own accounts at the Fed. Banks are *required* to hold some minimum fraction of their transactions deposits in reserve. Nearly all of these reserves are held in accounts at the regional Federal Reserve banks. Only a small amount of reserves is held as cash in a bank's vaults. These accounts at the Fed provide greater security and convenience for bank reserves. They also enable the Fed to monitor the actual level of bank reserves.

- *Providing currency.* Because banks hold very little cash in their vaults, they turn to the Fed to meet sporadic cash demands. A private bank can simply call the regional Federal Reserve bank and order a supply of cash, to be delivered (by armored truck) before a weekend or holiday. The cash will be deducted from the bank's own account at the Fed. When all the cash comes back in after the holiday, the bank can reverse the process, sending the unneeded cash back to the Fed.

- *Providing loans.* The Federal Reserve banks may also loan reserves to private banks. This practice, called "discounting," will be examined more closely in a moment.

The Board of Governors

At the top of the Federal Reserve System's organization chart (Figure 14.2) is the Board of Governors. The Board of Governors is the key decision-maker for monetary policy. The Fed Board, located in Washington, D.C., consists of seven members appointed by the president of the United States and confirmed by the U.S. Senate. Board members are appointed for fourteen-year terms and cannot be reappointed. Their exceptionally long tenure is intended to give the Fed governors a measure of political independence. They are not beholden to any elected official and will hold office longer than any president.

FIGURE 14.2
Structure of the Federal Reserve System

The broad policies of the Fed are determined by the seven-member Board of Governors. Alan Greenspan is the chairman of the Fed Board.

The twelve Federal Reserve banks provide central-banking services to individual banks in their respective regions. The private banks must follow Fed rules on reserves and loan activity.

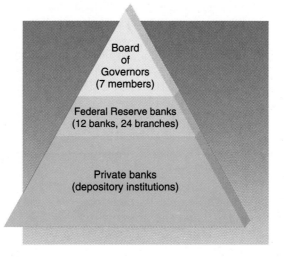

Board of Governors (7 members)

Federal Reserve banks (12 banks, 24 branches)

Private banks (depository institutions)

The intent of the Fed's independence is to keep control of the nation's money supply beyond the immediate reach of politicians (especially members of Congress, elected for two-year terms). The designers of the Fed system feared that political control of monetary policy would cause wild swings in the money supply and macro instability. Critics argue, however, that the Fed's independence makes it unresponsive to the majority will.

The Fed Chairman

The most visible member of the Fed system is the Board's chairman. The chairman is selected by the president of the United States for a four-year term. The chairman may be reappointed for additional terms during his or her fourteen-year term as a governor. The occasions for reappointment typically entail a lot of debate among the Fed, the Congress, and the president about the conduct of monetary policy. President Ronald Reagan first made Alan Greenspan the Fed chairman in 1987 and President George Bush reappointed him for another four-year term in 1991. When his second term expired in 1996, President Clinton had the opportunity to reappoint him for a third term or select another Fed chairman.

MONETARY TOOLS

> **money supply (M1):** Currency held by the public, plus balances in transactions accounts.

Our immediate interest is not in the structure of the Federal Reserve System but in the way the Fed can use its powers to alter the **money supply (M1).** The levers of the Fed's power include

- Reserve requirements
- Discount rates
- Open-market operations

Reserve Requirements

> **required reserves:** The minimum amount of reserves a bank is required to hold by government regulation; equal to required reserve ratio times transactions deposits.

We have already emphasized the need for banks to maintain some minimal level of reserves. The Fed requires private banks to keep some stated fraction of their deposits "in reserve." These **required reserves** are held either in the form of actual vault cash or, more commonly, as credits (deposits) in the bank's "reserve account" at a regional Federal Reserve bank.

The Fed's authority to set reserve requirements gives it great power over the lending behavior of individual banks. ***By changing the reserve requirement, the Fed can directly alter the lending capacity of the banking system.***

Recall that the ability of the banking system to make additional loans—create deposits—is determined by two factors: (1) the amount of excess reserves banks hold and (2) the money multiplier—that is

- $$\text{Available lending capacity of banking system} = \text{excess reserves} \times \text{money multiplier}$$

Changes in reserve requirements affect both variables on the right side of this equation.

The impact of reserve requirements on the first of these variables is straightforward. **Excess reserves** are simply the difference between total reserves and the amount required by Fed rules—that is

> **excess reserves:** Bank reserves in excess of required reserves.

- $$\text{Excess reserves} = \text{total reserves} - \text{required reserves}$$

money multiplier: The number of deposit (loan) dollars that the banking system can create from $1 of excess reserves; equal to 1 ÷ required reserve ratio.

Accordingly, with a given amount of total reserves, *a decrease in required reserves increases excess reserves.* The opposite is equally apparent: an increase in the reserve requirement reduces excess reserves.

A change in the reserve requirement also increases the **money multiplier.** Recall that the **money multiplier** is simply the reciprocal of the reserve requirement (i.e., 1 ÷ reserve requirement). Hence *a lower reserve requirement directly increases the value of the money multiplier.* Both determinants of bank lending capacity thus are affected by reserve requirements.

The impact of a decrease in the required reserve ratio is summarized in Table 14.1. In this case, the required reserve ratio is decreased from 25 to 20 percent. Notice that this change in the reserve requirement has no effect on the amount of initial transactions deposits in the banking system (row 1 of Table 14.1) or the amount of total reserves (row 2). They remain at $100 billion and $30 billion, respectively.

What the decreased reserve requirement *does* affect is the way those reserves can be used. Before the increase, $25 billion in reserves was *required,* leaving $5 billion of *excess* reserves. Now, however, banks are required to hold only $20 billion (0.20 × $100 billion) in reserves, leaving them with $10 billion in excess reserves. Thus a decrease in the reserve requirement immediately increases excess reserves, as illustrated in row 4 of Table 14.1.

There is a second effect also. Notice what happens to the money multiplier (1 ÷ reserve ratio). Previously it was 4 (1 ÷ 0.25); now it is 5 (1 ÷ 0.20). Consequently, a lower reserve requirement not only increases excess reserves but boosts their lending power as well.

A change in the reserve requirement, therefore, hits banks with a double whammy. *A change in the reserve requirement causes*

- *A change in excess reserves*
- *A change in the money multiplier*

These changes lead to a sharp rise in bank lending power. Whereas the banking system initially had the power to increase the volume of loans by only $20 billion ($5 billion of excess reserves × 4), it now has $50 billion ($10 billion × 5) of unused lending capacity, as noted in the last row of Table 14.1.

Changes in reserve requirements are a powerful weapon for altering the lending capacity of the banking system. The Fed uses this power sparingly, so as not to cause abrupt changes in the money supply and severe disruptions of banking activity. From 1970 to 1980, for example, reserve requirements were changed only twice, and then only by half a percentage point

TABLE 14.1
The Impact of a Decreased Reserve Requirement

A decrease in the required reserve ratio raises both excess reserves (row 4) and the money multiplier (row 5). As a consequence, changes in the reserve requirement have a substantial impact on the lending capacity of the banking system.

		Required Reserve Ratio	
		25 Percent	**20 Percent**
1.	Total deposits	$100 billion	$100 billion
2.	Total reserves	30 billion	30 billion
3.	Required reserves	25 billion	20 billion
4.	Excess reserves	5 billion	10 billion
5.	Money multiplier	4	5
6.	Unused lending capacity	$20 billion	$50 billion

each time (e.g., from 12.0 to 12.5 percent). In December 1990, the Fed lowered reserve requirements, hoping to create the extra lending power that might push the stalled economy out of recession. The Headline below describes how this same policy lever was used in Japan.

The Discount Rate

Banks have a tremendous incentive to maintain their reserves at or close to the minimum established by the Fed. Money held in reserve earns no interest, but loans and bonds do. Hence a profit-maximizing bank seeks to keep its excess reserves as low as possible, preferring to put its reserves to work. In fact, banks have demonstrated an uncanny ability to keep their reserves close to the minimum federal requirement (see Figure 14.3).

Because banks continually seek to keep excess reserves at a minimum, they run the risk of falling below reserve requirements. A large borrower may be a little slow in repaying a loan, or the rate of deposit withdrawals and transfers may exceed expectations. At such times a bank may find that it doesn't have enough reserves to satisfy Fed requirements.

Banks could ensure continual compliance with reserve requirements by maintaining large amounts of excess reserves. But that is an unprofitable procedure. On the other hand, a strategy of maintaining minimum reserves runs the risk of violating Fed rules. Banks can pursue this strategy only if they have some last minute source of extra reserves.

There are three possible sources of last-minute reserves. A bank that finds itself short of reserves can turn to other banks for help. If a reserve-poor bank can borrow some reserves from a reserve-rich bank, it may be able to bridge its temporary deficit and satisfy the Fed. Another option available to reserve poor banks is the sale of securities. Banks use some of their excess reserves to buy government bonds, which pay interest. If a bank needs more reserves to satisfy federal regulations, it may sell these securities and deposit the proceeds at the regional Federal Reserve bank. Its reserve position is thereby increased.

HEADLINE

RESERVE REQUIREMENTS

Japanese Central Bank Cuts Reserve Requirements

Rare Move Taken to Widen Access to Credit

TOKYO, Oct. 1—In a rare move aimed at making credit more widely available, the Bank of Japan today announced that it will slash by about 40 percent the amount of money that commercial banks must keep in reserve at the central bank.

The cut in reserve requirements, which will become effective Oct. 16, is the first by the Bank of Japan in more than five years, and economists said it is the most dramatic of a series of actions the central bank has taken

since midyear to ensure that the economy's current slowdown doesn't turn into something more severe. . . .

"There's a tremendous liquidity squeeze out there, and this is an expression by the monetary authorities that, in spite of what they have said, they are concerned about the tightness of liquidity in the economy," said Kenneth Courtis, chief economist at Deutsche Bank's Tokyo office. "Since banks will . . . keep less money on reserve at the central bank, it means they will have more money to lend out to the economy as a whole."

—Paul Blustein

The Washington Post, October 2, 1991, p. C1. © 1991, The Washington Post. Reprinted with permission.

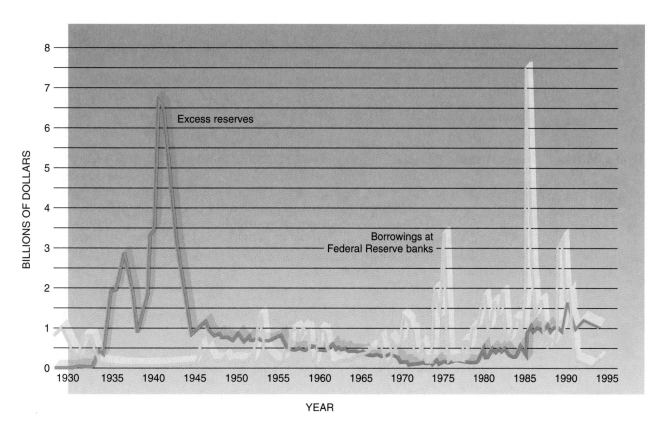

FIGURE 14.3
Excess Reserves and Borrowings

Excess reserves represent unused lending capacity. Hence banks strive to keep excess reserves at a minimum. The one exception to this practice occurred in the Great Depression, when banks were hesitant to make any loans.

In trying to minimize excess reserves, banks occasionally fall short of required reserves. At such times they may borrow from other banks (the federal funds market) or they may borrow reserves from the Fed. Borrowing from the Fed is called "discounting."

Source: Federal Reserve System.

A third option for avoiding a reserve shortage lies in the structure of the Federal Reserve System itself. The Fed not only establishes certain rules of behavior for banks but also functions as a central bank, or banker's bank. Banks maintain accounts with the regional Federal Reserve banks, much the way you and I maintain accounts with a local bank. Individual banks deposit and withdraw "reserve credits" from these accounts, just as we deposit and withdraw dollars. Should a bank find itself short of reserves, it can go the Fed's "discount window" and borrow some reserves. This process is called **discounting.** Discounting means the Fed is lending reserves directly to private banks.

The discounting operation of the Fed provides private banks with an important source of reserves, but not without cost The Fed, too, charges interest on the reserves it lends to banks, a rate of interest referred to as the **discount rate.**

The discount window provides a mechanism for directly influencing the size of bank reserves. ***By raising or lowering the discount rate, the Fed changes the cost of money for banks and therewith the incentive to bor-***

discounting: Federal Reserve lending of reserves to private banks.

discount rate: The rate of interest charged by the Federal Reserve banks for lending reserves to private banks.

row reserves. At high discount rates, borrowing from the Fed is expensive. High discount rates also signal the Fed's desire to restrain the money supply and an accompanying reluctance to lend reserves. Low discount rates, on the other hand, make it profitable to acquire additional reserves and to exploit one's lending capacity to the fullest. Low discount rates also indicate the Fed's willingness to support credit expansion.

Open-Market Operations

Reserve requirements and discount-window operations are important tools of monetary policy. But they do not come close to open-market operations in day-to-day impact on the money supply. *Open-market operations are the principal mechanism for directly altering the reserves of the banking system.* Since reserves are the lifeblood of the banking system, open-market operations are of immediate and critical interest to private banks and the larger economy.

Portfolio Decisions. To appreciate the impact of open-market operations, you have to think about the alternative uses for idle funds. Just about everybody has some idle funds, even if they amount to a few measly dollars in your pocket or a minimal balance in your checking account. Other consumers and corporations have great amounts of idle funds, even millions of dollars at any time. What we're concerned with here is what people decide to do with such funds.

People (and corporations) do not hold all of their idle funds in transactions accounts or cash. Idle funds are also used to purchase stocks, build up savings-account balances, and purchase bonds. These alternative uses of idle funds are attractive because they promise some additional income in the form of interest, dividends, or capital appreciation (e.g., higher stock prices).

Hold Money or Bonds? The open-market operations of the Federal Reserve focus on one of the portfolio choices people make—whether to deposit idle funds in transactions accounts or to purchase government bonds. In essence, the Fed attempts to influence this choice by making bonds more or less attractive, as circumstances warrant. It thereby induces people to move funds from banks to bond markets, or vice versa. In the process, reserves either enter or leave the banking system, thereby altering the lending capacity of banks.

Figure 14.4 depicts the general nature of Federal Reserve open-market operations. The process of deposit creation begins when people deposit money in the banking system. They can deposit either cash or checks. They cannot deposit bonds. Hence the size of potential deposits depends on how much of their wealth people hold in the form of money and how much in the form of bonds. The Fed's objective is to alter this portfolio decision by buying or selling bonds. *When the Fed buys bonds from the public, it increases the flow of deposits (reserves) to the banking system. Bond sales by the Fed reduce the flow.*

Open-Market Activity. The basic premise of open-market activity is that market participants will respond to changes in bond prices. People will want to sell bonds when bond prices are high and buy bonds when prices are low. Hence *changes in bond prices will alter portfolio choices.* Accordingly, the Fed can induce people to buy more bonds by offering to sell

FIGURE 14.4
An Open-Market Purchase

The Fed can increase bank reserves by buying government securities from the public. The Fed check used to buy securities (Step 1) gets deposited in a private bank (Step 2). The bank returns the check to the Fed (Step 3), thereby obtaining additional reserves. To decrease bank reserves, the Fed would sell securities, thus reversing the flow of reserves.

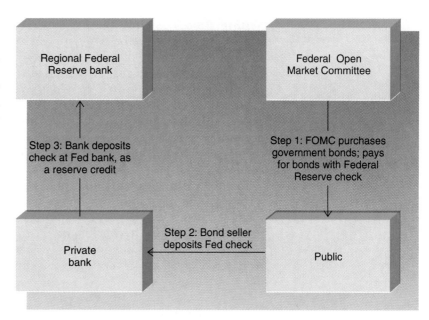

open-market operations: Federal Reserve purchases and sales of government bonds for the purpose of altering bank reserves.

them at lower prices. As people buy more bonds, their money balances decline and their bond holdings rise.

The reverse adjustments occur when the Fed offers to buy bonds at high prices. People will sell their bonds, thereby reducing their bond holdings and increasing their money balances.

The Fed's interest in portfolio choices originates in its concern over bank reserves. The more money people hold in the form of bank deposits, the greater the reserves and lending capacity of the banking system. If people hold more bonds and smaller bank balances, banks will have fewer reserves and less lending power. Recognizing this, ***the Fed buys or sells bonds in order to alter the level of bank reserves.*** This is the purpose of this bond market activity. In other words, **open-market operations** entail the purchase and sale of government securities (bonds) for the purpose of altering the flow of reserves into and out of the banking system.

Buying Bonds. Suppose the Fed wants to increase the money supply. To do so, it must persuade people to deposit a larger share of their financial assets in banks and hold less in other forms, particularly government bonds. How can the Fed do this? The solution lies in bond prices. If the Fed offers to pay a high price for bonds, people will sell some of their bonds to the Fed. They will then deposit the proceeds of the sale in their bank accounts. This influx of money into bank accounts will directly increase bank reserves.

Figure 14.4 illustrates the details of open-market operations. Notice that when the Fed buys a bond from the public, it pays with a check written on itself. The bond seller must deposit the Fed's check in his bank account if he wants to use part of the proceeds or simply to hold the money for safekeeping. The bank, in turn, deposits the check at a regional Federal Reserve bank, in exchange for a reserve credit. The bank's reserves are directly increased by the amount of the check. Thus ***by buying bonds, the Fed increases bank reserves.*** These reserves can be used to expand the money supply still further, as banks put their newly acquired reserves to work making loans.

Selling Bonds. Should the Fed desire to slow the growth in the money supply, it can reverse the whole process. Instead of offering to *buy* bonds, the Fed in this case will try to *sell* bonds. If it sets the price sufficiently low, individuals, corporations, and government agencies will convert some of their transactions deposits into bonds. When they do so, they write a check, paying the Fed for the bonds. The Fed then returns the check to the depositor's bank, taking payment through a reduction in the bank's reserve account. The reserves of the banking system are thereby diminished. So is the capacity to make loans. Thus **by selling bonds, the Fed reduces bank reserves.**

To appreciate the significance of open-market operations, one must have a sense of the magnitudes involved. The volume of trading in U.S. government securities exceeds $100 *billion* per day. The Fed alone owned over $350 billion worth of government securities at the beginning of 1995 and bought or sold enormous sums daily. Thus open-market operations involve tremendous amounts of money and, by implication, potential bank reserves.

Powerful Levers

The three levers of monetary policy are

- Reserve requirements
- Discount rates
- Open-market operations

By using these levers, the Fed can change the level of bank reserves and their lending capacity. Since bank loans are the primary source of new money, **the Fed has effective control of the nation's money supply.** The question then becomes, what should the Fed do with this policy lever?

SHIFTING AGGREGATE DEMAND

The ultimate goal of all macro policy is to stabilize the economy at its full-employment potential. Monetary policy contributes to the goal by increasing or decreasing the money supply as economic conditions require.

Expansionary Policy

Suppose the economy is in recession, producing less than its full-employment potential. Such a situation is illustrated by the equilibrium point E_1 in Figure 14.5. The objective in this situation is to stimulate the economy, increasing the rate of output from Q_1 to Q_F.

We earlier saw how fiscal policy can help bring about the desired expansion. Were the government to increase its own spending, **aggregate demand** would shift to the right. A tax cut would also stimulate aggregate demand by giving consumers and business more disposable income to spend.

> **aggregate demand:** The total quantity of output demanded at alternative price levels in a given time period, *ceteris paribus*.

Monetary policy may be used to shift aggregate demand as well. If the Fed lowers reserve requirements, drops the discount rate, or buys more bonds, it will increase bank lending capacity. The banks in turn will try to use that expanded capacity and make more loans. By offering lower interest rates or easier approvals, the banks can encourage people to borrow and spend more money. In this way, an increase in the money supply will result in a rightward shift of the aggregate demand curve. In Figure 14.5 the resulting shift propels the economy out of recession (Q_1) to its full-em-

**FIGURE 14.5
Demand-Side Focus**

Monetary-policy tools change the size of the money supply. Changes in the money supply, in turn, shift the aggregate demand curve. In this case, an increase in M1 shifts demand from AD_1 to AD_2, restoring full employment (Q_F).

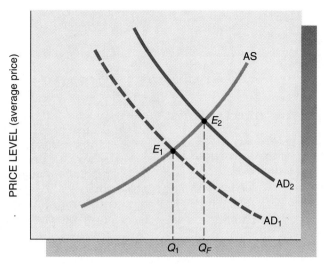

RATE OF OUTPUT (real GNP per time period)

ployment potential (Q_F). The Headline on page 292 illustrates how the Bank of Japan used this policy lever to help end the recession in that country.

Restrictive Policy

Monetary policy may also be used to cool an overheating economy. Excessive aggregate demand may put too much pressure on our production capacity. As market participants bid against each other for increasingly scarce goods, prices will start rising. The resulting inflation will redistribute real incomes (perhaps unfairly) and may disrupt investment and consumption plans.

The goal of monetary policy in this situation is to reduce aggregate demand, that is, to shift the AD curve leftward. To do this, the Fed can reduce the money supply by (1) raising reserve requirements, (2) increasing the discount rate, or (3) selling bonds in the open market. All of these actions will reduce bank lending capacity. The competition for this reduced pool of funds will drive up interest rates. The combination of higher interest rates and lessened loan availability will curtail investment consumption and even government spending. This was the intent of the Fed's monetary restraint in 1994. As the accompanying Headline indicates, the Fed was worried that the U.S. economy was growing so fast that it would overshoot the full-employment goal. To avert those inflationary pressures, it reduced money-supply growth and raised interest rates. The essence of this restrictive policy is captured in the accompanying cartoon.

The Dropouts—reprinted by permission of Howard Post.

HEADLINE

MONETARY RESTRAINT

Fed Increases Two Key Interest Rates

The Federal Reserve raised two key interest rates a half percentage point each yesterday to make sure inflation stays under control. . . .

In a statement, the Fed said its actions were "designed to maintain favorable trends in inflation and thereby sustain the economic expansion."

The Fed raised the discount rate, the rate the central bank charges on loans to financial institutions, from 3 percent to 3.5 percent, and lifted its target for the federal funds rate, the rate financial institutions pay one another on overnight loans, from 3.75 percent to 4.25 percent. . . .

Greenspan and other central bank officials have indicated that they want to make sure that the economy does not grow so fast that shortages of production capacity and tight labor markets cause inflation to worsen.

Most Fed officials expect the economy will expand at about a 3 percent rate this year, the same as the administration's forecast. That is fast enough to cause unemployment, which was 6.4 percent last month, to fall slowly, according to the forecasts.

But by next year, some Fed officials want growth to be running at about a 2.5 percent to 2.75 percent pace, which they estimate is about how fast the economy's capacity to produce will be increasing. Thus, growth of that sort would not keep pushing the unemployment rate downward, the officials have said, or be likely to trigger an acceleration of inflation.

—John M. Berry

The Washington Post, May 18, 1994, p. 1. © 1992, The Washington Post. Reprinted with permission.

PRICE VS. OUTPUT EFFECTS

The successful execution of monetary policy depends on two conditions. The first condition is that aggregate demand will respond (shift) to changes in the money supply. The second prerequisite for success is that the aggregate supply curve have the right shape.

Aggregate Demand

The first prerequisite—responsive aggregate demand—usually isn't a problem. An increase in the money supply is typically gobbled up by consumers and investors eager to increase their spending. Only in rare times of economic despair (e.g., the Great Depression of the 1930s) do banks or their customers display a reluctance to use available lending capacity. In such situations, anxieties about the economy may overwhelm low interest rates and the ready availability of loans. If this happens, monetary policy will be no more effective than "pushing on a string." In more normal times, however, increases in the money supply can shift aggregate demand rightward.

Aggregate Supply

aggregate supply: The total quantity of output producers are willing and able to supply at alternative price levels in a given time period, *ceteris paribus.*

The second condition for successful monetary policy is not so assured. Now we must confront **aggregate supply.** *The effects of an aggregate demand shift on prices and output depend on the shape of the aggregate supply curve.*

Notice in Figure 14.5 what happened to output and prices when aggregate demand shifted rightward. This expansionary monetary policy *did* succeed in increasing output to its full-employment level. In the process, however, prices also rose. The price level of the new macro equilibrium (E_2) is higher than before the monetary stimulus (E_1). Hence the economy suffers from inflation as it moves toward full employment. The monetary-policy intervention is not an unqualified success.

Figure 14.6 illustrates how different slopes of the aggregate supply curve could change the impact of monetary policy. Figure 14.6a depicts the shape often associated with Keynesian theory. In Keynes's view, producers would not need the incentive of rising prices during a recession. They would willingly supply more output at prevailing prices, just to get back to full pro-

FIGURE 14.6
Contrasting Views of Aggregate Supply

(a) In the simple Keynesian model, the rate of output responds fully and automatically to increases in demand until full employment (Q_F) is reached. If demand increases from AD_1 to AD_2, output will expand from Q_1 to Q_F without any inflation. Inflation becomes a problem only if aggregate demand increases beyond capacity—to AD_3, for example.

(b) Some critics assert that changes in the money supply affect prices but not output. They regard aggregate supply as a fixed rate of output, positioned at the long-run, "natural" rate of unemployment (here noted as Q_N). Accordingly, a shift of demand (from AD_4 to AD_5) can affect only the price level (from P_4 to P_5).

(c) The eclectic view concedes that the AS curve may be horizontal at low levels of output and vertical at capacity. In the middle, however, the AS curve is upward-sloping. In this case, both prices and output are affected by monetary policy.

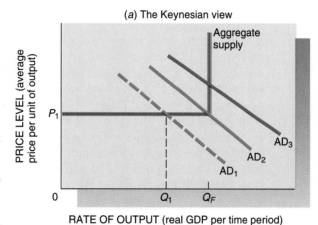

(a) The Keynesian view

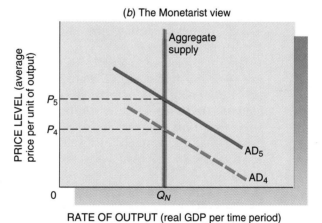

(b) The Monetarist view

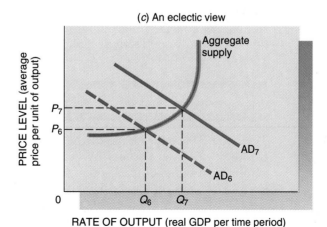

(c) An eclectic view

duction. Only when capacity was reached would producers start raising prices. In this view, the aggregate supply curve is horizontal until full employment is reached, when it shoots up.

The horizontal aggregate supply curve in Figure 14.6*a* creates an ideal setting for monetary policy. If the economy is in recession (e.g., Q_1), expansionary policy (e.g., AD_1 to AD_2) increases output but not prices. If the economy is overheated, restrictive policy (e.g., AD_3 to AD_2) lowers prices but not output. In each case, the objectives of monetary policy are painlessly achieved.

Although a horizontal AS curve is ideal, there is no guarantee that producers and workers will behave in that way. The relevant AS curve is the one that mirrors producer behavior. Economists are in disagreement, however, about the true shape of the AS curve.

Figure 14.6*b* illustrates a different theory about the shape of the AS curve, a theory that gives the Fed nightmares. The AS curve is completely vertical in this case. The argument here is that the quantity of goods produced is primarily dependent on production capacity, labor-market efficiency, and other "structural" forces. These structural forces establish a "natural" rate of unemployment that is fairly immune to short-run policy intervention. From this perspective, there is no reason for producers to depart from this "natural" rate of output when the money supply increases. Producers are smart enough to know that both prices and costs will rise when spending increases. Hence rising prices will not create any new profit incentives for increasing output. Firms will just continue producing at the "natural" rate, with higher (nominal) prices and costs. As a result, increases in aggregate demand (e.g., AD_4 to AD_5) are not likely to increase output levels. Expansionary monetary policy only causes inflation in this case; the rate of output is unaffected.

The third picture in Figure 14.6 is much brighter. The AS curve in Figure 14.6*c* illustrates a middle ground between the other two extremes. This upward-sloping AS curve renders monetary policy effective, but not perfectly so. **With an upward-sloping AS curve, expansionary policy causes some inflation and restrictive policy causes some unemployment.** There are no clear-cut winners or losers here. Rather, monetary (and fiscal) policy confronts a tradeoff between the goals of full employment and price stability.

Many economists believe Figure 14.6*c* best represents market behavior. The Keynesian view (horizontal AS) assumes more restraint in raising prices and wages than seems plausible. The Monetarist vision (vertical AS) assumes instantaneous wage and price responses. The eclectic view (upward-sloping AS), on the other hand, recognizes that market behavior responds gradually and imperfectly to policy interventions.

POLICY PERSPECTIVES

Fixed Rules or Discretion?

The debate over the shape of the aggregate supply curve spotlights a central policy debate. Should the Fed try to fine-tune the economy with constant adjustments of the money supply? Or should the Fed instead simply keep the money supply growing at a steady pace?

Discretionary Policy

The argument for active monetary intervention rests on the observation that the economy itself is constantly beset by expansionary and recessionary forces. In the absence of active discretionary policy, it is feared, the economy would tip first one way, then the other. To reduce such instability, the Fed can "lean against the wind," restraining the economy when the wind accelerates, stimulating the economy when it stalls. This view of market instability and the attendant need for active government intervention reflects the Keynesian perspective. Applied to monetary policy, it implies the need for continual adjustments to the money supply.

Fixed Rules

Critics of discretionary monetary policy raise two objections. Their first argument relies on the vertical AS curve (Figure 14.6b). They contend that expansionary monetary policy inevitably leads to inflation. Producers and workers can't be fooled into believing that more money will create more goods. With a little experience, they'll soon realize that when more money chases available goods, prices rise. To protect themselves against inflation, they will demand higher prices and wages whenever they see the money supply expanding. Such defensive behavior will push the AS curve into a vertical position.

Suppose that you could fool most of the people most of the time. Specifically, suppose that producers and workers would not push prices up when the money supply expanded. Critics argue that *even in these circumstances* discretionary policy would not be appropriate.

Even if one concedes that the AS curve isn't necessarily *vertical*, one still has to determine how much slope it has. This inevitably entails some guesswork and the potential for policy mistakes. If the Fed thinks the AS curve is less vertical than it really is, its expansionary policy might cause too much inflation. Hence discretionary policy is as likely to cause macro problems as to cure them. Critics conclude that fixed rules for money-supply management are less prone to error. These critics, led by Milton Friedman, urge the Fed to increase M1 by a constant (fixed) rate each year.

The Fed's Eclecticism

For a brief period (1979–82) the Fed adopted the policy of fixed money-supply targets. On October 6, 1979, the chairman of the Fed (Paul Volcker) announced that the Fed would begin focusing on the money supply, seeking to keep its growth within tight limits. The Fed's primary goal was to reduce inflation, which was then running at close to 14 percent a year. To slow the inflationary spiral, the Fed decided to limit sharply growth of the money supply.

The Fed succeeded in reducing money-supply growth and the inflationary spiral. But its tight-money policies sent interest rates soaring and pushed the economy into a deep recession (1981–82). Exactly three years after adopting fixed rules, the Fed abandoned them.

Instead of fixed rules for money-supply growth, the Fed has adopted an eclectic combination of (flexible) rules and (limited) discretion. Each year the Fed announces targets for money-supply growth. But the targets are very broad and not very stable. At the beginning of 1986, for example, the Fed set a target of 3 to 8 percent growth for M1. That wide target gave it plenty of room to adjust to changing interest rates and cyclical changes. But the Fed actually missed the target by a mile—M1 increased by 15 percent in 1986. In explaining this mile-wide miss to Congress, Chairman Volcker emphasized pragmatism. "Success in my mind," he asserted, "will not be measured by whether or not we meet some preordained, arbitrary target" but by our macroeconomic performance. Since the economy was growing steadily in 1987, and inflation was not increasing, he concluded that monetary policy had been a success. He ended his testimony by telling Congress that the Fed would no longer set targets for M1 but would instead keep an eye on broader money-supply measures and interest rates. In other words, the Fed would do whatever it thought necessary to promote price stability and economic growth.

Alan Greenspan is committed to the same brand of eclecticism. In early 1992, he refused to set a target for growth of the narrowly defined money supply (M1) and set very wide targets (2.5–6.5 percent) for broader measures of the money supply (M2). He wanted to stimulate the economy but also to keep a rein on inflation. To achieve this balancing act, Greenspan proclaimed that the Fed could not be bound to any one theory but must instead use a mix of money-supply and interest-rate adjustments to attain desired macro outcomes.

SUMMARY

- The Federal Reserve System controls the nation's money supply by regulating the loan activity (deposit creation) of private banks (depository institutions).
- The core of the Federal Reserve System is the twelve regional Federal Reserve banks, which provide check-clearance, reserve deposit, and loan ("discounting") services to individual banks. Private banks are required to maintain minimum reserves on deposit at one of the regional Federal Reserve banks.
- The general policies of the Fed are set by its Board of Governors. The Board's chairman is selected by the U.S. president and confirmed by Congress. The chairman serves as the chief spokesman for monetary policy.
- The Fed has three basic tools for changing the money supply: reserve requirements, discount rates, and open-market operations (buying and selling of Treasury bonds). With these tools, the Fed can change bank reserves and their lending capacity.
- Changes in the money supply directly affect aggregate demand. Increases in M1 shift the aggregate demand curve rightward; decreases shift it to the left.
- The impact of monetary policy on macro outcomes depends on the slope of the aggregate supply curve. If the AS curve has an upward slope, a tradeoff exists between the goals of full employment and price stability.
- Advocates of discretionary monetary policy say the Fed must counter market instabilities. Advocates of fixed policy rules warn that discretionary policy may do more harm than good.

Terms to Remember   Define the following terms:

monetary policy	money multiplier	open-market operations
money supply (M1)	discounting	aggregate demand
required reserves	discount rate	aggregate supply
excess reserves		

Questions for Discussion   1. Why do banks want to maintain as little excess reserves as possible? Under what circumstances might banks desire to hold excess reserves? (Hint: see Figure 14.3.)

2. Why do people hold bonds rather than larger savings-account or checking-account balances? Under what circumstances might they change their portfolios, moving their funds out of bonds into bank accounts?
3. If the Federal Reserve banks mailed everyone a brand-new $100 bill, what would happen to prices, output, and income? Illustrate with aggregate demand and supply curves.
4. Why might the Fed want to reduce the money supply?
5. How does an increase in the money supply get into the hands of consumers? What do they do with it?
6. What functions do the regional Federal Reserve banks perform?

Problems

1. Assume that the following data describe the condition of the commercial banking system:

   Total reserves: $200 billion
   Transactions deposits: $800 billion
   Cash held by public: $100 billion
   Reserve requirement: 0.20

   (a) How large is the money supply (M1)?
   (b) Are the banks fully utilizing their lending capacity? Explain.
   (c) What would happen to the money supply *initially* if the public deposited another $50 billion in cash in transactions accounts? Explain.
   (d) What would the lending capacity of the banking system be after such a portfolio switch?
   (e) How large would the money supply be if the banks fully utilized their lending capacity?
   (f) What three steps could the Fed take to offset that potential growth in M1?

2. Suppose the Federal Reserve decided to purchase $10 billion worth of government securities in the open market.
   (a) How will M1 be affected initially?
   (b) How will the lending capacity of the banking system be affected if the reserve requirement is 25 percent?
   (c) How will banks induce investors to utilize this expanded lending capacity?

3. Suppose the economy is initially in equilibrium at an output level of 100 and price level of 100. The Fed then manages to shift aggregate demand rightward by 20.
   (a) Illustrate the initial equilibrium (E_1) and the shift of AD.
   (b) Show what happens to output and prices if the aggregate supply curve is (1) horizontal, (2) vertical, and (3) upward-sloping.

4. Illustrate the effects on bank reserves of an open-market sale (see Figure 14.4).

Chapter 15

Economic Growth

Economic growth is the fundamental determinant of the long-run success of any nation, the basic source of rising living standards, and the key to meeting the needs and desires of the American people.

—*Economic Report of the President*, 1992

Twenty years ago there were no fax machines, no cellular phones, no miniaturized TVs, and no DATs. Personal computers were still on the drawing board, and laptops weren't even envisioned. Home video didn't exist, and no one had yet produced microwave popcorn. Biotechnology hadn't yet produced any blockbuster drugs, and people used the same pair of athletic shoes for most sports.

New products are symptoms of our economic progress. Over time, we produce not only *more* goods and services but also *new* and *better* goods and services. In the process, we get richer: our material living standards rise.

Rising living standards are not inevitable, however. According to World Bank estimates, over 3 *billion* people—over half the world's population—continue to live in abject poverty. Worse still, living standards in many of the poorest countries have *fallen* in the last decade. Living standards also fell in Eastern Europe when communism collapsed and a painful transition to market economies began. The former communist-bloc countries are counting on the power of free markets to jump-start their economies and raise living standards.

The purpose of this chapter is to take a longer-term view of economic performance. Most macro policy focuses on the *short-run* variations in output and prices we refer to as business cycles. There are *long-run* concerns as well. As we ponder the future of the economy beyond the next business cycle, we have to confront the prospects for economic growth. In that longer-run context we consider three questions:

- How important is economic growth?
- How does an economy grow?
- What policies promote economic growth?

We develop answers to these questions by first examining the nature of economic growth and then examining its sources and potential.

THE NATURE OF GROWTH

Economic growth refers to increases in the output of the economy. But there are two distinct ways in which output increases, and they have very different implications for our economic welfare.

Short-Run Changes in Capacity Use

> **production possibilities:** The alternative combinations of final goods and services that could be produced in a given time period with all available resources and technology.

The easiest kind of growth comes from increased use of our productive capabilities. At any given moment there is a limit to an economy's potential output. This limit is determined by the quantity of resources available and our technological know-how. We illustrate these short-run limits to output with a **production-possibilities** curve, as in Figure 15.1a. By using all of our available resources and our best expertise, we can produce any combination of goods on the production-possibilities curve.

We do not always take full advantage of our productive capacity, however. The economy often produces a mix of output that lies *inside* our production possibilities, like point A in Figure 15.1a. When this happens, the major short-run goal of macro policy is to achieve full employment—to move us from point A to some point on the production-possibilities curve (e.g., point B). In the process, we produce more output.

Long-Run Changes in Capacity

As desirable as full employment is, there is an obvious limit to how much additional output we can obtain in this way. Once we are fully utilizing our productive capacity, further increases in output are attainable only if we *expand* that capacity. To do so, we have to *shift* the production possibilities outward, as in Figure 15.1b. Such shifts imply an increase in *potential* GDP—that is, our productive capacity.

Over time, increases in capacity are critical. Short-run increases in the utilization of existing capacity can generate only modest increases in out-

FIGURE 15.1
Two Types of Growth

Increases in output may result from increased use of existing productive capacity or from increases in that capacity itself. In part *a* the initial mix of output at point *A* does not make full use of our production possibilities. Hence we can grow—get more output—by employing more of our available resources or using them more efficiently. This is illustrated by point *B* (or any other point on the curve). Once we are on the production-possibilities curve, we can increase output further only by *increasing* our productive capacity. This is illustrated by the *shift* of the production-possibilities curve in part *b*.

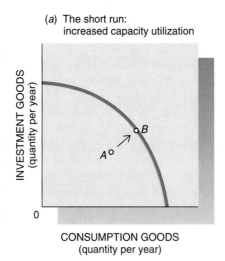

(*a*) The short run: increased capacity utilization

INVESTMENT GOODS (quantity per year)

CONSUMPTION GOODS (quantity per year)

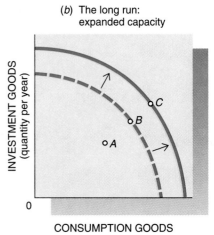

(*b*) The long run: expanded capacity

INVESTMENT GOODS (quantity per year)

CONSUMPTION GOODS (quantity per year)

put. Even "high" unemployment rates (e.g., 7 percent) leave little room for increased output. ***To achieve large and lasting increases in output we must push our production possibilities outward.*** For this reason, economists tend to define **economic growth** in terms of changes in *potential* GDP.

economic growth: An increase in output (real GDP); an expansion of production possibilities.

The unique character of economic growth can also be illustrated with aggregate supply and demand curves. Short-run macro policies focus on the aggregate demand (AD) curve. Fiscal- and monetary-policy levers are used to shift the AD curve, trying to achieve the best possible combination of full employment and price stability. As we have observed, however, the aggregate supply (AS) curve sets a limit to demand-side policy. In the short run, the slope of the aggregate supply curve determines how much inflation we have to "pay" to get more output. In the long run, the position of the AS curve limits total output. To get a long-run increase in output, we must move the AS curve.

Figure 15.2 illustrates the supply-side focus of economic growth. Notice that ***economic growth—sustained increases in total output—is possible only if the AS curve shifts rightward.***

Nominal vs. Real GDP

nominal GDP: The total value of goods and services produced within a nation's borders, measured in current prices.

We refer to *real* GDP, not *nominal* GDP, in our concept of economic growth. **Nominal GDP** is the current dollar value of output—that is, the average price level (*P*) multiplied by the quantity of goods and services produced (*Q*). Accordingly, increases in nominal GDP can result from either increases in the price level or increases in the quantity of output. In fact, nominal GDP can rise even when the quantity of goods and services falls. This was the case in 1991, for example. The total quantity of goods and services produced in 1991 was less than the quantity produced in 1990. Nevertheless, prices rose enough during 1991 to keep nominal GDP growing.

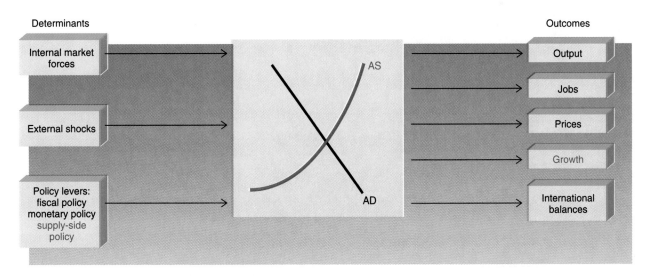

FIGURE 15.2
Supply-Side Focus

Short-run macro policy uses shifts of the aggregate demand curve to achieve economic stability. To achieve long-run *growth*, however, the aggregate supply curve must be shifted as well.

real GDP: The inflation-adjusted value of GDP; the value of output measured in constant prices.

Real GDP refers to the actual quantity of goods and services produced. Real GDP avoids the distortions of inflation by valuing output in *constant* prices.

GROWTH INDEXES

The GDP Growth Rate

growth rate: Percentage change in real GDP from one period to another.

Typically, changes in real GDP are expressed in percentage terms, as a growth *rate*. The **growth rate** is simply the change in real output between two periods divided by total output in the base period. In 1990, for example, real GDP was $4.885 trillion when valued in constant prices of 1987. Real GDP fell to $4.848 trillion in 1991, again measured in constant 1987 prices. Hence the growth rate between 1990 and 1991 was

$$\text{Growth rate} = \frac{\text{change in real GDP}}{\text{base period GDP}} = \frac{-.037 \text{ trillion}}{4.885 \text{ trillion}} = -0.7\%$$

The negative growth rate in 1991 was far below the long-term average for the United States (just over 3 percent). As Figure 15.3 illustrates, growth rates are usually positive, although they vary greatly from year to year. Years of actual decline in real GDP (e.g., 1974, 1975, 1980, 1982, 1991) are relatively rare. They are a serious setback to economic growth, however, and always lower living standards.

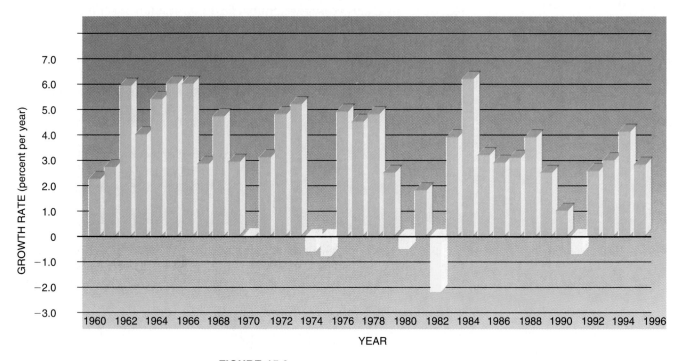

FIGURE 15.3
Recent U.S. Growth Rates

Total output typically increases from one year to another. The focus of policy is on the growth *rate*—that is, how fast real GDP increases from one year to the next. In the 1960s, real GDP grew an average of 4.2 percent per year. In the 1970s, the growth rate declined to 3.2 percent, and total output actually fell in two years (1970 and 1975). Growth in the 1980s was even slower, largely due to two recessions at the start of the decade. Will the 1990s be better? Only if the decade finishes a lot stronger than it started.

The challenge for the remainder of the 1990s is to maintain higher rates of economic growth. After the recession of 1990–1991, the U.S. economy got back on its long-term growth track. The growth rate even moved up to 4 percent in 1994. As the economy approached full employment, however, it became increasingly difficult to maintain such momentum.

The Exponential Process. At first blush, the "challenge" of raising the growth rate from 1 or 2 percent to 3 percent may appear neither difficult nor important. Indeed, the whole subject of economic growth looks rather dull when you discover that "big" gains in economic growth are measured in fractions of a percent. However, this initial impression is not fair. First of all, even one year's "low" growth implies lost output. Consider the recession of 1991 (see Figure 15.3). If we had just *maintained* the rate of total output in 1991—that is, "achieved" a *zero* growth rate rather than a 0.7 percent decline—we would have had $37 billion more worth of goods and services. That works out to $148 worth of goods and services per person. Lots of people would have liked that extra output.

Second, economic growth is a *continuing* process. Gains made in one year accumulate in future years. It's like interest you earn at the bank. If you leave your money in the bank for several years, you begin to earn interest on your interest. Eventually you accumulate a nice little bankroll.

The process of economic growth works the same way. Each little shift of the production-possibilities curve broadens the base for future GDP. As shifts accumulate over many years, the economy's productive capacity is greatly expanded. Ultimately, we discover that those "little" differences in annual growth rates generate tremendous gains in GDP.

This cumulative process, whereby interest or growth is compounded from one year to the next, is called an "exponential process." To get a feel for its impact, consider the longer-run difference between annual growth rates of 3 and 5 percent. In thirty years, a 3 percent growth rate will raise our GDP to $18 trillion (in 1995 dollars). But a 5 percent growth rate would give us $30 trillion of goods and services in the same amount of time. Thus, in a single generation, 5 percent growth translates into a standard of living that is 70 percent higher than 3 percent growth. From this longer-term perspective, "little" differences in growth rates look very big.

GDP per Capita: A Measure of Living Standards

> **GDP per capita:** Total GDP divided by total population; average GDP.

The exponential process might look even more meaningful if we translated it into *per capita* terms. **GDP per capita** is simply total output divided by total population. In 1994, the total output of the U.S. economy was $6.7 trillion (measured in 1994 dollars). Since there were 260 million of us to share that output, GDP per capita was

$$\text{1994 GDP per capita} = \frac{\$6.7 \text{ trillion of output}}{260 \text{ million people}} = \$25,769$$

This does not mean that every man, woman, and child in the United States received $25,769 worth of goods and services in 1994. Rather, it simply indicates how much output was potentially available to the "average" person. ***Growth in GDP per capita is attained only when the growth of output exceeds population growth.*** In the United States, this condition is usually achieved. In the 1980s, our population grew by an average of only 1 percent a year. Hence our average economic growth rate of 3 percent was more than sufficient to ensure steadily rising living standards. Faster growth of GDP—or slower population growth—would have generated even larger gains in GDP per capita. The accompanying Headline indicates some of the ways past GDP growth has changed the way we live—*and* how long we live.

Less developed countries do not enjoy such rapid growth. Most of these countries suffer from both slower growth of GDP and faster rates of population growth. Ethiopia, for example, is one of the poorest countries in the world, with GDP per capita of less than $200. Yet its population continues to grow more rapidly (2.7 percent per year) than GDP (2.2 percent growth), further depressing living standards. The population of Zambia

HEADLINE

IMPROVED LIVING STANDARDS

What Economic Growth Has Done for U.S. Families

As the economy grows, living standards rise. The changes are so gradual, however, that few people notice.

After twenty years of growth, though, some changes are remarkable. We now live longer, work less, and consume a lot more. Some examples:

	1970	1990
Average size of a new home (square feet)	1,500	2,080
New homes with central air conditioning	34%	76%
People using computers	< 100,000	75.9 million
Households with color TV	33.9%	96.1%
Households with cable TV	4 million	55 million
Households with VCRs	0	67 million
Households with two or more vehicles	29.3%	54%
Median household net worth (real)	$24,217	$48,887
Housing units lacking complete plumbing	6.9%	1.1%
Homes lacking a telephone	13%	5.2%
Households owning a microwave oven	< 1%	78.8%
Heart transplant procedures	< 10	2,125
Average work week	37.1 hours	34.5 hours
Average daily time working in the home	3.9 hours	3.5 hours
Work time to buy gas for 100-mile trip	49 minutes	31 minutes
Annual paid vacation and holidays	15.5 days	22.5 days
Number of people retired from work	13.3 million	25.3 million
Women in the work force	31.5%	56.6%
Recreational boats owned	8.8 million	16 million
Manufacturers' shipments of RVs	30,300	226,500
Adult softball teams	29,000	188,000
Recreational golfers	11.2 million	27.8 million
Attendance at symphonies and orchestras	12.7 million	43.6 million
Americans finishing high school	51.9%	77.7%
Americans finishing four years of college	13.5%	24.4%
Employee benefits as a share of payroll	29.3%	40.2%
Life expectancy at birth (years)	70.8	75.4
Death rate by natural causes (per 100,000)	714.3	520.2

Federal Reserve Bank of Dallas, *1993 Annual Report.*

grew by more than 3 percent per year in the 1980s, while GDP grew at a slower rate of only 0.5 percent. As a consequence, GDP per capita *declined* more than 2 percent per year.

By comparison with these countries, the United States has been most fortunate. Our GDP per capita has more than doubled since John F. Kennedy was president. This means that the average person today has twice as many goods and services as the average person had only a generation ago.

What about the future? Will we continue to enjoy substantial gains in living standards? It all depends on how fast output continues to grow in relation to population. Table 15.1 indicates some of the possibilities. If GDP per capita continues to grow at 1.8 percent per year—as it did in the 1980s—our average income will double again in thirty-nine years. If GDP per capita grows just half a percent faster, say, by 2.3 percent per year, our standard of living will double in only thirty-one years.

GDP per Worker: A Measure of Productivity

labor force: All persons over age sixteen who are either working for pay or actively seeking paid employment.

productivity: Output per unit of input, e.g., output per labor hour.

The increases in total output depicted in Table 15.1 will not occur automatically. Someone is going to have to produce more output if we want GDP per capita to rise. One reason our living standard rose in the 1980s is that the **labor force** grew faster than the population. Those in the World War II baby boom had reached maturity and were entering the labor force in droves. At the same time, more women took jobs outside the home. As a consequence, the number of workers grew faster than the population. This increase in the proportion of workers in the economy helped to increase GDP per capita.

The percentage of people who participate in the labor market cannot increase forever. At the limit, everyone would be in the labor market, and no further workers could be found. Sustained increases in GDP per capita are more likely to come from increases in output *per worker*. The total quantity of output produced depends not only on how many workers are employed but also on how productive each worker is. If **productivity** is increasing, then GDP per capita is likely to rise as well. Productivity gains have been the major source of economic growth in the past. The average worker today produces nearly *twice* as much output as his or her parents did (see Figure 15.4).

TABLE 15.1
The Rule of 72

Small differences in annual growth rates cumulate into large differences in GDP. Shown here are the number of years it would take to double GDP at various growth rates.

Doubling times can be approximated by the "rule of 72." Seventy-two divided by the growth rate equals the number of years it takes to double.

Growth Rate (percent)	Doubling Time (years)
0.0	Never
0.5	140
1.0	70
1.5	47
2.0	35
2.5	30
3.0	24
3.5	20
4.0	18
4.5	16
5.0	14

FIGURE 15.4
Productivity Gains

During the 1980s, manufacturing output per U.S. worker increased by 3.1 percent a year. This was an improvement over the 1970s and comparable to productivity gains in other countries. Japan and several other Asian countries enjoyed particularly fast productivity gains.

Source: U.S. Bureau of Labor Statistics.

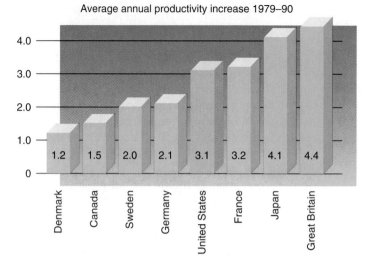

Average annual productivity increase 1979–90

Denmark	Canada	Sweden	Germany	United States	France	Japan	Great Britain
1.2	1.5	2.0	2.1	3.1	3.2	4.1	4.4

SOURCES OF PRODUCTIVITY GROWTH

If we want GDP per capita to keep going up, productivity will have to continue rising. Will it?

To answer this question, we need to examine the sources of productivity gains. *The sources of productivity gains include*

- *Higher skills*—an increase in labor skills
- *More capital*—an increase in the ratio of capital to labor
- *Improved management*—better use of available resources in the production process
- *Technological advance*—the development and use of better capital equipment

Labor Quality

In 1950, less than 8 percent of all U.S. workers had completed college. Today over 20 percent of the work force has completed four years of college. In addition to this advance in general education, there has been a substantial increase in vocational training, both in the public sector and by private firms. These improvements in labor quality have been a major source of productivity gains.

Capital Investment

investment: Expenditures on (production of) new plant and equipment (capital) in a given time period, plus changes in business inventories.

No matter how educated workers are, they still need tools, computers, and other equipment to produce most goods and services. Thus *capital* **investment** *is a prime determinant of both productivity and growth.* More investment gives the average worker more and better tools to work with.

While labor-force growth accelerated in the 1970s, the growth of capital slowed. As Table 15.2 indicates, the capital stock increased by 4.1 percent per year in the late 1960s. In the 1970s, however, the growth of capital slowed to only 2.5 percent per year; and in the early 1980s, it slowed even further. The stock of capital was still growing faster than the labor force (compare columns 1 and 2), but the difference was getting smaller. This means that although the average worker was continuing to get more and

TABLE 15.2
Average Annual Growth Rate of Labor, Capital, and Productivity, 1959–85

In the 1970s, the rate of capital growth slowed while the rate of labor growth increased. As a consequence, productivity gains declined. These trends were reversed in the late 1980s.

Period	Average Annual Percentage Change In		
	Labor Stock	Capital Stock	Output per Labor Hour
1959–65	0.9	3.8	3.3
1965–69	1.2	4.1	2.2
1969–73	0.4	3.5	2.6
1973–79	1.6	2.5	0.8
1979–85	1.6	2.2	0.9

Source: *Economic Report of the President*, 1988.

better machines, the rate at which he was getting them was slower. As a consequence, productivity growth declined (see column 3). By contrast, Korea and Japan invested more and grew more rapidly (see Headline).

Management

The quantity and quality of factor inputs do not completely determine the rate of economic growth. Resources, however good and abundant, must be organized into a production process and managed. Hence entrepreneurship and the quality of continuing management are major determinants of economic growth.

It is difficult to characterize differences in management techniques or to measure their effectiveness. However, much attention has been focused in recent years on the alleged shortsightedness of American managers. U.S. firms, it is said, focus too narrowly on short-term profits, neglecting long-

HEADLINE

COMPARATIVE INVESTMENT

Investment and Growth

Investment in new plant and equipment is essential for economic growth. In general, countries that allocate a larger share of output to investment will grow more rapidly. In the 1980s, Korea and Japan had the highest investment and growth rates.

Country	Investment as Percentage of GDP (average, 1980–90)	Growth Rate of GDP (average, 1980–92)
Korea (South)	30.7	9.4
Japan	29.8	4.1
United States	**17.9**	**2.7**
Great Britain	17.5	2.7
Germany	20.4	2.6
Ethiopia	13.5	1.2

Source: World Bank and Organization for Economic Cooperation and Development.

term gains in productivity. They also emphasize quantity over quality of output. And they fail to include workers in key decisions, thus depriving themselves of important insights and good will. By contrast, firms in Japan and elsewhere concentrate on longer-term gains, quality control, and strong bonds between labor and management. As a consequence, Japanese firms enjoy remarkably good labor and customer relations, intense worker loyalty, and faster productivity gains.

No single management style can be characterized as "best." The recent critiques of traditional management styles, however, have led to some new approaches. American labor unions and managers have experimented with some new cooperative approaches. These include "quality-of-work" circles and other collective efforts to improve relationships and productivity. In some cases workers have even assumed a direct role in management or ownership. At the same time, U.S. firms have put renewed emphasis on product quality, vowing to keep American-made goods "second to none" in consumer satisfaction. Although not always successful, such commitments tend to keep managers alert to innovation and quality control. The end result is often more and better products.

Research and Development

A fourth and vital source of productivity advance is research and development (R&D). R&D is a broad concept that includes scientific research, product development, innovations in production technique, and the development of management improvements. R&D activity may be a specific, identifiable activity (e.g., in a research lab), or it may be part of the process

---

HEADLINE

R&D PAYOFFS

New "Super Rice" Nearing Fruition

Big Boost Is Predicted for World Food Supply

Researchers at the International Rice Research Institute (IRRI) have developed a prototype breed of "super rice" that yields 25 percent more food per acre than today's best varieties. If planted in all suitable parts of the world's rice-growing regions, agronomists estimate, it could yield 100 million tons more grain than is now grown—enough to sustain an additional 450 million people a year.

Moreover, work is underway to modify the variety in a way that promises to achieve another 25 percent boost in yield.

And, according to Klaus Lampe, director general of the Philippines-based institute where the new variety was developed, super rice requires significantly less fertilizer than do today's varieties.

"This new rice will go a long way toward feeding the world's people through the next century, especially in Asia where rice is the staple," said Ismail Serageldin, chairman of the Consultative Group on International Agricultural Research

Additional plant breeding is underway to produce subvarieties with the various cooking qualities and flavors preferred by different cultures. Also, the individual grains must be made a little larger to suit most of the world's rice eaters. These are the kinds of adaptations that are routine with most new varieties of any crop.

Lampe said the new breed is needed because the world has little or no additional land on which to grow rice—the primary food of the part of the world where the population is growing in the largest numbers. In fact, some of the best rice land has been lost to urban sprawl. The area planted in rice worldwide has not increased since 1980.

—Boyce Rensberger

The Washington Post, October 24, 1994, p. 1. © 1994, The Washington Post. Reprinted with permission.

of "learning by doing." In either case, the insights developed from R&D generally lead to new products and cheaper ways of producing them. Over time, R&D is credited with the greatest contributions to economic growth. In his study of U.S. growth during the period 1929–82, Edward Denison concluded that 26 percent of *total* growth was due to "advances in knowledge." The relative contribution of R&D to productivity (output per worker) was probably twice that much.

Sometimes R&D generates startling advances in productivity. As the accompanying Headline describes, scientists discovered in 1994 how to increase rice yields by 25 percent. Such discoveries not only expand U.S. production possibilities but those of the whole world as well.

There is an important link between R&D and capital investment. Part of each year's gross investment compensates for the depreciation of existing plant and equipment. However, new machines are rarely identical to the ones they replace. Instead, new capital equipment tends to embody improved technology. Indeed, the availability of improved technology is often a major motivation for new investment, long before old machines have literally worn out. From this perspective, R&D and capital investment make a joint contribution to productivity advance.

POLICY LEVERS

To a large extent, the pace of economic growth is set by market forces—by the education, training, and investment decisions of market participants. Government policy plays an important role as well. Indeed, ***government policies can have a major impact on whether and how far the aggregate supply curve shifts.***

Education and Training

As noted earlier, the quality of labor largely depends on education and training. Accordingly, government policies that support education and training contribute directly to growth and productivity. From a fiscal-policy perspective, money spent on schools and training has a double payoff: it stimulates the economy in the *short* run (like all other spending) and increases the *long*-run capacity to produce. Tax incentives for training have the same effect.

Immigration Policy

Both the quality and the quantity of labor are affected by immigration policy. Close to a million people immigrate to the United States each year. This influx of immigrants has been a major source of growth in the U.S. labor force—and thus a direct contributor to an outward shift of our production possibilities.

The impact of immigration on our productive capacity is not just a question of numbers but also the quality of these new workers. Recent immigrants have much lower educational attainments than native-born Americans and are less able to fill job vacancies in growing industries. This is largely due to immigration policy, which sets only country-specific quotas and gives preference to relatives of U.S. residents. The accompanying Headline suggests that the United States should pay more attention to the edu-

HEADLINE

LABOR SUPPLY

Let's Change the Immigration Law—Now

Millions of Eastern Europeans and Soviets—educated and talented for the most part—are likely to try to start fresh lives in the West as barriers to free emigration continue to tumble. The U.S. sorely needs immigrant talent as a way to compensate for the shrinking birthrate common to the West and to replenish the stagnating pool of skilled labor. But to get that talent, America will have to change its immigration policies and open her doors to those with proven skills.

America's outdated immigration law simply is not geared to admit the very ones the country needs most. Following a principle that has remained unchanged since 1952, the law offers the right of immigration based on family preference. As a result, the vast majority of new arrivals are spouses, children, and siblings of earlier immigrants—and the system self-perpetuates: Once they become citizens, they in turn bring in *their* families. Since these immigrants' skills are never a factor in whether or not they are admitted, any benefits that they bring to the U.S. economy are coincidental. Of last year's 650,000 new immigrants, just 54,000 qualified solely on the basis of their education or ability.

A more sensible policy would be to expand opportunities for those immigrants who possess skills in short supply, as Canada and Australia have recently done.

Some anti-immigrant sentiment has already boiled up in various communities around America. If the U.S. government doesn't bring the law into line with the nation's needs, that sentiment could spread while the country loses the chance to welcome newcomers who could bring with them the skills that are in critically short supply.

—Louis S. Richman

Fortune, January 29, 1990, p. 12. ©1990 Time Inc. All rights reserved.

cational and skill levels of immigrants and set preferences on the basis of potential productivity. In any case, we have to recognize that the sheer number of people entering the country makes immigration policy an important growth-policy lever.

Investment Incentives

Government policy also affects the supply of capital. As a rule, lower tax rates encourage people to invest more—to build factories, purchase new equipment, and construct new offices. Hence *tax policy is not only a staple of short-term stabilization policy but a determinant of long-run growth as well.*

The tax treatment of capital gains is one of the most debated supply-side policy levers. Capital gains are increases in the value of assets. When stocks, land, or other assets are sold, any resulting gain is counted as income, subject to a tax rate of 28 percent. In 1995, the Republican leadership in the U.S. Congress proposed a cut in the capital gains tax, arguing that a tax rate of 28 percent discourages people from investing. They claimed that a lower tax rate would stimulate more investment and also encourage people to reallocate their assets more often, thus increasing efficiency. Many countries—including Japan, Italy, South Korea, Taiwan, and the Netherlands—do not levy any taxes on capital gains. The rest of the European Union and Canada impose lower capital gains taxes than does the United States.

Critics argue that a capital gains tax cut would overwhelmingly favor the rich, who own most stocks, property, and other wealth. This inequity, they assert, would outweigh any efficiency gains. The "fairness" aspect of tax incentives designed to spur economic growth continues to stir intense debates. Advocates of growth-stimulating tax incentives say a little more in-equality in the short run is justified if the resulting economic growth makes everyone better off in the long run.

Savings Incentives

saving: That part of disposable income not spent on current consumption; disposable income less consumption.

Another prerequisite for faster growth is more **savings.** At full employment, a greater volume of investment is possible only if the rate of consumption is cut back. In other words, additional investment requires additional saving. Hence *supply-side economists favor tax incentives that encourage saving as well as greater tax incentives for investment.* This kind of perspective contrasts sharply with the Keynesian emphasis on stimulating consumption.

In the early 1980s Congress greatly increased the incentives for saving. First, banks were permitted to increase the rate of interest paid on various types of savings accounts. Second, the tax on earned interest was reduced. And finally, new forms of tax-free saving were created (e.g., Individual Retirement Accounts [IRAs]).

Despite these incentives, the U.S. savings rate declined during the 1980s. Household saving dropped from 6.2 percent of disposable income in 1981 to a low of 2.5 percent in 1987. Neither the tax incentives nor the high interest rates that prevailed in the early 1980s convinced Americans to save more. As a result, the U.S. saving rate fell considerably below that of other nations. Although saving rates have risen since then, American households continue to save relatively little (see Headline).

Budget Deficits

The dependence of economic growth on investment and savings adds an important dimension to the debate over budget deficits. When the government borrows money to finance its spending, it dips into the nation's savings pool. Hence the government ends up borrowing funds that could have been used to finance investment. If this happens, the government deficit

HEADLINE

SAVING RATES

Americans Save Little

American households save very little. On average, Americans spend roughly 96 cents out of every dollar of disposable income, leaving only 4 cents for saving. This saving rate is far below that in most other countries. As shown here, the United States ranked at the bottom of the savers' list in 1992.

Supply-siders are especially concerned about low saving rates. They argue that Americans must save more, to finance increased investment and economic growth. Otherwise, they fear, the United States will fall behind other countries in the progression toward higher productivity levels and living standards.

Country	Saving Rate (1992)
Italy	18.8%
Japan	15.0
France	12.7
Germany	12.6
Great Britain	12.0
Canada	10.3
United States	**4.9**

Note: Saving rate equals household saving divided by disposable income.

Source: Central Intelligence Agency, *Handbook of International Economic Statistics, 1993.*

crowding out: A reduction in private-sector borrowing (and spending) caused by increased government borrowing.

effectively "crowds out" private investment. This process of **crowding out**—of diverting available savings from investment to government spending—directly limits private investment. From this perspective, government budget deficits act as a constraint on economic growth.

Government deficits don't necessarily substitute for investment, however. In recessions, the primary macro concern is that people are not spending all available funds. Typically, consumers are saving more than business desires to invest. Indeed, this spending shortfall is the primary motivation for stepped-up government spending. In these recessionary circumstances, deficit-financed government spending doesn't crowd out private investment.

Even government spending that does crowd out private investment isn't necessarily antigrowth. The government may use the borrowed funds to build schools, highways, airports, or other infrastructure that *expands* our productive capacity.

Although budget deficits don't necessarily crowd out (private) investment, that possibility must be considered. Hence *fiscal and monetary policies must be evaluated in terms of their impact not only on short-run aggregate demand but also on long-run aggregate supply.*

Deregulation

There are still other mechanisms for stimulating economic growth. The government intervenes directly in supply decisions by *regulating* employment and output behavior. In general, such regulations limit the flexibility of producers to respond to changes in demand. Government regulation also tends to raise production costs. The higher costs result not only from required changes in the production process but also from the expense of monitoring government regulations and filling out endless government forms. The budget costs and the burden of red tape discourage production and so limit aggregate supply. From this perspective, deregulation would shift the AS curve rightward.

Factor Markets. Minimum-wage laws are one of the most familiar forms of factor-market regulation. The Fair Labor Standards Act of 1938 required employers to pay workers a minimum of 25 cents per hour. Over time, Congress has increased the coverage of that act and the minimum wage itself repeatedly. In 1990, the minimum wage was increased to $3.80 per hour, and then to $4.25 in 1991. In 1995, President Clinton proposed to increase it again, to $5.15 an hour by 1997.

The goal of the minimum-wage law is to ensure workers a decent standard of living. But the law has other effects as well. By prohibiting employers from using lower-paid workers, it limits the ability of employers to hire additional workers. This hiring constraint limits job opportunities for immigrants, teenagers, and low-skill workers. Without that constraint, more of these workers would find jobs and gain valuable experience, shifting the AS curve rightward.

Government regulation of factor markets extends beyond minimum-wage laws. The government also sets standards for workplace safety and health. The Occupational Safety and Health Administration (OSHA), for example, sets limits on the noise levels at work sites. If noise levels exceed these limits, the employer is required to adopt administrative or engineering controls to reduce the noise level. Personal protection of workers (e.g., earplugs or earmuffs), though much less costly, will suffice only if source controls are not feasible. All such regulations are intended to improve the welfare of workers. In the process, however, these regulations raise the costs of production and inhibit supply responses.

Product Markets. The government's regulation of factor markets tends to raise production costs and inhibit supply. The same is true of regulations imposed directly on product markets. A few examples illustrate the impact.

TRANSPORTATION COSTS. At the federal level, various agencies regulate the output and prices of transportation services. Until 1984 the Civil Aeronautics Board (CAB) determined which routes airlines could fly and how much they could charge. The Interstate Commerce Commission (ICC) has had the same kind of power over trucking, interstate bus lines, and railroads. The routes, services, and prices for ships (in U.S. coastal waters and foreign commerce) have been established by the Federal Maritime Commission. In all these cases the regulations constrained the ability of producers to respond to increases in demand. Existing producers could not increase output at will, and new producers were excluded from the market. The easing of these restrictive regulations has spurred more output, lower prices, and innovation in air travel, telecommunications, and land transportation.

FOOD AND DRUG STANDARDS. The Food and Drug Administration (FDA) has a broad mandate to protect consumers from dangerous products. In fulfilling this responsibility, the FDA sets health standards for the content of specific foods. A hot dog, for example, can be labeled as such only if it contains specific mixtures of skeletal meat, pig lips, snouts, and ears. By the same token, the FDA requires that chocolate bars must contain no more than 60 microscopic insect fragments (including rat feces) per 100 grams of chocolate. The FDA also sets standards for the testing of new drugs and evaluates the test results. In all three cases, the goal of regulation is to minimize health risks to consumers.

Like all regulation, however, the FDA standards entail real costs. The tests required for new drugs are very expensive and time-consuming. Getting a new drug approved for sale can take years of effort and require a huge investment. The net results are that (1) fewer new drugs are brought to market and (2) those that do reach the market are more expensive than they would be in the absence of regulation. In other words, the aggregate supply of goods is shifted to the left.

Many—perhaps most—of these regulatory activities are beneficial. In fact, all were originally designed to serve specific public purposes. As a result of such regulation, we do get safer drugs, cleaner air, and less deceptive advertising. We must also consider the costs involved, however. All regulatory activities impose direct and indirect costs. These costs must be compared to the benefits received. *The basic contention of supply-side economists is that regulatory costs are too high.* To improve our economic performance, they assert, we must *deregulate* the production process, thereby shifting the aggregate supply curve to the right again.

POLICY PERSPECTIVES

Is More Growth Desirable?

The government clearly has a powerful set of levers for promoting faster economic growth. Many people wonder, though, whether more economic growth is really *desirable*. Those of us who commute on congested highways, breathe foul air, and can't find a secluded camping site may raise a loud chorus of no's. But before reaching a conclusion let us at least determine what it is people don't like about the prospect of continued growth.

Is it really economic growth per se that people object to or, instead, the specific ways GDP has grown in the past? To state the question this way may provoke a few second thoughts.

First of all, let us distinguish very clearly between economic growth and population growth. Congested neighborhoods, dining halls, and highways are the consequence of too many people, not of too many goods and services. And there's no indication that population growth will cease any time soon. As the accompanying Headline notes, the U.S. population is likely to increase by another 60 million people by the year 2030.

Who's going to feed, clothe, and house all these people? Are we going to redistribute the current level of output, leaving everyone with less? Or should we try to produce *more* output so living standards don't fall? Indeed, if we had *more* goods and services—if we had more houses and transit systems—much of the population congestion we now experience might be relieved. Maybe if we had enough resources to meet our existing demands *and* to build a solar-generated "new town" in the middle of Montana, people might move out of the crowded neighborhoods of Chicago and St. Louis. Well, probably not, but at least one thing is certain: with fewer goods and services, more people will have to share any given quantity of output.

Which brings us back to the really essential measure of growth, GDP per capita. Are there any serious grounds for desiring less GDP per capita, a reduced standard of living? And don't say yes just because you think we already have too many cars on our roads or calories in our bellies. That argument refers to the *mix* of output again and does not answer the question of whether or not we want *any* more goods or services per person. Increasing GDP per capita can take a million forms, including the educational services you are now consuming. The rejection of economic growth per se implies that none of those forms is desirable.

We could, of course, acquire more of the goods and services we consider beneficial simply by cutting back on the production of the things we consider unnecessary. But who is to say which mix of output is "best," and how

HEADLINE

POPULATION GROWTH

World May Have 3 Billion More People by 2030

By the year 2030, the world will have nearly 3 billion more people—2 billion of them in countries where the average person earns less than $2 a day, the World Bank predicts.

Its report, issued yesterday, estimates the global population total will reach 8.5 billion, compared with 5.7 billion in 1995.

People will live longer too. The average African baby born today can expect to live to age 54; one born in 2030 should survive to 63.

The World Bank estimates the U.S. population will grow from 263.1 million next year to 327.9 million in 2030. Life expectancy in North America should increase to 82 years from 77, it reported.

The population of Europe is due to increase from 731 million to 742 million by 2030, the bank says, while Africa's will grow from 720 million to 1.6 billion.

The Washington Post, August 4, 1994, p. A9. © 1994, The Washington Post. Reprinted with permission.

are we going to bring about the desired shift? The present mix of output may be considered bad because it is based on a maldistribution of income, deceptive advertising, or failure of the market mechanism to account for external costs. If so, it would seem more efficient (and politically more feasible) to address those problems directly rather than to attempt to lower our standard of living.

SUMMARY

- Economic growth refers to increases in real GDP. Short-run growth may result from increases in capacity utilization (e.g., less unemployment). In the long run, however, growth requires increases in capacity itself—rightward shifts of the long-run aggregate supply curve.
- GDP per capita is a basic measure of living standards. By contrast, GDP per worker gauges our productivity. Over time, increases in productivity have been the primary cause of rising living standards.
- Productivity gains can originate in a variety of ways. These sources include better labor quality, increased capital investment, research and development, and improved management.
- The policy levers for increasing growth rates include education and training, immigration, and investment and saving incentives. All of these levers may increase the quantity or quality of resources.
- Budget deficits may inhibit economic growth by "crowding out" investment. This occurs when government borrowing absorbs savings that would otherwise finance investment.
- The goal of economic growth implies that macroeconomic policies must be assessed in terms of their long-run supply impact as well as their short-term demand effects.
- Continued economic growth is desirable as long as it brings a higher standard of living for people and an increased ability to produce and consume socially desirable goods and services.

Terms to Remember

Define the following terms:

production possibilities	growth rate	investment
economic growth	GDP per capita	saving
nominal GDP	labor force	crowding out
real GDP	productivity	

Questions for Discussion

1. In what specific ways (if any) does a college education increase a worker's productivity?
2. Why don't we consume all of our current output instead of sacrificing some present consumption for investment?
3. In 1866, Stanley Jevons predicted that economic growth would come to a halt when England ran out of coal, a doomsday that he reckoned would occur in the mid-1970s. How have we managed to avert that projection?
4. Fertility rates in the United States have dropped so low that we are approaching zero population growth, a condition that France has maintained for decades. How will this affect our economic growth? Our standard of living?

5. Suppose that economic growth could only be achieved by increasing inequality (e.g., via tax incentive for investment). Would economic growth still be desirable?
6. Is limitless growth really possible? What forces do you think will be most important in slowing or halting economic growth?
7. Notice in the Headline on p. 310 how the time spent working on the job and at home has declined. How are these changes indicative of economic growth?

Problems

1. If real GDP is growing at 3 percent a year, how long will it take for
   (a) Real GDP to double?
   (b) Real GDP *per capita* to double if the population is increasing each year by
       (i) 0 percent?
       (ii) 1 percent?
       (iii) 2 percent?
2. Suppose that every additional 5 percentage points in the investment rate (I ÷ GDP) boost economic growth by 1 percentage point. Assume also that all investment must be financed with consumer saving. The economy is now characterized by

GDP:	$6 trillion
Consumption:	5 trillion
Saving:	1 trillion
Investment:	1 trillion

   If the goal is to raise the growth rate by 1 percent
   (a) By how much must investment increase?
   (b) By how much must consumption decline for this to occur?
   (c) Are consumers better or worse off as a result?
3. Suppose that the labor force expands by 1 percent each year solely as a result of immigration. How will average GDP per worker be affected if immigrants are always
   (a) Half as productive as native-born workers?
   (b) As productive as native-born workers?
   (c) Twice as productive as native-born workers?
   How large are the differences between (a), (b), and (c) after 10 years?

Chapter 16

Theory and Reality

There is no one solution. It isn't just a question of the budget. It isn't just the question of inflationary labor rates. It isn't just the question of sticky prices. It isn't just the question of what the Government does to keep prices up or to make regulations that tend to be inflationary. It isn't just the weather or just the drought. It is all these things. The interaction of these various factors is what is so terribly difficult for us to understand and, of course, what is so terribly difficult for us to deal with.

—Former Secretary of the Treasury W. Michael Blumenthal

Macroeconomic theory is supposed to explain the business cycle and show policymakers how to control it. But something is obviously wrong. We have repeatedly failed to achieve our goals of full employment, price stability, and vigorous economic growth. No matter how hard we try, the business cycle seems to persist.

What accounts for this discrepancy between economic theory and economic performance? Are our theories no good? Or is sound economic advice being ignored?

Many people blame the economists. They point to the conflicting theories and advice that economists offer and wonder what theory is supposed to be followed. If economists themselves can't agree, it is asked, why should anyone else listen to them?

Not surprisingly, economists see things a bit differently. First of all, they point out, the **business cycle** isn't as bad as it used to be. Since World War II, the economy has had many ups and downs, but none has been as severe as the Great Depression or earlier catastrophes. Second, economists place most of the responsibility for continuing business-cycle problems on the real world, not on their theories. They complain that "politics" takes precedence over good economic advice. Politicians are reluctant, for example, to raise taxes or cut spending in order to control inflation. Their concern is winning the next election, not solving the country's economic problems.

business cycle: Alternating periods of economic growth and contraction.

President Jimmy Carter anguished over another problem—the complexity of economic decision making. In the real world, neither theory nor politics can keep up with all our economic goals. As President Carter observed: "We cannot concentrate just on inflation or just on unemployment or just on deficits in the federal budget or our international payments. Nor can we act in isolation from other countries. We must deal with all of these problems simultaneously and on a worldwide basis."

The purpose of this chapter is to confront these and other frustrations of the real world. In so doing, we will try to provide answers to the following questions:

- What is the ideal "package" of macro policies?
- How well does our macro performance live up to the promises of that package?
- What kinds of obstacles prevent us from doing better?

POLICY LEVERS

The macroeconomic tools available to policymakers are summarized in Table 16.1. Although this list is brief, we hardly need a reminder at this point of how powerful each instrument can be. Every one of these major policy instruments can significantly alter the dimensions of the economy. Their use may not only affect inflation and unemployment rates but may also change our answers to the basic economic questions of WHAT, HOW, and FOR WHOM to produce.

Fiscal Policy

> **fiscal policy:** The use of government taxes and spending to alter macroeconomic outcomes.

The basic tools of **fiscal policy** are contained in the federal budget. Tax cuts are supposed to stimulate spending by putting more income in the hands of consumers and businesses. Tax increases are intended to curtail spending and thus reduce inflationary pressures. Some of the major tax changes implemented in recent years are summarized in Table 16.2.

The expenditure side of the federal budget provides another fiscal-policy tool. From a Keynesian perspective, increases in government spending raise aggregate demand and so encourage more production. A slowdown in government spending is supposed to restrain aggregate demand, lessening any inflationary pressures that might exist. With government spending exceeding $1.6 trillion a year, changes in the federal budget can influence aggregate demand significantly.

TABLE 16.1
The Policy Levers

Economic policymakers have access to a variety of policy instruments. The challenge is to choose the right tools at the right time. The mix of tools required may vary from problem to problem.

Type of Policy	Policy Instruments
Fiscal	Tax cuts and increases
	Changes in government spending
Monetary	Open-market operations
	Reserve requirements
	Discount rates
Supply-side	Tax incentives for investment and saving
	Deregulation
	Education and training
	Immigration

TABLE 16.2
Fiscal-Policy Milestones

1981	Economic Recovery Tax Act	Three-year consumer tax cut of $213 billion plus $59 billion of business tax cuts
1982	Tax Equity and Fiscal Responsibility Act	Raised business, excise, and income taxes by $100 billion over three years
1983	Social Security Act Amendments	Increased payroll taxes and cut future retirement benefits
1984	Deficit Reduction Act	Increased income, business, and excise taxes by $50 billion over three years
1985	Gramm-Rudman-Hollings Act	Required a balanced budget by 1991 and authorized automatic spending cuts
1986	Tax Reform Act	Major reduction in tax rates coupled with broadening of tax base
1987	Gramm-Rudman-Hollings Reaffirmation	Postponed balanced-budget target until 1993
1990	Budget Enforcement Act	Eliminated deficit ceilings; imposed limit on discretionary spending
1993	Clinton's "New Direction"	Tax increases and spending cuts to reduce deficit, 1994–97
1994	"Contract with America"	Republicans propose tax cuts for personal income and capital gains

Automatic Stabilizers. Changes in the budget don't necessarily originate in presidential decisions or congressional legislation. Tax revenues and government outlays also respond to economic events. ***When the economy slows, tax revenues decline, and government spending increases automatically.*** The recession of 1990–91, for example, displaced 2 million workers and reduced the incomes of millions more. As their incomes fell, so did their tax liabilities. As a consequence, government tax revenues fell.

The recession also caused government spending to *rise*. The swollen ranks of unemployed workers increased outlays for unemployment insurance benefits, welfare, food stamps, and other transfer payments. None of this budget activity required new legislation. Instead, the benefits were increased *automatically* under laws already written. No *new* policy was required.

These recession-induced changes in tax receipts and budget outlays are referred to as **automatic stabilizers.** Such budget changes help stabilize the economy by increasing after-tax incomes and spending when the economy slows. Specifically, ***recessions automatically***

- ***Reduce tax revenues***
- ***Increase government outlays***
- ***Widen budget deficits***

Economic expansions have the opposite effect on government budgets. When the economy booms, people have to pay more taxes on their rising incomes. They also have less need for government assistance. Hence tax receipts rise and government spending drops automatically when the economy heats up. These changes tend to shrink the budget deficit and help "cool" the economy.

Discretionary Policy. Automatic changes in taxes and spending do not reflect current fiscal-policy decisions; they reflect laws already on the books. Current fiscal policy entails *new* tax and spending decisions. Specifically, ***fiscal policy refers to deliberate changes in tax or spending legislation.*** These changes can be made only by the U.S. Congress. Every year the pres-

automatic stabilizer: Federal expenditure or revenue item that automatically responds countercyclically to changes in national income—e.g., unemployment benefits, income taxes.

fiscal year (FY): The twelve-month period used for accounting purposes; begins October 1 for federal government.

ident proposes specific budget and tax changes, negotiates with Congress, then accepts or vetoes specific acts that Congress has passed. The resulting policy decisions represent "discretionary" fiscal policy. Policymakers deserve credit (or blame) only for the effects of the discretionary policy decisions they make (or fail to make).

The distinction between automatic stabilizers and discretionary spending helps explain why the federal budget deficit jumped from $221 billion in **fiscal year** 1991 to nearly $270 billion in fiscal 1992. Ironically, Congress had *increased* tax rates in fiscal 1992, hoping to trim the deficit somewhat. Congress had also planned to slow the growth of government spending. Hence discretionary fiscal policy was slightly restrictive. These discretionary policies were overwhelmed, however, by the force of the recession. Automatic stabilizers caused huge shortfalls in tax revenues and increased government transfer payments as well. The net result was a much larger budget deficit in fiscal 1992, the opposite of what Congress had intended. The swollen deficit was a symptom of the economy's weakness, not a measure of fiscal-policy stimulus.

The opposite occurred in 1994 and 1995. The economy grew faster in those years than anticipated. As a result, tax revenues increased, transfer payments declined, and the budget deficit shrank more than expected. Although President Clinton claimed credit for the deficit reduction, much of it was due to the automatic stabilizers that accompany economic growth.

Monetary Policy

monetary policy: The use of money and credit controls to influence macroeconomic activity.

money supply (M1): Currency held by the public, plus balances in transactions accounts.

The policy arsenal described in Table 16.1 also contains monetary tools. The tools of **monetary policy** include open-market operations, discount-rate changes, and reserve requirements. The Federal Reserve uses these tools to change the **money supply.** In so doing, the Fed strives to shift the aggregate demand curve in the desired direction.

The effectiveness of both fiscal and monetary policy depends on the shape of the aggregate supply (AS) curve. If the AS curve is horizontal, changes in the money supply (and related aggregate demand shifts) affect output only. If the AS curve is vertical, money-supply changes will affect prices only. In the most typical case of an upward-sloping AS curve, changes in the money supply will affect both prices and output.

HEADLINE

POLICY ADJUSTMENTS

Greenspan Sees an End to Rate Increases

WASHINGTON—Federal Reserve Chairman Alan Greenspan, cheering financial markets and pleasing politicians, told Congress that the Fed might refrain from raising interest rates further even if inflation measures move up a bit.

Mr. Greenspan didn't rule out further increases in rates, and explicitly cautioned that "the jury is still out on whether the slowing" of the economy that has recently become evident "will be sufficient to contain inflationary pressures."

But just as the Fed raised short-term rates "to head off inflationary pressures not yet evident in the data," he said "there may come a time when we hold our policy stance unchanged, or even ease, despite adverse price data, should we see signs that underlying forces are acting ... to reduce inflationary pressures."

—David Wessel

Rules vs. Discretion. Disagreements about the actual shape of the AS curve raise questions about how to conduct monetary policy. Some economists urge the Fed to play an active role in adjusting the money supply to changing economic conditions. Others suggest that we would be better served by fixed rules for money-supply growth. Fixed rules would make the Fed more of a passive mechanic rather than an active policymaker.

There are clear risks of error in discretionary policy. In 1979 and again in 1989 the Fed pursued restrictive policies that pushed the economy into recessions. In both cases, the Fed had to reverse its policies. (In Table 16.3 compare October 1982 to October 1979 and 1991 to 1989.) The Fed tried to avert such a mistake in 1995 by easing off the monetary brake before all signs of inflation were gone (see Headline).

The debate over rules versus discretion concerns not only possible mistakes but also the potential effectiveness of monetary policy. In 1991, the Fed moved aggressively to stimulate aggregate demand with lower interest rates. But consumers and investors were unpersuaded. They used the lower interest rates to reduce their debts rather than buy more goods and services. Critics used the occasion to point out that discretionary monetary policy was not only error-prone but also likely to be ineffective when needed. Advocates of discretionary policy urged patience to give the markets more time to respond to monetary stimulus.

Supply-Side Policy

> **supply-side policy:** The use of tax rates, (de)regulation, and other mechanisms to increase the ability and willingness to produce goods and services.

Supply-side theory offers the third major set of policy tools. We have seen how ***the shape of the aggregate supply curve limits the effectiveness of fiscal and monetary policies.*** Shifts of the aggregate supply curve are also a prerequisite for economic growth. Supply-side policy focuses directly on these constraints. The goal of **supply-side policy** is to shift the aggregate supply curve to the right. Such rightward shifts not only promote long-term growth but also make short-run policy intervention more successful.

TABLE 16.3
Monetary-Policy Milestones

August 1979	Paul Volcker becomes Fed chairman
October 1979	Fed adopts monetarist approach, tightening money supply; interest rates soar
July 1982	Deep into recession, Fed votes to ease monetary restraint
October 1982	Volcker abandons pure monetarist approach and expands money supply rapidly
June 1983	Reagan reappoints Volcker
1984	Reagan administration and Fed criticize each other's policies: Fed criticized for being too tight; Reagan criticized for being too stimulative
1986	Money supply increases by 15 percent
May 1987	Volcker abandons money-supply targets as policy guides
June 1987	Volcker resigns; replaced by Alan Greenspan; money-supply growth decreases; discount rate increased
1989	Greenspan announces goal of "zero inflation"; slows money-supply growth
1990	Bush administration urges Fed to reduce interest rates; Fed urges smaller budget deficits
1991	In midst of recession Greenspan reverses monetary policy; interest rates fall to their lowest level in decades
1994	As growth accelerates and unemployment dips, Fed raises interest rates substantially

The supply-side toolbox is filled with a variety of tools. Tax cuts designed to stimulate work effort, saving, and investment are among the most popular and powerful supply-side tools. Deregulation may also reduce production costs and stimulate investment. Expenditure on education, training, and research also expands our capacity to produce. Immigration policy alters the size and skills of the labor force and thus affects aggregate supply as well.

In the 1980s, tax rates were reduced dramatically. The maximum marginal tax rate on individuals was cut from 70 percent to 50 percent in 1981, and then still further, to 28 percent, in 1987. The 1980s also witnessed major milestones in the deregulation of airlines, trucking, telephone service, and other industries (see Table 16.4). All of these policies helped shift the AS curve rightward.

Government policies can also shift the AS curve leftward. When the minimum wage jumped to $4.25 an hour in 1991, the cost of supplying goods and services went up. A 1991 increase in the payroll tax intended to help pay for Medicare boosted production costs as well. In the early 1990s, private employers were also burdened with higher labor costs associated with government-mandated fringe benefits (Family Leave Act of 1993) and accommodations for handicapped workers (Americans with Disabilities Act). All of these policies restrained aggregate supply.

President Clinton argued that the productive capacity of the economy could be expanded with greater investment in both *physical* capital and *human* capital. His "Rebuild America" program stepped up spending on highways and other public infrastructure. He also increased spending on education and urged private employers to provide more worker training.

Because tax rates are a basic tool of supply-side policy, fiscal and supply-side policies are often intertwined. When Congress changes the tax laws, it almost always alters marginal tax rates and thus changes production in-

TABLE 16.4
Supply-Side Milestones

1978	Airline Deregulation Act	Phased out federal regulations of airline routes, fares, and entry
1980	Motor Carrier Act	Eliminated federal restrictions on entry, routes, and fares in the trucking industry
1981	Economic Recovery Tax Act	Decreased marginal tax rates by 30 percent
1982	AT&T breakup	AT&T monopoly on phone service ended via antitrust action
1986	Tax Reform Act	Eliminated most tax preferences for investment and saving, but sharply reduced marginal tax rates
1989	Fair Labor Standards Act amended	Congress increases minimum wage to $3.80 in 1990 and $4.25 in 1991
1990	Social Security Act amendments implemented	Payroll tax increased to 7.65 percent
1990	Americans with Disabilities Act	Employers must provide more handicap access
1990	Immigration Act	Increased immigration quotas, new preference for skilled workers
1990	Clean Air Act	Toughened pollution standards
1991	Surface Transportation Act	Accelerated highway and rail improvements
1993	Rebuild America Program	Increased infrastructure investment
1993	Family Leave Act	Employers required to offer unpaid leave
1995	Minimum wage increase	President Clinton proposes hike to $5.15

centives. Notice, for example, that tax legislation appears in Table 16.4 as well as in Table 16.2. The Tax Reform Act of 1986 not only changed total tax revenues (fiscal policy) but also restructured production and investment incentives (supply-side policy). Congress also has broad authority over regulatory policies, although the president and the executive agencies make day-to-day decisions on how to interpret and enforce these policies.

IDEALIZED USES

These fiscal, monetary, and supply-side tools are potentially powerful levers for controlling the economy. In principle, they can cure the excesses of the business cycle. To see how, let us review their use in three distinct macroeconomic settings.

Case 1: Recession

When output and employment levels fall far short of the economy's full-employment potential, the mandate for public policy is clear. Total spending must be increased so that producers can sell more goods, hire more workers, and move the economy toward its productive capacity. At such times the most urgent need is to put people to work, and relatively little concern is expressed for other, possibly conflicting economic goals.

How should people be put to work? Pure Keynesians emphasize the need to stimulate aggregate demand. They seek to shift the aggregate demand curve rightward by cutting taxes or boosting government spending. The resulting stimulus will set off a **multiplier** reaction, propelling the economy to full employment.

multiplier: The multiple by which an initial change in aggregate spending will alter total expenditure after an infinite number of spending cycles; $1/(1 - MPC)$.

Modern Keynesians acknowledge that monetary policy might also help. Specifically, increases in the money supply may lower interest rates and thus give investment spending a further boost. All of these actions can be taken simultaneously. To give the economy a really powerful stimulus, we might want to cut taxes, increase government spending, and expand the money supply all at the same time. By taking such convincing action, we might also increase consumer confidence, raise investor expectations, and induce still greater spending and output.

By MAL. © Associated Features. Inc.

Other economists offer different advice. So-called Monetarists and other critics of government intervention see no point in discretionary policies. As they see it, the aggregate supply curve is vertical at the "natural" rate of unemployment. "Quick fixes" of monetary or fiscal policy may shift the aggregate demand curve but won't change the aggregate supply curve. Monetary or fiscal stimulus will push the price level up (more inflation) without reducing unemployment. In this view, the appropriate policy response to a recession is patience. As sales and output slow, interest rates will decline, and new investment will be stimulated.

Supply-siders confront these objections head-on. In their view, policy initiatives should focus on changing the shape and position of the aggregate supply curve. Supply-siders would emphasize the need to improve production incentives. They would urge cuts in marginal tax rates on investment and labor. They would also look for ways to reduce government regulation.

Case 2: Inflation

An overheated economy elicits a similar assortment of policy prescriptions. In this case, one task of policy is to restrain aggregate demand—that is, shift the aggregate demand curve to the left. Keynesians would do this by raising taxes and cutting government spending, relying on the multiplier to cool down the economy. Monetarists would simply cut the money supply. If the AS curve is really vertical, changes in the money supply alter prices, not output. Therefore, inflation must reflect excessive money-supply growth or the anticipation of such growth. The role of public policy, Monetarists would assert, is not only to reduce money-supply growth but to convince market participants that a more cautious monetary policy will be continued.

Supply-siders would point out that inflation implies both "too much money" and "not enough goods." They would look at the supply side of the market for ways to expand productive capacity. In a highly inflationary setting, they would propose more incentives to save. The additional savings would automatically reduce consumption while creating a larger pool of investable funds. Supply-siders would also cut taxes and regulations, which raise production costs, and lower import barriers, which keep out cheaper foreign goods.

Case 3: Stagflation

stagflation: The simultaneous occurrence of substantial unemployment and inflation.

Although serious inflations and recessions provide reasonably clear options for economic policy, there is a vast gray area between these extremes. All too often the economy suffers from both inflation and unemployment at the same time—a condition called **stagflation.** If the aggregate supply curve starts sloping upward before full employment is reached, inflation emerges even when unemployment is too high. In this case, any demand-side effort to attain full employment worsens inflation. Likewise, restrictive demand policies increase unemployment. Although any upward-sloping AS curve poses such a tradeoff, the position of the curve also determines how difficult the choices are. Figure 16.1 illustrates this stagflation problem.

There are no simple solutions for stagflation. Any demand-side initiatives must be designed with care, seeking to balance the competing threats of inflation and unemployment. This requires more attention to the specific nature of the supply constraints. Perhaps the early rise in the AS curve is due to **structural unemployment.** Prices may be rising in the telecommunications industry, for example, while unemployed workers are abun-

structural unemployment: Unemployment caused by a mismatch between the skills (or location) of job seekers and the requirements (or location) of available jobs.

FIGURE 16.1
Stagflation

Both unemployment and inflation may occur at the same time. This is always a potential problem with an upward-sloping AS curve. The further the AS curve is to the left, the worse the stagflation problem is likely to be. The curve AS_1 implies higher prices than AS_2 at any given rate of unemployment (e.g., Q_u).

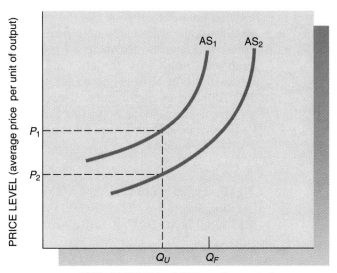

REAL OUTPUT (real GDP per time period)

dant in the housing industry. The higher prices and wages in telecommunications function as a signal to transfer resources from the housing industry into telecommunications. Such resource shifts, however, may not occur smoothly or quickly. In the interim, public policy can be developed to alter the structure of supply or demand.

On the demand side, the government could decrease the demand for telecommunications by increasing excise taxes on phone and other transmission services, buying fewer terminals for government use, or raising installment-loan interest rates. It could increase the demand for houses by providing housing subsidies to poor people, greater home-related tax deductions for everyone, or lower interest rates in the mortgage market. This was the demand-side intent of President Bush's 1992 proposal to give first-time home buyers a $5,000 tax credit. On the supply side, the government could offer tax credits for housing construction, teach construction workers how to install and operate telecommunications equipment, or speed up the job-search process.

High tax rates or costly regulations might also contribute to stagflation. If either of these constraints exists, high prices (inflation) may not be a sufficient incentive for increased output. In this case, reductions in tax rates and regulation could shift the AS curve rightward, easing the stagflation pressures. This is the basic goal of all supply-side policies.

Stagflation may have arisen from a temporary contraction (leftward shift) of aggregate supply that both reduces output and drives up prices. In this case, neither structural unemployment nor excessive demand is the culprit. Rather, an "external shock" (such as a natural disaster) or an abrupt change in world trade (such as an oil embargo) is the cause of stagflation. The high oil prices and supply disruptions that occurred during the Gulf War (1990–91) illustrate this problem. In these circumstances, conventional policy tools are unlikely to provide a complete "cure." In most cases the economy simply has to adjust to a temporary setback.

Fine-Tuning

Everything looks easy on the blackboard. Indeed economic theory seems to have all the answers for our macro problems. Some people even imag-

fine-tuning: Adjustments in economic policy designed to counteract small changes in economic outcomes; continuous responses to changing economic conditions.

ine that economic theory has the potential to "fine-tune" the economy, that is, to correct any and all macro problems that arise. Such **fine-tuning** would entail continual adjustments to policy levers. When unemployment is the problem, simply give the economy a jolt of fiscal or monetary stimulus; when inflation is worrisome, simply apply the fiscal or monetary brakes. To fulfill our goals for content and distribution, we simply pick the right target for stimulus or restraint. With a little attention and experience, the right speed could be found and the economy guided successfully down the road to prosperity.

THE ECONOMIC RECORD

The economy's track record does not live up to the high expectations of fine-tuning. To be sure, the economy has continued to grow and we have attained an impressive standard of living. We have also had some great years when both unemployment and inflation rates were low, as in 1994 and 1995. Nor can we lose sight of the fact that even in a "bad" year our per capita income greatly exceeds the realities and even the expectations in most other countries of the world. Nevertheless, we must also recognize that our economic history is punctuated by periods of recession, high unemployment, inflation, and recurring concern for the distribution of income and mix of output. We have witnessed a significant gap between the potential and the reality of economic policy.

The graphs in Figure 16.2 provide a quick summary of our experiences since 1946, the year the Employment Act committed the federal government to macro stability. It is evident that we have not successfully fulfilled our major economic goals during this period. In the 1970s we rarely came close. Although we approached our inflation and growth goals in the 1980s, our economic performance was far from perfect. Two recessions sent unemployment to post–World War II heights in the early 1980s. Then inflation accelerated at the end of the 1980s, despite the fact that we were still a long way from the avowed goal of 4 percent unemployment. When more restrictive monetary and fiscal policies were implemented, the economy stumbled into another recession (1990–91).

In terms of real economic growth, the record is equally spotty. Output actually declined (i.e., recessions) in eight years and grew less than 3 percent in another fifteen. The 1990s got underway with virtually zero growth as the seven-year expansion of the 1980s petered out. Moreover, the distribution of income in 1994 looked virtually identical to that of 1946, and over 36 million people were still officially counted as poor in the later year. Accordingly, we must acknowledge that the potential of economic policy to fulfill our goals has not yet been fully realized.

The economic performance of the United States is similar to that of other Western nations. The economies of most countries did not grow as fast as the U.S. economy in the 1980s. But, as the accompanying Headline shows, some countries did a better job of restraining prices or reducing unemployment.

WHY THINGS DON'T ALWAYS WORK

We have already noted the readiness of economists and politicians to blame each other for the continuing gap between our economic goals and per-

FIGURE 16.2
The Economic Record

The Full Employment and Balanced Growth Act of 1978 established specific goals for unemployment (4 percent), inflation (3 percent), and economic growth (4 percent). We have rarely attained those goals, however, as these graphs illustrate. Measurement, design, and policy implementation problems help explain these shortcomings.

Source: *Economic Report of the President*, 1995.

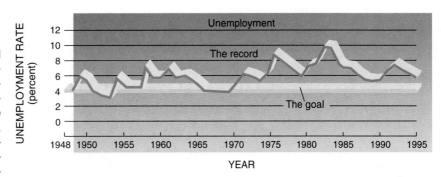

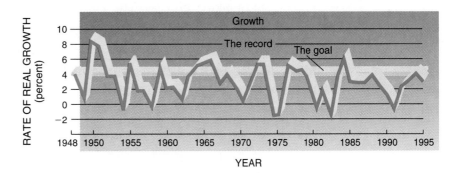

formance. Rather than taking sides, however, we may note some general constraints on successful policy making. In this regard, we can distinguish *four obstacles to policy success:*

- *Goal conflicts*
- *Measurement problems*
- *Design problems*
- *Implementation problems*

Goal Conflicts

The first factor to note is potential conflicts in policy priorities. Suppose for the moment that the economy was suffering from stagflation and, further, that all macro policies involved some tradeoff between unemployment and inflation. Should we try to cure inflation, unemployment, or just a bit of both? Answers are likely to vary. Unemployed people will put the highest priority on attaining full employment. Bankers, creditors, and people

HEADLINE

COMPARATIVE PERFORMANCE

Macro Performance in the 1980s

The performance of the U.S. economy in the 1980s was similar to that of other developed economies. Germany had the greatest success in restraining inflation (2.6 percent) but suffered from very slow growth. The Japanese economy grew rapidly (3.7 percent) and kept unemployment low (2.5 percent), but it had a relatively high rate of inflation (6.1 percent). The U.S. inflation rate was less (4.6 percent), but growth (2.9 percent) and unemployment (7.2 percent) performance were above average. In the early 1990s, America's relative performance improved on all three measures.

Performance (annual average percentage)	U.S.	Japan	Germany	United Kingdom	France	Italy	Canada
Real growth	2.9	3.7	1.1	2.1	0.8	1.2	3.3
Inflation	4.6	6.1	2.6	6.2	6.5	10.1	6.1
Unemployment	7.2	2.5	6.1	9.9	9.3	6.5	9.3

Source: *Economic Report of the President, 1995.*

on fixed incomes will demand an end to inflation. There is no "right" solution to this goal conflict. As a result, we cannot completely succeed.

In practice, these goal conflicts are often institutionalized in the decision-making process. The Fed is traditionally viewed as the guardian of price stability and tends to favor policy restraint. The president and Congress worry more about people's jobs and government programs, so lean toward policy stimulus. Thus a basic institutional conflict exists about the direction of policy (see entries for 1984 and 1990 in Table 16.3).

Distributional goals may also conflict with macro objectives. Antiinflationary policies may require cutbacks in programs for the poor, the elderly, or needy students. These cutbacks may be politically impossible. Likewise, tight-money policies may be viewed as too great a burden for small businesses. In either case, policy decisions will be constrained by basic goal conflicts.

Although the policy levers listed in Table 16.1 are powerful, they cannot grant all our wishes. Since we still live in a world of scarce resources, ***all policy decisions entail opportunity costs.*** This means that we will always be confronted with tradeoffs; the best we can hope for is a set of compromises that yields optimal outcomes, not ideal ones.

Even if we all agreed on policy priorities, success would not be assured. We would still have to confront the more mundane problems of measurement, design, and implementation.

Measurement Problems

The measurement problems that plague economic policy have little to do with economic theory. Although our theoretical perspectives are by no means complete, they are adequately developed to deal with major economic problems. As long as we can diagnose the major dimensions of a problem, economic theory is equipped to provide a fairly reliable set of policy guidelines.

A good many of our problems arise in the diagnosis stage, however. One reason fire fighters are pretty successful in putting out fires before whole cities burn down is that fires are highly visible phenomena. Such visibility is not characteristic of economic problems, at least not in their more moderate manifestations. An increase in the unemployment rate from 5 to 6 percent, for example, is not the kind of thing you notice while crossing the street. Unless you lose your own job, the increase in unemployment is not likely to attract your attention. The same is true of prices; small increases in product prices are unlikely to ring many alarms. Hence both inflation and unemployment may worsen considerably before anyone takes serious notice. Were we as slow and ill equipped to notice fires, whole neighborhoods would burn before someone rang the alarm.

Measurement problems are a very basic policy constraint. To formulate good economic policy, we must first determine the nature of our problems. To do so, we must measure employment changes, output changes, price changes, and other macro outcomes. Although the government spends vast sums of money to collect and process such data, the available information is always dated and incomplete. ***At best, we know what was happening in the economy last month or last week.*** The processes of data collection, assembly, and presentation take time, even in this age of high-speed computers. The average recession lasts about eleven months, but official data generally do not even confirm the existence of a recession until eight months after a downturn starts! The recession of 1990–91 was no exception, as the accompanying Headline shows.

President Clinton expressed his frustration with this measurement problem at the very outset of his presidency. His successful election campaign was based on the perception that the economy was faltering and that a Clinton-designed stimulus was needed. Immediately after the November 1992 election, however, the U.S. Commerce Department reported that the economy was growing faster than previously thought. These revised figures caused Clinton to reverse his promise of fiscal stimulus (tax cuts) and pursue fiscal restraint (tax increase) instead.

Forecasts. In an ideal world, policymakers would not only respond to economic problems that occur but also *anticipate* their occurrence and act to

HEADLINE

MEASUREMENT PROBLEMS

This Just In: Recession Ended 21 Months Ago

WASHINGTON—Here's proof that economics is an inexact science. An official panel of economists determined today that the nation's ninth postwar recession ended a month before they realized it had started. And it took 21 months to sort all this out.

The dating committee of the National Bureau of Economic Research declared today that the recession had ended in March 1991—the month before it even announced there was a recession. The committed determined in April 1991 that the recession had begun in the previous July.

—Robert D. Hershey, Jr.

avoid them. If we foresee an inflation emerging, for example, we want to take immediate action to keep aggregate demand from increasing. That is to say, the successful fire fighter not only responds to fires but also looks for hazards that might start one.

Unfortunately, economic policymakers are again at a disadvantage. Their knowledge of future problems is even worse than their knowledge of current problems. **In designing policy, policymakers must depend on economic forecasts,** that is, informed guesses about what the economy will look like in future periods.

Macro Models. Those guesses are often based on complex computer models of how the economy works. These models—referred to as *econometric macro models*—are mathematical summaries of the economy's performance. The models try to identify the key determinants of macro performance, then show what happens to macro outcomes when they change.

An economist "feeds" the computer two essential inputs. One is a model of how the economy allegedly works. Such models are quantitative summaries of one or more macro theories. A Keynesian model, for example, will include equations that show multiplier spending responses to tax cuts. A monetarist model will show that tax cuts raise interest rates ("crowding out"), not total spending. And a supply-side model stipulates labor-supply and production responses. The computer can't tell which theory is right; it just predicts what it is programmed to see. In other words, the computer sees the world through the eyes of its economic master.

The second essential input in a computer forecast is the assumed values for critical economic variables. A Keynesian model, for example, must specify how large a multiplier to expect. All the computer does is carry out the required mathematical routines, once it is told that the multiplier is relevant and what its value is. It cannot discern the true multiplier any better than it can pick the right theory.

Given the dependence of computers on the theories and perceptions of their economic masters, it is not surprising that computer forecasts often differ greatly. It's also not surprising that they are often wrong.

Even policymakers who are familiar with both economic theory and computer models can make some pretty bad calls. In January 1990, Fed Chairman Alan Greenspan assured Congress that the risk of a recession was as low as 20 percent. Although he said he "wouldn't bet the ranch" on such a low probability, he was confident that the odds of a recession were below 50 percent. Five months after his testimony, the 1990–91 recession began.

Design Problems

Forget all these bad forecasts for a moment and just pretend that we can, somehow, get a reliable forecast of where the economy is headed. The outlook, let us suppose, is bad. Now we are in the driver's seat, trying to steer the economy past looming dangers. We need to chart our course—to design an economic plan. What action should we take? How will the marketplace respond to any specific action we take? Will the aggregate demand curve respond as expected? What shape will the aggregate supply curve have? Which macro theory should we use to guide policy decisions?

Suppose, for example, that we adopt a Keynesian approach to ending a recession. Specifically, we cut income taxes to stimulate consumer spending. How do we know that consumers will respond as anticipated? Perhaps the marginal propensity to consume has changed. Maybe the level of consumer confidence has dropped. Any of these changes could frustrate even the best-intentioned policy. The successful policymaker needs a very good crystal ball—one that will also foretell how market participants are going to respond to any specific actions taken.

Implementation Problems

Measurement and design problems can break the spirit of even the best policymaker (or his economic advisers). Yet measurement and design problems are only part of the story. A good idea is of little value unless someone puts it to use. Accordingly, to understand why things often go wrong, we must also consider the difficulties of implementing a well-designed (and credible) policy initiative.

Congressional Deliberations. Suppose that the president and his Council of Economic Advisers (perhaps in conjunction with the secretary of the Treasury and the director of the Office of Management and Budget) decide that the rate of aggregate spending is slowing down. A tax cut, they believe, is necessary to stimulate demand for goods and services. Can they simply go ahead and cut tax rates? No, because all tax changes must be legislated by Congress. Once the president decides on the appropriate policy initiative, he must ask Congress for authority to take the required action. This means a delay in implementing policy, and possibly no policy at all.

At the very least, the president must convince Congress of the accuracy of his own perspectives and the appropriateness of his suggested action. The tax proposal must work its way through separate committees of both the House of Representatives and the Senate, get on the congressional calendar, and be approved in each chamber. If there are important differences in Senate and House versions of the tax-cut legislation, they must be compromised in a joint conference. The modified proposal must then be returned to each chamber for approval.

The same kind of process applies to the outlay size of the budget. Once the president has submitted his budget proposals (in January), Congress reviews them, then sets its own spending goals. After that, the budget is broken down into thirteen different categories, and a separate appropriations bill is written for each one. These bills spell out in detail how much can be spent and for what purposes. Once Congress passes them, they go to the president for acceptance or veto.

In theory, all of these budget deliberations are to be completed in nine months. Budget legislation requires Congress to finish the process by October 1 (the beginning of the federal fiscal year). Congress rarely meets this deadline, however. In most years the budget debate continues well into the fiscal year. In some years, the budget debate is not resolved until the fiscal year is nearly over! The final budget legislation is typically over 1,000 pages long and so complex that few people understand all its dimensions.

This description of congressional activity is not an outline for a civics course; rather, it is an important explanation of why economic policy is not fully effective. ***Even if the right policy is formulated to solve an emerging economic problem, there is no assurance that it will be implemented. And if it is implemented, there is no assurance that it will take effect at the right time.*** One of the most frightening prospects for economic policy is that a policy design intended to serve a specific problem will be implemented much later, when economic conditions have changed. The policy's effect on the economy may then be the opposite of what was intended.

Figure 16.3 is a schematic view of why things don't always work out as well as economic theory suggests they might. There are always delays be-

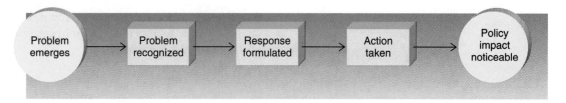

FIGURE 16.3
Policy Response: A Series of Time Lags

Even the best-intentioned economic policy can be frustrated by time lags. It takes time for a problem to be recognized, time to formulate a policy response, and still more time to implement that policy. By the time the policy begins to affect the economy, the underlying problem may have changed.

tween the time a problem emerges and the time it is recognized. There are additional delays between recognition and response design, between design and implementation, and finally between implementation and impact. Not only may mistakes be made at each juncture, but even correct decisions may be overcome by changing economic conditions.

Politics vs. Economics. Last but not least, we must confront the politics of economic policy. Tax hikes and budget cuts rarely win votes. On the other hand, tax cuts and pork-barrel spending tend to make voters happy. Accordingly, savvy politicians tend to stimulate the economy before elections, then tighten the fiscal restraints afterward. This creates a kind of *political* business cycle—a two-year pattern of short-run stops and starts. The conflict between the urgent need to get reelected and the necessity to manage the economy results in a seesaw kind of instability.

The political content of fiscal policy was very visible in 1995. The Republican party had scored stunning victories in the 1994 congressional elections by promising tax cuts and spending reductions. Shortly after the election results were in, President Clinton jumped on the tax-cut bandwagon, too. The Democrats and Republicans then competed to see who could promise the largest tax cut. Meanwhile, the economy was closing in on full employment, and economists were wondering how much fiscal *restraint* might be needed to keep price levels from rising. The politicians would hear nothing of fiscal restraint, however, when voters had responded so eagerly to the lure of tax cuts. As the accompanying Headline suggests, you don't win votes with fiscal restraint.

In theory, the political independence of the Fed's Board of Governors provides some protection from ill-advised but politically advantageous policy initiatives. In practice, however, the Fed's relative obscurity and independence may backfire. The president and the Congress know that if they don't take effective action against inflation—by raising taxes or cutting government spending—the Fed can and will take stronger action to restrain aggregate demand. This is a classic case of having one's cake and eating it too. Elected officials win votes for not raising taxes or cutting some constituent's favorite spending program. They also take credit for any reduction in the rate of inflation brought about by Federal Reserve policies. To top it off, Congress and the president can also blame the Fed for driving up interest rates or starting a recession if monetary policy becomes too restrictive.

HEADLINE

POLITICS VS. ECONOMICS

For Clinton, the Politics of a Tax Cut Are Sure to Clash with the Economics

WASHINGTON—Can Bill Clinton, looking for ways to boost his popularity, resist taking a bite from the tax-cut apple?

Administration officials acknowledge that President Clinton will be tempted by his advisers this fall with a proposal to revive his broken campaign promise to cut taxes for middle-class families.

Conflicting Views

When the debate is joined in the fall, it is likely to pit some of Mr. Clinton's political advisers, who like the politics of a tax cut, against some of his economic advisers, who dislike the economics.

The biggest obstacle is that middle-class tax cuts are expensive because the American middle class is so large. "The first thing [White House chief of staff] Leon Panetta is going to say is: 'How are you going to pay for it?'" says one administration official. To pay for a tax credit of $300 for each child under age 18—just $5.77 a week—Mr. Clinton would have to come up with offsetting spending cuts or tax increases of about $14 billion a year. Limiting the tax break to families with younger children would be cheaper.

The case for a tax cut is simple: To boost the chances of re-election, Mr. Clinton needs to reshape his image and return to the themes that played well in 1992. "Pushing for family tax relief would refocus the Clinton administration on its 'New Democrat' roots," says Will Marshall, head of the Progressive Policy Institute, the centrist Democratic think-tank. It would, he says, restore Mr. Clinton as the candidate of the "forgotten middle class."

—David Wessel

The Wall Street Journal, September 6, 1994, p. A3. Reprinted by permission of *The Wall Street Journal*, © 1994 Dow Jones & Company, Inc. All Rights Reserved Worldwide.

Finally, we must recognize that policy design is obstructed by a certain lack of will. Neither the man in the street nor the elected public official is constantly attuned to economic goals and activities. Even students enrolled in economics courses have a hard time keeping their minds on the economy and its problems. The executive and legislative branches of government, for their part, are likely to focus on economic concerns only when economic problems become serious or voters demand action. Otherwise, policymakers are apt to be complacent about economic policy as long as economic performance is within a "tolerable" range of desired outcomes.

POLICY PERSPECTIVES

Hands Off or Hands On?   In view of the goal conflicts and the measurement, design, and implementation problems that policymakers confront, it is less surprising that things sometimes go wrong than that things often work out right. The maze of obstacles through which theory must pass before it becomes policy explains a great many of our collective shortcomings. On this basis alone, we may conclude that ***consistent fine-tuning of the economy is not compatible with either our design capabilities or our decision-making procedures.*** We have exhibited a strong capability to avoid major economic disruptions in the last four decades. We have not, however, been able to make all the minor adjustments necessary to fulfill our goals completely. As Arthur Burns, former chairman of the Fed's Board of Governors, said:

There has been much loose talk of "fine-tuning" when the state of knowledge permits us to predict only within a fairly broad level the course of economic development and the results of policy actions.[1]

Hands-off Policy

Some critics of economic policy take this argument a few steps further. If fine-tuning isn't really possible, they say, we should abandon discretionary policies altogether. Typically, policymakers seek minor adjustments in interest rates, unemployment, inflation, and growth. The pressure to "do something" is particularly irresistible in election years. In so doing, however, policymakers are as likely to worsen the economic situation as to improve it. Moreover, the potential for such short-term discretion undermines people's confidence in the economy's future.

Critics of discretionary policies say we would be better off with fixed policy rules. They would require the Fed to increase the money supply at a constant rate. Critics of fiscal policy would require the government to maintain balanced budgets, or at least to offset deficits in sluggish years with surpluses in years of high growth. Such rules would prevent policymakers from over- or understimulating the economy, and the risks of economic instability would be reduced.

Milton Friedman has been one of the most persistent advocates of fixed policy rules instead of discretionary policies. With discretionary authority, Friedman argues,

> the wrong decision is likely to be made in a large fraction of cases because the decision-makers are examining only a limited area and not taking into account the cumulative consequences of the policy as a whole. On the other hand, if a general rule is adopted for a group of cases as a bundle, the existence of that rule has favorable effects on people's attitudes and beliefs and expectations that would not follow even from the discretionary adoption of precisely the same policy on a series of separate occasions.[2]

The case for a hands-off policy stance is based on practical, not theoretical, arguments. Everyone agrees that flexible, discretionary policies *could* result in better economic performance. But Friedman and others argue that the practical requirements of monetary and fiscal management are too demanding and thus prone to failure. Moreover, required policies may be compromised by political pressures.

Hands-on Policy

Critics of fixed rules acknowledge occasional policy blunders but emphasize that the historical record of prices, employment, and growth has improved since active fiscal and monetary policies were adopted. Without flexibility in the money supply and the budget, they argue, the economy would be less stable and our economic goals would remain unfulfilled. They say the government must maintain a "hands-on" policy of active intervention.

The historical evidence does not provide overwhelming support for either policy stance. Victor Zarnowitz showed that the U.S. economy has been much more stable since 1946 than it was in earlier periods (1875–1918 and 1919–45). Recessions have gotten shorter and economic expansions longer. But a variety of factors—including a shift from manufacturing to services, a larger government sector, and automatic stabilizers—have contributed to

---

[1] *Newsweek*, August 27, 1973, p. 4.

[2] Milton Friedman, *Capitalism and Freedom* (Chicago: University of Chicago Press, 1962), p. 53.

this improved macro performance. The contribution of discretionary macro policy is less clear. It is easy to observe what actually happened but almost impossible to determine what would have occurred in other circumstances. It is also evident that there have been noteworthy occasions—World War II, for example—when something more than fixed rules for monetary and fiscal policy was called for, a contingency even Professor Friedman acknowledges. Thus occasional flexibility is required, even if a nondiscretionary policy is appropriate in most situations.

Finally, one must contend with the difficulties inherent in adhering to any fixed rules. How is the Fed, for example, supposed to maintain a steady rate of growth in M1? The supply of money (M1) is not determined exclusively by the Fed. It also depends on the willingness of market participants to buy and sell bonds, to maintain bank balances, and to borrow money. Since all of this behavior is subject to change at any time, maintaining a steady rate of M1 growth is an impossible task.

The same is true of fiscal policy. Government spending and taxes are directly influenced by changes in unemployment, inflation, interest rates, and growth. These automatic stabilizers make it virtually impossible to maintain any fixed rule for budget balancing. Moreover, if we eliminated the automatic stabilizers, we would risk greater instability.

Modest Expectations

The clamor for fixed policy rules is more a rebuke of past policy than a viable policy alternative. We really have no choice but to pursue discretionary policies. Recognition of measurement, design, and implementation problems is important for an understanding of the way the economy functions. But even though it is difficult or even impossible to reach all our goals, we cannot abandon conscientious attempts to get as close as possible to goal fulfillment. If public policy can create a few more jobs, a better mix of output, a little more growth and price stability, or an improved distribution of income, those initiatives are worthwhile.

SUMMARY

- The government possesses an array of policy levers, each of which can significantly alter macroeconomic outcomes. To end a recession, we can cut taxes, expand the money supply, or increase government spending. To curb inflation, we can reverse each of these policy levers. To overcome stagflation, we can combine fiscal and monetary levers with improved supply-side incentives.
- Although the potential of economic theory seems impressive, the economic record does not look so good. Persistent unemployment, recurring economic slowdowns, and nagging inflation suggest that the realities of policymaking are more difficult than theory implies.
- To a large extent, the "failures" of economic policy are a reflection of scarce resources and competing goals. Even when consensus exists, however, serious obstacles to effective economic policy remain. These obstacles include:

  (*a*) Measurement problems. Our knowledge of economic performance is always dated and incomplete. We must rely on forecasts of future problems.

(b) Design problems. We don't know exactly how the economy will respond to specific policies.

(c) Implementation problems. It takes time for Congress and the president to agree on an appropriate plan of action. Moreover, the agreements reached may respond more to political needs than to economic needs.

For all these reasons, the fine-tuning of economic performance rarely lives up to its theoretical potential.

- Many people favor rules rather than discretionary macro policies. They argue that discretionary policies are unlikely to work and risk being wrong. Critics respond that discretionary policies are needed to cope with ever-changing economic circumstances.

Terms to Remember

Define the following terms:

business cycle	monetary policy	stagflation
fiscal policy	money supply (M1)	structural unemployment
automatic stabilizer	supply-side policy	fine-tuning
fiscal year (FY)	multiplier	

Questions for Discussion

1. Should economic policies respond immediately to any changes in reported unemployment or inflation rates? When should a response be undertaken?
2. Suppose that it is an election year and that aggregate demand is growing so fast that it threatens to set off an inflationary movement. Why might Congress and the president hesitate to cut back on government spending or raise taxes, as economic theory suggests is appropriate?
3. In his fiscal 1994 budget, President Clinton proposed decreases in defense spending to help reduce the budget deficit. Should military spending be subject to macroeconomic constraints? What programs should be expanded or contracted to bring about needed changes in the budget? Is this feasible?
4. Are we better off or worse off as a result of the discretionary macro policies of the last two years? How can you tell?
5. Suppose that the economy is slumping into recession and needs a fiscal-policy boost. Voters, however, are opposed to larger federal deficits. What should policymakers do?
6. Outline a macro policy package for attaining full employment and price stability in the next twelve months. What obstacles, if any, will impede attainment of these goals?
7. Does the monetary policy described in the Headline on page 328 resemble "fine tuning"? Did it work?

Problem

1. The following table presents hypothetical data on government expenditure, taxes, exports, imports, inflation, unemployment, and pollution for three levels of equilibrium income (GDP). A government decision-maker is trying to determine the optimal level of government expenditures, with each of the three columns being a possible choice. At the time of the choice the inflation index is 1.0. Dollar amounts are in billions per year.

	Nominal GDP		
	$7,000	**$8,000**	**$9,000**
Government expenditure	$700	$800	$900
Taxes	$600	$800	$1,000
Exports	$300	$300	$300
Imports	$100	$300	$500
Inflation (index)	1.00	1.04	1.15
Unemployment rate	10%	4%	3.5%
Pollution index	1.00	1.80	2.00

(a) Compute the federal budget balance, balance of trade, and real GDP for each level of nominal GDP.

(b) What government expenditure level would best accomplish each of the following goals?

Lowest taxes
Largest trade surplus
Lowest pollution
Lowest inflation rate
Lowest unemployment rate
Highest amount of public goods and services
Highest real income
Balancing the federal budget
Achieving a balance of trade
Maintaining price stability
Achieving full employment

(c) What government expenditure levels would most flagrantly violate each of the preceding goals?

(d) Which policy would be in the best interests of the country?

(e) What policies, in addition to changes in government expenditures, might the government use to attain more of its desired goals?

SECTION IV

INTERNATIONAL

Chapter 17

International Trade

Passions ran high during the 1993 debate over the North American Free Trade Agreement (NAFTA). President Clinton argued that the removal of trade barriers between the United States, Mexico, and Canada would accelerate U.S. economic growth and create millions of new jobs. Ross Perot railed against the agreement, arguing that it would send U.S. jobs and factories to Mexico where labor was cheap. If NAFTA were signed, Perot warned, "the next thing you hear will be a giant sucking sound as the remainder of our manufacturing jobs get pulled across our southern border."

Ross Perot's dire warnings about the consequences of freer trade struck a responsive chord. Most Americans are convinced that the United States gets a bad deal in international trade. They complain that cheap foreign labor threatens American jobs and that foreign nations unfairly restrict U.S. exports.

Most of the goods and services we buy from other countries we could in fact produce ourselves. Why, then, do we purchase them from other countries? For that matter, why does the rest of the world buy computers, tractors, chemicals, airplanes, and wheat from us rather than produce such products for themselves? Wouldn't we all be better off relying on ourselves for the goods we consume (and the jobs we need), rather than buying and selling products in international markets? Or is there some advantage to be gained from international trade? If so, what is the nature of that advantage, and who reaps the benefits?

In this chapter we first survey the nature of international trade patterns—what goods we trade, and with whom. Then we address basic issues related to such trade:

- What benefit, if any, do we get from international trade?
- How much harm do imports cause, and to whom?
- Should we protect ourselves from "unfair" trade by limiting some or all imports?

After examining the arguments for and against international trade, we try to draw some general conclusions about trade policy. As we shall see, international trade tends to increase our *average* incomes, although it may diminish the job and income opportunities of specific industries and workers.

U.S. TRADE PATTERNS

Imports

imports: Goods and services purchased from foreign sources.

In 1994, the United States imported nearly $670 billion of merchandise (goods). We also imported $135 billion of services such as foreign travel, transportation, and banking. Although total **imports** of goods and services represent only 12 percent of total GDP, they often account for much larger shares of specific product markets. Coffee is a familiar example. Since all coffee is imported, Americans would have a harder time staying awake without imports. Likewise, there would have been no aluminum if we hadn't imported bauxite, no chrome bumpers if we hadn't imported chromium, no tin cans without imported tin, and a lot fewer computers without imported components. We couldn't even play the all-American game of baseball without imports, since baseballs are no longer made in the United States!

Exports

exports: Goods and services sold to foreign buyers.

While we are buying baseballs, coffee, bauxite, computer components, and oil from the rest of the world, foreigners are buying our **exports.** In 1994, we exported $500 billion of goods, including farm products (wheat, corn, soybeans), tobacco, machinery (computers), aircraft, automobiles and auto parts, raw materials (lumber, iron ore), and chemicals. We also exported nearly $200 billion of such services as tourism, insurance, and software.

As with our imports, our exports represent a relatively modest fraction of total GDP. Whereas we export about 10 percent of total output, other developed countries export as much as one-fourth of their output (see Headline). Here, again, however, the relatively low ratio of exports to total sales disguises our heavy dependence on exports in specific industries. We export 25 to 50 percent of our rice, corn, and wheat production each year, and still more of our soybeans. Clearly, a decision by foreigners to stop eating American agricultural products could devastate a lot of American farmers. Such companies as Boeing (planes), Caterpillar Tractor (construction and farm machinery), Weyerhaeuser (logs, lumber), Eastman Kodak (film), Dow (chemicals), and Sun Microsystems (computer workstations) sell over one-fourth of their output in foreign markets. Pepsi and Coke are battling it out in the soft-drink markets of such unlikely places as Egypt, Abu Dhabi, and the various nations of the former Soviet Union.

Trade Balances

trade deficit: The amount by which the value of imports exceeds the value of exports in a given time period.

As the figures indicate, our imports and exports were not equal in 1994. Quite the contrary: we had a large imbalance in our trade flows, with many more imports than exports. The trade balance is computed simply as the difference between exports and imports; that is

$$\bullet \quad \frac{\text{Trade}}{\text{balance}} = \text{exports} - \text{imports}$$

During 1994, we imported more than we exported and so had a negative trade balance. A negative trade balance is called a **trade deficit.** In 1994, the United States had a negative trade balance of $108 billion. As Table

HEADLINE

EXPORT RATIOS

Exports in Relation to GDP

Exports of goods and services account for 10 percent of total U.S. output. Although substantial, this trade dependence is relatively low by international standards.

Germany, for example, exports one-third of its total output, while Malaysia exports nearly 80 percent of its annual production.

World Bank, *World Development Report 1994.*

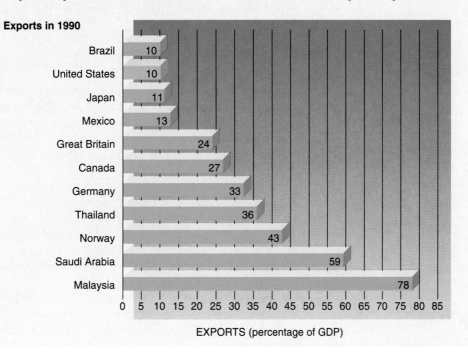

Exports in 1990

Country	Exports (percentage of GDP)
Brazil	10
United States	10
Japan	11
Mexico	13
Great Britain	24
Canada	27
Germany	33
Thailand	36
Norway	43
Saudi Arabia	59
Malaysia	78

EXPORTS (percentage of GDP)

17.1 shows, this overall trade deficit reflected divergent patterns in goods and services. The United States had a very large deficit in *merchandise* trade, mostly due to auto imports and imported oil. In *services* (e.g., travel, finance, consulting), however, we enjoyed a substantial surplus. When the merchandise and services accounts are combined, the United States ends up with a trade deficit.

If the United States has a trade deficit with the rest of the world, then other countries must have an offsetting **trade surplus.** On a global scale,

trade surplus: The amount by which the value of exports exceeds the value of imports in a given time period.

TABLE 17.1
Trade Balances

Both merchandise (goods) and services are traded between countries. The United States typically has a merchandise deficit and a services surplus. When combined, an overall trade deficit remained in 1994.

Product Category	Exports	Imports	Surplus (Deficit)
Merchandise	503	669	(166)
Services	193	135	58
Total Trade	696	804	(108)

Source: U.S. Department of Commerce.

imports must equal exports, since every good exported by one country must be imported by another. Hence **any imbalance in America's trade must be offset by reverse imbalances elsewhere.**

The U.S. trade balance has been in deficit since the mid-1970s. Prior to that, America generally exported more goods than it imported. Hence the United States was a net exporter and the rest of the world was a net importer. Today, the trade imbalances are reversed.

Whatever the overall balance in our trade accounts, bilateral balances vary greatly. For example, our 1994 trade deficit incorporated a huge bilateral trade deficit with Japan and large deficits with Taiwan, Germany, China, and Canada also. As Table 17.2 shows, however, we had trade surpluses with Belgium, Argentina, Australia, and the Netherlands.

MOTIVATION TO TRADE

Many people wonder why we trade so much, particularly since (1) we import many of the things we also export (e.g., computers, airplanes, clothes); (2) we *could* produce many of the other things we import; and (3) we seem to worry so much about imports and trade deficits. Why not just import those few things that we cannot produce ourselves, and export just enough to balance that trade?

Although it might seem strange to be importing goods we could or do produce ourselves, such trade is imminently rational. Indeed, our decision to trade with other countries arises from the same considerations that motivate individuals to specialize in production. Why don't you become self-sufficient, growing all your own food, building your own shelter, recording your own songs? Presumably because you have found that you can enjoy a much higher standard of living (and better music) by producing only a few goods and buying the rest in the marketplace. When countries engage in international trade, they are expressing the same kind of commitment to specialization, and for the same reason: **specialization increases total output.**

To demonstrate the economic gains obtainable from international trade, we may examine the production possibilities of two countries. We want to

TABLE 17.2
Bilateral Merchandise Trade Balances

The U.S. merchandise trade deficit of $166 billion in 1994 was the net result of bilateral deficits and surpluses. We had very large trade deficits with Japan and China, but small trade surpluses with the Netherlands, Belgium, Australia, and Argentina. International trade is multinational, with surpluses in some countries being offset by trade deficits elsewhere.

Country	Merchandise Trade Balance (in billions of dollars)
TOP DEFICIT COUNTRIES	
Japan	−65.7
China	−29.5
Canada	−14.5
Germany	−12.5
Taiwan	−9.6
TOP SURPLUS COUNTRIES	
Netherlands	+7.4
Australia	+6.6
Belgium	+4.6
Argentina	+2.7
Great Britain	+1.8

Source: U.S. Department of Commerce.

demonstrate that two countries that trade can together produce more output than they could in the absence of trade. If they can, ***the gain from trade will be increased world output and thus a higher standard of living in both countries.***

Production and Consumption Without Trade

> **production possibilities:** The alternative combinations of final goods and services that could be produced in a given time period with all available resources and technology.

Consider the production and consumption possibilities of just two countries—say, the United States and France. For the sake of illustration, we shall assume that both countries produce only two goods, bread and wine. To keep things simple, we will also transform the familiar **production-possibilities** curve into a straight line, as in Figure 17.1.

The "curves" in Figure 17.1 and our own intuition suggest that the United States is capable of producing much more bread than France is. After all, we have a greater abundance of labor, land, and other factors of production. With these resources, we assume that the United States is capable of producing up to 100 zillion loaves of bread per year, if we devote all of our resources to that purpose. This capability is indicated by point *A* in Figure 17.1*a* and the accompanying production-possibilities schedule. France (Figure 17.1*b*), on the other hand, confronts a *maximum* bread production of only 15 zillion loaves per year (point *G*) because it has little available land, less fuel, and fewer potential workers.

The assumed capacities of the two countries for wine production are 50 zillion barrels for us (point *F*) and 60 zillion for France (point *L*), largely reflecting France's greater experience in tending vines. Both countries are also capable of producing alternative *combinations* of bread and wine, as evidenced by their respective production-possibilities curves (points *B–E* for the United States and *H–K* for France).

We have seen production-possibilities curves before. We are looking at them again to emphasize that

- The production-possibilities curve defines the limits to what a country can produce.
- In the absence of trade, a country cannot consume more than it produces.

> **consumption possibilities:** The alternative combinations of goods and services that a country could consume in a given time period.

Accordingly, a production-possibilities curve also defines the **consumption possibilities** for a country that does not engage in international trade. In the absence of trade, each country focuses simply on WHAT mix of output to produce and consume from its limited choices.

International trade opens a whole new set of options. International trade breaks the link between *production* possibilities and *consumption* possibilities. As we'll discover,

- ***With trade, a country's consumption possibilities exceed its production possibilities.***

To see how this startling outcome emerges, we'll examine how countries operate without trade and then with trade.

In the absence of trade, each country must choose a mix of output to consume from its limited production possibilities. Assume that Americans choose point *D* on their production-possibilities curve. At point *D* we would produce and consume 40 zillion loaves of bread and 30 zillion barrels of wine each year. The French, on the other hand, prefer the mix of output represented by point *I* on their production-possibilities curve. At that point they produce and consume 9 zillion loaves of bread and 24 zillion barrels of wine.

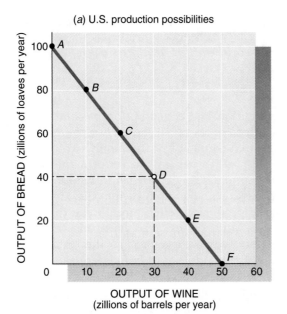

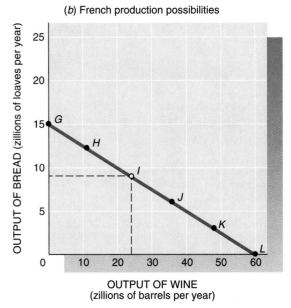

U.S. Production Possibilities				French Production Possibilities			
	Bread (zillions of loaves)	+	Wine (zillions of barrels)		Bread (zillions of loaves)	+	Wine (zillions of barrels)
A	100	+	0	G	15	+	0
B	80	+	10	H	12	+	12
C	60	+	20	I	9	+	24
D	40	+	30	J	6	+	36
E	20	+	40	K	3	+	48
F	0	+	50	L	0	+	60

FIGURE 17.1
Consumption Possibilities Without Trade

In the absence of trade, a country's consumption possibilities are identical to its production possibilities. The assumed production possibilities of the United States and France are illustrated in the graphs and the corresponding schedules. Before entering into trade, the United States chose to produce and consume at point *D*, with 40 zillion loaves of bread and 30 zillion barrels of wine. France chose point *I* on its own production-possibilities curve. By trading, each country hopes to increase its consumption beyond these levels.

Our primary interest here is in the combined annual output of the United States and France. Given their respective decisions on WHAT to produce, we can tally up world output as follows:

	BREAD OUTPUT (ZILLIONS OF LOAVES)	WINE OUTPUT (ZILLIONS OF BARRELS)
U.S. (at point *D*)	40	30
France (at point *I*)	9	24
World total	49	54

What we want to know is whether world output would increase if France and the United States abandoned their isolation and started trading. Could either country, or both, be made better off by engaging in a little trade?

Trade Increases Specialization and World Output

Trying to eke out a little extra wine and bread from this situation might not appear very promising. Both countries, after all, are already fully using their limited production possibilities. Such pessimism is unwarranted, however. Take another look at the production possibilities confronting the United States, as reproduced in Figure 17.2. Suppose that the United States were to produce at point *C* rather than point *D*. At point *C* we could produce 60 zillion loaves of bread and 20 zillion barrels of wine. That combination is clearly possible, even if less desirable (as evidenced by the fact that the United States earlier chose point *D*).

Suppose the French were also to change their mix of output. The French earlier produced at point *I*. Now we will move them to point *K*, where they can produce 48 zillion barrels of wine and 3 zillion loaves of bread. This change in the mix of output may not be desired, but it is *possible*.

Two observations are now called for. The first is simply that output mixes have changed in each country. The second, and more interesting, is that total world output has increased. When the United States and France were at points *D* and *I*, their *combined* annual output consisted of

	BREAD OUTPUT (ZILLIONS OF LOAVES)	WINE OUTPUT (ZILLIONS OF BARRELS)
U.S. (at point *D*)	40	30
France (at point *I*)	9	24
Total output before specializing	49	54

FIGURE 17.2
Consumption Possibilities With Trade

A country can increase its consumption possibilities through international trade. Each country alters its mix of domestic output to produce more of the good it produces best. As it does so, total world output increases, and each country enjoys more consumption. In this case, trade allows U.S. consumption to move from point *D* to point *N*. France moves from point *I* to point *M*.

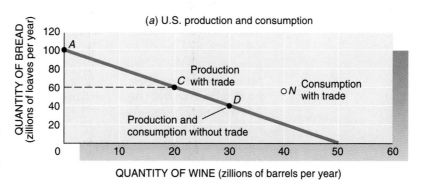

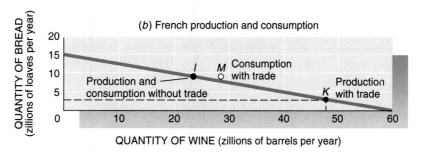

After moving along their respective production-possibilities curves to points C and K, the combined world output becomes

	BREAD OUTPUT (ZILLIONS OF LOAVES)	WINE OUTPUT (ZILLIONS OF BARRELS)
U.S. (at point C)	60	20
France (at point K)	3	48
Total output after specializing	63	68

Total world output has increased by 14 zillion loaves of bread and 14 zillion barrels of wine. Just by changing the mix of output in each country, we have increased *total* world output. This additional output creates the potential for making both countries better off than they were in the absence of trade.

The reason the United States and France weren't producing at points C and K before is that they simply didn't want to consume those particular combinations of output. The United States wanted a slightly more liquid combination than that represented by point C and the French could not survive long at point K. Hence they chose points D and I. Nevertheless, our discovery that points C and K result in greater *total* output suggests that everybody can be happier if we all cooperate. The obvious thing to do is to specialize in production, then start exchanging wine for bread in international trade.

Trade Possibilities

Suppose that we are the first to discover the potential benefits that result from trade. Using Figure 17.2 as our guide, we suggest to the French that they move their mix of output from point I to point K. As an incentive for making such a move, we promise to give them 6 zillion loaves of bread in exchange for 20 zillion barrels of wine. This would leave them at point M, with as much bread to consume as they used to have, plus an extra 4 zillion barrels of wine. At point I they had 9 zillion loaves of bread and 24 zillion barrels of wine. At point M they can have 9 zillion loaves of bread and 28 zillion barrels of wine. Thus, by altering their mix of output (from point I to point K) and then trading (point K to point M), the French end up with more goods and services than they had in the beginning. Notice in particular that the new consumption possibility made available through international trade (point M) lies *outside* France's domestic production-possibilities curve.

The French will obviously be quite pleased with their limited trading experience, but where does this leave us? Do we gain from trade as well? The answer is yes. By trading, we too end up consuming a mix of output that lies outside our production-possibilities curve.

Note that at point C we *produce* 60 zillion loaves of bread per year and 20 zillion barrels of wine. We then export 6 zillion loaves to France. This leaves us with 54 zillion loaves of bread to consume. In return for our exported bread, the French give us 20 zillion barrels of wine. These imports, plus our domestic production, permit us to *consume* 40 zillion barrels of wine. Hence we end up *consuming* at point N, enjoying 54 zillion loaves of bread and 40 zillion barrels of wine. Thus, by first changing our mix of output (from point D to point C), then trading (point C to point N), we end up with 14 zillion more loaves of bread and 10 zillion more barrels of wine than we started with! International trade has made us better off, too.

There is no sleight of hand going on here. Rather, ***the gains from trade are due to specialization in production.*** When each country goes it alone, it is a prisoner of its own production-possibilities curve; it must make its production decisions on the basis of its own consumption desires. When international trade is permitted, however, each country can concentrate on those goods it makes best. Then the countries trade with each other to acquire the goods they desire to consume.

In other words, international trade allows each country to focus on what it does best, with the resultant specialization increasing total world output. In this way each country is able to escape the confines of its own production possibilities curve, to reach beyond it for a larger basket of consumption goods. ***When a country engages in international trade, its consumption possibilities exceed its production possibilities.*** These additional consumption possibilities are emphasized by the position of points *N* and *M outside* the production-possibilities curves (Figure 17.2). If it were not possible for countries to increase their consumption by trading, there would be no incentive for trading, and thus no trade.

COMPARATIVE ADVANTAGE

Although international trade can make every country better off, it is not so obvious what goods should be traded, or on what terms. In our previous illustration, the United States ended up trading bread for wine on terms that were decidedly favorable to us. Why did we choose to export bread rather than wine, and how did we end up getting such a good deal?

Opportunity Costs

> **comparative advantage:** The ability of a country to produce a specific good at a lower opportunity cost than its trading partners.

> **opportunity cost:** The most desired goods or services that are forgone in order to obtain something else.

The decision to export bread is based on **comparative advantage,** that is, the *relative* cost of producing different goods. Recall that we can produce a maximum of 100 zillion loaves of bread per year or 50 zillion barrels of wine. Thus the domestic opportunity cost of producing 100 zillion loaves of bread is the 50 zillion barrels of wine we forsake in order to devote our resources to bread production. In fact, at every point on the U.S. production-possibilities curve (Figure 17.2 *a*), the **opportunity cost** of a loaf of bread is $1/2$ barrel of wine. That is to say, we are effectively paying $1/2$ barrel of wine to get a loaf of bread.

Although the opportunity costs of bread production in the United States might appear outrageous, note the even higher opportunity costs that prevail in France. According to Figure 17.2*b*, the opportunity cost of producing a loaf of bread in France is a staggering 4 barrels of wine. To produce a loaf of bread, the French must use factors of production that could have been used to produce 4 barrels of wine.

A comparison of the opportunity costs prevailing in each country exposes the nature of what we call comparative advantage. The United States has a *comparative* advantage in bread production because less wine has to be given up to produce bread in the United States than in France. In other words, the opportunity costs of bread production are lower in the United States than in France. ***Comparative advantage refers to the relative (opportunity) costs of producing particular goods.***

A country should specialize in what it is *relatively* efficient at producing, that is, goods for which it has the lowest opportunity costs. In this case, the United States should produce bread because its opportunity cost ($1/2$ barrel of wine) is less than France's (4 barrels of wine). Were you the production manager for the whole world, you would certainly want each country to exploit its relative abilities, thus maximizing world output. Each country can arrive at that same decision itself by comparing its own opportunity costs to those prevailing elsewhere and offering to trade to mutual advantage. ***World output, and thus the potential gains from trade, will be maximized when each country pursues its comparative advantage.*** It does so by exporting goods that entail low domestic opportunity costs and importing goods that involve higher domestic opportunity costs.

Absolute Costs Don't Count

> **absolute advantage:** The ability of a country to produce a specific good with fewer resources (per unit of output) than other countries.

In assessing the nature of comparative advantage, notice that we needn't know anything about the actual costs involved in production. Have you seen any data suggesting how much labor, land, or capital is required to produce a loaf of bread in either France or the United States? For all you and I know, the French may be able to produce both a loaf of bread and a barrel of wine with fewer resources than we are using. Such an **absolute advantage** in production might exist because of their much longer experience in cultivating both grapes and wheat, or simply because they have more talent.

We can envy such productivity, but it should not alter our production and international trade decisions. All we really care about are *opportunity costs*—what we have to give up in order to get more of a desired good. If we can get a barrel of imported wine for less bread than we have to give up to produce that wine ourselves, we have a comparative advantage in producing bread. In other words, as long as we have a *comparative* advantage in bread production, we should exploit it. It doesn't matter to us whether France could produce either good with fewer resources. For that matter, even if France had an absolute advantage in *both* goods, we would still have a *comparative* advantage in bread production, as we have already confirmed. The absolute costs of production were omitted from the previous illustration because they were irrelevant.

To clarify the distinction between absolute advantage and comparative advantage, consider this example. When Charlie Osgood joined the Willamette Warriors' football team, he was the fastest runner ever to play football in Willamette. He could also throw the ball farther than most people could see. In other words, he had an *absolute advantage* in both throwing and running that made all other football players look like second-string water boys. Without extolling Charlie's prowess any further, let it stand that Charlie would have made the greatest quarterback *or* the greatest end ever to play football. *Would have.* The problem was that he could play only one position at a time, just as our resources can be used to produce only one good at a time. Thus the Willamette coach had to play Charlie either as a quarterback or as an end. He reasoned that Charlie could throw only a bit farther than some of the other top quarterbacks but could far outdistance all the other ends. In other words, Charlie had a *comparative advantage* in running and was assigned to play as an end.

TERMS OF TRADE

It definitely pays to pursue one's comparative advantage and trade with the rest of the world on that basis. It may not yet be clear, however, how we got such a good deal with France. We are clever traders, to be sure. But be-

terms of trade: The rate at which goods are exchanged; the amount of good *A* given up for good *B* in trade.

yond that, is there any way to determine the **terms of trade,** the quantity of good *A* that must be given up in exchange for good *B*? In our previous illustration, the terms of trade were very favorable to us; we exchanged only 6 zillion loaves of bread for 20 zillion barrels of wine. The terms of trade were thus 6 loaves = 20 barrels.

Limits to the Terms of Trade

The terms of trade with France were determined by our offer and France's ready acceptance. France was willing to accept our offer because the attendant terms of trade permitted France to increase its wine consumption without giving up any bread consumption. In other words, our offer to trade 6 loaves for 20 barrels was an improvement over France's domestic opportunity costs. France's domestic possibilities required it to give up 24 barrels of wine in order to produce 6 loaves of bread (see Figure 17.2*b*). Getting bread via trade was simply cheaper for France than producing bread at home. As a result, France ended up with an extra 4 zillion barrels of wine.

Our first clue to the terms of trade, then, lies in each country's domestic opportunity costs. *A country will not trade unless the terms of trade are superior to domestic opportunity costs.* In our example, the opportunity cost of wine in the United States is 2 loaves of bread. Accordingly, we will not export bread unless we get at least 1 barrel of wine in exchange for every 2 loaves of bread we ship overseas. In other words, we will not play the game unless the terms of trade are superior to our own opportunity costs, thus providing us with some benefit.

No country will trade unless the terms of exchange are better than its domestic opportunity costs. Hence we can predict that *the terms of trade between any two countries will lie somewhere between their respective opportunity costs in production.* That is to say, a loaf of bread in international trade will be worth at least $\frac{1}{2}$ barrel of wine (the U.S. opportunity cost) but no more than 4 barrels (the French opportunity cost). In point of fact, the terms of trade ended up at 1 loaf = 3.33 barrels (that is, at 6 loaves = 20 barrels). This represented a very large gain for the United States and a small gain for France.

The Market Mechanism

Relatively little trade is subject to such direct negotiations between countries. More often than not, the decision to import or export a particular good is left up to the market decisions of individual consumers and producers.

Individual consumers and producers are not much impressed by such abstractions as comparative advantage. Market participants tend to focus on prices, always trying to allocate their resources in order to maximize profits or personal satisfaction. As a result, consumers tend to buy the products that deliver the most utility per dollar of expenditure, while producers try to get the most output per dollar of cost. Everybody's looking for a bargain.

So what does this have to do with international trade? Well, suppose that Henri, an enterprising Frenchman, visited the United States before the advent of international trade. He noticed that bread was relatively cheap, while wine was relatively expensive, the opposite of the price relationship prevailing in France. These price comparisons brought to his mind the opportunity for making a fast franc. All he had to do was bring over some

French wine and trade it in the United States for a large quantity of bread. Then he could return to France and exchange the bread for a greater quantity of wine. *Alors!* Were he to do this a few times, he would amass substantial profits.

Our French entrepreneur's exploits will not only enrich him but will also move each country toward its comparative advantage. The United States ends up exporting bread to France and France ends up exporting wine to the United States, exactly as the theory of comparative advantage suggests. The activating agent is not the Ministry of Trade and its 620 trained economists, however, but simply one enterprising French trader. He is aided and encouraged, of course, by the consumers and producers in each country. The American consumers are happy to trade their bread for his wines. They thereby end up paying less for wine (in terms of bread) than they would otherwise have to. In other words, the terms of trade Henri offers are more attractive than the prevailing (domestic) relative prices. On the other side of the Atlantic, Henri's welcome is equally warm. French consumers are able to get a better deal by trading their wine for his imported bread than by trading with the local bakers.

Even some producers are happy. The wheat farmers and bakers in America are eager to deal with Henri. He is willing to buy a lot of bread and even to pay a premium price for it. Indeed, bread production has become so profitable in the United States that a lot of people who used to grow and mash grapes are now starting to grow wheat and knead dough. This alters the mix of U.S. output in the direction of more bread, exactly as suggested earlier in Figure 17.2a.

In France the opposite kind of production shift is taking place. French wheat farmers start to plant grapes so they can take advantage of Henri's generous purchases. Thus Henri is able to lead each country in the direction of its comparative advantage, while raking in a substantial profit for himself along the way.

Where the terms of trade and the volume of exports and imports end up depends in part on how good a trader Henri is. It will also depend on the behavior of the thousands of individual consumers and producers who participate in the market exchanges. In other words, trade flows depend on both the supply and the demand for bread and wine in each country. ***The terms of trade, like the price of any good, will depend on the willingness of market participants to buy or sell at various prices.***

PROTECTIONIST PRESSURES

Although the potential gains from world trade are perhaps clear, we should not conclude that everyone will be smiling at the Franco-American trade celebration. On the contrary, some people will be very upset about the trade routes that Henri has established. They will not only boycott the celebration but actively seek to discourage us from continuing to trade with France.

Microeconomic Losers

Consider, for example, the winegrowers in western New York. Do you think they are going to be very happy about Henri's entrepreneurship? Recall that Americans can now buy wine more cheaply from France than they can from New York. New York winegrowers are apt to be outraged at some foreigner cutting into their market. Before long we may hear talk about unfair foreign competition or about the greater nutritional value of American grapes (see Headline). The New York winegrowers may also emphasize the importance of maintaining an adequate grape supply and a strong wine industry at home, just in case of nuclear war.

Joining with the growers will be the farm workers and all of the other workers, producers, and merchants whose livelihood depends on the New York wine industry. If they are aggressive and clever enough, the growers will also get the governor of the state to join their demonstration. After all, the governor must recognize the needs of his people, and his people definitely don't include the wheat farmers in Kansas who are making a bundle from international trade. New York consumers are, of course, benefiting from lower wine prices, but they are unlikely to demonstrate over a few cents a bottle. On the other hand, those few extra pennies translate into millions of dollars for domestic wine producers.

The winegrowers in western New York (not to mention those in California) will gather additional support from abroad. The wheat farmers in France are no happier about international trade than are the winegrowers in the United States. They would dearly love to sink all those boats bringing wheat from America, thereby protecting their own market position.

If we are to make sense of international trade policies, then, we must recognize one central fact of life: some producers have a vested interest in restricting international trade. In particular, *workers and producers who compete with imported products—who work in import-competing industries—have an economic interest in restricting trade.* This helps to explain why GM, Ford, and Chrysler are unhappy about trade in Toyotas and Mercedes, and why workers in Massachusetts want to end the importation of Italian shoes. It also explains why the textile producers in South Carolina think Taiwan and Korea are behaving irresponsibly when they sell cotton shirts and dresses in the United States.

Microeconomic resistance to international trade, then, arises from the fact that imports typically mean fewer jobs and less income for some domestic industries. At the same time, however, exports represent increased

HEADLINE

IMPORT COMPETITION

Whining over Wine

A new type of wine bar has sprung up on Capitol Hill, and it's not likely to tickle the palate of a dedicated oenophile. California wine makers are hawking a bill that could slap higher tariffs on imported wine, and Congress shows some sign of becoming intoxicated with what the wine makers have to offer. First introduced last summer, the Wine Equity Act, as the measure is called, is already sponsored by 345 Congressmen and 60 Senators.

The wine makers aren't putting all their grapes into one bottle. Behind the scenes they have been making common cause with the American Grape Growers Al-

liance for Fair Trade, a group that represents many of the farmer cooperatives that supply domestic wineries. In a suit they filed with the Commerce Department and International Trade Commission in January, the growers complained that the Europeans, and particularly the Italians, are unfairly subsidizing their wine producers. If their suit is upheld, the ITC could impose stiff duties on the imports. The importers say there is no good evidence of substantial government subsidies.

Fortune, February 20, 1984, p. 41. © 1984 Time Inc. All rights reserved.

jobs and incomes for other industries. Producers and workers in export industries gain from trade. Thus on a microeconomic level, there are identifiable gainers and losers from international trade. ***Trade not only alters the mix of output but also redistributes income from import-competing industries to export industries.*** This potential redistribution is the source of political and economic friction.

The Net Gain

We must be careful to note, however, that the microeconomic gains from trade are greater than the microeconomic losses. It's not simply a question of robbing Peter to enrich Paul. On the contrary, we must remind ourselves that consumers in general are able to enjoy a higher standard of living as a result of international trade. As we saw earlier, trade increases world efficiency and total output. Accordingly, we end up slicing up a larger pie rather than just reslicing the same old smaller pie. Although this may be little consolation to the producer or worker who ends up getting a smaller slice than before, it does point up an essential fact. The gains from trade are large enough to make everybody better off if we so choose. Whether we actually choose to undertake such a distribution of the gains from trade is a separate question, to which we shall return shortly. We note here, however, that ***trade restrictions designed to protect specific microeconomic interests reduce the total gains from trade.*** Trade restrictions leave us with a smaller pie to split up.

BARRIERS TO TRADE

The microeconomic losses associated with imports give rise to a constant clamor for trade restrictions. People whose jobs and incomes are threatened by international trade tend to organize quickly and air their grievances. Moreover, they are assured of a reasonably receptive hearing, both because of the political implications of well-financed organizations and because the gains from trade are widely diffused. If successful, such efforts can lead to a variety of trade restrictions.

Tariffs

tariff: A tax (duty) imposed on imported goods.

One of the most popular and visible restrictions on trade is the **tariff,** a special tax imposed on imported goods. Tariffs, also called "customs duties," were once the principal source of revenue for governments. In the eighteenth century, tariffs on tea, glass, wine, lead, and paper were imposed on the American colonies to provide extra revenue for the British government. The tariff on tea led to the Boston Tea Party in 1773 and gave added momentum to the independence movement. In modern times, tariffs have been used primarily as a means of import protection to satisfy specific microeconomic or macroeconomic interests. The current U.S. tariff code specifies tariffs on 8,753 different products—nearly 70 percent of all U.S. imports. Although the average tariff is only 5 percent, individual tariffs vary widely. The tariff on cars, for example, is only 2.5 percent, while polyester sweaters confront a 34.6 percent tariff.

The attraction of tariffs to import-competing industries should be obvious. ***A tariff on imported goods makes them more expensive to domestic consumers, and thus less competitive with domestically produced goods.*** Among familiar tariffs in effect in 1995 were $0.20 per gallon on

HEADLINE

TRADE RESISTANCE

A Litany of Losers

Some excerpts from congressional hearings on trade:

In the past few years, sales of imported table wines . . . have soared at an alarming rate. . . . Unless this trend is halted immediately, the domestic wine industry will face economic ruin. . . . Foreign wine imports must be limited.

—Wine Institute

The apparel industry's workers have few other alternative job opportunities. They do want to work and earn a living at their work. Little wonder therefore that they want their jobs safeguarded against the erosion caused by the increasing penetration of apparel imports.

—International Ladies' Garment Workers' Union

We are never going to strengthen the dollar, cure our balance of payments problem, lick our high unemployment, eliminate an ever-worsening inflation, as long as the U.S. sits idly by as a dumping ground for shoes, TV sets, apparel, steel and automobiles, etc. It is about time that we told the Japanese, the Spanish, the Italians, the Brazilians, and the Argentinians, and others who insist on flooding our country with imported shoes that enough is enough.

—United Shoe Workers of America

We want to be friends with Mexico and Canada. . . . We would like to be put in the same ball game with them. . . . We are not trying to hinder foreign trade . . . (but) plants in Texas go out of business (17 in the last 7 years) because of the continued threat of fly-by-night creek bed, river bank Mexican brick operations implemented overnight.

—Brick Institute of America

Trade policy should not be an absolute statement of how the world ought to behave to achieve a textbook vision of "free trade" or "maximum efficiency." It should . . . attempt to achieve the best results for Americans.

—United Auto Workers

Scotch whiskey and $1.17 per gallon on imported champagne. These tariffs made American-produced spirits look like relatively good buys and thus contributed to higher sales and profits for domestic distillers and grape growers. In the same manner, imported baby food is taxed at 34.6 percent, orange juice at 36 percent, footwear at 20 percent, and imported stereos at rates ranging from 4 to 6 percent. In each of these cases, domestic producers in import-competing industries gain. The losers are domestic consumers, who end up paying higher prices; foreign producers, who lose business; and world efficiency, as trade is reduced.

Quotas

quota: A limit on the quantity of a good that may be imported in a given time period.

Tariffs help to reduce the flow of imports by raising import prices. As an alternative barrier to trade, a country can impose import **quotas,** restrictions on the quantity of a particular good that may be imported. The United States maintained a quota on imported petroleum from 1959 to 1973. Other goods that have been (and most of which still are) subject to import quotas in the United States are sugar, meat, dairy products, textiles, cotton, peanuts, steel, cloth diapers, and even ice cream. According to the U.S. Department of State, approximately 12 percent of our imports are subject to import quotas.

Quotas, like all barriers to trade, reduce world efficiency and invite retaliatory action. Moreover, quotas are especially pernicious because of their impact on competition and the distribution of income. To see this impact, we may compare market outcomes in four different contexts: no trade, free trade, tariff-restricted trade, and quota-restricted trade.

equilibrium price: The price at which the quantity of a good demanded in a given time period equals the quantity supplied.

Figure 17.3a depicts the supply-and-demand relationships that would prevail in a closed (no-trade) economy. In this situation, the **equilibrium price** of textiles is completely determined by domestic demand and supply curves. The equilibrium price is p_1, and the quantity of textiles consumed is q_1.

Suppose now that trade begins and foreign producers are allowed to sell textiles in the American market. The immediate effect of this decision will be a rightward shift of the market supply curve, as foreign supplies are added to domestic supplies (Figure 17.3b). If an unlimited quantity of textiles can be bought in world markets at a price of p_2, the new supply curve will look like S_2 (infinitely elastic at p_2). The new supply curve (S_2) inter-

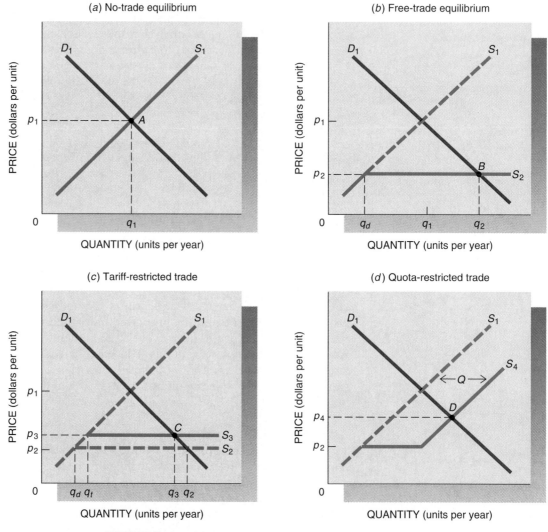

FIGURE 17.3
The Impact of Trade Restrictions

In the *absence of trade*, the domestic price and sales of a good will be determined by domestic supply and demand curves (point *A* in part *a*). Once trade is permitted, the market supply curve will be altered by the availability of imports. With *free trade* and unlimited availability of imports at price p_2, a new market equilibrium will be established at world prices (point *B*).

Tariffs raise domestic prices and reduce the quantity sold (point *C*). *Quotas* put an absolute limit on imported sales and thus give domestic producers a great opportunity to raise the market price (point *D*).

sects the old demand curve (D_1) at a new equilibrium price of p_2 and an expanded consumption of q_2. At this new equilibrium, domestic producers are supplying the quantity q_d while foreign producers are supplying the rest ($q_2 - q_d$). Comparing the new equilibrium to the old one, we see that the initiation of trade results in reduced prices and increased consumption.

Domestic textile producers are unhappy, of course, with their foreign competition. In the absence of trade, the domestic producers would sell more output (q_1) and get higher prices (p_1). Once trade is opened up, the willingness of foreign producers to sell unlimited quantities of textiles at the price p_2 puts a limit on the price behavior of domestic producers. Accordingly, we can anticipate some lobbying for trade restrictions.

Figure 17.3c illustrates what would happen to prices and sales if the United Textile Producers was successful in persuading the government to impose a tariff. Let us assume that the tariff has the effect of raising imported textile prices from p_2 to p_3, making it more difficult for foreign producers to undersell so many domestic producers. Domestic production expands from q_d to q_t, imports are reduced from $q_2 - q_d$ to $q_3 - q_t$, and the market price of textiles rises. Domestic textile producers are clearly better off, whereas consumers and foreign producers are worse off. In addition, the U.S. Treasury will be better off as a result of increased tariff revenues.

Now consider the impact of a textile *quota*. Suppose that we eliminate tariffs but decree that imports cannot exceed the quantity Q. Because the quantity of imports can never exceed Q, the supply curve is effectively shifted to the right by that amount. The new curve S_4 (Figure 17.3d) indicates that no imports will occur below the world price p_2, and that above that price the quantity Q will be imported. Thus the *domestic* supply curve determines subsequent prices. Foreign producers are precluded from selling greater quantities as prices rise further. This outcome is in marked con-

—from HERBLOCK AT LARGE (Pantheon Books, 1987).

trast to that of tariff-restricted trade (Figure 17.3c), which at least permits foreign producers to respond to rising prices. Accordingly, *quotas are a much greater threat to competition than tariffs, because quotas preclude additional imports at any price.* The accompanying Headline suggests how costly such protection can be.

Voluntary Restraint Agreements

> **voluntary restraint agreement (VRA):** An agreement to reduce the volume of trade in a specific good; a "voluntary" quota.

A slight variant of quotas has been used in recent years. Rather than imposing quotas on imports, the U.S. government asks foreign producers to limit their exports "voluntarily." These so-called **voluntary restraint agreements** have been negotiated with producers in Japan, South Korea, Taiwan, China, the European Economic Community, and other countries. Korea, for example, agreed to reduce its annual shoe exports to the United States from 44 million pairs to 33 million pairs. Taiwan reduced its shoe exports from 156 million pairs to 122 million pairs per year. In 1989, China agreed to slow its exports of clothing, limiting its sales growth to 3 percent a year. For their part, the Japanese agreed to reduce sales of color television sets in the United States from 2.8 million to 1.75 million per year.

All of these "voluntary export restraints," as they are often called, represented an informal type of quota. The only difference is that they are negotiated rather than imposed, and they often include provisions for later increases in sales. But these differences are lost on consumers, who end up paying higher prices for these goods. The voluntary limit on Japanese auto exports to the United States alone cost consumers $15.7 billion in only four years.

Nontariff Barriers

Embargoes, export controls, tariffs, and quotas are the most visible barriers to trade, but they are far from the only ones. Indeed, the variety of pro-

---

HEADLINE

IMPORT QUOTAS

Sugar Quota a Sour Deal

Very little sugarcane is grown in the United States. Most domestically produced sugar comes from the sugar beet. The rest of our sugar is imported from tropical countries.

The 12,000 domestic sugar beet growers have convinced Congress to protect their industry to ensure a secure supply of sugar in a war. The U.S. Department of Agriculture guarantees the sugar beet growers a minimum of 18 cents per pound for their output. To keep prices at that level, the U.S. Congress limits sugar imports. As a result, domestic sugar prices are typically twice as high as world sugar prices. In early 1990, the price of sugar in U.S. markets was 22 cents per pound, versus only 10 cents in world markets. This price dif-

ference cost American consumers nearly $1 billion in 1990 alone. Foreign producers and workers who were excluded from the U.S. market also lost out. Between 1983 and 1990, over 400,000 workers in Caribbean nations lost their jobs as a result of shrinking U.S. sugar quotas.

Who benefits from these sugar quotas? The list includes

- The 12,000 American sugar beet farmers
- Producers of sugar substitutes (e.g., corn syrups)
- Those nations and producers that get a share of the U.S. quota
- Former and current members of Congress who receive fees and campaign contributions for perpetuating the sugar quota system

tectionist measures that have been devised is testimony to the ingenuity of the human mind. At the turn of the century, the Germans were officially committed to a policy of extending equal treatment to all trading partners. The Germans, however, wanted to lower the tariff on cattle imports from Denmark without extending the same break to Switzerland. Accordingly, the Germans created a new and higher tariff on "brown and dappled cows reared at a level of at least 300 meters above sea level and passing at least one month in every summer at an altitude of at least 800 meters." The new tariff was, of course, applied equally to all countries. But Danish cows never climb that high, so they were not burdened with the new tariff.

With the decline in tariffs over the last twenty years, nontariff barriers have increased. The United States uses product standards, licensing restrictions, restrictive procurement practices, and other nontariff barriers to restrict roughly 15 percent of imports. Japan makes even greater use of nontariff barriers, restricting nearly 30 percent of imports in such ways.

POLICY PERSPECTIVES

Lowering Trade Barriers: GATT and NAFTA

Trade policy is a continuing conflict between the benefits of comparative advantage and pleadings of protectionists. Free trade promises more output, greater efficiency, and lower prices. At the same time, free trade threatens profits, jobs, and wealth in specific industries.

Politically, the battle over trade policy favors protectionist interests over consumer interests. Few consumers understand how free trade affects them and are unlikely to organize political protests just because the price of orange juice is 35 cents per gallon higher. By contrast, import-competing industries have a large economic stake in trade restrictions and can mobilize political support easily. After convincing Congress to pass new quotas on textiles in 1990, the Fiber Fabric Apparel Coalition for Trade (FFACT) mustered 250,000 signatures and 4,000 union members to march on the White House demanding that President Bush sign the legislation.

President Clinton faced similar political resistance when he sought congressional approval of NAFTA in 1993 and GATT in 1994. Indeed, the political resistance to free trade was so intense that Congress delayed a vote on GATT until after the November 1994 elections. This forced President Clinton to convene a special postelection session of Congress for the sole purpose of ratifying the GATT trade agreement.

GATT

The political resistance to free trade is not unique to the United States. As we have observed, international trade creates winners and losers in every trading nation. Recognizing this, the countries of the world decided long ago that multinational agreements were the most effective way to overcome domestic protectionism. Broad trade agreements can address the entire spectrum of trade restrictions, rather than focusing on one industry at a time. Multinational agreements can also muster political support by offering greater *export* opportunities as *import* restrictions are lifted.

In 1947, the General Agreement on Tariffs and Trade (GATT) was signed by twenty-three of the world's largest trading nations. The GATT pact committed these nations to pursue free-trade policies and to extend equal access ("most favored nation" status) to domestic markets for all GATT members. Today, more than 100 nations have joined GATT.

The GATT goal of lowering trade barriers is pursued with periodic "rounds" of multinational trade agreements. The latest (eighth round) negotiations began in Uruguay in November 1986 and so are referred to as the "Uruguay Round." Each round entails protracted negotiations about how to lower trade barriers. Whereas earlier rounds focused on manufactured goods, the Uruguay Round extended trade agreements to farm products and "intellectual property" such as copyrighted books, music, and computer software. As always, import-competing industries attempted to maintain trade restrictions while export interests petitioned for more market access. The Uruguay Round was particularly long, because European and Japanese farmers opposed free trade in farm products while the United States refused to abandon textile quotas. In November 1992, negotiations got so heated that a brief trade war erupted between the United States and the European Economic Community.

After nearly eight years of tense and highly detailed negotiations, 117 nations initiated a final agreement on April 15, 1994. The final pact included

- A further reduction in import tariffs
- An expansion of the scope of free-trade rules to agriculture and services
- The creation of a new organization (the World Trade Organization) to police and enforce trade rules

When GATT was first signed, in 1947, tariff rates in developed countries averaged 40 percent. The first seven GATT rounds pushed tariffs down to an average of 6.3 percent, and the Uruguay Round lowered them further, to 3.9 percent. As these trade barriers continue to fall, the volume of trade expands and the gains from trade increase. By the year 2000, U.S. incomes should be 1 to 3 percent higher as a result of GATT-increased trade.

NAFTA

The United States, Canada, and Mexico have sought similar gains from the North American Free Trade Agreement (NAFTA), signed in December 1992. The ultimate goal of NAFTA is to eliminate all trade barriers between these three countries. At the time of signing, intraregional tariffs averaged 11 percent in Mexico, 5 percent in Canada, and 4 percent in the United States. NAFTA requires that all tariffs between the three countries be eliminated within fifteen years. The pact also requires the elimination of specific nontariff barriers.

Although NAFTA will ultimately eliminate trade barriers, it maintains and even increases some trade restrictions in the short run. The 1,000-page agreement has specific provisions for more than 9,000 products. The 35-cents-per gallon U.S. tariff on imported orange juice, for example, won't be phased out completely for fifteen years. Other industries (autos, textiles, electronics) will get new protection from so-called domestic-content rules. These rules restrict the amount of non–North American parts in products allowed "free-trade" access. Such provisions have been characterized as "political ransom" required to get a broader free-trade agreement.

The greater trade and efficiency attributed to NAFTA will increase employment and incomes in all three countries. Not everyone will gain, however. American workers in low-wage industries like apparel and electronics assembly may lose jobs, while U.S. employment increases in farming, trucking, and finance. Although these are the kinds of resource reallocations that occur whe., nations pursue comparative advantage, the workers who lose jobs seldo·ι welcome their role in promoting world trade.

Adjustment Assistance

> **adjustment assistance:** Compensation to market participants for losses imposed by international trade.

One way to overcome resistance to free trade is to compensate those who lose jobs when trade barriers fall. This is the goal of **adjustment assistance.** The objective of trade, we should remember, is to reallocate resources in such a way to increase world output and domestic consumption. To this end, each country is expected to shuffle its capital and labor from one industry to another, in the direction of comparative advantage (see Headline). As we observed in Figure 17.2, this simply entails a move from one point on the production-possibilities curve to another point. Unfortunately, such shuffling from one industry to another is more difficult in practice than it is along the dimensions of a textbook graph.

In our illustration of Franco-American trade, vineyards were transformed instantaneously into wheat fields, vats into ovens, and grape pickers into wheat threshers. A nice trick if you can manage it, but few people can. Indeed, were such instantaneous resource reallocations possible, there would be no microeconomic resistance to international trade. Everyone would be able to share in the jobs and profits associated with comparative advantage. *The resistance to trade arises from the fact that resource reallocations are difficult and costly in practice,* both in human and in financial terms. The nature of resistance to trade is evident in a few grim statistics. In a recent survey of workers who lost their jobs as a result of import competition, it was found that 26 percent had gone for at least a year without work. Those who had found jobs had worked, on the average, only 50 percent of the time.

The objective of adjustment assistance is to speed up the reallocation of resources and to make the transition less painful for affected workers. For this purpose, workers may be taught new skills, assisted in finding new

HEADLINE

RESOURCE SHIFTS

**NAFTA Reallocates Labor:
Comparative Advantage at Work**

The lowering of trade barriers between Mexico and the United States will change the mix of output in both countries. New export opportunities will create jobs in some industries while increased imports will eliminate jobs in other industries. (Estimated gains and losses are during the first five years of NAFTA, 1993–1997.)

More Jobs in These Industries		But Fewer Jobs in These Industries	
Agriculture	+10,600	Construction	−12,800
Metal products	+ 6,100	Medicine	− 6,000
Electrical appliances	+ 5,200	Apparel	− 5,900
Business services	+ 5,000	Lumber	− 1,200
Motor vehicles	+ 5,000	Furniture	− 400

Source: Congressional Budget Office

jobs, aided in moving to new areas, and provided with interim income maintenance. In the case of older workers whose skills are not easily transferred, early retirement and pension benefits may be the most efficient kind of adjustment assistance.

All such assistance is expensive, of course. The Trade Expansion Act of 1962 permitted displaced workers to receive 70 percent of their previous wages for a period of up to 18 months, plus training and relocation allowances. Between 1975 and 1981 over 1 million workers received nearly $3 billion in such assistance. Nevertheless, many labor unions have dismissed the program as "burial insurance." They argue that benefits are too low, and that in any case many workers can neither return nor relocate without considerable hardship. As John Mara, head of the Boot and Shoe Workers' Union, put it after seeing ninety shoe factories shut down in Massachusetts: "Retraining for what? I want the economists to tell me what alternatives are available. Picking tomatoes in California?" *The critical issue in trade adjustment is whether alternative jobs exist and whether we are prepared to help workers get them.* Income maintenance, retraining assistance, job-search aid, relocation subsidies, and a strong economy are all required for a smooth transition.

SUMMARY

- International trade permits each country to concentrate its resources on those goods it can produce relatively efficiently. This kind of productive specialization increases world output. For each country, the gains from trade are reflected in the fact that its consumption possibilities exceed its production possibilities.
- In determining what to produce and offer in trade, each country will exploit its comparative advantage—its *relative* efficiency in producing various goods. One way to determine where comparative advantage lies is to compare the quantity of good *A* that must be given up in order to get a given quantity of good *B* from domestic production. If the same quantity of *B* can be obtained for less *A* by engaging in world trade, we have a comparative advantage in the production of good *A*. Comparative advantage rests on a comparison of relative opportunity costs.
- The terms of trade—the rate at which goods are exchanged—are subject to the forces of international supply and demand. The terms of trade will lie somewhere between the opportunity costs of the trading partners. Once established, the terms of trade will help to determine the share of the gains from trade received by each trading partner.
- Resistance to trade emanates from workers and firms that must compete with imports. Even though the country as a whole stands to benefit from trade, these individuals and companies may lose jobs and incomes in the process.
- The means of restricting trade are many and diverse. Tariffs discourage imports by making them more expensive. Quotas limit the quantity of a good that may be imported. Voluntary restraint agreements (VRAs) act just like quotas.
- Trade-adjustment assistance is a mechanism for compensating people who incur economic losses as a result of international trade; thus it represents an alternative to trade restrictions.

Terms to Remember

Define the following terms:

imports	consumption	tariff
exports	possibilities	quota
trade deficit	comparative advantage	equilibrium price
trade surplus	opportunity cost	voluntary restaint
production	absolute advantage	agreement (VRA)
possibilities	terms of trade	adjustment assistance

Questions for Discussion

1. Suppose a lawyer can type faster than any secretary. Should the lawyer do her own typing? Can you demonstrate the validity of your answer?
2. Can you identify three services Americans import? How about three exported services?
3. Suppose we refused to sell goods to any country that reduced or halted its exports to us. Who would benefit and who would lose from such retaliation? Can you suggest alternative ways to ensure import supplies?
4. Domestic producers often base their claim for import protection on the fact that workers in country X are paid substandard wages. Is this a valid argument for protection?
5. How much adjustment assistance should a displaced worker receive? For how long?
6. Based on the Headline on p. 369, how do American furniture manufacturers feel about NAFTA? How about farmers?

Problems

1. Suppose the following table reflects the domestic supply and demand for compact discs (CDs):

Price ($)	16	14	12	10	8	6	4	2
Quantity supplied	8	7	6	5	4	3	2	1
Quantity demanded	2	4	6	8	10	12	14	16

   (a) Graph these market conditions and identify the equilibrium price and sales.
   (b) Now suppose that foreigners enter the market, offering to sell an unlimited supply of CDs for $6 apiece. Illustrate and identify (1) the market price, (2) domestic consumption, and (3) domestic production.
   (c) If a tariff of $2 per CD is imposed, what will happen to (1) the market price, (2) domestic consumption, and (3) domestic production?
2. Alpha and Beta, two tiny islands off the east coast of Tricoli, produce pearls and pineapples. The production-possibilities schedules on the next page describe their potential output in tons per year:
   (a) Graph the production possibilities confronting each island.
   (b) What is the opportunity cost of pineapples on each island (before trade)?
   (c) Which island has a comparative advantage in pearl production?
   (d) Graph the consumption possibilities of each island if unrestricted trade is permitted.
3. Suppose the two islands in problem 2 agree that the terms of trade will be 1 pineapple for 1 pearl and that trade soon results in an exchange of 10 pearls for 10 pineapples.

(a) If Alpha produced 6 pearls and 15 pineapples and Beta produced 30 pearls and 8 pineapples before they decided to trade, how much would each be producing after trade became possible? Assume that the two countries specialize just enough to maintain their consumption of the item they export, and make sure each island trades the item for which it has a comparative advantage.

(b) How much would each island be consuming after specializing and trading?

(c) How much would the combined production of pineapples increase for the two islands due to trade? How much would the combined production of pearls increase?

(d) How could both countries produce and consume even more?

(e) Assume the two islands are able to trade as much as they want with the rest of the world, with the terms of trade at 1 pineapple for 1 pearl. Draw the ultimate consumption-possibilities curve for each island.

Alpha		Beta	
Pearls	Pineapples	Pearls	Pineapples
0	30	0	20
2	25	10	16
4	20	20	12
6	15	30	8
8	10	40	4
10	5	45	2
12	0	50	0

Glossary

Numbers in parentheses indicate the chapters in which the definitions appear.

A

absolute advantage: The ability of a country to produce a specific good with fewer resources (per unit of output) than other countries. (*17*)

adjustment assistance: Compensation to market participants for losses imposed by international trade. (*17*)

aggregate demand: The total quantity of output demanded at alternative price levels in a given time period, *ceteris paribus*. (*11*) (*12*) (*13*) (*14*)

aggregate supply: The total quantity of output producers are willing and able to supply at alternative price levels in a given time period, *ceteris paribus*. (*11*) (*14*)

antitrust: Government intervention to alter market structure or prevent abuse of market power. (*9*)

automatic stabilizer: Federal expenditure or revenue item that automatically responds countercyclically to changes in national income—e.g., unemployment benefits, income taxes. (*16*)

average total cost (ATC): Total cost divided by the quantity produced in a given time period. (*5*)

B

bank reserves: Assets held by a bank to fulfill its deposit obligations. (*13*)

barriers to entry: Obstacles that make it difficult or impossible for would-be producers to enter a particular market, e.g., patents. (*6*) (*7*)

barter: The direct exchange of one good for another, without the use of money. (*13*)

budget deficit: The amount by which government expenditures exceed government revenues in a given time period. (*12*)

budget surplus: An excess of government revenues over government expenditures in a given time period. (*12*)

business cycle: Alternating periods of economic growth and contraction. (*10*) (*11*) (*16*)

C

ceteris paribus: The assumption of nothing else changing. (*1*) (*3*) (*4*)

comparative advantage: The ability of a country to produce a specific good at a lower opportunity cost than its trading partners. (*17*)

competitive firm: A firm without market power, with no ability to alter the market price of the goods it produces. (*6*)

competitive market: A market in which no buyer or seller has market power. (*6*)

competitive profit-maximization rule: Produce at that rate of output where price equals marginal cost. (*6*)

Consumer Price Index (CPI): A measure (index) of changes in the average price of consumer goods and services. (*10*)

consumption: Expenditure by consumers on final goods and services. (*12*)

consumption possibilities: The alternative combinations of goods and services that a country could consume in a given time period. (*17*)

contestable market: An imperfectly competitive industry subject to potential entry if prices or profits increase. (*7*)

crowding out: A reduction in private-sector borrowing (and spending) caused by increased government borrowing. (*15*)

D

deflation: A decrease in the average level of prices of goods and services. (*10*)

demand: The ability and willingness to buy specific quantities of a good at alternative prices in a given time period, *ceteris paribus*. (*3*) (*4*)

demand curve: A curve describing the quantities of a good a consumer is willing and able to buy at alternative prices in a given time period, *ceteris paribus*. (*3*) (*4*)

demand for labor: The quantities of labor employers are willing and able to hire at alternative wage rates in a given time period, *ceteris paribus*. (*8*)

demand schedule: A table showing the quantities of a good a consumer is willing and able to buy at alternative prices in a given time period, *ceteris paribus*. (*3*)

deposit creation: The creation of transactions deposits by bank lending. (*13*)

derived demand: The demand for labor and other factors of production results from (depends on) the demand for final goods and services produced by these factors. (*8*)

discounting: Federal Reserve lending of reserves to private banks. (*14*)

discount rate: The rate of interest charged by the Federal Reserve banks for lending reserves to private banks. (*14*)

disposable income: After-tax income of consumers. (*12*)

E

economic cost: The value of all resources used to produce a good or service; opportunity cost. (*5*)

economic growth: An increase in output (real GDP); an expansion of production possibilities. (*2*) (*15*)

economics: The study of how best to allocate scarce resources among competing uses. (*1*)

economies of scale: Reductions in minimum average costs that come about through increases in the size (scale) of plant and equipment. (*7*)

efficiency (technical): Maximum output of a good from the resources used in production. (*6*)

emission charge: A fee imposed on polluters, based on the quantity of pollution. (*9*)

equilibrium (macro): The combination of price level and real output that is compatible with both aggregate demand and aggregate supply. (*11*) (*12*)

equilibrium price: The price at which the quantity of a good demanded in a given time period equals the quantity supplied. (*3*) (*6*) (*17*)

equilibrium wage: The wage at which the quantity of labor supplied in a given time period equals the quantity of labor demanded. (*8*)

excess reserves: Bank reserves in excess of required reserves. (*13*) (*14*)

exports: Goods and services sold to foreign buyers. (*2*) (*17*)

externalities: Costs (or benefits) of a market activity borne by a third party; the difference between the social and private costs (or benefits) of a market activity. (*2*) (*9*)

F

factor market: Any place where factors of production (e.g., land, labor, capital, entrepreneurship) are bought and sold. (*3*)

factors of production: Resource inputs used to produce goods and services, e.g., land, labor, capital, entrepreneurship. (*1*) (*5*)

fine-tuning: Adjustments in economic policy designed to counteract small changes in economic outcomes; continuous responses to changing economic conditions. (*16*)

fiscal policy: The use of government taxes and spending to alter macroeconomic outcomes. (*11*) (*12*) (*16*)

fiscal year (FY): The twelve-month period used for accounting purposes; begins October 1 for federal government. (*16*)

fixed costs: Costs of production that do not change when the rate of output is altered, e.g., the cost of basic plant and equipment. (*5*)

free rider: An individual who reaps direct benefits from someone else's

purchase (consumption) of a public good. (*9*)

full employment: The lowest rate of unemployment compatible with price stability; variously estimated at between 4 and 6 percent unemployment. (*10*)

functional distribution of income: The division of income among factors of production, especially between capital and labor. (*2*)

G

GDP per capita: Total GDP divided by total population; average GDP. (*15*)

government failure: Government intervention that fails to improve economic outcomes. (*1*) (*3*) (*9*)

gross domestic product (GDP): The total value of goods and services produced within a nation's borders in a given time period. (*2*)

growth rate: Percentage change in real GDP from one period to another. (*15*)

I

imports: Goods and services purchased from foreign sources. (*2*) (*17*)

income transfers: Payments to individuals for which no current goods or services are exchanged; e.g., Social Security, welfare, unemployment benefits. (*2*)

inflation: An increase in the average level of prices of goods and services. (*10*) (*11*)

inflation rate: The annual rate of increase in the average price level. (*10*)

in-kind income: Goods and services received directly, without payment in a market transaction. (*2*)

investment: Expenditures on (production of) new plant and equipment (capital) in a given time period, plus changes in business inventories. (*2*) (*12*) (*15*)

investment decision: The decision to build, buy, or lease plant and equipment; to enter or exit an industry. (*5*)

L

labor force: All persons over age sixteen who are either working for pay or actively seeking paid employment. (*10*) (*15*)

labor supply: The willingness and ability to work specific amounts of time at alternative wage rates in a given time period, *ceteris paribus*. (*8*)

laissez faire: The doctrine of "leave it alone," of nonintervention by government in the market mechanism. (*1*) (*3*)

law of demand: The quantity of a good demanded in a given time period increases as its price falls, *ceteris paribus*. (*3*) (*4*)

law of diminishing marginal utility: The marginal utility of a good declines as more of it is consumed in a given time period. (*4*)

law of diminishing returns: The marginal physical product of a variable input declines as more of it is employed with a given quantity of other (fixed) inputs. (*5*) (*8*)

law of supply: The quantity of a good supplied in a given time period increases as its price increases, *ceteris paribus*. (*3*)

long run: A period of time long enough for all inputs to be varied (no fixed costs). (*5*)

M

macroeconomics: The study of aggregate economic behavior, of the economy as a whole. (*1*) (*10*) (*11*)

marginal cost (MC): The increase in total cost associated with a one-unit increase in production. (*5*) (*6*)

marginal cost pricing: The offer (supply) of goods at prices equal to their marginal cost. (*6*) (*7*)

marginal physical product (MPP): The change in total output associated with one additional unit of input. (*5*) (*8*)

marginal propensity to consume (MPC): The fraction of each additional (marginal) dollar of disposable income spent on consumption. (*12*)

marginal propensity to save (MPS): The fraction of each additional (marginal) dollar of disposable income not spent on consumption; $1 - MPC$. (*12*)

marginal revenue (MR): The change in total revenue that results from a one-unit increase in quantity sold. (*7*)

marginal revenue product (MRP): The change in total revenue associated with one additional unit of input. (*8*)

marginal utility: The change in total utility obtained from an additional (marginal) unit of a good or service consumed. (*4*)

market demand: The total quantities of a good or service people are willing and able to buy at alternative prices in a given time period; the sum of individual demands. (*3*) (*4*) (*7*)

market failure: An imperfection in the market mechanism that prevents optimal outcomes. (*1*) (*9*)

market mechanism: The use of market prices and sales to signal desired outputs (or resource allocations). (*1*) (*3*) (*6*) (*9*)

market power: The ability to alter the market price of a good or service. (*6*) (*7*) (*9*)

market shortage: The amount by which the quantity demanded exceeds the quantity supplied at a given price; excess demand. (*3*)

market structure: The number and relative size of firms in an industry. (*6*)

market supply: The total quantities of a good that sellers are willing and able to sell at alternative prices in a given time period, *ceteris paribus*. (*3*) (*6*)

market supply of labor: The total quantity of labor that workers are willing and able to supply at alternative wage rates in a given time period, *ceteris paribus*. (*8*)

market surplus: The amount by which the quantity supplied exceeds the quantity demanded at a given price; excess supply. (*3*)

microeconomics: The study of individual behavior in the economy, of the components of the larger economy. (*1*)

mixed economy: An economy that uses both market and nonmarket signals to allocate goods and resources. (*1*)

monetary policy: The use of money and credit controls to influence macroeconomic activity. (*11*) (*14*) (*16*)

money: Anything generally accepted as a medium of exchange. (*13*)

money multiplier: The number of deposit (loan) dollars that the banking system can create from $1 of excess reserves; equal to 1 ÷ required reserve ratio. (*13*) (*14*)

money supply (M1): Currency held by the public, plus balances in transactions accounts. (*13*) (*14*) (*16*)

monopoly: A firm that produces the entire market supply of a particular good or service. (*2*) (*6*) (*7*)

multiplier: The multiple by which an initial change in aggregate spending will alter total expenditure after an infinite number of spending cycles; 1/(1 − MPC). (*12*) (*16*)

N

natural monopoly: An industry in which one firm can achieve

economies of scale over the entire range of market supply. (*7*)

net exports: Exports minus imports ($X - M$). (*12*)

nominal GDP: The total value of goods and services produced within a nation's borders, measured in current prices. (*15*)

nominal income: The amount of money income received in a given time period, measured in current dollars. (*10*)

O

open-market operations: Federal Reserve purchases and sales of government bonds for the purpose of altering bank reserves. (*14*)

opportunity cost: The most desired goods and services that are forgone in order to obtain something else. (*1*) (*3*) (*6*) (*8*) (*9*) (*17*)

opportunity wage: The highest wage an individual would earn in his or her best alternative job. (*8*)

optimal mix of output: The most desirable combination of output attainable with existing resources, technology, and social values. (*9*)

P

patent: Government grant of exclusive ownership of an innovation. (*7*)

per capita GDP: Total GDP divided by total population; average GDP. (*2*)

personal distribution of income: The way total personal income is divided up among households or income classes. (*2*)

price ceiling: Upper limit imposed on the price of a good. (*3*)

price elasticity of demand: The percentage change in quantity demanded divided by the percentage change in price. (*4*)

price floor: Lower limit imposed on the price of a good. (*3*)

price stability: The absence of significant changes in the average price level; officially defined as a rate of inflation of less than 3 percent. (*10*)

private costs: The costs of an economic activity directly borne by the immediate producer or consumer (excluding externalities). (*9*)

private good: A good or service whose consumption by one person excludes consumption by others. (*9*)

production decision: The selection of the short-run rate of output (with existing plant and equipment). (*5*) (*6*) (*7*)

production function: A technological relationship expressing the maximum quantity of a good attainable from different combinations of factor inputs. (*5*)

production possibilities: The alternative combinations of final goods and services that could be produced in a given time period with all available resources and technology. (*1*) (*15*) (*17*)

productivity: Output per unit of input, e.g., output per labor hour. (*15*)

product market: Any place where finished goods and services (products) are bought and sold. (*3*)

profit: The difference between total revenue and total cost. (*5*) (*6*)

profit-maximization rule: Produce at that rate of output where marginal revenue equals marginal cost. (*7*)

progressive tax: A tax system in which tax rates rise as incomes rise. (*2*)

public good: A good or service whose consumption by one person does not exclude consumption by others. (*9*)

Q

quota: A limit on the quantity of a good that may be imported in a given time period. (*17*)

R

real GDP: The inflation-adjusted value of GDP; the value of output measured in constant prices. (*2*) (*10*) (*11*) (*15*)

real income: Income in constant dollars; nominal income adjusted for inflation. (*10*)

recession: A decline in total output (real GDP) for two or more consecutive quarters. (*10*)

regressive tax: A tax system in which tax rates fall as incomes rise. (*2*)

relative price: The price of one good in comparison with the price of other goods. (*10*)

required reserves: The minimum amount of reserves a bank is required to hold by government regulation; equal to required reserve ratio times transactions deposits. (*13*) (*14*)

reserve ratio: The ratio of a bank's reserves to its total transactions deposits. (*13*)

S

saving: That part of disposable income not spent on current consumption;

disposable income less consumption. (*12*) (*15*)

Say's Law: Supply creates its own demand. (*11*)

scarcity: Lack of available resources to satisfy all desired uses of those resources. (*1*)

shift in demand: A change in the quantity demanded at any (every) given price. (*3*)

short run: The period in which the quantity (and quality) of some inputs cannot be changed. (*5*)

social costs: The full resource costs of an economic activity, including externalities. (*9*)

stagflation: The simultaneous occurrence of substantial unemployment and inflation. (*16*)

structural unemployment: Unemployment caused by a mismatch between the skills (or location) of job seekers and the requirements (or location) of available jobs. (*16*)

supply: The ability and willingness to sell (produce) specific quantities of a good at alternative prices in a given time period, *ceteris paribus*. (*3*) (*5*) (*6*)

supply-side policy: The use of tax rates, (de)regulation, and other mechanisms to increase the ability and willingness to produce goods and services. (*11*) (*16*)

T

tariff: A tax (duty) imposed on imported goods. (*17*)

terms of trade: The rate at which goods are exchanged; the amount of good *A* given up for good *B* in trade. (*17*)

total cost: The market value of all resources used to produce a good or service. (*5*)

total revenue: The price of a product multiplied by the quantity sold in a given time period, $p \times q$. (*4*) (*6*)

total utility: The amount of satisfaction obtained from entire consumption of a product. (*4*)

trade deficit: The amount by which the value of imports exceeds the value of exports in a given time period. (*17*)

trade surplus: The amount by which the value of exports exceeds the value of imports in a given time period. (*17*)

transactions account: A bank account that permits direct payment to a third party (e.g., with a check). (*13*)

transfer payments: Payments to individuals for which no current goods or services are exchanged, e.g., Social Security, welfare, unemployment benefits. (*9*)

U

unemployment: The inability of labor-force participants to find jobs. (*10*) (*11*)

unemployment rate: The proportion of the labor force that is unemployed. (*10*)

utility: The pleasure or satisfaction obtained from a good or service. (*4*)

V

variable costs: Costs of production that change when the rate of output is altered, e.g., labor and material costs. (*5*)

voluntary restraint agreement (VRA): An agreement to reduce the volume of trade in a specific good; a "voluntary" quota. (*17*)

Index

Note: **Boldface** indicates glossary terms defined in text.

G